The Mail Tool Men

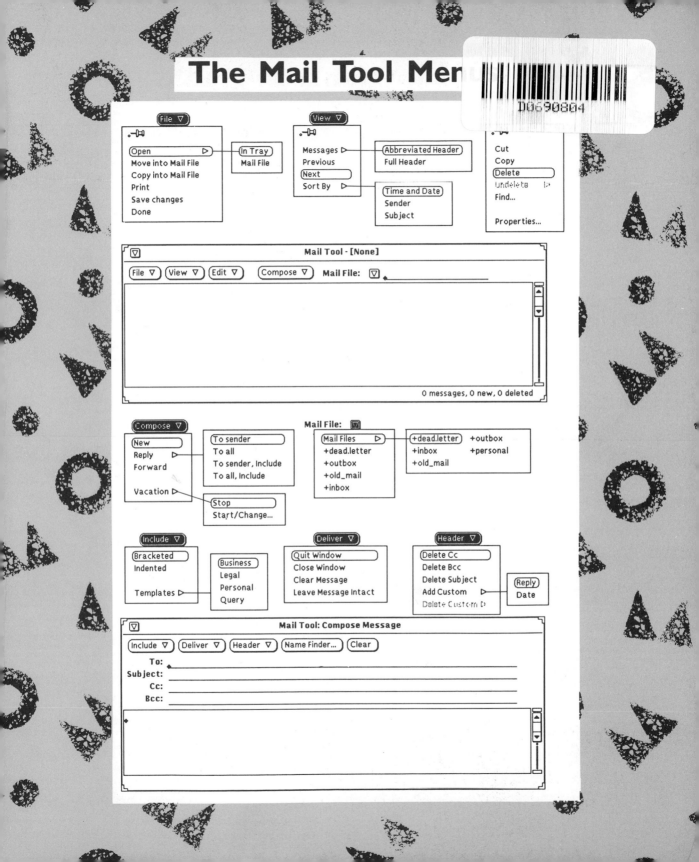

File ▽

Open ▷ → In Tray / Mail File
Move into Mail File
Copy into Mail File
Print
Save changes
Done

View ▽

Messages ▷ → Abbreviated Header / Full Header
Previous
Next
Sort By ▷ → Time and Date / Sender / Subject

Cut
Copy
Delete
Undelete ▷
Find...

Properties...

Mail Tool - [None]

File ▽   View ▽   Edit ▽   Compose ▽   Mail File: ▽

0 messages, 0 new, 0 deleted

Compose ▽

New
Reply ▷ → To sender / To all / To sender, Include / To all, Include
Forward

Vacation ▷ → Stop / Start/Change...

Mail File: ▽

Mail Files ▷ → +dead.letter / +inbox / +old_mail
+dead.letter → +outbox / +personal
+outbox
+old_mail
+inbox

Include ▽

Bracketed
Indented

Templates ▷ → Business / Legal / Personal / Query

Deliver ▽

Quit Window
Close Window
Clear Message
Leave Message Intact

Header ▽

Delete Cc
Delete Bcc
Delete Subject
Add Custom ▷ → Reply / Date
Delete Custom ▷

Mail Tool: Compose Message

Include ▽   Deliver ▽   Header ▽   Name Finder...   Clear

To:
Subject:
Cc:
Bcc:

Mastering
SunOS

MASTERING SUNOS

Brent D. Heslop
David Angell

SYBEX

San Francisco • Paris • Düsseldorf • Soest

Acquisitions Editor: Dianne King
Developmental Editor: Vince Leone
Copy Editor: Ami Knox
Technical Editor: John A. Pew
Word Processors: Scott Campbell and Winnie Kelly
Book Designer: Julie Bilski
Chapter Art and Production Layout: Eleanor Ramos
Technical Art: Delia Brown
Screen Graphics: Cuong Le
Desktop Publishing Production: Daniel Brodnitz
Proofreader: Lisa Jaffe
Indexer: Nancy Anderman Guenther
Cover Designer and Photographer: David Bishop

SYBEX is a registered trademark of SYBEX, Inc.

TRADEMARKS: SYBEX has attempted throughout this book to distinguish proprietary trademarks from descriptive terms by following the capitalization style used by the manufacturer.

SYBEX is not affiliated with any manufacturer.

Every effort has been made to supply complete and accurate information. However, SYBEX assumes no responsibility for its use, nor for any infringement of the intellectual property rights of third parties which would result from such use.

The text of this book is printed on recycled paper.

Library of Congress Card Number: 90-70330
ISBN: 0-89588-683-9

Manufactured in the United States of America
10 9 8 7 6 5 4 3 2

To Kim for her love, patience, and understanding
B.D.H.
To Frank Merritt Angell, who inspired me before I even realized it
D.A.

Acknowledgements

We wish to express our sincere appreciation to all the people who helped make this book a reality. A special thanks to Jeff Horan, Software Design Engineer (who unfailingly provided technical and moral support); John Loiacono, Press Relations Manager for Platforms and Graphics; Mark Pinone, X11/NeWS Product Manager; Julie Sarbacker, DeskSet Product Manager; Janice Winsor, Senior Technical Writer; Cathleen Beall Garfield, Public Relations Manager for Desktop Software Products; Carrie Dillon, Public Relations Specialist for Platforms and Graphics; and Rich Piziali, Lead Technical Support Engineer, and Keith Abbey, Technical Support Engineer at Sun Microsystems, all of whom went the extra mile. Thanks to Robert David, Steve Biblehiemer, Scott Mattoon, and Martha Venegas at Sun Microsystems Technical Support for their patient and cheerful support. We are also grateful to Dennis Freeman, Press Relations Manager for Networking SunOS and Distribution; Carl Swirsding, Manager of Creative Services; and Cyndi Jung, European Marketing Liaison for their assistance.

We also want to express our gratitude to Christine Hinton, Marketing Communications Coordinator at Pacific Data Products, for use of the PostScript Language Emulation Cartridge for the HP LaserJet Series II printer; Stephanie Guigou at TOPS for providing the TOPS network; Stephanie Hafner at NOVELL for helping us network the Sun system; Paul Eddington at Word-Perfect Corporation for the use of WordPerfect; and Beverly Toms, Marketing Communications Specialist at FRAME Technology, who supplied us with FrameMaker 2.0 during this project.

At SYBEX, we want to acknowledge Dianne King, Acquisitions Editor and Rudy Langer, Vice President and Editor-in-Chief, who gave us the opportunity to work on this exciting project. We are also grateful to Vince Leone, Developmental Editor, for his encouragement and advice while seeing this book through production. Thanks also to Ami Knox for her professional copyediting.

Thanks to Jeff House for his friendship and the editorial skills he provided throughout this book. Lastly, but in placement only, we are indebted to Larry Goodman, who wrote the useful SunOS Command Reference contained in Chapter 14.

Contents at a Glance

Table of Contents

Introduction

Sun Microsystems is the fastest growing Fortune 500 computer company in history. Sun stands for Stanford University Network, a name given to a printed circuit board developed in 1981 that was designed to run the popular UNIX operating system. This board was instrumental in bringing UNIX to the desktop. Sun Microsystems' continued success is based on manufacturing low-cost workstations utilizing a new generation of microprocessors that support the powerful UNIX operating system. Previously available only on expensive mainframes and minicomputers, Sun's UNIX-based operating system, known as SunOS, harnesses the powerful microprocessors that have enabled Sun's low-cost workstations to dominate the workstation market. As Sun workstations enter new markets in growing numbers, more and more new users are faced with the challenge of mastering SunOS.

What is SunOS?

SunOS is a collection of programs that control the Sun workstation and provide a link between the user, the workstation, and its resources. A core of SunOS programs manage the computer system and remain hidden from the user. The remaining programs are known as *utility programs*—these provide the user with tools for working with SunOS. SunOS is analogous to a building manager who attends to the needs of the tenants in each of the building's rooms and manages the utilities, such as the flow of heat and water. SunOS provides the platform for running application programs such as Computer Aided Design (CAD) programs.

The Evolution of SunOS

SunOS has its roots firmly placed in the two most popular UNIX families: Berkeley UNIX, commonly known as BSD (Berkeley Software Distribution), and AT&T's System V, commonly known as SVID (System V Interface Definition).

UNIX is a constellation of modular programs that allows users to select and use programs to fit their precise needs. Because of its modular design, UNIX has evolved from a mini and mainframe programmer's environment into a platform for a variety of applications. UNIX was created by Ken Thompson and Dennis Ritchie at AT&T's Bell Labs to provide an environment that promoted efficient program development. Thompson later brought UNIX to the University of California at Berkeley, where it began a life of its own and eventually became known as Berkeley UNIX. Over time, UNIX matured into an easier-to-use, increasingly powerful operating system, incorporating such key features as portability, networking, security, and a friendly user interface.

Earlier versions of SunOS were a refinement of the UNIX operating system that blended the best of both AT&T and Berkeley UNIX, as well as added enhancements. AT&T and Sun Microsystems later worked together to create a new industry standard, AT&T Unix System V Release 4 (SVR4).

The Structure of SunOS

SunOS comes pre-installed on Sun workstations and is loaded into memory when the system is turned on, a process commonly referred to as *booting up*. SunOS consists of a broad range of general and specialized programs; not everyone needs the entire range of programs. In fact, storing a complete version of SunOS takes up a large amount of disk space—over 50 megabytes. (A megabyte is equal to 1,048,576 characters.)

To save storage space, SunOS is divided into two packages: Application SunOS and the Developer's Toolkit. This book focuses on Application SunOS. Regardless of the package your system is using, SunOS is composed of three major parts: the kernel and file system, shells and graphical interfaces, and utility programs.

The Kernel and the File System

The kernel is the heart of SunOS; it resides in memory and manages the system's hardware, such as terminals, printers, drives, and other devices. It schedules and terminates processes (programs being run) and keeps track of the file system and other important functions.

The file system is integrated with the kernel and provides the organizing structure that stores your data. It enables you to organize files in a logical and structured manner, utilizing a hierarchical file system that allows related files to be grouped together in directories. These files are stored on a disk and organized into different levels with parent directories and subordinate directories called subdirectories, similar in structure to a family tree.

SunOS Shells and Graphical User Interfaces

The shell is a program, called a command interpreter, that manages the interaction of the user with the kernel. The shell first accepts, then interprets, and finally executes commands entered at the command-line prompt. There are three primary SunOS shells: the C Shell, the Bourne Shell, and the KORN Shell. The C Shell and the Bourne Shell come with SunOS. The Bourne shell was developed for AT&T's System V UNIX and usually displays a dollar sign prompt ($) when it's active. The C Shell was developed for Berkeley UNIX and usually displays a percent sign prompt (%) when it's active. This book assumes that you are working with the C Shell because it's the standard shell used with SunOS. However, most of the features discussed are common to both the Bourne and C Shell.

BOURNE SHELL $
C SHELL %

Graphical User Interfaces (GUIs) provide a friendlier interface than the command prompt. SunOS uses the OPEN LOOK GUI, which makes working with SunOS substantially easier by allowing you to use a mouse to work with icons, menus, and windows. OPEN LOOK is the GUI for Sun's DeskSet, a collection of graphical-based applications (which includes windows for performing command line operations).

The DeskSet is available for both the SunView and Open-Windows environments. These windowing environments provide a foundation for running GUIs. SunView (Sun Visual Integrated Environment Windows) is Sun's proprietary window environment. The newer environment, OpenWindows, was developed to run on a variety of platforms, provided they follow the industry standard, AT&T Unix System V Release 4 (SVR4).

You can perform routine SunOS tasks, such as file management, sending mail, and text editing using either the command line or the DeskSet. In most cases, the DeskSet provides a quicker route to accomplishing these tasks. The command line, however, offers additional power, enabling you to combine commands and options to perform operations not available using DeskSet applications.

Utility Programs

Over 300 utility programs are supplied with SunOS. These programs are lists of instructions and data that are interpreted by the computer. These utility programs share the same names as the commands used to execute them. Commands can be in the form of an English-like statement or presented as an option in a graphical menu system. SunOS provides programs for file management, editing, electronic mail, performing calculations, and many other specialized functions.

How to Use This Book

Mastering SunOS explains working with SunOS from the traditional command-line prompt or using the newer graphical-based applications of the DeskSet. The first seven chapters cover SunOS fundamentals and use of the command line to perform tasks, such as managing files, sending mail, and editing text. Chapters 8 through 13 explain how to use the applications in the DeskSet, such as the File Manager, Mail Tool, and Text Editor. Chapter 14 provides a handy alphabetical command reference that allows you to easily look up command information, including the syntax to follow, a description of the command, options the command can take, and examples of how to use the command.

Throughout this book you will find brief notes in the margins that provide you with extra information. There are three kinds of notes, and each is distinguished by an icon, as shown in the margin next to this paragraph. The following list explains the purpose of each type of note:

 This is the Note icon.

 This is the Tip icon.

This is the Warning icon.

- *Notes*: These provide reminders and cross references.
- *Tips*: These explain shortcuts and hints to simplify your work.
- *Warnings*: These point out possible hazards to avoid.

Mastering SunOS will serve as useful companion for effectively using SunOS, regardless of your previous computer experience. Its easy-to-follow examples progressively build SunOS skills, yet allow you the freedom to skip to the topic appropriate to your needs. This comprehensive tutorial and reference book is designed to give the reader the flexibility to work with SunOS using either the friendly graphical user interface or the standard command-line approach.

CHAPTER 1

Getting Started
with SunOS

GETTING STARTED WITH SUNOS IS LIKE LEARNING to drive a car. You need to sit in the SunOS "driver's seat" to get the feel of using SunOS. In this chapter, you take SunOS out for a test spin by using the command line. The *command line* is the line on which you enter commands so SunOS can translate them into instructions the computer understands. The percent sign (%) is the SunOS command line prompt that indicates SunOS is ready for your next command. Your SunOS test spin will take you through the basics of logging in and out of SunOS, entering commands, working with several useful SunOS utility programs, and sending and receiving electronic mail.

Before You Start

This test spin assumes you can log in to SunOS on your terminal. Before using SunOS, you need an *account* set up by a *system administrator*, a person responsible for managing the system. In setting up your account, the system administrator instructs SunOS to accept you as a user and establishes certain parameters for your use of the system. When your account is established, you are assigned a user name and password. Your *user name* identifies you to the system and usually consists of the initial of your first name and your complete last name. Your *password* prevents the use of your account by unauthorized users. You can change your password anytime, as explained later in this chapter.

Logging In to SunOS

Once you've created a user name and a password, after being assigned an account, you are ready to start working with SunOS. The process of getting into SunOS is called *logging in.* To log in to SunOS requires just a few simple steps.

⊙ Keep in mind that SunOS is *case sensitive,* meaning that it treats lowercase and uppercase characters as two distinct character types.

1. At the **username** login prompt, type in your user name in lowercase characters (usually your first initial and last name) and then press Return. SunOS then prompts you to enter your password. If you type in the wrong character(s) and haven't pressed Return, use the Delete key to erase the incorrect characters and then type the correct character(s).

2. At the **password** login prompt, type in your password, then press Return. Your password is not displayed as you type it. On some systems number symbols (**#**) are displayed on the screen instead of the characters in your password to prevent anyone from seeing it.

3. SunOS logs you in and displays the prompt, indicating that you are ready to start using the system.

The SunOS System Prompt

Most of the examples in this book will not include the system prompt. Just be aware that this prompt will be displayed on your screen as you follow the exercises presented here.

The system prompt is SunOS's way of saying it is ready and waiting for a command. How your SunOS prompt appears depends on which shell your system is using. A *shell* is the interface between you and SunOS; it translates commands you enter from the keyboard for the operating system. The *C Shell* usually uses the percent sign (%) as the system prompt symbol and is generally the standard shell for Sun workstations. However, your system may be using the *Bourne Shell*, which usually displays a dollar sign ($) as its prompt. Most of the commands in this chapter are common to both the Bourne and C Shell. A system prompt may incorporate a system host name (also known as the name of the *file server*, the central computer on the network which enables you to access files throughout the system) followed by the percent sign (%) symbol for the C Shell. This is displayed as

```
bookware%
```

System Login Messages

After you've logged in to SunOS, you may see a login message displayed on your screen just before the system prompt. A *login message* usually displays information from the system administrator about important system events, such as when the system will be shut down for maintenance. There may also be a message indicating you have mail, which is electronic mail sent to you by other users on the system. SunOS mail features are covered later in this chapter.

Logging Out of SunOS

After completing a SunOS session, it's important to *log out*. Otherwise anyone walking by your terminal can gain unauthorized access to your files. To log out of SunOS, first make sure the system prompt is displayed, then type Control-D or

```
logout
```

and press Return. The system displays the login screen again. If the system prompts you with the message **there are stopped jobs**, type **logout** two or three more times. If the system prompts you with the message **not login shell**, type **exit**, then type **logout**. For more information on logging out with stopped jobs, see Chapter 7, "Multitasking and Customizing SunOS."

Changing Your Password

It's a good idea to change your password periodically to prevent anyone from gaining unauthorized access to your files. Your password is entirely your choice and can be changed as often as you like. For convenience, pick a password that is easy to remember, yet not easily deduced by others. If you use a password less than six characters in length, SunOS prompts you to use a longer password. However, you can use a shorter password if you enter it each time SunOS prompts you to enter a longer password (usually three times). Remember, SunOS is case sensitive; if you mix upper- and lowercase letters in your password, you'll have to type them in exactly the same way to log in. The following steps explain how to change your password:

1. At the system prompt, type in the command **passwd** in lowercase characters, then press Return. SunOS displays the message **Changing password for *username*** (where ***username*** is your user name).

2. SunOS prompts you to type in your current password. Type it in, then press Return. The system will not display the characters you type in.

3. The system prompts you for your new password. Type it in, then press Return. The system next prompts you

to retype your new password to verify its correctness. Type in your new password again, then press Return.

If you forget your password, see your system administrator.

Entering SunOS Commands

Options and expressions will be explained when commands that use them are introduced.

When you type in characters at the system prompt, you're entering characters into an area of memory called the *command-line buffer*. Pressing Return instructs SunOS to *execute* the command—to accept the contents of the command line in the buffer and process it. The command line can contain simple one-word commands or more complex commands that include *arguments*. Arguments modify commands and may be *options, expressions*, and *file names*. For example, adding a file name after a command identifies the file to be affected by the command.

The terms *commands* and *programs* are used interchangeably in SunOS because the names of the individual programs that make up the operating system are also the commands used to execute them.

Keep in mind that the terms *commands* and *programs* are used interchangeably in SunOS because the names of the individual programs that make up the operating system are also the commands used to execute them. The general format for SunOS commands is as follows:

```
Command Option(s) Expression(s) Filename(s)
```

Correcting Mistakes

There are several keyboard commands you can use to correct mistakes in the command line. The key combinations vary depending on how your system administrator has set up your system and account. Pressing the Delete key allows you to erase characters from the command line right to left. To erase an entire command line (as long as you haven't pressed Return), press Control-U. If you mistype a command and press Return, SunOS gives you an error message, such as **Command not found**. You can then retype the command. However, if you have typed in the wrong command, SunOS may execute a program you do not want to run. To terminate an executed program, press Control-C.

Useful SunOS Programs

SunOS contains over 300 utility programs that perform a wide variety of functions. To familiarize yourself with the SunOS environment, try running the utility programs described in this section. These programs enable you to display the date and time, display a calendar, establish who is using the system, remind you of an appointment, and repeat commands you have entered previously.

Displaying the Date and Time

To display the current date and time, type **date** at the system prompt, then press Return. SunOS uses a 24-hour clock and gives the time to the second. For example, SunOS might display the current date and time as

```
Tue Jan 30 10:52:35 PST 1999
```

Displaying a Calendar

The **cal** command displays a calendar on your screen for the month and year specified. Typing **cal** and then pressing Return displays the calendar for the current month. You can enter arguments to the **cal** command to specify a particular month and year. There must be at least one space between the command and argument. The year can be in the range from 0 to 9999 a.d. The months are numbered **01** to **12**, though you can use a one- or two-digit number for single digit months, such as **5** or **05** for the month of May. To display the calendar for just one month of any year, enter

```
cal month_number year
```

To see the calendar for October 1999, enter

```
cal 10 1999
```

SunOS displays the calendar for October 1999 as follows:

```
     October 1999
 S   M  Tu  W Th  F   S
                  1   2
 3   4   5  6  7  8   9
10  11  12 13 14 15  16
17  18  19 20 21 22  23
24  25  26 27 28 29  30
31
```

Entering the command

```
cal 1999
```

displays the entire calendar for the year 1999.

Who Is Using the System?

SunOS is a multiuser system, which means more than one person can use the system at any one time. The **who** and **finger** commands are useful if you need to know a user's login name to send mail but only know their real name.

The **who** command lists the people logged into the system at that moment. The list contains user names, which terminals are being used, and the date and time each user logged in. To execute the **who** command, enter

```
who
```

SunOS displays a listing of current system users of your host machine. If your user name was **lbird**, the system might display

```
lbird      tty06      Aug 30   11:35
mjohnson   tty15      Aug 30   09:02
mjordan    tty19      Aug 29   15:06
```

The **finger** command provides more detailed user information than the **who** command. Depending on what your system administrator has directed this command to display, it may list a user's full name, user name, terminal location, idle time, home directory, and more. To execute the **finger** command, enter

```
finger
```

SunOS then displays a **finger** command listing, such as

```
Login      Name            TTY    Idle   When
lbird      Larry Bird      06     12     Tue 10:30
mjohnson   Magic Johnson   15     0      Wed 12:55
mjordan    Michael Jordan 19     20     Wed 15:06
```

An Appointment Reminder

The **leave** command notifies you when it's time to leave for an appointment. To activate **leave**, simply enter the command followed by the time you want to leave. You may enter the time in either 12- or 24-hour formats, but the **leave** command converts any time entered into a 12-hour format and assumes the time specified is within the next twelve hours. For example, to execute the **leave** command to remind you of a 12:15 appointment, enter

```
leave 1215
```

SunOS displays a confirmation message, such as

```
Alarm set for Tue Jan 30 12:15:24 1999
```

At five minutes before 12:15, **leave** warns you of your upcoming appointment time. At one minute before your scheduled appointment, **leave** again reminds you of your upcoming appointment. At exactly 12:15, **leave** tells you it is time to leave. The **leave** command then displays this warning each minute for the next ten minutes:

```
You're going to be late!
```

Then the **leave** command displays the final message

```
That was the last time I'll tell you. Bye.
```

Repeating Commands

SunOS stores a list of previously issued commands that can be redisplayed on your screen and executed using the **history** command. This timesaving feature speeds up the task of reentering commands. You can set or change the number of commands you want the **history** command to remember during a session by entering in the following:

```
set history = n
```

The letter *n* indicates the number of commands you would like the system to remember. For example, entering

```
set history = 20
```

instructs the system to remember the last 20 commands executed. You can reexecute any command in the **history** command list. To see a list of previous commands which have been captured by the **history** command, type **history** at the system prompt, then press Return. This displays a list of all the commands now available for you to reexecute. For example, if you have entered each of the commands discussed in this chapter in the order in which they were introduced, entering **history** would produce this list:

```
1 date
2 cal 10 1999
3 cal 1999
4 who
5 finger
6 leave 1215
7 set history = 20
```

This list is dynamic, which means that it changes as you enter more commands at the system prompt. The commands issued first are the first to scroll off the list. To execute the last command in the list, type **!!** at the system prompt and press Return. To execute any command in the list, type **!n** and press Return, where **n** is the number of the command in the list. For example, typing **!5** and pressing Return executes the fifth command in the **history** command list.

Sending and Receiving Electronic Mail

SunOS's **mail** program allows you to send mail messages, called *electronic mail* or *E-mail*, to other users on the network and receive electronic mail in return. When you execute the **mail** program for either sending or receiving mail, it displays its own prompt, the ampersand (**&**) symbol. This program prompt indicates that you are working in the **mail** program. Whenever you log in, SunOS checks the system mailbox. If any mail is addressed to your user name, you may see the message **You have mail** displayed on your screen. You can then display a listing of your mail messages and read your mail or ignore the mail message prompt and read your mail at any time later. You can send mail messages to other users whether they are on line or not.

Reading Your Mail

If you get a message notifying you that you have mail, someone has sent you a mail message through the SunOS mail system. In order to read your mail, at the system prompt enter

```
mail
```

The system displays a list of mail message headers followed by the **mail** program prompt, as shown below.

```
Mail version 4.0 Mon Feb 17 00:20:20:58 ST 1992  Type ? for
help.
"+inbox": 3 messages 3 new
```

```
N  1lbird      Tue Dec 12 09:08  12/281  Game tonight
N  2mjohnson   Wed Jan 16 15:55  19/610  No game this week
N  3mjordan    Mon Jan 25 16:51  20/619  Game tomorrow night
&
```

The following describes what information is provided in each of the columns from left to right in the above mail headers list:

Column	Description
Letter status	New (**N**) or unread (**U**) mail messages (**U** denotes old messages that you haven't read yet)
Letter number	Number you use to specify which letter you want to read
Sender	Name of user who sent letter (for example, **1bird**)
Time sent	Date and time sender sent the letter
Size	Number of lines and characters in the letter (for example, letter 1 contains 12 lines and 281 characters)
Subject	Subject of the letter

You can choose the mail message you want to read by entering the mail message number at the mail prompt (**&**). For example, if you want to read mail message number 2, type **2** at the mail prompt. The mail program then displays mail message number 2, as shown below.

```
Message 2:
From mjohnson Wed Jan 16 15:55 1992
From mjohnson (Magic Johnson)
Subject: No game this week

Just a reminder that we won't be playing any basketball
games this week. So get some work done.
```

Once a mail message is read, it is normally moved to a file named **mbox** or **old_mail** located in the your home directory. You can then press Return to view the next mail message or type a specific mail message number. Typing **h** (headers) displays the mail headers list again. Type **q** at the mail program prompt to exit the mail program and return to the system prompt.

Sending Mail

You send mail by specifying the user name of the person or persons you want to receive the mail in the **mail** command. You can use the **who** or **finger** command as explained earlier in this chapter to find a user's name if you don't know it. When you send mail to another user, it is stored in the recipient's electronic mailbox, and that person is notified that they have mail. The following steps explain how to send mail to another user.

1. At the system prompt, type **mail *username(s)***, then press Return. To send the same mail message to multiple users, separate each user name with a space. The mail program prompts you for the mail message subject.

2. Type in the subject of your mail message at the **Subject:** prompt, then press Return. If you decide you want to cancel your mail message, press Control-C twice.

3. Type in the text of your mail message. If you want to create a new line, simply press Return at any point.

The difference between specifying other users immediately after **mail** or after **Cc:** is relevant because the easiest method of replying to a message allows you to choose whether your reply should go to those on the **Cc:** list. See Chapter 4 for details.

4. When you've finished entering your mail message text, press Return to move the cursor to a new line, and then press Control-D. The **mail** program may then display the **Cc:** prompt. You can enter the names of other users you want to send copies of the mail message to. To specify more than one user, separate each user name with a space. When you are finished entering user names, press Return to end your mail message and send it. The system prompt returns to your screen.

Summary

In this chapter you have developed a feel for working with SunOS from the command line. You should now know how to perform these basic SunOS procedures:

- Log in to SunOS, change your password, and log out of SunOS
- Enter, execute, and stop SunOS commands. You also learned how to correct mistakes in the command line.
- Use the SunOS utility programs **date**, **cal**, **who**, **finger**, **leave**, and **history**
- Read and send mail to other users on the system

Table 1.1 lists the commands covered in this chapter and their functions.

Table 1.1: Commands Covered in Chapter 1

Command	Result
cal	Displays calendar for month or year specified
date	Displays current time and date
finger	Lists detailed information about users currently on the system
history	Lists commands previously executed
leave	Reminds user when to leave for an appointment
logout	Allows user to log out

Table 1.1: Commands Covered in Chapter 1 (continued)

Command	Result
`mail`	Allows user to read or send electronic mail
`passwd`	Changes password
`who`	Lists users currently logged in to system

CHAPTER 2

Understanding the SunOS File System

ONE OF THE MAJOR STRENGTHS OF SUNOS IS ITS sophisticated file system. This chapter explains the three major components of this file system: directories, subdirectories, and files. It provides hands-on examples that show you how to navigate the file system's paths and discusses how to create and work with directories and files. Using the information in this chapter, you can create, copy, compare, and rename directories and files as well as remove unwanted directories and files. Timesaving tips and techniques for locating files are included to help you speed up the process of working with files and directories. This chapter also explains how to protect your directories and files by setting access permissions and working with links.

An Overview of the SunOS Hierarchical File System

SunOS uses a hierarchical file structure, an inverted tree structure with the base of the tree at the top similar to the structure of a family tree. A *file* is a "container" that holds text or programs. *Directories* are files that contain indexes to aid SunOS in locating files. It's helpful if you think of directories as file cabinets and files as file folders containing the information that you want to access. That is, though directories really only contain indexes to files, you can think of them as actually containing the files themselves.

The topmost parent directory of the tree is known as the *root* directory and is indicated by a slash (**/**). The root directory contains files and *subdirectories*. Although every directory except the root directory is a subdirectory, subdirectories can be referred to as directories. In other words, the term subdirectory and directory are often used interchangeably. Your system may have a directory called **home** that contains home directories for all users. The names of these individual home directories are usually based on the names of the users.

Distinguishing between Directories, Files, and Programs

In SunOS you add an option to a command by typing a space and then a hyphen before the first option letter.

To help you quickly identify the different directories, files, and programs (executable files), enter the **ls** (list) command with the **-F** option, **ls -F**. The hyphen is used by SunOS to add options to commands. The **-F** option instructs SunOS to display the subdirectories and files for the directory in which you are located. Directories are marked with a slash (**/**), while executable files are marked with an asterisk (*****). Symbolic links—used primarily by programmers—are marked with an at sign (**@**).

Text files appear without an identifying mark. When you enter **ls -F**, a directory listing such as this one appears on your screen:

```
Desktop*     examples/    info*     memo
clients      final        mail/     textfile
```

Types of Directories

SunOS relies on specific system directories to operate. In most cases, the system administrator organizes and restricts access to these directories. The following list explains the primary types of directories that exist on a SunOS system.

/ (root) The first slash represents the top of the file system, or the root directory. The root directory contains the program **vmunix**, which is also known as the *kernel*. The kernel is the heart of SunOS; it manages the system's hardware and schedules and terminates processes.

/dev This is the device directory, which contains files that support such devices as the screen (**/dev/tty**), the mouse (**/dev/mouse**), and the window system (**dev/win**).

/etc This directory is specifically used by the system administrator for system maintenance. For example, the **/etc/printcap** subdirectory is used to add or remove printers from the system.

/export The **/export** directory contains files and file systems that a file server shares with other work stations on the network.

/tmp   Temporary files are stored in this directory and are either periodically removed by your system administrator or deleted when you reboot your computer.

/usr   This is a general purpose directory that contains several important subdirectories for users. For example, **/usr/bin** contains many of the SunOS command programs, and **/usr/share/man** contains the online help manual.

/var   This directory is maintained by the system administrator.

Navigating Directories

When you want to move to another directory, enter the **cd** (change directory) command followed by the name of directory you want to move to. The following sections describe more fully the **cd** command and explain additional techniques that you can use to move quickly through the file system. They also include a discussion of absolute and relative pathnames, on-screen displays of your current working directory, and shortcuts for returning to your home directory.

Navigating with Pathnames

Every file has a pathname. A pathname tells SunOS which paths to take to find a specific directory or file, and so is similar to an address on a letter because both give specific directions for a final destination. You change from one directory to another by invoking the **cd** command with a pathname. A pathname consists of a directory name or series of directory names separated by slashes (**/**). For example, **/usr** indicates the directory **usr**, which is a subdirectory immediately below the root directory (indicated by the forward slash). There are two types of pathnames: absolute and relative.

Navigating with Absolute Pathnames

You can construct the pathname of a file by tracing a path from the root directory to the directory where the file resides. An *absolute pathname* always begins with a slash (**/**) and lists the file name after the final slash. For example, **/home/bozo/letter** is the absolute pathname for the file **letter** in the directory **/home/bozo**.

Navigating with Relative Pathnames

Unless you specify an absolute pathname by beginning the pathname with a slash, SunOS assumes you are using a relative pathname. A relative pathname describes a path that starts from the directory in which you're currently working. In other words, relative pathnames trace the path from the working directory to the desired file or directory. Relative pathnames save you the time of typing in a complete, or absolute, pathname to access a directory or file beneath the directory you are currently located in. For example, in the directory **/home/bozo**, the command

```
cd reports
```

moves you to the subdirectory **/home/bozo/reports**.

Moving to Your Home Directory

Usually your user name is also the name of your home directory. Do not confuse this with the *home* directory, which contains directories for all users.

Your *home directory* is the directory that was created for you when you first logged into the system. Every user is assigned a home directory. Entering the **cd** command by itself moves you directly to your home directory. The tilde character (**~**) can be used as a shortcut for typing in the entire pathname for your home directory. For example, typing **cd ~/reports** moves you to the

reports subdirectory of your home directory. You can also access another user's home directory by following the tilde character with the person's user name. For example, **cd ~dquayle** moves you to Dan Quayle's home directory.

Displaying the Working Directory

The *working directory* is not a fixed directory but the directory in which you are currently located. A useful SunOS command is **pwd**, which prints on the screen the name of your working directory. When you use the **ls** command with the **a** option to list the contents of a directory, SunOS may indicate the working directory pathname as a single dot (.).

Moving to a Parent Directory

The *parent directory* is the directory located one level above your working directory. You can specify the pathname of the parent directory of your working directory with two consecutive periods (. .). For example, entering **cd . .** moves you up one directory level. The following example prints the working directory before and after moving up a directory level using the double-dot shortcut. If entering the **pwd** command displays

```
/home/users/bozo
```

issuing the command **cd . .** then the **pwd** command displays

```
/home/users
```

Backtracking through Directories

When you are changing directories often, use the **pushd** command to store a list of directories in a directory stack so that you can easily revisit them. To move and store the name of a directory that you'll want to return to, enter

```
pushd directoryname
```

where ***directoryname*** is the name of the directory that you want to return to at a later time. Unlike the **cd** command, you need to specify a destination directory (even when returning to your home directory). The **pushd** command changes to the new directory while keeping track of which directory you changed from and which you changed to. The new directory name and previous directory name are displayed immediately after you execute the **pushd** command as shown in the following two examples.

```
/home/
pushd dquayle
/home/dquayle ~

pushd /
/ /home/dquayle ~
```

Notice in the first **pushd** example that the tilde indicates that the user issued the **pushd** command while in his home directory. In the second example, the user moved to the root directory as indicated by the first forward slash (**/**). Notice that the directory from which you start (**~** in this case) continues to be displayed.

To backtrack to a previous directory, type the command **popd**. Issuing **popd** twice with the previous example displays

```
popd
/home/dquayle ~

popd
~
```

The tilde by itself in the last example indicates the user has returned to their home directory.

If you lose track of where you have been, enter **dirs**. SunOS will list the directories in your directory stack. You can also have SunOS list the full pathnames of stacked directories by adding the **-l** (long) option to the **dirs** command as shown below

```
dirs -l
/home/gbush
```

Working with Directories

Now that you know how to use absolute and relative pathnames, you can use several helpful commands to conveniently and strategically organize your files. Your ability to perform actions on a given file is governed by the type of access you have to that file. The type of access you have is controlled by *permissions* settings.

- *Read* permission allows you to view or copy the contents of a file.
- *Write* permission enables you to add or delete directories.
- *Execute* permission allows you to move into a directory and execute programs.

In most cases, if you try to move, copy, or remove a file for which you don't have these permissions, SunOS will respond with a **Permission denied** message. Permissions are covered in detail later in this chapter.

Listing a Directory's Contents

The **ls** command by itself lists the contents of the working directory. You can also specify a directory after the **ls** command to get a listing for that directory. For example, **ls /home/files/bozo** lists the files for the directory **bozo** no matter which directory you're using. There are a number of arguments the **ls** command can accept to display different information.

Option	*Result*
-a (all)	Lists all subdirectories and hidden files (special system files that have a file name beginning with a dot or a period)
-l (long)	Displays a long listing of the contents of the directory
-lg	Shows the group ownership of a file in a long listing
-R	Recursively lists the contents of each subdirectory under a specified directory. Each subdirectory name is followed by its relative pathname and a listing of the contents of that subdirectory until SunOS reaches the last level of the hierarchical structure.
-r	Reverses order of listing to display a reverse alphabetical directory listing
-t (time)	Lists a directory sorted in order of newest to oldest files

Below is a sample listing produced by **ls -l**.

```
-rw-r--r-- 1 jcool      1094 Dec  1 17:08 clients
drwxr-sr-x 2 jcool         0 Nov  9 19:52 DeskTop*
-rw-r--r-- 1 jcool         0 Dec  1 17:08 info*
drwxr-sr-x 2 jcool       512 Jan 30 19:52 mail/
```

The different components of this listing are explained in the "Listing File and Directory Permissions" section later in this chapter.

Creating a Directory

The **mkdir** command creates directories. By creating directories you are making the equivalent of a file drawer where you can keep related files. Before creating a directory, make sure you are in your home directory by typing **cd** and pressing

Return. Enter **mkdir** followed by the name you want to give your new directory. For example, in the directory **/home/bozo**, entering

```
mkdir reports
```

creates the subdirectory **/home/bozo/reports**. If you attempt to make a new directory with a directory name that already exists, the message **mkdir:** *directoryname:* **File exists** appears where *directoryname* is the name that you tried to use. In order to create a directory outside your home directory, you must have write and execute permissions in the parent directory.

Copying a Directory

You can duplicate the contents of any directory using the **cp** (copy) command and the **-r** (recursive) option. This guarantees that all files and subdirectories of the source directory are duplicated. For example, in the directory **/home/felix**, issuing the command **cp -r portfolio record** copies all files and subdirectories from the **portfolio** directory to the directory named **record**, where **record** and **portfolio** are subdirectories of **/home/felix**. If the directory to which the copies are supposed to be sent doesn't exist, the **cp** command first creates it and then copies the files and directories to the new directory. If the directory to which the copies are supposed to be sent already exists, any existing files already there are overwritten. To allow you to avoid mistakenly overwriting existing files, use the **-i** (interactive) option. This option causes SunOS to ask if you really want to overwrite files in a directory that already exists. Pressing any key other than Y causes the **cp** process to terminate.

As with many SunOS commands, you can use more than one option with the **cp** at a time. When you use multiple options you only need to precede the list of options with a single hyphen. For example, if you enter **cp -ir portfolio record**, the **-i** causes SunOS to ask if you really want to overwrite the existing files in **record**. Press Y, and the **-r** (/) recursive option then copies all the files and subdirectories of the **portfolio** directory to the **record** directory until SunOS reaches the last level of the hierarchical structure.

You can maintain the original modification times and permission modes of files and directories by using the **-p** (preserve) option. If you don't use the **-p** option, the files are assigned the current date and default permission modes. To interactively and recursively copy the contents of the directory **bozo** to the directory **clone**, while preserving the original modification times and permission modes, enter

```
cp -ipr /bozo /clone
```

Beware of a recursive copy that doesn't specify files to be copied, such as **cp -r source source/backup**. This copy command can ruin your day by recursively creating new **backup** subdirectories and copying files until it fills the entire file system.

Removing a Directory

Be careful when using the **-r** and **-f** options. All subdirectories are permanently deleted when you use these options. Before removing a directory, use the **ls** command with the **-a** (all) option to guarantee that the directory doesn't contain subdirectories or files that you'll later need. Then use the **rm** command with the **-ir** options to ensure you don't accidently remove needed directories and files.

You can delete a directory using the remove directory command, **rmdir**. The directory that you want to remove cannot be the working directory (the directory in which you're located). To remove a directory with **rmdir**, the directory needs to be empty; that is, it cannot contain any subdirectories or files. When removing subdirectories from your current directory, remember that you can refer to subdirectories using the shorthand convention of relative pathnames. For example, to remove the empty subdirectory **reports** from your current directory, simply enter **rmdir reports**. Adding the **-i** option causes SunOS to ask if you want the directory to be removed before SunOS deletes the directory. If you attempt to remove a directory that isn't empty, SunOS displays the message **rmdir:** *directoryname* **Directory not empty**.

To remove directories that contain files or subdirectories, use **rm** with the **-r** (recursive) option, which deletes all existing files and subdirectories and then removes the directory. To interactively remove a directory and its contents, enter the command **rm -ir *directoryname*.** You can force files to be removed without SunOS displaying permissions, asking questions, and reporting errors by using the **-f** (force) option.

Working with Files

Manipulating files is the essence of SunOS. SunOS provides commands to perform just about any operation on a file you can imagine. The following section only scratches the surface in explaining the most essential commands and options you can use when working with files, such as displaying a file's type or contents, or copying, renaming, moving, or removing files. In many ways, working with files is similar to working with directories. Most of the commands you use with directories are the same as the commands you use with files.

Listing Files

The command for listing files is the same as that for listing the contents of a directory. You can list the files for any directory by following the **ls** command with the absolute or relative pathname and any of the **ls** options. If the directory is empty and you use **ls -a** to list all your files, a single period (.) indicating the current directory and two consecutive periods (..) indicating the parent directory are displayed.

Determining File Types

If you enter **file** followed by a file name, SunOS lists that file's *type*, such as ASCII text, program files, or directory. For example, issuing the command

```
file clients
```

causes SunOS to display

```
clients: ascii text
```

indicating that clients is an ASCII text file. If the file is a program file, the command also lists the language it was written in and any pertinent information about the file.

File Name Conventions

A file name must be unique in the directory where it resides. File names can be up to 256 characters long, but it is recommended that you keep them under fourteen characters to save time entering them. You can assign a file any name you want, provided you avoid using special characters such as – * ? < > ! / \. Remember, SunOS is a case-sensitive operating system, so you need to enter the file name exactly as you created it in order to use it again. File names that begin with a period (.) indicate special hidden files that are used by the system and do not appear when you use **ls** by itself to list the files. Otherwise you can use a period anywhere else in a file name, and it will not become a hidden file.

Be careful when naming files. To create file names that are easy to remember and avoid conflicting with SunOS's special characters, it is best to restrict file names to letters, digits, underscores, and periods (except as the first character). Don't create a file name that contains a nonprinting character, or a *control character*, by pressing a Control-key combination, such as Control-A. Although in most cases SunOS would substitute the control character with a question mark on screen, a file name with nonprintable characters can make that file inaccessible.

Creating a File

You can use a text editor, such as **vi**, to create a file, or you can use the **cat** command. The **cat** command is an abbreviation of *concatenate*, which means to link or connect in a series.

To create a file with the **cat** command, type **cat > *filename*,** where ***filename*** is the name you want your file to have. After typing the name for your file and pressing Return, you can begin entering the text you want your file to contain. When you are finished entering the text, press Control-D. For example, to create a file using the **cat** command, type in the following:

> **cat >myfile** (press Return)
>
> **My first text file.** (press Return)
>
> (press Control-D)

The greater-than sign is a *redirection operator* that channels your text into the file **myfile**. Control-D signals the end of the text that is to be put into the file. If you accidentally type **cat** without a redirection symbol or a file name, press Control-D to exit the **cat** command.

Displaying the Contents of a File

Many SunOS files are binary files that contain instructions only the computer can understand. When you try to display these files, they appear as text resembling what you might find in a cartoon balloon to indicate cursing.

Once you've created a file, you can look at its contents by entering the **cat** command followed by the file name. If you misspell the name of the file you want to view, SunOS displays the file name you typed followed by the message **No such file or directory**. If the file contains more lines than the screen can display, the beginning text scrolls off the screen, leaving only the last screen of text visible. The following key combinations are useful in this situation:

> Control-S   Temporarily halts scrolling
>
> Control-Q   Resumes scrolling
>
> Control-C   Cancels scrolling

You can display more than one file in sequence on the screen by typing in the names of all the files you want to see after **cat**, making sure to separate the file names with a space. For example, **cat doc1 doc2** displays the contents of the file **doc1**, followed by the contents of the file **doc2**.

The following options are available when using the **cat** command:

Option	Result
-b	Numbers the lines but omits line numbers for blank lines
-e	Displays nonprinting characters as the **-v** option does and displays a **$** character at the end of each line
-n	Precedes each line with a line number, starting at 1
-s	Substitutes a single blank line for consecutive, multiple blank lines
-t	Displays non-printing characters as the **-v** option does and tab characters as **^I**
-v	Lists invisible characters, such as **^b** for Control-B

Conveniently Displaying a Long File

A convenient way to look at a long file is to use the **more** filter A *filter* is a command that accepts text as input, manipulates that text in some way, and then outputs new text. The **more** filter simply transforms text into screen-sized blocks so the text of a file can be displayed one screen at a time. To use the **more** command, type **more *filename(s)***, where ***filename(s)*** indicates the file or files you want to display. If you want to display multiple files, remember to separate each file name with a space. For example, **more doc1 doc2** displays the contents of **doc1**, followed by the contents of **doc2**, one screenful of text at a time. To display the next screenful of text, press spacebar. As you view a file using the **more** filter, the percentage of text that has been displayed is listed at the bottom of the screen in parentheses. To exit the **more** filter, type **Q**.

Once you have started the **more** filter, you can display a specific number of lines at a time by typing in the number and pressing the spacebar or Return. For example, typing the number **5** and pressing the spacebar displays the next five lines of the file. You can change the display size by typing the number of lines you want the screen to show followed by **d** or Control-D. You can scroll backwards by indicating the number of lines to go back and pressing Control-B. If you are displaying a large file, backwards scrolling can be excruciatingly slow.

Displaying the First or Last Lines of a File

If you want a quick look at the beginning or ending of a file, use the **head** or **tail** filters. The **head** filter displays the top ten lines of a file by default. For example, **head jaeger** lists the first ten lines of the file named **jaeger**. Adding a minus sign followed by a number before the file name lists that number of lines from the top of the file. For example, **head -12 jaeger** lists the top twelve lines of the **jaeger** file.

The **tail** filter shows the tail end of a file. If you issue the **tail** filter without an option followed by the name of the file you want to view, **tail** lists the last ten lines of the file. You can change this display length by adding a minus sign and the number of lines you want displayed before the file name. For example, **tail -20 stocks** displays the last twenty lines of the file named **stocks**. If you precede the number with a plus sign instead of a minus sign, **tail** starts at that specified line number and displays all lines from there to the end of the file. For example, **tail +5 bonds** displays all lines from line 5 to the end of the **bonds** file. If you use the **+** option and indicate a number greater than the number of lines in the file, **tail** will not display anything.

Copying Files

You copy files with the **cp** command. To copy one of your files, type **cp** the name of the file to be copied, and the file name you want to copy this file to. For example, **cp rocky smooth** copies the file **rocky** to a file with the name **smooth**, leaving **rocky** intact. Unless you use the **-p** (preserve) option to record the original modification time and permission modes, the file is created with the current date and default permission modes. (Permission modes are explained later in this chapter.) When copying files, use the **-i** (interactive) option to ensure that the target name for the copy doesn't already exist. That way if the file does exist, SunOS inquires if you really want to overwrite the existing file. Pressing any key other than Y causes the copying process to terminate. You can also copy more than one file. To copy two or more files at once, list all the files after the command **cp**, making sure you separate each file name with a space. For example, to interactively copy the files **onefile twofile** to your home directory, enter

```
cp -i onefile twofile ~
```

If the file names exist in your home directory, SunOS asks you, one file at a time, whether or not to overwrite the existing file. Pressing any key other than Y aborts the copy process for that file, and SunOS then asks if you want to overwrite the next existing file.

Comparing Text Files

Once you have copied a text file, you can use the **diff** command to ensure that the files are exactly the same. The **diff** command displays line-by-line differences between a pair of text files. You can check to make sure that a file has been copied using the **ls** command, but the **diff** command is helpful if you have two copies of a file and can't readily determine the differences between them. Entering the command

```
diff fileone filetwo
```

causes SunOS to display the differences between **fileone** and **filetwo**. If no differences are found, the prompt is redisplayed without a message. Use the **diff3** command to display the differences between three files, such as **diff3 fileone filetwo filethree**. The following example shows the result of using **diff** on two files beginning with the same first line but with differences in the next three lines of text. The line containing numbers and an alphabetical character indicates the number of the lines and type of edits needed to make both files identical. If the letter **a** appears, it indicates that text needs to be appended. The letter **d** indicates text needs to be deleted. The letter **c** indicates text needs to be changed. In the following example, the first line indicates that lines 2 through 4 of **file1** need to be changed to match lines 2 through 4 of **file2**. The less-than signs (<) identify the differing lines in **file1**. The greater-than signs (>) identify the differing lines in **file2**.

```
diff fileone filetwo
2, 4c2, 4
< The second line contains the word incongruous
< The third line contains the word disparate
< The fourth line contains the word different
---
> The second line contains the word analogous
> The third line contains the word similar
> The fourth line contains the word corresponding
```

Moving and Renaming Files

Moving a file and renaming a file both use the same command, **mv** (move). To move a file, type **mv** followed by the name of the file you want to move, then type the directory you want to move the file to. If you want to rename a file, type **mv** followed by the file name you want to rename and then type the new name. For example, the command **mv sunrise sunset** changes the file name **sunrise** to **sunset**. The **mv** (move) command deletes the original file after copying the file and moving it to its new location. Use the **-i** option to ensure that you don't move a file to another file that already exists and overwrite the text there. You can't rename more than one file at a time. You can, however, move several files at one time by listing all the files you want to move before the destination directory and separating each file name with a space. For example, if you are in Dan Quayle's home directory, entering the command

```
mv letter1 letter2 memo dquayle/letters
```

moves the files **letter1**, **letter2**, and **memo** to the **letters** subdirectory of **dquayle**.

Removing Files

Be careful using the **-r** and **-f** options. Files and sub directories are permanently deleted when you use these options. When removing files, use the **-i** option to ensure you don't accidentally remove the wrong files.

The **rm** command deletes one or more files. To remove a file you need to have write permission in the directory that contains the file as well as in the file itself. If you don't have write permission for the file, and you created the file, SunOS asks you whether or not to override the permissions feature and remove the file. To remove more than one file, list all the files you want to delete and separate each file name with a space. The command **rm junk trash** removes the files **junk** and **trash** from the working directory. The **rm -i** (interactive) option prompts you with the question **Remove *filename*?**. Type Y to remove the file; any other response will cause SunOS to ask if you want to remove the next file in an argument list or, if you only have one file in the list, aborts the removal process. You can force files to be removed without displaying access permissions or having SunOS ask questions or report errors by using the **-f** (force) option. To remove all the files and subdirectories in the current directory, use the **rm -r** (recursive) option.

Searching for Files

Several facilities are built into SunOS to help you locate files using special characters called *metacharacters* or *wildcard* characters. Wildcard characters are analogous to the joker card in card games, where the joker can be any card. These characters can be used to indicate one character of a file name or parts of file names.

File Name Metacharacters

The special characters used most often for pattern or wildcard searches are the question mark (**?**) and the asterisk (*****). The **?** represents any single character. Entering the command **ls letter?** lists all files beginning with the word **letter** and ending with one additional character, such as **letter1** and **letterA**.

The asterisk character (*****) matches any series of characters. Issuing the **ls** command followed by a single asterisk, **ls ***, lists every file in the working directory, except for hidden files. Entering the command **ls b*** lists every file beginning with the letter **b**—for example, **bard**, **beta**, **botany**, and **business**.

Place characters within braces, separated by commas, before an asterisk to match specific character strings of any length. For example, **{sun, night, light}*** lists all files beginning with sun, night, or light, such as **sunlight**, **nighttime**, and **lighter**. You can also add wildcards within the braces and nest braces within strings. For example, **{{n,l}ight, sun}*** is another way to match the files beginning with night, light, or sun.

Character Class

Another way to search for files is to use the character-class option. A single character, or a string of characters enclosed in brackets, is known as a *character class*. When you use brackets, you're instructing SunOS to match any character within the brackets. For example, **ls [Aabc]*** matches all file names beginning with an uppercase **A** or lowercase **a**, **b**, or **c**. You can also indicate a range of alphabetical characters by separating the beginning and ending range with a hyphen. For example, **ls [A-Z]*** matches all file names that begin with an uppercase alphabetical character, **ls [a-m]*** matches all file names that begin with lowercase alphabetical characters ranging from **a** through **m**, and **ls [1-9]** matches any numbers ranging from one to nine.

Permissions

Because SunOS allows users to share the file system, it protects files and directories by defining types of users and access permission modes. Every file and directory has three types of users and four types of access permission modes. By changing permission modes, you can selectively share files and directories with some or all of the people on the system.

Listing File and Directory Permissions

By adding the **-1** (long) option to the **ls** (list) command, you can list permissions information about files. Entering **ls -1** displays a long format for your directory listing. This option can be used alone or used in conjunction with the other options. This next example shows a listing of files using the **-1** (long) and **-a** (all) options with **ls (ls -al)** followed by an explanation of each of the file attributes from left to right.

```
-rw-r--r-- 1 jcool      1094 Dec  1 17:08 clients
drwxr-sr-x 2 jcool         0 Nov  9 19:52 DeskTop*
-rw-r--r-- 1 jcool         0 Dec  1 17:08 info*
drwxr-sr-x 2 jcool       512 Jan 30 19:52 mail/
-rw-r--r-- 1 jcool      1094 Dec  1 17:08 memo
drwxr-sr-x 2 jcool       512 Jul  4 12:26 temp/
-rw-r--r-- 1 jcool       179 Mar  1 10:35 test
-rw-r--r-- 1 jcool      1327 Mar  1 15:00 textfile
```

Permissions   Permissions are displayed in the *permissions list*, which is the first ten characters in the listing. The first character that appears in the leftmost column indicates the file type (regular, directory, or device). The remaining nine characters in the series specify the permission modes for the three types of users: yourself, group, and others (three characters for each user type).

Links	The number that follows the first ten characters lists the number of files and directories linked to that file. Links are covered later in this chapter.
Owner	The user name of the person who created or owns the file
Group	Users can be organized into groups. This enables members of a particular department to share access to files and directories. There can only be one group associated with a file or directory.
Bytes	The size of the file (a byte equals one character)
Date	The date and time the file was created or last modified
File name	The name of the file or directory

File and Directory Types

The first character in the permissions list indicates the file type. The most common types of files are referred to as *standard* files and are indicated by a hyphen (-). A directory is identified by the letter **d**. Outside your home directory you are likely to encounter other types of files. Here are some of the letters used to identify these other types of files on the system.

Letter	Description
b or **c**	Indicates that the file is a device file (a program file that controls a device, such as a printer)
s	Identifies the file as a socket file, used for communication between running programs

Letter	Description
`l`	Indicates the file is a link used to link one file with another (links are discussed later in this chapter)

Types of Permissions

There are four types of permissions you can assign to your files or directories. By assigning different permissions, you can limit the access others have to that directory or file. Here is a list of the four permission modes and the letters that represent them in a permissions list.

r (read)	The read privilege allows a user to list the contents of the directory or file. The read permission is also necessary to copy a file from one location to another.
w (write)	The write permission allows a user to change the contents of a file or directory. This permits a user to create, append, and remove existing files.
x (execute)	The execute permission allows a user to execute a file. The ability to search through directories is also a function of the execute permission. A directory can be read from or written to, but unlike a file, it can't be executed. When applied to a directory, the execute access permission allows you to search through and list the contents of the directory.
− (no access)	This permission is also referred to as the protection mode. It prevents a user from reading, writing to, or executing a file.

Ownership of Files

File access is defined for three types of users: owner, group, and others. The following lists descriptions for each of these three types of ownership, and also includes examples of permissions modes.

Owner   This refers to the creator of the file or directory. The first three characters after the file type character list the types of permissions available to the owner. For example, a permissions list beginning with **-rw-** indicates the owner has read and write permissions but not execute permission.

Group   Each user is a member of a group defined by the system administrator. The fifth, sixth, and seventh characters in the list indicate the permissions available to users who are in the same group as the owner. For example, a file beginning with **-rw-r--** indicates that group members have read, but not write or execute permissions. To find out which group or groups you belong to, enter the command **groups**.

Others   This means all other users. The third set of three characters after the file type lists the types of permissions available to users who are not members of the same group as the owner. For example, a file with **-rw-r-----** permissions indicates that users outside the owner's group have no access to the file.

Changing Permission Modes

The owner of a file controls which users have permission to access and work with that file. You use the **chmod** command to change the permission modes of a file or directory. The permission modes of a file can only be changed by the person who created the file or by someone who has **superuser** privileges (additional access to files beyond those of a normal system user); usually this is your system administrator.

There are two forms of the **chmod** command you can use to change file and directory permission modes: the symbolic form and the numeric form.

Changing Permission Modes Using Symbolic Notation

The format for changing permission modes with symbolic notation is as follows:

```
chmod class(es) operation permission(s) filename(s)
```

Use the following abbreviations to identify the class for which you want to change permission modes:

u   User

g   Groups

o   Others

You then use operators to assign **r** for read, **w** for write, and **x** for execute permission modes. Table 2.1 shows abbreviations for the possible arguments that can be added to the **chmod** command to assign, add, or remove permissions from a file using symbolic notation. If you omit class, the setting is applied to all three classes (user, group, and others).

The following example lists **chmod** commands to assign the file named **populace** read, write, and execute permissions for all classes of users and to remove all permissions for everyone but the user (owner) of the file **restricted**:

```
chmod a=rwx populace
chmod go-rwx restricted
```

Table 2.1: Arguments Used with **chmod** to Change Permission Modes

Class	Operations	Permissions
u User (owner)	**=** assigns a permission	**r** read
g Group	**+** adds a permission	**w** write
o Others	**–** removes a permission	**x** execute
a All		

The command

```
chmod a=rx testfile
```

changes the mode of **testfile** so that it can be accessed and read but not written to by all users on the system. It's important to note that if you use **=** and do not specify all types of permissions (that is, if you omit **r**, **w**, or **x**), the permissions for the omitted types will be turned off. You can also change permissions for multiple files, provided you want them to have the same access permissions. You must separate the file names with a single space.

The following combines several aspects of **chmod**:

```
chmod u=rw, o=r redfish bluefish
```

This command

- Allows the owner of the files redfish and bluefish to read and write to them

- Allows everyone else to read (but not write to) these files

- Prevents everyone, including the owner, from executing the files (because **x** was not specified)

Changing Permission Modes Using Numeric Notation

To assign permissions using numeric notation, you enter numbers to specify the permissions you want. If you enter only one number after **chmod**, that permission will apply to the others class. If you enter two numbers, the first number will specify permissions for the group and the second will set the permissions for others. If you enter three numbers, the first number will set the owner's permissions, the second number will set group permissions, and the third number will apply to all others. The numeric values that can be used to change permissions are listed in Table 2.2.

To change modes using numeric notation, enter the **chmod** command followed by the numbers indicating the mode you

Table 2.2: Numbers Assigned to Permission Modes

Values	Permissions	Definition
7	rwx	read, write, execute
6	rw-	read, write
5	r-x	read, execute
4	r- -	read only
3	-wx	write and execute
2	-w-	write only
1	- -x	execute only
0	- - -	no access

want to assign to each class of user. For example, entering **chmod 750 fugu** indicates that the file named **fugu** can be read, written to, and executed by the owner, because the first number indicates the owner's permission mode is equal to 7. The next number, 5, indicates that the file can be read and executed by a member of the owner's group. The last number, 0, indicates there are no permissions for others on the system.

Here are two other examples of using the **chmod** command to change permissions mode:

```
chmod 64 project
```

assigns both read and write permissions to the group with access to the file **project** and assigns only the read permission to all other users. (Since only two numbers were entered after **chmod**, no permissions were assigned to the owner.)

```
chmod 544 document
```

assigns read and execute permissions for the owner of the file **document** and only read permission to both the group and all others.

Links

If two users are working on a linked file simultaneously, only the user who first accessed the file will be able to write to it.

A *link* is a directory entry that acts as a pointer to locate files. A link is automatically created when you create a file. In SunOS, you can create different names for a single file (that is, you can create additional links) by using the **ln** (link) command. For example, if you and another member of your group are both working on a file, you can have the file listed (under the same or different names) in both of your home directories. This ensures that two different versions of a file don't exist and also saves disk space. When you list files using the list command with the **-l** option, **ls -l**, the number displayed between the permissions modes and the file owner's name indicates the number of links to that file. In the following file listing, the file named **unite** has 2 links and **sole** has one.

```
-rw-r--r--  2 tcleaver     1024 Apr  1 19:05 unite
-rw-r--r--  1 tcleaver      256 Apr  1 19:35 sole
```

Creating a Link

When you create a file, SunOS places the file name in the appropriate directory and creates a link, or pointer, that points to the file so SunOS can locate it. When you remove a file, the link is broken and the pointer is removed from the directory. Each file has at least one link, but other links can be created. To create a link to a file, you must have execute permission for the directory in which you want to create a link. The syntax for the link command is as follows:

```
ln pathname_filename pathname_otherfilename
```

The **ln** command makes a file available from the directory in which you created the link. Once a file has been linked, it can be referenced without a path from that directory. If you wanted to link the file **chip** with the file **dale**, you would enter

```
ln chip dale
```

If the file originally named **chip** is the only file in the directory, entering **ls -l** would display

```
-rw-r--r--  2 cporter      23 May  5 12:35 chip
-rw-r--r--  2 cporter      23 May  5 12:35 dale
```

Removing Links

Using the remove command, **rm**, to delete a file removes a single link. For instance, entering

```
rm dale
```

removes the link to the file **chip** created in the previous example. If a file has more than one link, you can remove one file name and still access the file from the other link. Once a file is down to a single link, however, the next time you use the **rm** command specifying that file, it is removed.

Summary

In this chapter, you explored the SunOS hierarchical file system and learned a number of commands and options to create and manipulate directories and files. Understanding how to create and manage SunOS files and directories provides a solid foundation for building your SunOS skills as you work with more powerful commands to manipulate your files. This chapter presented these essential file system topics and commands:

- Work with absolute or relative pathnames to change directories with the **cd** command, use the tilde (~) as a substitute for typing your home directory name, and use the double-dot shortcut (..) to quickly move up directories

- Print the working directory on your screen using the **pwd** command

- List a directory's contents with the **ls** command. You also learned about several options that can be used in conjunction with the **ls** command, such as **-al** to list all files using a long format.

- Create a directory using the **mkdir** command or remove a directory with the **rmdir** command

- Recursively copy the contents of a directory using the **cp -r** command

- Create, name, and view a file using the **cat** command

- Display a file using the **more** command and display any portion of the beginning or ending of a file using the **head** and **tail** commands

- Copy and compare files using the **cp** and **diff** commands

- Move and rename files with the **mv** command, and remove files with the **rm** command

- Use the **?** and ***** wildcard characters to locate files and search directories together with brackets to indicate a character class

- Protect your files by changing the read, write, and execute permissions modes using the **chmod** command with either numeric or symbolic notations

- Create links using the ln command to share files and allow easier access to files from other directories

Table 2.3 lists the commands covered in this chapter.

Table 2.3: Commands Covered in Chapter 2

Command	Result
. .	Moves user to parent directory of working directory
~	Changes working directory to user's home directory
cat	Creates a file and displays a file's contents
cd	Allows user to change directories
chmod	Allows user to change permission modes of a file or directory
cp	Copies contents of directories and files
diff	Compares and displays differences between files

Table 2.3: Commands Covered in Chapter 2 (continued)

Command	Result
`file`	Lists file type of a given file
`head`	Displays top lines of a file
`ln`	Creates links between files
`ls`	Lists directories and files
`mkdir`	Creates directories
`more`	Displays text one screenful at a time
`mv`	Moves and renames files
`pwd`	Prints the working directory on screen
`rm`	Removes files and links to files
`rmdir`	Removes directories
`tail`	Displays last lines of a file

CHAPTER 3

Beyond the
Fundamentals

THIS CHAPTER EQUIPS YOU WITH A VARIETY OF helpful commands, tips, and techniques to improve your productivity. It reveals several ways to control the input and output of SunOS using redirection as well as explaining the concepts of pipes and filters.

Getting the Most from the Command Line

With the command line you can repeat or modify a recent command, which allows you to perform an assortment of operations with only a few keystrokes. The SunOS features described in this section enable you to edit command-line entries, perform multiple commands in the same command line, repeat commands using matching characters, repeat parts of commands, and quickly fix commands incorrectly entered.

Performing Multiple Commands

To place more than one command on the command line, separate each command with a semicolon (;). When two or more commands are separated by a semicolon, they are treated as if they were sequentially entered on separate lines. For example, typing **cd; pwd; ls -la** and pressing Return brings you to your home directory, displays the directory name, and displays a long listing of all the files in that directory.

The history Mechanism

In Chapter 1, you learned how to use the **history** command to store and repeat your commands using the **!** metacharacter. You can set the number of commands the **history** mechanism remembers by typing **set history = *n***, where *n* is the number of commands you want **history** to remember. For example, **set history = 20** makes the **history** mechanism remember the last 20 commands.

Repeating Commands

Typing **! !** repeats the last command, and typing **!** followed by a number repeats the command with the corresponding number in the **history** list. To see a listing of your most recent commands, enter **history**. The following shows a sample listing of commands displayed using the **history** command.

```
1 cd; pwd; ls -la
2 set history = 20
3 history
```

⦿ Be careful using the **!** metacharacter. If you recently copied a file, cleared the screen, and didn't specify between the two commands using the second letter of the command, entering **!c** will cause the metacharacter to match the most recent command beginning with the letter c. If an incorrect command is executed, press Control-C to abort the command.

The **!** metacharacter is the basis for other sophisticated timesaving techniques.

- Following **!** with a negative number repeats previous commands. For example, **!-3** repeats the third from the last command on the **history** list.

- You can also repeat a command by matching the first few characters of a previous command. For example, typing **!c** after entering the **clear** command to clear your screen causes SunOS to reissue the **clear** command.

- Following the **!** metacharacter with a string of characters surrounded by question marks also allows you to repeat any command in the **history** list by matching characters embedded in the command line. For example, typing

      !?mem?

  will repeat the last command that contained the string **mem** anywhere within it. For example, it would repeat the following command:

      cp ~bozo/project/memorandum ~

  This would recopy the file **memorandum** from **bozo**'s home directory to your home directory.

Repeating the Last Word of a Command

When you want to repeat only the last word from the previous command line, type **!$**. For example, typing **cat article** and pressing Return, and then entering the command **head !$**, is the same as entering **head article**, which displays the first ten lines of the file named **article**.

Changing Command-Line Entries

Use the command substitution character, the caret (**^**), to change a portion of a command line. To correct the misspelling of the word *more* in the following command line

```
mroe thesis
```

type

```
^ro^or
```

and press Return. The carets (**^**) tell SunOS to substitute the characters between the first and second carets with the characters after the second caret.

If you want to edit a command besides the previous command, use the **:s** (substitute) modifier to make your changes. To substitute the file named **letter** with the file named **report** in the 12th command in the **history** command list, enter

```
!12:s/letter/report/
```

The first occurrence of the file named **letter** in the 12th command of the **history** list is replaced with the file named **report**.

You can globally replace all occurrences of a string in a command line by using the global substitute indicator **:gs**. For example, the command

```
!!:gs/acct/account
```

changes every occurrence of the string **acct** to **account** in the last command line.

Command and File Name Numbering

Each string of characters on a command line that are separated by a space are referred to as *words*. SunOS numbers the words in each command starting at **0**, as in Figure 3.1.

Remember that the command is considered the first word and is assigned the number 0; the second string of characters is considered word number 1.

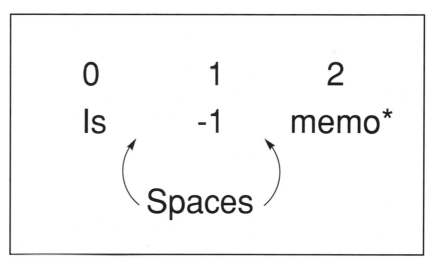

Figure 3.1: Numbering words in commands

You can refer to individual words with **:n**, where **n** is the word number. For example, say you just finished entering the following command:

```
cat file1
```

The command

```
mv !!:1 newfile
```

takes the file name that is word number 1 in the previous command line (**file1**) and renames it **newfile**.

You can also specify a range of words by entering the number of the word you want to begin with, followed by a hyphen and a dollar sign. For example, the modifier **3-$** refers to all words starting with word number 3 to the end of the command line. The following examples show how to change permission modes of three files by listing three files and then using the **-$** modifier to specify a range of words. Issuing the command

```
12% ls -l contract resume stats
```

It can be helpful to have the prompt display the current **history** command number. If you enter the command **set prompt = '\!%'** the prompt will be the command number followed by a percent sign, as shown in the accompanying example.

results in this listing

```
-rw-rw-r-- lbird     1 1024 Dec 23 10:30 contract
-rw-rw-r-- lbird     1 1024 Jan 22 11:30 resume
-rw-rw-r-- lbird     1 1024 Jan 23 12:30 stats
```

Following this with the command

```
13% chmod g-w !ls:2-$
```

would delete the group's write permissions to all files listed when you last used the **ls** command (**g** specifies that the command affect the group's permissions). To see the effects of this change in this example, you would enter **!12** to repeat the **ls -l contract resume stats** command issued in command number 12.

```
14% !12

-rw-r--r-- lbird     1 1024 Dec 23 10:30 contract
-rw-r--r-- lbird     1 1024 Jan 22 11:30 resume
-rw-r--r-- lbird     1 1024 Jan 23 12:30 stats
```

The sixth character in the permissions list for each file is now a **-**, indicating that the group does not have write permission for these files.

An asterisk character (*****) refers to all the words in a command except word 0. Keep in mind that SunOS considers word 0 a command. For example, if the last command was

```
15% cat scratch temp
```

entering

```
16% rm !!:*
```

is the same as issuing the command

```
rm scratch temp
```

Both versions remove the files named **scratch** and **temp**.

Spell Checking

SunOS provides two commands to check your spelling. The **look** command lists all the words in SunOS's 25,000 word dictionary that begin with the letters you enter. To use the **look** command, type the first few letters of a word of which you want to check the spelling. The **look** command displays the words closest to the spelling you have indicated, including proper nouns. For instance, entering

```
look suns
```

displays

```
sunscreen
sunset
sunshade
sunshine
sunshiny
sunspot
```

The **spell** command checks an entire text file for words that don't match any of the words in the system dictionary. To check the spelling of a text file, type **spell**, followed by the name of the file you want to spell check. If the spelling program hasn't been loaded into your system, SunOS displays the message **spell: command not found**. The **spell** command produces a list of words that don't match the entries in the SunOS online dictionary. For example, entering the command **spell brochure**, where **brochure** is a file than contains misspellings of the words *travel*, *oasis*, and *cruise*, displays the following results:

```
cruize
osais
travl
```

Counting Words in a File

Another helpful program for working with text files is the **wc** (word count) command. The **wc** command counts and displays the number of lines, words, and characters in a file. You can use these options with **wc**:

Option	Result
-l (line)	Counts lines only
-c (characters)	Counts characters only
-w (word)	Counts words only

The following shows the results of using **wc** on a file named **jumbo**.

```
1625    2805    50545    jumbo
```

This indicates there are 1625 lines, 2805 words, and 50,545 characters in **jumbo**.

Locating Files

SunOS is a large file system. If you are working in several directories, it is easy to misplace a file, but you can discover where a file is located using the **find** command. The **find** command searches for files that meet conditions you specify, starting at the top of the current or specified directory and automatically searching each subdirectory. A condition could be a file name matching a specific pattern, a file owned by a specific user or belonging to a specific group, or a file that has been modified within a specific time frame. The more specific your criteria, the narrower the field search becomes. The syntax for the **find** command is

```
find directory options
```

The **find** options create a criterion for selecting a file. To see which files within the current directory and its subdirectories end in the letter **s**, type

```
find ~/ -name '*s' -print
```

~/	Indicates the search should begin at the top of your home directory. The tilde specifies your home directory and the front slash begins the search at the highest directory.
-name '*s'	Instructs **find** to find all filenames ending with the letter **s**. If wildcards are used, as in this example, the file name character string and wildcard characters must be surrounded by single quotation marks.
-print	Indicates that you want the results to be displayed on your screen.

Table 3.1 lists options that can be added to the **find** command to locate files.

Using \! to reverse the effect of an option does not work with hidden files (files that begin with a period). In this example, hidden files ending with the letter **s** are still displayed.

You can reverse the meaning of an option by inserting a backslash and an exclamation point before the option. The backslash is referred to as an *escape character*. It indicates that the special character or symbol following it has a different meaning than its normal "metacharacter" meaning. In this instance, the exclamation point after the backslash indicates that SunOS should select files for which the option does *not* apply. For example, the command

```
find ~/ \! -name '*s' -print
```

finds file names in your home directory and any subdirectories that *don't* end with the letter **s**.

You can also use **find** to execute commands on the files it finds by adding the following option:

```
-exec command '{}' \;
```

For example, you can use **find** to locate and remove files that are named consistently. If the name of the files you want to remove begin with the string **junk** (such as **junk1**, **junk2**, and

Table 3.1: The find Command Options

Option	Result
-exec **command "{ } \;"**	Applies any command you specify to the files **find** calls up
-group *group*	Finds files belonging to the specified group
-mtime *n*	Selects files that have been modified in the last *n* days
-name *filename*	Finds files that have names matching the character string you specify in single quotes
-never *filename*	Finds files that have been modified after the file specified
-user *username* or *user_number*	Selects files belonging to the user indicated

The quoted braces tell the command (**rm** in this case) to operate on the files that **find** selects.

junk3) the following command line finds and removes them from the current directory:

```
find . -name 'junk*' -exec rm '{}' \;
```

Remember that a single period (.) refers to the working directory.

Locating Text in Files

The **grep** command is a powerful pattern searching command that locates text in files. You can have **grep** search for an exact string of text, or you can use wildcards and brackets to broaden the search pattern. You must tell **grep** which files it should search through. The most basic **grep** syntax is

```
grep search_string filename(s)
```

If **grep** only searches through one file, it will simply display any lines that contain the search string. If it searches more than one file, it will display the matching lines and also tell you the names of the files in which they occur.

Within a search string, a period (**.**) matches any single character in the same way the question mark (**?**) is used in file name substitution. For example, the command **grep .s namelist** matches all lines in which the letter **s** is preceded by a character (any character) in the file **namelist**. The equivalent of the asterisk wildcard is a period preceding an asterisk (**.***). For example, **grep 't.*' testfile** locates every word in **testfile** containing the letter **t**. Note that the letter **t** and ***** wildcard character must be put in quotes.

A caret (**^**) instructs the pattern to match only the beginning of the line. The command **grep ^v** matches any line beginning with the letter **v**. A search string followed by a dollar sign (**$**) matches only those lines with that expression at the end of the line. For example, **grep s$ slist** displays all lines ending with the letter **s** in the file named **slist**. The command **grep ^v$** matches any line in which **v** is the only character.

Use double or single quotes to surround text that contains spaces. For example, if you use **grep** to search all files for the phrase **good work**, you would enter **grep 'good work'**. If you did not use the quotes, **grep** would only search for **good** and would consider **work** to be a file name.

Bracketed lists and ranges work just as they do for file name substitutions. For example, **grep '[BH]' namelist,** where the file **namelist** contains the names **Beck**, **Hendrix**, and **Clapton**, displays both **Beck** and **Hendrix**, but not **Clapton**. Note that you must place quotation marks around the search string when you use brackets this way.

The characters &, !, $, ? ., ;, and \ need to be preceded by a backslash when you want them to be treated as ordinary (literal) characters.

Table 3.2 shows the characters that can be used to match or escape characters using the **grep** command.

Table 3.2: Special grep Pattern-Search Characters

Character	Matches
^	The beginning of a text line
.	Any single character
[ ]	Any character in the bracketed list or range
[^]	Any character not in the list or range
*	The preceding character or expression
.*	Any characters
\	Escapes special meaning of next character
$	Any matching characters at the end of a line

Using Options to Tailor grep's Output

There are several options that you can use to change **grep**'s output to better fit your needs. The most useful of these are explained below. When you employ these options, use the following syntax:

```
grep option(s) search_string filename(s)
```

Option	*Result*
-v	Displays all lines that *don't* contain the search string
-l	Causes **grep** to display only the names of any of the specified files that contain the search string. Does not display the lines that contain the search string.
-c	Causes **grep** to display the number of lines that contain the search string. If more than one file contains the string, displays the names of these files and the number of matching lines in each.

Redirection

When you execute commands, the results are displayed on your screen. The screen is considered to be the *standard output.* A command normally gets information from the keyboard, which is referred to as *standard input.* You can control standard input and output and redefine where information is sent once a command has processed it. For example, you can store the output of commands into files for reviewing or editing. You can send output from one command into another and further process the data, such as formatting text to be sent to a printer.

Redirecting Output to a File

The greater-than symbol (**>**), also known as "to," sends output from commands into a specified file rather than to the screen. For example,

```
ls -a > myfiles
```

sends the output of the **ls -a** (list all) command to a file named **myfiles**. When you redirect output to a file, because the output is redirected to the target file, it isn't displayed on the screen.

Specifying a target file automatically creates the target file with the name you specify (if a file with that name does not exist). SunOS normally doesn't allow you to redirect and save information to a file that already exists.

You can force an existing file to be overwritten by following the greater-than symbol with an exclamation point (**>!**). For example, **cat file1 >! newfile** redirects the contents of **file1** to **newfile**, overwriting the contents of **newfile** if that file already exists.

When you use **>!** to redirect output to a file that already exists, the contents of that file will be overwritten.

Adding Text to an Existing File

Two greater-than symbols in succession can be used to append text to the end of an existing file. This append feature is useful for keeping running logs or for accumulating information in a single file. The command

```
cat clients >> newclients
```

appends the file **clients** to a file named **newclients**.

Using Files as Input to Commands

Just as you can redirect the output of a command, you can also have a file or device provide input to a command. The less-than sign (**<**), referred to as "from," redirects the standard input of a command.

Input redirection is valuable for the few commands that don't use file name arguments. For example, the command

```
mail bozo < reply
```

mails the contents of the file **reply** to **bozo**. Another command that reads from a file instead of the terminal is the **tr** (translate) command. The following example sends the file **filei** to the **tr** command and translates all lowercase i's in the file to uppercase I's.

```
tr i I < filei
```

Redirecting the Standard Error

When a command performs without problems, it produces results as standard output to your screen. When a command encounters a problem, it uses a different channel to send error messages, or diagnostic output, to the screen. If you are using the C shell, you can redirect the standard error output to a file for review later by using the greater-than redirection sign followed by an ampersand (**>&**). For example,

```
cat testfile >& errorfile
```

redirects the standard output and standard error to the file named **errorfile**. If **testfile** doesn't exist, **errorfile** contains the error message:

```
testfile: No such file or directory.
```

You can use command grouping to redirect the standard output to one file and the standard error output to another. For example,

```
(cat testfile > stdoutfile) >& errorfile
```

The **cat** command output is redirected to the **stdoutfile** file and any error messages are sent to the file named **errorfile**.

You can also redirect error messages to the system wastebasket file. This file is located in the device directory and named **null** (**/dev/null**). Any output you redirect to this file disappears—you can send output here when you don't want it displayed.

Table 3.3 lists and explains redirection commands with examples.

Table 3.3: Redirection Command Examples

Command	Function	Example
>	Redirects the standard output	`cat file1 > file2`
>!	Forces redirection, even if the file exists	`cat file1 >! file2`
>>	Appends the standard output to the file	`cat file2 >> file1`
>>!	Appends the standard output, creating the file if necessary	`cat file1 >>! file3`
>&	Redirects the standard output and the standard error	`cat file1 >& errorfile`
>>&	Appends both the standard output and the standard error	`cat file1 >>& errorfile1`
<	Redirects the standard input	`tr a A < filea`

Using Pipes to Combine Commands

The output of one command can be fed in directly as input to another. A set of commands strung together is called a *pipeline*. The symbol for this connection is a solid vertical bar (|), called a *pipe*. The pipe (|) key is to the right of the F12 key on many keyboards. Pipes have a wide variety of uses. You can string multiple commands with pipes, as long as the command line does not exceed 256 characters.

Piping is a convenient alternative to a multiline command. A pipe passes output from one command to the input of another. Instead of having to store data into temporary work files and perform several operations, you can join commands together so that output from one is used as input for another. For example, the command **ls -l | more** allows the user to view a long directory listing page by page. You can even connect groups of commands this way.

In addition to using pipes for file processing, you can pipe commands to simplify daily SunOS operations. For example, suppose you want a quick list of all the files you have changed today in your home directory. You can pipe the output of a long directory listing (**ls -l**) into **grep** and produce a list of files matching today's date. For example, if today is July 19, you can obtain a list of files using the following:

```
ls -l | grep 'July 19'
```

The listing produced might look something like this:

```
-rw-rw-rw- 1 jcool      1640   Jul 19 03:09 project
-rw-r-xr-- 1 jcool        64   Jul 19 10:10 style
-rwxr-xrw- 1 jcool       256   Jul 19 12:07 clients
```

Redirecting Combined Commands

When you want to redirect the output of a group of commands, enclose the group of commands in parentheses. An example of the output of grouped commands being sent to a file instead of the screen might appear as follows:

```
(ls -l | grep 'Jul 19') > todaysfile
```

You can combine any commands this way to consolidate output into a single file. Output from grouped commands can also be piped to other commands. For example, typing

```
(ls -l | grep 'Jul 19') | lpr
```

prints the listing. Not all SunOS applications accept standard input, which means you can't pipe information into them. You can, however, pipe information into the **lpr** (printing) command, because this command accepts standard input. Piping is also effective for all DOS commands and applications running under SunOS.

Directing Data to More than One Place

Like pipes, the **tee** command is a term borrowed from the plumbing trade to describe a single pipe that splits into two directions. The **tee** command splits output into two or more separate destinations. As **tee** stores data in a file, it also displays the output on the screen or channels it to another selected destination. This ability to split output is useful in many situations. For example, you can use it to send a sorted list to two files instead of one, or to view the list on the screen while simultaneously saving the data in a file. The command

```
who | tee userfile
```

displays a listing of who is using the system and also sends the listing to a file named **userfile**. The command creates **userfile** if it doesn't already exist and overwrites its data if it does.

If you use the **-a** option, **tee** appends the data into an existing file. For instance, the command

tee overwrites files.

```
ls -l | tee -a userfile
```

displays a long directory listing and also adds this listing to the existing file **userfile**.

Filters

Filters are commands that accept text as input, transform it in some way, and then produce text as output. You've already used a number of filters; the **more**, **head**, **tail**, and **spell** commands are all examples of filters. Filters send their output to the screen by default; of course the standard output can be redirected to files or system devices. Figure 3.2 shows a simple example of how a filter might process text.

Sorting a File

One of the most commonly used SunOS filters is the **sort** command. You can alphabetically sort the contents of a file in ascending order by issuing the **sort** command followed by the

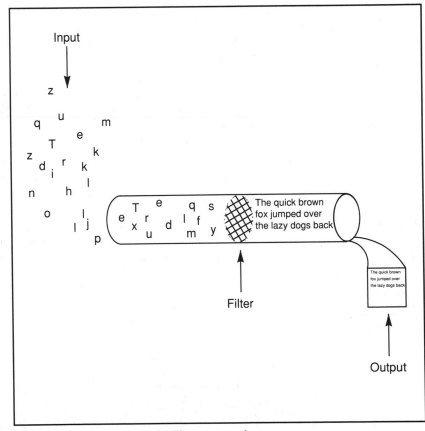

Figure 3.2: An example of a filter processing text

file name to be sorted. The proper way to sort a file is to break the operation into two lines, as shown in the following example:

```
sort clients > temp
mv temp clients
```

⊙ Make sure the output file has a different name from the file you are processing. Otherwise, the original file will be wiped out.

Make sure the output file has a name different from the file you are processing. For example, if you are sorting a file called **clients**, do not send output to a file of the same name. This wipes out the original file before the information is sorted.

To sort a file named **clients** and store the result in a new file called **sclients**, you would type

```
sort clients > sclients
```

Because the sorted clients information is directed into a file, it does not appear on the screen as it would if you simply typed **sort clients**. You can easily examine the **sclients** file using the **cat** or **more** commands or view the sorted information as it is sent to **sclients** by entering

```
sort clients | tee sclients
```

Selecting a Sort Field

Remember that the **sort** command begins numbering fields with the number zero. The second string of characters is considered field number one.

The **sort** command allows you to sort by characters other than those at the beginning of a line. For example, say you have a file named **clients** in which you keep the following list of clients:

```
hugh jones
martha applebee
daniel newton
ursula smith
pippi schwartz
```

If you entered the command **sort clients**, the file would be sorted alphabetically by the first names of your clients. To sort the file by the last names, you have to specify which field to perform the sort on. *Fields* are character strings separated by spaces. The file **clients** contains two fields. The first field (field 0) comprises the first names and the second field (field 1) comprises the last names. The numbering scheme used with fields is illustrated in Figure 3.3.

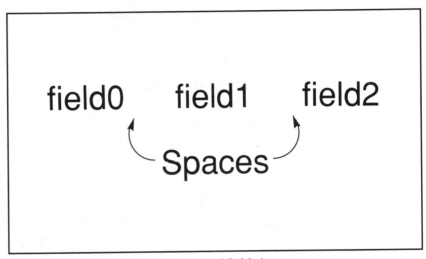

Figure 3.3: The numbering scheme of fields in sorts

To specify where a sort begins, use this syntax:

```
sort +field_number filename
```

The plus sign (**+**) followed by the field number indicates the field with which the sort begins. If you wanted to sort your list of clients by their last names, you would enter

```
sort +1 clients
```

where the number 1 specifies that the sort be performed on the field containing the last names. The output of this command, the sorted list, will then appear on the screen. Most likely you will want to save the sorted list to another file, in which case you will have to enter a command like this one:

```
sort +1 clients > sclients
```

Here the output of sort, the sorted list of **clients**, is redirected to a new file named **sclients**.

In some instances, it is inconvenient to have spaces serve as field separators. For example, if your list of clients also included the name Joe Van Gogh and you tried to use the previous command to sort the list by last name, **sort** would only recognize Van and not include Gogh in the sort criteria. Of course, this would not affect the outcome of the sort on the current list, but if the file also contained the names Ella Vance, Jack Vance, and Jerry Van Heusen, it would cause problems. Fortunately you can change the field separator to another character with the **-t***c* option, where *c* is used to identify the new field separator. To add an option to the sort command, follow this general syntax:

```
sort options(s) +field_number filename
```

If you inserted a symbol, say a colon, between the first and last names on your list and you specify the colon as the new field separator, you could sort by first or last names without worrying about spaces affecting the sort.

With the **sort** command you can sort on any range of characters you want as long as you specify where you want the sort to begin and end. This means you must indicate both the field number and character number to begin and end on. Use the following syntax to perform a sort on a specific range of characters:

```
sort option(s) +field_number.character_number
        -field_number.character_number filename
```

Here the plus sign (**+**) indicates which field and character number to start the sort on and the minus sign (**-**) indicates which field and character number to end the sort on.

Let's say you added the amount of revenue of each client to the **sclients** file. Your list might look like this:

```
martha applebee:$1000.00
hugh jones:$500.00
daniel newton:$250.00
pippi schwartz:$600.00
ursula smith:$4500.00
```

The first character in a field is numbered 0.

To produce a list of clients in order of lowest to highest revenue, enter

```
sort -t: -n +1.1 -1.5 sclients > revenues
```

Here the **-t:** indicates that the colon serves as the field separator, separating the list into two fields: names of clients and revenue. The **-n** (numeric) option allows you to sort in ascending numerical order. The **+1.1** specifies that the sort begin with the second field (field 1) and second character of the field (character 1), or at the first number after the dollar sign. The **-1.5** indicates that the sort ends with the sixth character (character 5) of the second field. The output of the command is then sent to the file **revenues**.

The following list reviews some of the options you can use with **sort**:

Option	*Result*
-f	Causes **sort** to ignore case when performing a sort. Otherwise the sort is performed according to ASCII number.
-n (numeric)	Instructs **sort** to sort in numerical order
-r (reverse)	Produces a list sorted in descending order (see next section)
-t*c*	Indicates the fields are separated by *c*. In the previous example the fields are separated by the colon (:) character.

Reverse Sorts

When you sort a file containing a field of numbers you may want to sort the file in descending numeric order to see the fields with the largest amounts first. Suppose you want to select the top three clients with the largest revenue from **sclients**. You can sort the file in reverse numeric order using the **-r** (reverse) and

-n (numeric) options to produce a highest-to-lowest listing and then use the **head** command to select the top three entries. By using a pipe to separate the **sort** and **head** commands, you can get a list of the top three clients in the **sclients** file by entering the command

```
sort -t: -r -n +1.1 -1.5 sclients | head -3
```

which displays this result:

```
ursula smith:$4500.00
martha applebee:$1000.00
pippi schwartz:$600.00
```

Summary

Table 3.4 lists useful SunOS filters, some of which were covered in earlier chapters. While this table primarily uses examples of filters processing files, keep in mind that filters can just

Table 3.4: Examples of Useful SunOS Filters

Purpose of Filter	Example
cat	
Displays a file	`cat file2`
Creates a file from information typed at the keyboard	`cat > newfile`
Merges two or more files	`cat file1 file2 > file3`
echo	
Displays a message on the screen	`echo 'Hi SunOS'`

Table 3.4: Examples of Useful SunOS Filters (continued)

Purpose of Filter	Example
grep	
Searches a file or group of files for information you specify	`grep 'Clients' file 1`
head	
Displays the beginning lines of a file	`head file1`
more	
Displays one or more files, one screen at a time	`more longfile`
sort	
Sorts a file	`sort clients`
Sorts and merges multiple files	`sort clients prospects > contacts`
tail	
Displays the final lines of a file	`tail prospects`
tee	
Duplicates output to a file in addition to displaying output on the screen.	`sort comm | tee temp`

Table 3.4: Examples of Useful SunOS Filters (continued)

Purpose of Filter	Example
Sends output to two files at once	`cat file1| tee register log`
tr	
Translates one character or group of characters for another	`tr a b < temp`
wc	
Lists the number of lines, words, and characters in a file	`wc temp`

as easily handle input from the keyboard or other commands.

In this chapter, you've extended your inventory of helpful SunOS commands. You learned tips and techniques using the history mechanism to repeat commands. You also learned about redirecting output and input and filtering information from files using filters or stringing together commands using pipes. You learned how to

- Perform multiple commands by separating commands with a semicolon (;)

- Repeat commands and parts of commands using the ! metacharacter, such as !! and !$, and use carets (^) or the :s command to substitute portions of previous commands

- Perform spell checks on files or look up the spelling of a word with the **look** command, and use the **wc** command to count words, lines, and characters in a file

- Locate files with the **find** command
- Locate text within files with the **grep** command
- Redirect output of files and commands, including redirecting a standard error message using the **<** and **>** symbols
- Join multiple commands with pipes (**|**), making one command's output the next command's input
- Direct data to the screen and other files using the **tee** command
- Perform a group of commands by enclosing them within parentheses
- Sort files with one or more fields and perform numeric and reverse sorts using the **sort** command

The commands that you explored in this chapter are like building blocks that enable you to control SunOS rather than having SunOS control you. Most SunOS commands are similar to the commands you've learned in this chapter. Table 3.5 lists all of these commands.

Table 3.5: Commands Covered in Chapter 3

Command	Result
! *n*	Repeats the command with the corresponding number in the **history** list
! *char-acter(s)*	Repeats the last command that matches the character string specified
!$	Repeats the last word from the previous command line
!!	Repeats the last command

Table 3.5: Commands Covered in Chapter 3 (continued)

Command	Result
>	Redirects output
>>	Appends text to the end of an existing file
>&	Redirects standard error output
<	Redirects input
		Takes command output and channels it into another command
clear	Clears the screen
find	Locates files
grep	Searches for specific patterns in text files
history	Lists commands previously used
look	Lists all the words from the system dictionary that begin with the characters the user specifies
sort	Sorts files
spell	Checks a text file for words that do not match those in the system dictionary
tee	Sends output to two destinations
tr	Changes characters in a text file
wc	Counts the number of lines, words, and characters in a file

CHAPTER 4

Electronic Mail and Messages

ONE OF SUNOS'S MOST USEFUL FEATURES IS ITS ability to send and receive electronic mail and messages. *Electronic mail* allows you to send and receive mail letters, including files, to and from other SunOS users, whether they're logged on or not. *Electronic messaging* allows you to interactively communicate with other users who are currently logged into SunOS. In this chapter, you'll learn how to receive, send, and manage your electronic mail using the **mail** program. You'll also learn how to communicate with other users online using the **talk** and **write** commands.

Overview of SunOS's Electronic Mail

Using SunOS's **mail** program is similar to sending mail through the post office. When you send an electronic letter, the **mail** program, like the post office, delivers your letter directly to the recipient's mailbox. The user name serves as the unique address of every user on the system. Each user on the system has a mailbox to receive electronic mail. This mailbox is usually a file called **inbox**, located in the **mail** subdirectory of your home directory. Depending on how your system is set up, when someone on the system sends you mail, SunOS notifies you that you have mail in your mailbox (**inbox**). Once you've read your mail, the **mail** program automatically stores these letters into a special storage file called **mbox** or **old_mail**, which is located in your home directory. When you execute the **mail** program, it displays its own unique prompt, the ampersand symbol (**&**). After executing the **mail** program, a working buffer is created in memory, where all tasks you perform within **mail**, such as moving and deleting mail messages, are temporarily stored. These changes are stored to disk only when you quit the **mail** program.

Getting Help in the mail Program

You can request help by entering a question mark (**?**) at the **mail** prompt (**&**). Entering **?** displays a list of available mail program commands with descriptions, as shown below.

```
cd [directory]         chdir to directory or home if none
                       given
d [message list]       delete messages
e [message list]       edit messages
f [message list]       show from lines of messages
h                      print out active message headers
m [user list]          mail to specific users
n                      goto and type next message
p [message list]       print messages
pre [message list]     make messages go back to system
                       mailbox
```

q	quit, saving unresolved messages in mbox
r [message list]	reply to sender (only) of messages
R [message list]	reply to sender and all recipients of messages
s [message list] file	append messages to file
t [message list]	type messages (same as print)
top [message list]	show top lines of messages
u [message list]	undelete messages
v [message list]	edit messages with display editor
w [message list] file	append messages to file, without from line
x	quit, do not change system mailbox
z [-]	display next [previous] page of headers
!	shell escape

Quitting the mail Program

There are two commands for leaving the **mail** program: the **q** (quit) command and the **x** (exit) command. The **q** command

- Moves the letters you have read from your mailbox (**inbox**) and saves them in a file named **mbox** or **old_mail**.

- Saves any changes you've made to letters in your mailbox, such as deleting letters.

- Quits the **mail** program, and returns you to the system prompt.

If you have any unread mail in your mailbox, **mail** displays a message similar to the following

```
Held 3 messages in home/lbird/mail/inbox
```

The **x** (exit) command leaves the **mail** program but doesn't save any changes you made to mail in your mailbox, such as deleting a letter. It also doesn't move any letters you have already read into the **mbox** or **old_mail** file.

Receiving Mail

When you log in, your incoming mailbox, **inbox**, is checked for new mail. If there are any new letters, SunOS displays the message **You have mail** on your screen. If mail is sent to you while you're on the system, at the next SunOS prompt you are notified with the same message. SunOS checks your mailbox every few minutes to see if you have received mail. The time between these checks may vary, depending on how your system administrator has set up your account. You can choose to read your mail immediately after notification by SunOS or at a later time.

If you're prompted with the message **You have mail**, you can type **from** at the system prompt to find out who sent you mail. The **from** command brings up a list of users who sent you mail similar to the following example:

```
From lbird        Sun  Apr 1 8:45:12 1992
From mjordan      Sun  Apr 1 8:45:22 1992
From mjohnson     Sun  Apr 1 8:45:45 1992
```

Listing Your Mail

To begin reading your mail, type **mail** at the system prompt. If you don't have any mail, the **mail** program displays the message, **No mail for *username*.** If you do have mail, the **mail** program displays a list of mail headers from your **inbox** file followed by the **mail** program prompt, as shown below.

```
Mail version 4.0 Mon Feb 17 00:20:20:58 ST 1992  Type ? for
help.
"+inbox": 3 messages 2 new 1 unread
>N  1kmchale     Mon Jan 25 16:51  20/619  Game tomorrow
 N  2mjohnson    Wed Jan 16 15:55  19/610  No game this week
 U  3lbird       Tue Dec 12 09:08  12/281  Game tonight
&
```

New letters are indicated by **N**, as shown in the first column above. The **U** (Unread) status indicates the letter was new but was not read before quitting the **mail** program previously.

The **>** located to the far left of the first header in the list indicates the current letter. The current letter is either the first new letter in your mailbox or the last letter you read. The following list describes the information provided in each of the columns from left to right in the mail headers list:

Column	Description
Mail letter status	Status of a letter in the mailbox
Mail letter number	Number you can use to specify a letter
Sender	User name of the person who sent the letter
Time sent	Date and time the letter was sent
Size	Number of lines and number of characters in the letter (lines/characters)
Subject	Subject of the letter

If you have numerous letters in your mailbox, the header list may not show all of your mail headers. Instead, it displays one screenful of mail headers at a time. You can display the next screenful of mail headers with the command

    h+

You can display the previous screenful of mail headers with

    h-

You can redisplay the mail headers list at any time by typing

    h

Remember that if you enter **q** to quit **mail**, the letters you have read are moved to your **mbox** or **old_mail** file.

Reading Your Mail

After you've displayed the mail headers list, there are several ways to read the mail in your mailbox. The easiest way is simply to press Return. The current letter, indicated by the greater-than sign (**>**), is displayed. To continue reading your letters one by one, press Return again after each letter. You can redisplay the previous message by typing **p**. When you've reached the end of the letters, **mail** responds with the message **At EOF** (end of file), meaning **mail** couldn't find any more mail letters in your mailbox.

Another way to read your mail is to type the message number at the **mail** prompt (**&**). Letter numbers are displayed in the second column of the mail headers list. For example, if you want to read mail letter number 2, type **2** at the **mail** prompt. The **mail** program then displays the mail letter number 2:

```
Message 2:
From mjohnson Wed Jan 15 15:55 1992
From mjohnson (Magic Johnson)
Subject: No game this week

Just a reminder, we won't be playing any basketball games
this week. So get some work done.
```

Another way to read a letter that is longer than a single screen is to save it as a file (explained later in this chapter) then use the **more** command.

If a letter is longer than the screen, it quickly scrolls down your screen. You can use Control-S to freeze the screen and Control-Q to unfreeze it. You can check to see if a letter is longer than the screen by noting the number of lines in the size column of the mail headers list.

Replying to Mail

When you read your mail, **mail** allows you to send a reply to the originator of any letter. Use the **r** (reply) command to quickly send a reply to the original sender of a letter. For example, to send a reply to the creator of mail message number 2, type **r 2** at the **mail** prompt. The **mail** program responds with

```
To: mjohnson
Subject: Re: No game this week
```

The subject line of the reply will automatically hold the subject of the original letter, preceded by **Re:**. You can then type in your reply. When you complete your reply, press Return to place the cursor on a blank line, press Control-D, and then press Return. The **mail** program may then ask if you want to send any "carbon copies" by displaying a prompt such as **Cc:**. If you don't want to send duplicates of the reply to other users, simply press Return. The reply is sent to the author of the original letter.

Deleting Mail

After you've read or replied to mail letters, you may want to delete them rather than have then saved in your **mbox** or **old_mail** file. The **mail** program allows you to delete mail from your mailbox. You can delete the last letter you read by typing **d** at the **mail** prompt. By typing **h** (header) you can verify that the letter was deleted. You can delete specific letters by typing **d** followed by the letter number. For example, typing **d 3** deletes letter number 3. You can delete multiple letters, too. For example, if you wanted to delete letters 1 and 3, type **d 1 3**. You can also delete a range of letters. For example, to delete letters 2, 3, and 4, type **d 2-4**.

Undoing a Mail Deletion

If you accidentally delete letters, you can restore them using the **u** (undelete) command. To undo the last delete command, type **u** at the **mail** program prompt immediately after the deletion. For example, if the last deletion command was **d 4-7**, typing **u** undeletes messages 4, 5, 6, and 7.

The Mail Storage File

When you read a letter, it is marked to be moved to another file for storage. The default file name for this secondary mail file is **mbox**, and it is located in your home directory. Letters remain in the **mbox** file until you remove them. This mail storage file enables you to read your mail and store mail for reference at a later date, leaving your mailbox (**inbox**) uncluttered.

Managing the Mail Storage File

When you want to access mail in your secondary mail storage file, **mbox**, use the **mail** command with the **-f** option as follows:

```
mail -f mbox
```

Your screen then displays a headers list exactly like the headers list displayed when accessing your mailbox (**inbox**). You can read, save, or delete letters using the same commands as you did when you used the **mail** command without the **-f** option. ·

Holding Mail

To prevent letters from being automatically moved to your **mbox** or **old_mail** file after reading them, you can use the **ho** (hold) command. The **ho** (hold) command instructs the **mail** program to keep the letter(s) you have read in your **inbox** or **old_mail** file after quitting **mail** if you want to refer to the letter at a later time. Suppose you want to hold the last letter you've read; type **ho** at the **mail** prompt. Like deleting letters, you can hold single or multiple letters, or a range of letters. For example, to hold letter number 3, type **ho 3** at the **mail** prompt. If you wanted to hold multiple letters, such as letters 1 and 3, type **ho 1 3**. To hold a range of letters—for example, letters 2, 3, and 4—type **ho 2-4** at the **mail** prompt. The hyphen (-) separates the beginning and end of the range of letters to be held.

Saving Letters as Files

You may want to save a letter as a file for editing or printing. To save the last letter you've read, including the header, into a file in your working directory, at the mail prompt (**&**) type

```
s filename
```

In addition, you can save any letter by specifying its number from the mail headers list, as follows:

```
s 4 filename
```

You can also save several letters in the same file at the same time. For example, to save letters 2, 4, 5, and 6 in a file, at the **mail** prompt, type

```
s 2 4-6 filename
```

You can also save a letter to a file using the **w** (write) command. This command is almost identical to the **s** (save) command, except it doesn't put the letter header into the file.

Saved letters are marked in the mail headers list with an asterisk (*). When you leave the **mail** program using the **q** (quit) command, the marked letters are deleted from your mailbox (**inbox**) and saved in your **mbox** or **old_mail** file.

An Overview of Sending Mail

You send mail with the **mail** command by specifying the user name of the person or persons you want to receive a letter. You can use the **who**, **finger**, or **rusers** commands to find a user's address if you don't know it. When you send mail to another user, it is stored in the recipient's electronic mailbox, and that person is notified that they have mail.

Who Is Using the System?

The **who**, **finger**, and **rusers** commands are useful if you need to know a user's login name but only know their real name. If the users you want to send mail to are logged into the same file server, you can address them using just their user names.

The **who** command lists the users logged into the system using the same file server at that moment. The list contains user names, identities of terminals being used, and the date and time each user logged in. Below is a listing produced by entering **who**.

```
wcleaver   tty06      Jul  3 10:30
dreed      tty15      Jul  3 12:55
mbrady     tty19      Jul  3 12:56
```

▪ Idle time is the length of time in minutes since the last SunOS command was issued.

The **finger** command provides more detailed user information than the **who** command. Depending on what your system administrator has directed this command to display, it may list a user's full name, user name, terminal number, idle time, home directory, and more. When you enter the **finger** command, SunOS displays a listing of current system users, such as the following:

```
Login      Name            TTY       Idle    When
wcleaver   Ward Cleaver    06        12      Fri 10:30
dreed      Donna Reed      15        0       Fri 12:55
mbrady     Mike Brady      19        20      Fri 12:56
```

Listing Users on a Network

▪ If the person you want to send mail to is on a different computer on the same local network, you need to use both the user name and a *machine name*, separated by the at sign (@).

To find out who's logged in on other computers within your local network, use the **rusers** command. The **rusers** command by itself lists the machine name of each computer on the network, followed by the users currently on that computer. For example, entering **rusers** might display a listing similar to the one below. The left column lists the machine names.

```
russet        gpost
cortez        jvalez
bradybunch    sbrady       mbrady
spike         slee
magus         jfowles
beaver        wcleaver
```

If you know the relevant machine name but can't remember the specific user's name, enter **rusers** followed by the machine name to display user names for that specific computer.

You can also add to **rusers** the **-l** (long) option, which lists the user name, machine name, terminal name, date, and time the user logged on, idle time, and the name of the machine on which the user logged in. For example, entering **rusers -l bradybunch** might display

```
sbrady bradybunch:console Jul 3 11:00  12
mbrady bradybunch:ttyp0   Jul 3 11:46  03 (sitcom)
```

Sending Mail

Once you've established the user name and the machine name (if needed) of the person you want to send mail to, you can follow these four simple steps to send them electronic mail:

SunOS has a special system database known as Yellow Pages. A feature of this database known as *alias mapping* simplifies identifying users on the system. If your network supports this feature, you can send mail to users on other machines using just their user name. Try typing **ypwhich** at the system prompt to see if Yellow Pages services are available for your machine.

1. If the person you want to send a letter to is using the same machine, at the system prompt type **mail username**, then press Return. If the person is on another machine, type **mail username@machinename**. If you are already in the mail facility, you can simply type **m** followed by the user name of the person you want to send a letter to. To send the same letter to multiple users, separate each user name with a space. The **mail** program then prompts you for the subject of the letter.

2. Type in the subject of your letter at the **Subject:** prompt, then press Return.

3. Type in the text of your letter. If at any point you want to create a new line, simply press Return. Remember, even though a sentence may wrap on your screen, it is not considered a line until you press Return. Each line of text can be up to 256 characters long. If you exceed 256 characters on your system, your screen will freeze up and you will have to abort the letter by pressing Ctrl-C.

4. When you've finished entering your text, press Return to move the cursor to a new line, and then press Control-D

to end your letter. You can also type a period and press Return to end your letter. The **mail** program then displays the **Cc:** (carbon copy) prompt. You can then enter the names of other users to whom you want to send copies of the letter. To specify more than one user, separate each user name with a space. When you're finished entering user names, or if you don't want to send any copies to other users, press Return to send your letter. If you left the letter body blank, SunOS displays the message **Null message body; hope that's ok** and then displays the system prompt; otherwise the system prompt returns to your screen.

Aborting a Letter

If at any point you change your mind about sending a letter, press Control-C to abort the letter. The **mail** program displays the message **(Interrupt -- one more time to kill letter)**, asking you to press Control-C again to confirm aborting the letter. If you decide not to abort the letter, continue entering your text.

Undeliverable Mail

When you send a letter with an incorrect address through the postal service, it's either returned to you or ends up in a dead letter office. The SunOS mail system works much the same way. If you've created your letter and pressed Return, and have specified an incorrect user name, SunOS responds with the message *username*... **User unknown**, and the letter is returned to your mailbox (**inbox**). When you enter the **mail** command again, the header states that you have returned mail, similar to the following example:

```
N 1 Mailer-Daemon Wed Jul 3 12:55 19/61 Returned mail: User
unknown
```

When you view the returned letter, it will appear similar to the following returned mail message:

```
From dreed Fri Jul  3 12:53:21 1992
From: Mailer-Daemon (Mail Delivery Subsystem)
Subject: Returned mail: User unknown
To: dreed

----- Transcript of session follows -----
550 wardcleaver... User unknown

----- Unsent message follows -----
Return-Path: <dreed>
Received: by noname (4.0/SMI-4.0)
 id AA00305; Fri, 3 Jul 92 12:53:21 PST
Date: Fri, 3 Jul 92 12:53:21 PST
From: dreed (Donna Reed)
Message-Id: <9002060053.AA00305@noname>
To: wardcleaver
Subject: hot water

Meet me at the water fountain at 4:45.
```

The mail facility also sends this information without the letter's text to a person who is designated as the *postmaster* on your system. This person is usually the same as your system administrator. When a letter is interrupted by pressing Control-C or cannot be delivered as in the previous example, the file is also sent to a file named **dead.letter** in your home directory.

Sending Files through mail

If you have a file with information you want to accompany a letter, such as a letter requesting payment and a file containing a list of outstanding invoices, you can mail the contents of a file as though it were a letter using the following command syntax:

```
mail username < filename
```

The **username** is the name of the user you want to send the file to, and **filename** is the name of the file you want to send. For example, **mail lbird < invoice** redirects the contents of the file named **invoice** to **lbird's** mailbox.

When you send a file using the redirection symbol (**<**), **mail** doesn't prompt you for a subject. If you want to add a subject line to the file, use the **-s** option followed by the text you want added as the subject. If the subject contains spaces, surround your subject text with quotation marks. The following is an example of adding a subject to a redirected file:

```
mail -s "Outstanding 1992 invoices" lbird < invoice
```

Using Tilde Escape Commands

During the composition of a letter, that is, while you're entering the letter, you can use tilde escape commands to perform a variety of functions. A *tilde escape* command usually consists of the tilde character (~) followed by a single character and possibly an argument. If you want to add a literal tilde to your letter, type two tildes in succession; only one tilde appears in your letter. The following lists some helpful tilde escape commands:

Command	*Result*
~!	Escapes to the SunOS prompt
~.	Simulates Control-D or a period on a separate line to mark the end of the file (EOF)
~:*mail_command*	While in the **mail** program, performs the indicated mail command
~b *username*	Adds user name(s) to a blind carbon copy (**Bcc**) list. This is similar to the carbon copy (**Cc**) list, but the names in the **Bcc** list aren't shown in the header of the letter.
~c *username(s)*	Adds user name(s) to the carbon copy (**Cc**) list

Command	*Result*
~d	Reads the contents of **dead-.letter** file in your home directory into the letter
~h	Displays, one at a time, the header lines **Subject**, **To**, **Cc**, and **Bcc**. You can delete any header text by using the Back Space key and then enter any new text.
~m *message_list*	In the **mail** program, inserts the text from a letter into the current letter
~p	Prints the current letter to the screen
~q	The equivalent of pressing Control-C twice. If the body of the letter is not empty, the partial letter is saved in the **dead.letter** file.
~r *filename*	Reads text from filename into your letter
~s *subject*	Changes the contents of the subject line to *subject*
~w *filename*	Writes the letter text into *filename* without adding the header information
~x	Exits similar to **~q** but doesn't save the letter in the **dead.letter** file

Using Electronic Messages

There are three kinds of electronic messages: interactive, broadcast, and system. Interactive messages let you communicate with another person who is currently using a terminal on your machine or using another machine on your local network. Broadcast messages are for important announcements for all current users of a system, such as an announcement that the system will be down for maintenance. System messages are the only messages that will be displayed for users who log on after the message was generated.

Talking with Other Current Users

The **talk** command is an interactive way of sending messages, similar to talking on a telephone. You can use **talk** to communicate with other users who are currently on the system. To find out who is currently on the system, issue the **who** command. To talk to another user, enter

```
talk username
```

where ***username*** is the person on the system you want to talk to. If a user is on another computer in a network, enter the command **talk *username@machinename*** where ***machinename*** is the name for the computer they're using. After entering this command, **talk**'s interactive screen appears and displays the message **No connection yet** until **talk** connects with the other user's machine. If you incorrectly enter the user name, or the other person isn't on the network, **talk** displays the message: **[Your party is not logged on]**.

If the person you want to talk to is logged on, **talk** connects with the other user's computer or terminal, displays a line across the middle of your screen, and notifies you that it is still contacting the other user with the message **[Waiting for your party to respond]**. While this message is displayed on your screen, the other user's screen displays a message similar to the following:

```
Message from Talk_Daemon@bradybunch at 01:11 ...
talk: connection requested by wcleaver@beaver
talk respond with: talk wcleaver@beaver
```

While the user is being notified that you want to talk, another message informs you that it is "ringing" the other user as follows:

```
[Ringing your party again]
[Ringing your party again]
```

The other person confirms that they want to be connected by typing in the user name and machine name, as displayed in the last line of the **talk** notification message.

```
talk wcleaver@beaver
```

If the other user is busy or simply doesn't respond, then you can type Control-C to exit **talk**. If the other user responds, you will see the message **[Connection established]**.

Now both users can type messages on the screen at the same time. The messages you send appear on the upper half of the screen. The other user's messages appear in the lower half of the split screen as shown below.

```
[Connection established]


Ward How ya doin
Eddie Haskell and Wally invited my kids to a party at your
house last week and they had a great time.
_____


That's interesting, Mr. Brady, because June and I were in
Mexico last week.
```

The message you type appears on the other user's screen as you type it. You can correct any misspellings on a single line, but once you press Return the line is sent. (Remember, even though a sentence may wrap on your screen, it is not considered a line until you press Return.) When either party wants to finish talking on the network, they can press Control-C to abort the **talk** program.

Writing Messages

The **write** command limits you to writing messages to only those users using terminals connected to the same computer as you. The **write** command doesn't use the entire screen like the **talk** command. To use the **write** command to send a message to another user, type **write** followed by the user name of the person you want to send the message to. The **write** command then displays the cursor on the next line without the prompt so that you can enter your message text. After typing the message text and pressing Return, the message is sent to the other user. The other person receives notification of the message directly below the command line, similar to the following:

```
Message from pduke@brooklyn on ttyp3 at 11:58
When did you want that financial report?
```

If the other person wants to write you back, they can type **write**, followed by your (the receiver's) user name, press Return, and begin their reply message. The two users can then continue to send messages back and forth without reentering the **write** command. To stop conversing using the **write** command, type Control-D to end the session. When either user presses Control-D, the letters **EOF** (End of File) appear, indicating the end of the conversation. The other user must also press Control-D to get the system prompt back.

Broadcasting Messages

 Refrain from using **wall** unless your message is so important that everyone on the system should see it.

The **wall** (write to all) command allows you to broadcast messages to every user on your system. These messages should be reserved for important messages only, such as when the system is going to be down for maintenance. To broadcast a message to everyone, type **wall** then press Return. You can then enter the message you want to broadcast. Press Control-D and your message is sent immediately to every one who is currently logged in.

System Messages

Messages sent to you automatically (and possibly generated) by the SunOS system itself, such as error messages or a message informing you that you have mail, are known as *system messages*. If you are not logged on when such a message is sent, it will still appear when you do log on. The system administrator can also create system messages. The most common message of this type is the *message of the day*. This is an important or general interest message sent to all users of a system when they log in.

Summary

In this chapter, you've learned how to use SunOS's mail and message commands to communicate with other users on the system. You can now perform the following tasks:

- Retrieve and read your mail using the **mail** program
- Delete, hold, and save mail to a file
- Reply to a letter
- Locate users on the system and send them mail
- Send files to other users using the **mail** program
- Use tilde escape commands to perform various functions such as adding a file to your letter text
- Access and manage your secondary mail storage file **mbox**
- Talk interactively on the network using either the **talk** or **write** commands

Table 4.1 lists the commands covered in this chapter.

Table 4.1: Commands Covered in Chapter 4

Command	Result
?	Displays a list of available mail commands (at the mail prompt)
d	Deletes letters (at the mail prompt)
from	Brings up a list of users who sent mail
mail	Takes user into the **mail** program and displays mail headers from inbox file
h	Displays mail headers list once in the mail program (at the mail prompt)
ho	Holds letters in **inbox** file (at the mail prompt)
q	Moves read letters to **mbox**, saves changes to letters, then exits the **mail** program (at the mail prompt)
r	Mails a reply to sender of a letter (at the mail prompt)
rusers	Lists the machine name of each computer on the network
s	Saves letters as files (at the mail prompt)
talk	Allows user to communicate interactively with another user

Table 4.1: Commands Covered in Chapter 4 (continued)

Command	Result
u	Restores deleted letters (at the mail prompt)
wall	Allows user to broadcast messages to every user on your system
write	Sends a message to another user without using the entire screen
x	Exits the **mail** program without saving changes (at the mail prompt)

CHAPTER 5

Using
the vi Editor

vi's command-driven structure can be a demanding environment for creating and editing simple text files, such as memos and letters. SunOS's DeskSet text editor make these tasks easier.

SUNOS'S VI EDITOR (PRONOUNCED VEE-EYE) IS A powerful, all-purpose file editor that edits everything from simple text files to complex program files. This SunOS feature provides an extensive collection of commands, many with overlapping functions, that can easily overwhelm new users. The purpose of this chapter is to provide you with a commanding grasp of essential vi commands for editing and file management.

About vi

The vi (visual editor) is a screen editor designed to display a full screen of a file at a time. While providing features for creating text documents, vi was not designed to process text with the same ease associated with most commercial word processing software packages. For instance, vi cannot produce formatted printouts by itself. Instead, vi depends on the **nroff** program to format documents created or modified with vi before printing them. The **nroff** program is covered in Chapter 6. However, you can print files created or modified in vi using the SunOS **lpr** command, which prints the text just as you see it on the screen.

Starting vi

To create or modify a file using vi, type **vi *filename*** at the system prompt, then press Return. For example, entering

```
vi sports
```

executes vi and creates the new file, **sports**. The following shows the last lines of the vi screen displayed with this file.

The tilde (~) indicates empty lines.

```
~
~
~
~
~
~
~
~
~
"sports" [New file]
```

If you want to execute vi with an existing file, such as a file named **basketball**, enter

```
vi basketball
```

The resulting screen display might look something like the example below:

```
Magic Johnson is a great basketball player.
Larry Bird is a great basketball player.
Michael Jordan is a great basketball player.
~
~
```

```
~
~
~
~
~
~
"basketball" 3 lines, 67 characters
```

You can start vi without specifying a file name by simply entering **vi**. Later you can give your new file a name when you exit vi. A file name can include any characters except special characters (such as **– * ? < > /**) and can be up to 256 characters in length.

The Status Line

The line at the bottom of the screen is called the *status line*. The status line shows the file name and the number of lines and characters in the file, as shown in the previous example. If you start vi to create a new file without a file name, no status line is displayed. Once you fill the screen with text, or move the cursor to the end of the file, the status line disappears. You can bring up the status line by pressing Control-G, which displays a new status line such as this:

```
"sports" [Modified] line 5 of 10 --50%--
```

Command and Insert Modes

There are two modes of operation in vi, command mode and insert mode. *Command mode* allows you to enter commands for performing a wide range of vi functions, such as cursor movement and editing operations. *Insert mode* allows you to enter text into a file and is activated within vi by typing **i** while in command mode. vi doesn't indicate which mode you're in, but pressing Esc always places you in command mode.

Command Mode

▗ You don't need to press Return to enter a vi command unless it is preceded by a colon.

You start vi in command mode. Most vi commands consist of one or two letters and an optional number, with uppercase and lowercase versions that usually perform related but different functions. For example, typing **x** deletes the character at the cursor, while typing **X** deletes the character preceding the cursor. You don't need to press Return after entering most vi commands. However, commands preceded by a colon do require you to press Return after the command. For example, to use the command **:q!** to quit vi and abandon changes, you must press Return after typing the exclamation point.

Undoing a Command

If you enter an incorrect vi command, you can undo it by typing **u** immediately after the command you want to undo. (The insert mode command is an exception; if you mistakenly enter this command, press Esc to return to command mode.) For example, if you've mistakenly deleted a line, immediately type **u**, and your deleted line is restored. You can also undo your last undo command. Typing **U** undoes all edits on a single line, as long as the cursor remains on that line. Once you move off a line, you can't use the **U** command for that line. The **u** command can be used to undo the **U** command.

Repeating the Previous Command

Any time you repeat the same editing command, you can save time duplicating the command by typing the repeat command (**.**) while in command mode. To repeat a command, position the cursor where you want to repeat the command and type a period (**.**). Keep in mind that you can only repeat the last command you executed, and that this command doesn't work with cursor movement or scrolling commands.

Insert Mode

You leave command mode and enter insert mode by typing **i** (insert) while in command mode. Typing **i** allows you to begin entering text at the cursor location. Characters you type subsequently appear to the left of the cursor and push any existing characters to the right. Remember, if you try to type a command while you're in insert mode, the command characters are inserted as text. Press Esc anytime you want to exit insert mode and enter another command. vi offers several other insert command options discussed later in this chapter.

Exiting vi

When you're creating or editing a file, you're actually working on a copy of the file that is stored in a *work buffer*, an area temporarily set aside in memory. Any changes you make to a file using vi only affect the file in the buffer until you instruct vi to save your file to disk. In other words, your edits don't affect your original file until you save your work. You can exit vi and abandon any changes you've made simply by not saving the contents of the work buffer. To quit vi, you must be in command mode.

Exiting vi and Saving Changes

To save your changes to a file and quit vi, press Shift-ZZ while in command mode or type **:x** and then press Return to save your file and exit vi. Entering the command **:w** writes (saves) the buffer contents to the disk but doesn't exit vi.

 Use **:w** frequently during a work session to prevent losing your work in the event of a system crash or failure.

If you started vi without a file name, type **:w**, followed by a new file name to save your work to another file, but continue to edit the same file. If you attempt to exit and save a new file you haven't named, vi responds with the message, **No current file name**. You can also quit vi and save both an old version of a file and a new version of a file with your new edits. For example, if you made changes to a file originally named **sports**,

you can save your edits to a different file called **sports.new** by
typing the command

```
:w sports.new
```

and then pressing Return. Your old version of the file, **sports**,
remains unchanged, and the new file, **sports.new**, contains
the file with your changes.

If you don't have a write permission for the file you've edited,
when you use the Shift-ZZ command to exit vi and save the file,
SunOS displays the message, **Permission denied**. Enter **:w** with
a different file name to save your file changes to disk. If you don't
have write permission in the working directory, vi may still not be
able to write your file to disk. Enter the **:w** command again, this
time using a pathname and a new file name in your home directory in place of the existing file name. For example, type

```
:w /usr/sports/temp
```

Exiting vi and Abandoning Changes

You can quit vi without saving your changes by typing **:q!** and
then pressing Return. Entering **:q** and pressing Return quits vi
if you haven't made any edits to the file; otherwise, vi prompts
you with the message

```
No write since last change (:quit! overrides)
```

In this case, you can use the appropriate command to save your
changes or abandon them. Type **:x** to exit vi and save changes
or **:q!** to exit without saving your changes.

Recovering Text after a System Crash

If the system crashes while you're editing a file with vi, you can
recover text that was not saved to disk before the crash. After the

system is restored and you have a system prompt, type

```
vi -r filename
```

where **filename** is the name of the file you were working on when the system crashed. The displayed file reflects the changes you made, but did not save, before the system crash. Use the **:w** (write) command immediately to save the salvaged copy of the work buffer to disk. You can then continue to edit the file.

Units of Text in vi

As you will see, many vi commands affect specific units of text, such as characters, words, lines, sentences, and paragraphs. To improve your productivity using vi commands, it's helpful to understand how vi defines these units of text. Table 5.1 explains vi's defined units of text.

Table 5.1: Units of Text in vi

Unit	Description
Character	Whatever is stored in a single byte. The letter **a** is a character, a space is a character, and a tab is also considered a character.
Word	A string of one or more characters separated on each side by a punctuation mark, space, tab, digit, or newline character (Return). A word can also be defined to include adjacent punctuation marks. These punctuated words are separated by the space, tab, or newline (Return) characters only.
Line	A string of characters separated by a newline character (Return). A line can be more than the width of a line of text displayed across your screen.

Table 5.1: Units of Text in vi (continued)

Unit	Description
Sentence	A string of characters that ends at a period, exclamation point, or question mark, followed by two spaces or a newline (Return) character. If only one space follows the period, exclamation point, or question mark, vi doesn't recognize it as the end of a sentence.
Paragraph	A group of one or more lines of characters preceded and followed by a blank line. Two newline (Return) characters in a row create a blank line in the text, which vi considers as the division between two paragraphs. A paragraph can be a single line or up to 45 lines.

Cursor Movement

There are vi commands to move the cursor up, down, left, or right; forward or backwards; by units of text, such as characters, words, sentences, or paragraphs; and through an entire file. However, you can't move the cursor below a tilde (~), which indicates a line without text or hidden control characters, such as for spaces, tabs, or returns. Keep in mind that all movement commands are executed in command mode.

With most cursor movement commands you can specify the number of times you want the cursor movement repeated. You can't use a repeat factor on any control commands, such as Control-D, which scrolls the screen down, or on any commands that position the cursor at a specific point on the screen. vi provides an extensive inventory of movement commands, as listed in Table 5.2.

Table 5.2: Cursor Movement Commands

Command Key	Cursor Movement
spacebar	Right (forward) one character position
l	Right (forward) one character
h	Left (backward) one character
+	First character of next line
−	First character of previous line
↓	Same position in line below
↑	Same position in line above
j	Down to same position in line below; moves left to last position if line below is shorter
k	Up to same position in line above; moves left to last position if line above is shorter
w	Forward to first letter of next word
W	Forward to first letter of next word, including punctuation
b	Backward to first letter of previous word
B	Backward to first letter of previous word, including punctuation
$	End of current line
0	Beginning of current line
Return	Forward to beginning of next line

Table 5.2: Cursor Movement Commands (continued)

Command Key	Cursor Movement
(	Back to beginning of current sentence
)	Ahead to beginning of next sentence
{	Back to beginning of current paragraph
}	Ahead to beginning of next paragraph
H	Left end of top line on screen
M	Left end of middle line on screen
L	Left end of lowest line on screen
G	Last line in work buffer
*n*G	Move to line number *n*
Control-D	Down half screen
Control-U	Up half screen
Control-F	Down almost a full screen
Control-B	Up almost a full screen
Control-E	Scroll down one line at a time
Control-Y	Scroll up one line at a time
Z	Scroll up or down a screen while leaving cursor on same line

Moving by Characters and Words

The arrow keys provide the easiest method for moving the cursor through a file one character at a time. You can also use the keys h,j,k, and l as follows:

h   left

j   down

k   up

l   right

Adding a repeat factor multiplies the movement factor accordingly. For example, typing **7** before pressing the right arrow key moves the cursor seven characters to the right.

Typing the **w** command moves the cursor forward one word at a time, treating symbols and punctuation marks as words. Typing the **W** command moves the cursor forward one word at a time, ignoring symbols and punctuation. To move backward one word at a time, type the command **b**. This command also treats symbols and punctuation marks as words. Typing **B** moves the cursor backward one word at a time, ignoring symbols and punctuation marks. You can multiply the movement effects of the **w**, **W**, **b**, or **B** commands by entering a repeat factor before the command. For example, typing **3w** moves the cursor forward three words; typing **6B** moves the cursor back six words, ignoring punctuation marks.

Moving by Lines, Sentences, and Paragraphs

Typing **+** while in command mode moves the cursor to the next line's first character; typing **–** moves the cursor to the first character of the previous line. You can also use the up or down arrow keys to move through lines and add repeat factors to multiply their effect.

Typing **$** moves the cursor to the end of the current line. To move the cursor to the beginning of the current line, type **0**.

Remember, in vi a line isn't necessarily the same length as the visible line (usually 80 characters) that appears on the screen.

You can move to the beginning of the current sentence by typing an open parenthesis (( ). Typing a close parenthesis ( )) moves the cursor to the beginning of the next sentence. You can move back to the beginning of the current paragraph by typing an open curly bracket ({), or ahead to the beginning of the next paragraph with a closed curly bracket, (}). You can use repeat factors with any of these commands. If there is a sequence of blank lines, the cursor moves to the beginning of the first blank line.

Moving within a Screen Display

You can move the cursor to certain positions on the screen. Typing **H** moves the cursor to the home position in the upper-left corner of the screen. Typing **M** moves the cursor to the beginning of the middle line of the screen. Typing **L** moves the cursor to the beginning of the last line on the screen. You can't add a repeat factor to any of these commands.

Scrolling through a File

Several useful commands for scrolling through a file are provided by vi. Pressing Control-U scrolls up half a screen at a time. Pressing Control-D scrolls down half a screen at a time. To move up or down one screen at a time, press Control-F to see the next screen, and press Control-B to see the previous screen. To scroll down one line at a time, press Control-E. To scroll up one line at a time, press Control-Y.

If you want to scroll the screen up or down, but you want the cursor to remain where it is on the current line, use the **z** command. Pressing **z**, then Return, moves the current line to the top of the screen. Typing **z.** moves the current line to the center of the screen. Typing **z-** moves the current line to the bottom of the screen.

Line Numbering and Line Movement

In vi each line in a file is assigned a sequential line number. Line numbers, by default, are not displayed. They can be displayed on the screen by entering the command

```
:set nu
```

Line numbers are displayed in vi as shown in the example below:

```
1   Magic Johnson is a great basketball player.
2   Larry Bird is a great basketball player.
3   Michael Jordan is a great basketball player.
~
~
~
~
~
~
~
~
"basketball" 3 lines, 67 characters
```

Only lines that have text are assigned numbers. Blank lines, those starting with the tilde character (~), are not numbered. These line numbers appear on the screen for convenience only and do not become part of your file. You can also display the current line number in the status line by pressing Control-G, which displays the current line number, the total number of lines in the file, and the percentage of the total lines of the file above the current line position.

Using the **G** (GoTo) command, you can move directly to any line containing text. For example, typing **44G** moves the cursor to the beginning of line forty-four. Typing **G** without a line number moves the cursor to the last line of the file. Entering **:*n*,** where ***n*** is the specified line number, also moves the cursor to that line number in your file.

Editing Commands

Remember, you can save time duplicating an edit command by using the repeat command. Simply position the cursor where you want to repeat the command and type a period.

There are four basic editing functions performed in vi.

- Inserting text in insert mode
- Deleting text
- Changing and replacing text
- Cutting (or copying) and pasting text from one place to another in your file

Most vi editing commands can also be combined with movement commands and repeat factors to further improve your productivity.

Cleaning Up the Screen

Once you start making extensive changes to your file, the screen can get cluttered with leftover command symbols before vi redraws your screen. *Redrawing* a screen means updating the screen to reflect your changes and removing command symbols that have been executed. vi doesn't automatically redraw your screen when you make changes, but instead redraws your screen periodically. You can redraw your vi screen at any time by pressing

```
Control-L
```

Inserting and Appending Text

In vi there are several commands to insert text into your file. All these commands are executed from insert mode. To enter insert mode, first position the cursor at the location you want to insert text, then type **i** while in command mode. You are now ready to begin entering text at the cursor location. The characters you type appear to the left or before the cursor position and push any following characters to the right. You can press Return to create a new line at any point while you are entering text.

Another way to enter insert mode is by typing **a** for the append command. Characters you type after using the **a** (append) command are inserted to the right of the cursor. While in command mode, you can insert a new line in your text by typing the **o** (open) command, which opens a new line below the cursor and automatically puts you in insert mode. Typing **O** opens a new line above the cursor for text.

To leave insert mode and return to command mode, press Esc. Table 5.3 lists vi insert mode commands.

Table 5.3: Commands for Entering Insert Mode

Command Key	Insert Location
i	Before cursor
I	Before first nonblank character on line
a	After cursor
A	At end of line
o	Open a line next line down
O	Open a line next line up
Esc	Quits insert mode

Deleting Text

vi provides a complete set of delete commands, listed in Table 5.4. Delete commands are performed in command mode. After executing a delete command, vi remains in command mode. Keep in mind that the **u** (undo) command, as explained earlier, is particularly useful in undoing deletion commands.

Table 5.4: Delete Commands

Command Key	Deletion
x	Character at cursor
X	Character before cursor
dw	To end of word
dW	To end of word, including punctuation
db	To beginning of word
dB	To beginning of word, including punctuation
dd	Current line
d Return	Two lines, current and following
d0	From cursor to end of line
d$	From cursor to beginning of line
d)	To end of sentence
d (	To beginning of sentence
d}	To end of paragraph
d{	To beginning of paragraph
dL	To last line on screen
dH	To first line on screen
dG	To end of the file

Table 5.4: Delete Commands (continued)

Command Key	Deletion
d1G	To the beginning of the file
u	Undo a command
U	Undo an undo command

Deleting Characters and Words

Use the **x** command while in command mode to delete a single character. Typing **x** deletes only the character the cursor is positioned on, unless you use a repeat factor. Typing **X** deletes the character before the cursor. You can delete multiple characters by typing the number of characters you want to delete before the command. For example, typing **10x** deletes ten characters forward, starting with the character *at* the cursor; typing the command **8X** deletes eight characters backwards, starting with the first character *following* the cursor.

To delete units other than characters, you type **d**, usually in combination with an argument that specifies the unit to be deleted. To delete a word, first position the cursor on the first or last character and type **dw**. If you want to delete a word, including any adjacent punctuation, type **dW**. You can include a repeat factor in these delete commands to delete a multiple number of words. The number is placed following the **d** but preceding either the **w** or **b**, such as typing **d4w** to delete four words forward.

Deleting Lines and Sentences

Typing **dd** deletes the line where the cursor is currently located. If you type **d**, then press Return, vi deletes the entire line and the line following it. To delete more than two lines, precede the first **d** with the number of lines you want to delete. For example, typing **12dd** deletes twelve lines down, starting with the current line.

You can also delete a part of a line. Typing **d$** deletes from the cursor to the end of a line. Typing **d0** deletes from the beginning of the line to the cursor.

To delete a sentence from the cursor to the end of the sentence, type **d)**. To delete a sentence from the cursor to the beginning of the sentence, type **d(**.

Placing the cursor at the very beginning or end of a sentence, then using the appropriate sentence deletion command, deletes an entire sentence. For example, typing **d)** with the cursor at the very beginning of the sentence deletes the entire sentence. As with other delete commands, you can add repeat factors to delete more than one sentence at a time. For example, typing **d4)** with the cursor located at the very beginning of a sentence deletes that entire sentence and the following three sentences.

Deleting Paragraphs and Other Sections of Your File

As with deleting sentences, placing the cursor at the very beginning or end of a paragraph and typing the appropriate delete command deletes the entire paragraph. To delete from the beginning of a paragraph to the cursor, type **d{**. To delete from the cursor to the end of the paragraph, type **d}**. You can also use the repeat factor to delete multiple paragraphs. For example, typing **d3}** with the cursor at the beginning of a paragraph deletes all of the current paragraph along with the two following paragraphs.

You can delete parts of your vi file as displayed on your screen. Typing **dH** deletes text from the line the cursor is located on to the very top of the screen. Typing **dL** deletes text from the line the cursor is on down to the very last line on the screen. Typing **dG** deletes text from the line the cursor is on to the end of the file. Typing **d1G** deletes text from the line the cursor is located on to the very beginning of the file.

Changing and Replacing Text

vi provides two commands to change text, the **c** (change) command and the **r** (replace) command.

- The change command combines deleting and inserting text in one command.

- The replace command allows you to overtype existing text.

You invoke both commands while in command mode.

When you enter a change command, you specify what text will be replaced. The end of this text is then marked with a **$** (the cursor location marks the beginning of the text to be changed). You then overtype the marked text and then press Esc to complete the deletion and effect the change. Your changes can be shorter or longer than the marked text that will be deleted. You can use the change commands to change words, lines, sentences, and paragraphs. As with most vi editing commands, you can add repeat factors to change commands. Table 5.5 lists available change and replace commands.

Changing Words, Lines, Sentences, and Paragraphs

To change a word, type the command **cw**. The **cw** (change word) command instructs vi to delete the word at the cursor location and insert new text. You can change multiple words by adding a repeat factor for the number of words you want to change. For example, typing **c3w** allows you to change three words forward from the cursor.

To change an entire line, type the command **cc**, which marks the line and places you in the insert mode to begin entering replacement text. When you're finished entering text, press Esc. It doesn't matter where the cursor is located on the line; **cc** deletes the entire line of text and replaces it with the text you enter before pressing Esc. You can also use a repeat factor to change multiple lines. For example, typing **7cc** marks the current line and six following lines for deletion and then places you in the insert mode to begin replacing the lines.

You can remove part or all of a sentence or paragraph and enter insert mode by using the commands **c (** (from the cursor to the end

Table 5.5: Change and Replacement Commands

Command	Change or Replacement
cw	To end of word
cW	To end of word, including punctuation
cb	From beginning of word to cursor
cB	From beginning of word, including punctuation, to cursor
cc	Current line
c$	From the cursor to the end of the line
c0	From the cursor to the beginning of the line
c)	From the cursor to the end of the sentence
c (	From the cursor to the beginning of the sentence
c}	From the cursor to the end of the paragraph
c{	From the cursor to the beginning of the paragraph
r	Replaces character at cursor
R	Replaces characters until Esc is pressed

of the sentence), **c)** (from the cursor to the beginning of the sentence), **c{** (from the cursor to the end of the paragraph), and **c}** (from the cursor to the beginning of the paragraph). As with other change commands, you can also use repeat factors with sentence or paragraph change commands.

Replacing Text

The **r** (replace) command allows you to overtype a single character. You can multiply the effects of this command by typing the number of characters you want to affect before it. For example, typing **8r** allows you to replace eight characters forward from the cursor. Typing **R** is particularly useful because it allows you to overtype characters until Esc is pressed.

Changing Case in Command Mode

You can use the tilde command to change the case of any letter because it changes both lowercase letters to uppercase and uppercase letters to lowercase.

To change the case of a character without leaving command mode, position the cursor on the letter whose case you want to change and type **~**. The case of the letter changes, and the cursor moves to the next character. You *can't* add a repeat factor or an argument, such as **w** for a word, to the tilde command (**~**).

Joining Two Lines

You can merge shorter lines to form a longer line using the **J** (join) command. For example, to join two lines, first position the cursor anywhere on the first line, then type **J** to merge the line below it. You can also add a repeat factor to merge consecutive lines into one line and use the repeat command (**.**) to repeat the join command. To join these three lines

```
See Kevin run.
See Larry run.
See Robert run.
```

type **3J**, which results in the following:

```
See Kevin run. See Larry run. See Robert run.
```

Cutting and Pasting Text

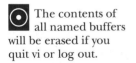 Don't confuse the general buffer with the work buffer, which holds your entire file in memory until you save it to disk.

The **u** (undo) command always uses text placed in the general buffer as its source.

Cutting and pasting text means you mark pieces of text, *yank* (copy) them, and then *put* (paste) them at another location. vi performs cutting and pasting tasks by storing the yanked (or deleted) text in buffers, which are areas set aside in memory to store text. There are two types of buffers for cutting and pasting text, the general buffer and named buffers. The *general buffer* stores only the last text manipulation you performed in memory. Because so many commands use the general buffer, such as delete and change commands, vi provides a way to create your own buffers for storing and retrieving text—these are called *named buffers.*

Using Named Buffers

You can establish up to 26 named buffers of your own, designated by lowercase letters ranging from **a** to **z**. These named buffers can store deleted, yanked, or changed text. You specify text stored in a named buffer by including a double quotation mark (**"**) and the name of the buffer before the delete, yank, or change command. For example, typing the command

```
"zd5
```

The contents of all named buffers will be erased if you quit vi or log out.

with the cursor at the beginning of a sentence deletes five sentences and stores them in a buffer named **z**.

Using a lowercase buffer name when instructing vi to save text to a named buffer *replaces* any text you have previously saved in that buffer. Using the uppercase version of a buffer name *appends* text you save to that buffer. For example, if you have text saved in a buffer named **z**, saving additional text by specifying **z** in the command appends this text to the existing text in the buffer named **z**. You can use this technique to collect separate lines in your file and use the uppercase name to place them together in a named buffer. Named buffers work as temporary buffers that are only active during your vi work session for a particular file.

Copying Text Using Buffers

To copy text from one location to another in your file, you use the **y** (yank) command. Yank commands copy a specified unit of text into the general buffer or a named buffer, leaving the original text in place. To paste the yanked text, move the cursor to the location you want to copy the yanked text, then use the **p** (put) command. The put command is explained below. Table 5.6 lists available yank commands. Each yank command puts the specified text into the general buffer unless you specify a named buffer.

Table 5.6: Yank Commands

Command	Text Yanked
yw	From the cursor to end of word
yW	From the cursor to end of word including punctuation
yb	From the cursor to beginning of word
yB	From the cursor to beginning of word including punctuation
yy	Current line
y Return	Two lines, current and following
Y$	From the cursor to end of a line

Table 5.6: Yank Commands (continued)

Command	Text Yanked
y0	From the cursor to beginning of a line
y)	From cursor to end of sentence
y(	From cursor to beginning of sentence
y}	From cursor to end of paragraph
y{	From cursor to beginning of paragraph
y6	To end of file

Retrieving Text from Buffers

The **p** (put) command by itself retrieves text from the general buffer into your file. If the contents of the general buffer are characters or words, typing **p** puts them *after* the character the cursor is located on. Typing **P** puts characters or words *before* the character the cursor is located on. If the general buffer contains lines, sentences, or paragraphs, typing **p** inserts the contents below the line, sentence, or paragraph the cursor is located on. Typing **P** inserts lines, sentences, or paragraphs from the general buffer above the line, sentence, or paragraph the cursor is located on. If your named buffer contains different units of text, such as a word and line, the put command places the buffer's text according to which unit of text was placed into the named buffer last. You can specify a named buffer to use with the put command. For example, typing the command **"tp** puts the contents of buffer **t** after the cursor in the appropriate location, depending on what units of text the buffer contains.

Inserting Text from Another File

With vi you can read in the contents of another file into the file you're currently working on using the `:r` (read) command

    :r filename

The read command inserts the contents of **filename**, starting on the line after the cursor position in the current file. For example, suppose your user name is **dquayle** and you are editing the file **sports** and want to read in a file called **basketball** from another directory. To read the file **basketball** into the file **sports**, first position the cursor one line above where you want the new data inserted in **sports**. In the command mode, enter

    :r /home/dquayle/basketball

The entire contents of the file **basketball** are read into your file **sports**.

You can also combine the read command with a SunOS command to read the results of a SunOS command into your file. For example, entering

    :r! date

will read in the system's date information into your file.

Searching vi Files

Two powerful tools are provided by vi for searching through your files for specified strings of characters—the search command and the global replacement command. Search commands search your file for a specified pattern. When a match is found, you can make changes, then search for the next occurrence of the string. Global replacement commands search your file for a specified pattern and automatically replace it with another pattern you specify.

◉ A forward search
continues until
the end of the file and
a backward search con-
tinues until the begin-
ning of the file. If you
begin in the middle of
a file, the entire file will
not be searched.

Searching vi Files for Patterns

Search commands search your file for a pattern match, which means vi searches for a string of characters that matches your specified text. To search forward through a file, type the forward slash character (/) while in command mode, followed by the pattern you want to search for. For example, type

```
/SunOS
```

then press Return. This instructs vi to search forward through the file to find the first occurrence of the pattern SunOS. Typing a question mark before the search pattern, as in the following

```
?SunOS
```

and then pressing Return searches backwards through your file for the specified pattern. If no match is found after executing a search command, the message **Pattern not found** is displayed in the status line. When a search command locates the first occurrence of a pattern, you can then perform an editing task such as changing or deleting the pattern. Typing **n** continues the search to find the next occurrence of a pattern in the same direction. Typing **N** changes the direction of the search. Table 5.7 lists vi search commands.

Global Replacement

vi provides a powerful tool for searching and replacing incorrect text entries. With one command you can automatically replace a string of characters, such as a misspelled word, wherever it occurs in the file. The global replacement command syntax is

```
:%s/old_pattern/new_pattern/
```

Once a global replacement command is entered, vi checks each line of a file for a given pattern. When the pattern is found, vi automatically replaces the old pattern with the new pattern

Table 5.7: Search Commands

Command	Result
/pattern Return	Searches forward in file
?pattern Return	Searches backward in file
n	Finds next pattern in same direction
N	Finds next pattern in opposite direction

you've specified. Suppose you wanted to search through your file and find each occurrence of the word **Harry** and change it to **Larry**. Type

```
:%s/Harry/Larry
```

then press Return. vi searches through the entire file for each occurrence of Harry and replaces it with Larry. If vi doesn't find any matches, it responds with the message **Substitute pattern match failed**.

Setting vi Parameters

You can adapt vi to your preferences for a vi work session by setting vi parameters, as vi offers a number of parameter options. You can list these options on your screen by typing the command

```
:set all
```

then pressing Return. The list shows the options available and their current status. You can set vi parameters to perform such functions as automatically inserting Returns, displaying line numbers, and displaying invisible characters such as tabs and end-of-line characters. To set a parameter while you're using vi, type **:set** followed by the option you want to change. For example, you can instruct vi to display line numbers by typing **:set nu** and pressing Return. To change back to the original set option, type **no** before the option. For example, typing the command

```
:set nonu
```

then pressing Return now instructs vi *not* to display line numbers. Table 5.8 lists several useful set command options.

Table 5.8: Useful Set Command Options

Option	Result
set all	Displays the complete list of options, including options that you have set as well as vi's default settings
:set Wrapmargin =n	Specifies the size of the right margin used to wrap text as you type, and saves manually entering Return after each line. A typical value for **n** is 10 or 15.
:set nu	Displays line numbers of a file
:set ic	Specifies that pattern searches should ignore case
:set window=x	Sets the number of lines shown in the screen window, where **x** is the number of lines
:set list	Displays invisible characters, with tabs displayed as **^I** and the end-of-line characters (Returns) displayed as **$**

Using SunOS Commands in vi

You can temporarily exit vi to execute SunOS commands, such as checking your mail, then return to your vi work session without having to quit vi. Typing the command `:sh` while in vi returns you to the SunOS system prompt. You can then execute other SunOS commands. When you want to return to vi, enter at the system prompt

```
exit
```

Save Time When Starting vi

There are several options available when starting vi beyond the basic **vi** *filename* start-up command. You can start up vi, open an existing file, then have the cursor move to a particular line in the file by typing

```
vi +nfilename
```

where **n** is the number of the line on which you want the cursor to be placed. You can also start up vi, open an existing file, and move the cursor to the last line of the file by typing **vi +*filename*.** The start-up command

```
vi +/pattern filename
```

opens a file at the first occurrence of a particular text pattern. For example, typing **vi +/fired letter** opens up the file **letter** and places the cursor at the first occurrence of the word **fired**.

Summary

In this chapter, you explored the fundamentals of SunOS's powerful, all-purpose editor, vi. A number of concepts and commands were presented to help you navigate through a file, perform the four major types of editing, search and replace text patterns, and customize vi's parameters. You learned to

- start up vi by entering **vi** at the system prompt

- exit vi and save changes (Shift-ZZ) or abandon changes (:**q!**)

- use the command and insert modes, repeat factors, and the **u** (undo) command

- use vi's units of text measurements in cursor movement and editing commands

- insert text with the **i** (insert) and **a** (append) commands

- delete and change text with the **d** (delete), **c** (change), and **r** (replace) commands and merge lines with the **J** (join) command

- cut and paste text using the **y** (yank) and **p** (put) commands and use named buffers to store cut text

- read text from another file into the current file with the :**r** (read) command

- use search and global replacement commands to search files for specific strings and replace them with another specified string

- customize vi's parameters with the :**set** command

- temporarily interrupt vi to execute SunOS commands with the :**sh** command

Table 5.9 lists the commands covered in this chapter that are not contained in the earlier tables.

Table 5.9: Miscellaneous Commands Covered in Chapter 5

Command	Result
.	Repeats previous command
Control-L	Redraws screen
:q!	Quits vi and abandons changes
Shift-ZZ	Quits vi and saves changes
vi	Allows user to enter vi
:w	Saves buffer contents without quitting vi

CHAPTER 6

Formatting and Printing

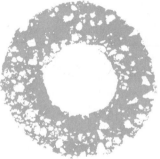

IN THE LAST CHAPTER, YOU WORKED WITH VI TO create and edit text files. In this chapter, you learn how to use the **nroff** and **troff** formatting programs to enhance the appearance of your printed files. With the **nroff** and **troff** commands you can perform a wide range of formatting tasks from boldfacing a single word to changing your entire document's page layout. This chapter teaches you a core of essential commands for performing basic formatting tasks. In addition, SunOS's printing commands and options are explained to provide you with a variety of ways to print your files.

An Overview of Formatting

SunOS provides several tools for formatting documents. The **nroff** and **troff** text formatting programs are two of these. One of the early text formatting commands in SunOS was named **roff**, which comes from the phrase to "run off" a document, used when a person wanted to format and print a document. **nroff** stands for "newer roff." **nroff** commands are primarily used with line printers—printers that print one line of text at a time in a single style of typeface. **troff** is an adaptation of **nroff** for typesetters and laser printers. These printers can print a page at a time and change typeface size and styles, commonly referred to as *fonts*.

Adding Formatting Requests to a File

Before you can use **nroff** or **troff**, you must insert requests in the document you want to format. A *request* is simply a formatting instruction embedded in the text of the document to be formatted. You insert requests in a file with a text editor, such as vi, placing a request on a blank line above the text you want formatted.

Remember to insert requests above the text to be formatted.

When you have finished embedding requests in your document, you return to the system prompt and enter the **nroff** command using this general syntax:

```
nroff filename | lpr -Pprintername
```

nroff then formats your text according to the embedded requests. These requests will not appear on the printout.

If you have a typesetter or laser printer, you use a similar general syntax command:

```
troff -t filename | lpr -Pprintername -t
```

where the **-t** option before the file name and after the print command indicate that the file contains **troff** formatting.

Using Macros to Format a File

Certain types of documents may need extensive formatting, and could require you to insert many requests in the text. Instead, use macros to save time in formatting your documents. For our purposes, we will define a *macro* as a sequence of **nroff** or **troff** requests. Macros are distinguished from **nroff** and **troff** requests by case—macros use uppercase letters. In SunOS, these macros are grouped together in *macro packages*. This chapter will cover some of the macros found in the **-ms** macro package.

You format text with macros the same way as with **nroff** and **troff** requests. Use a text editor to insert the macro above the text you want to format. Once you exit the text editor and return to the system prompt, you enter a command with this general syntax:

```
nroff -ms filename | lpr -Pprintername
```

Here the **-ms** indicates which macro package the macros embedded in your file belong to.

If you are using a laser printer, follow this syntax:

```
troff -ms -t filename | lpr -Pprintername -t
```

Character Formatting

If you're using a laser printer or a typesetter, you can use **troff** requests and **-ms** macros to print characters in different fonts (both sizes and styles). The following explains the **troff** commands that allow you to use different fonts, such as italic and bold. You can use some of these requests, such as the underline request, with **nroff**, but **nroff** ignores requests for fonts it can't handle. In other words, **nroff** doesn't change the size or style of your font.

Underlining Text

To underline text in a sentence, use the `.UL` macro; use the `.R` (roman) macro to stop underlining and return to a normal typeface. You can underline a certain number of words using the `nroff` request `.ul` *n*, where *n* is the number of words to underline. The following is an example of underlining a title in a text file.

```
To inquire how the editors liked the manuscript for
.UL
Les Miserables
.R
, Victor Hugo composed the following letter, quoted here in
its entirety: "?." The publisher responded: "!."
```

The text when printed then appears as follows:

To inquire how the editors liked the manuscript for <u>Les Miserables</u>, Victor Hugo composed the following letter, quoted here in its entirety: "?." The publisher responded: "!."

Italicizing Text

The `.I` macro is used to indicate italics. Italics are commonly used instead of underlining to indicate titles of books or magazine titles, or to set off a foreign word or expression, as shown in the following example.

```
The word "bug" in the slang expression "Don't bug me" comes
from the West African word
.I
bagu,
.R
meaning to annoy.
```

The text when printed then appears as follows:

The word "bug" in the slang expression, "Don't bug me" comes from the West African word *bagu,* meaning to annoy.

If you use the `.I` macro with **nroff**, italicized characters are converted to underline characters.

Boldfacing Text

Boldface is used to emphasize words or set headings apart from other text. To boldface text use the `.B` macro and the `.R` (roman) macro to return to normal roman typeface. The `.B` macro doesn't work with some line printers. For example

```
.B
Warning to all Personnel:
.R
Firings will continue until morale improves.
```

results in the printout

> **Warning to all Personnel:** Firings will continue until morale improves.

Changing the Size of a Font

If you're using a laser printer or a typesetter, you can change the size of your font using a few simple macros. The `.LG` macro makes the font two points larger. A *point* is $1/72$ of an inch. The `.SM` macro makes a font two points smaller, and the `.NL` macro returns your font to the normal size.

Formatting Lines

To **nroff** and **troff**, a file is only a stream of words. Both ignore the line breaks you made when you pressed Return while creating or editing a file. Instead **nroff** and **troff** format text by filling the lines to fit in the margins. This process is called *line filling*. When they encounter a space at the beginning of a line they interpret the space as a line break and stop filling the current line and begin a new line.

Filling and Justifying Lines

–ms by default inserts spaces between words to make lines end with a flush right margin; this is commonly known as *justification.* To produce a nonjustified (ragged) margin, use the request **.na** (nonadjusted). To return to a right margin alignment, add the request **.ad**. Look at the following example to see the effects of using **.ad** and **.na**.

```
.na
Traditionally dinosaurs have been thought of as being
cold-blooded reptiles. However, contemporary evidence on
posture, skeleton, and eating habits indicates some
dinosaurs may have been warm-blooded. It is a mistake
to think that dinosaurs and cave dwellers lived at the
same time.

.ad
Dinosaurs died out 65 million years ago, and the earliest
human dates back to no more than four million years.
It is also a myth that dinosaurs died during the Ice Age.
The last Ice Age, to which the myth presumably refers,
ended 10,000 years ago.
```

Here is how this example would be printed:

Traditionally dinosaurs have been thought of as being cold-blooded reptiles. However, contemporary evidence on posture, skeleton, and eating habits indicates some dinosaurs may have been warm-blooded. It is a mistake to think that dinosaurs and cave dwellers lived at the same time.

Dinosaurs died out 65 million years ago, and the earliest human dates back to no more than four million years. It is also a myth that dinosaurs died during the Ice Age. The last Ice Age, to which the myth presumably refers, ended 10,000 years ago.

When you want to stop lines from being joined together, use the **.nf** request. For example, when you put an address in a letter, you don't want the city and state to be added to the end of the street address on the previous line. To prevent **nroff** from filling lines, use **.nf** (no fill). The **.nf** request doesn't justify your text, but stops the filling process and prints your text with line breaks as they appear in the file. To restart line filling, use the **.fi** (fill) request.

Changing Line Spacing

nroff and **troff** both use single line spacing as the default. You can easily change the line spacing by adding the number of blank lines you want between each line using the request **.ls *n***, where ***n*** is the number of the spaces you want between each line. The following request begins double spacing text and then returns to single spacing:

```
.ls 2
A movie theater manager in Seoul, South Korea, decided that
the running time of the movie The Sound of Music was too
long, so he shortened it by cutting out all the songs.
.ls
```

The double-spaced text when printed appears as follows:

A movie theater manager in Seoul, South Korea, decided

that the running time of the movie The Sound of Music

was too long, so he shortened it by cutting out all the songs.

Inserting Blank Lines

You can insert any number of lines using the **.sp *n*** request. The letter ***n*** indicates the number of line spaces you want to insert in the text. For example,

```
Rough draft
.sp 3
It was a dark and stormy night.
```

adds three lines between the first line of text and the text following the **.sp 3** request, printed as follows:

Rough draft

It was a dark and stormy night.

Indenting Lines

To indent text from the left margin, use the **.in** request followed by the number of spaces to indent. You can add spaces to an indent by preceding the number in the argument with a plus (**+**) sign or decrease spaces with a minus sign (**-**). For example, **.in +5** increases the current indent by five spaces.

If you want to temporarily indent a single line of text, use the request **.ti** *n*, where *n* is the number of spaces you want to indent that one line.

Setting Tabs

You can set tabs using the **.ta** request followed by the tab position you want to set. For example,

```
.ta 1i 1.5i 2i 2.5i 3i 3.5i 4i 4.5i 5i 5.5i 6i
```

sets tabs every $\frac{1}{2}$ inch across a page. You can also set tabs relative to the previous tab stops by preceding the tab number with a plus (**+**) sign. For example,

```
.ta 1 +.5i +.5i +.5i +.5i +.5i +.5i +.5i +.5i +.5i
```

produces the same results as the previous **.ta** example. You can also create right-adjusted or centered tabs. To right-adjust a tab add the letter **R** after the tab setting. When you right-adjust a tab, the text following the tab is lined up against the right margin. To center a tab entry add the letter **C** after the tab setting.

The following shows how to create two columns of text using right-adjusted tabs. It is mandatory that you use the **.nf** (no fill) request at the beginning of this example to stop filling text. The **.fi** (fill) request at the end of this example is optional, depending on whether or not you want to resume filling text.

```
.nf
.ta 3.5iR
Date        Holiday
Jan 1       New Years Day
Jan 15      Martin Luther King Jr. Day
Feb 12      Lincoln's Birthday
Feb 14      Valentine's Day
Feb 19      Washington's Birthday
Mar 17      St. Patrick's Day
.fi
```

When printed this looks like this:

Date	Holiday
Jan 1	New Years Day
Jan 15	Martin Luther King Jr. Day
Feb 12	Lincoln's Birthday
Feb 14	Valentine's Day
Feb 19	Washington's Birthday
Mar 17	St. Patrick's Day

Centering Lines

The **.ce** request centers a single line of text. You can center multiple lines of text by following **.ce** with the number of lines of text you want centered. Blank lines are not counted when using the **.ce** request.

```
.ce 2
Men have become tools of their tools.
Thoreau
```

When printed this appears as follows:

>Men have become tools of their tools.
>Thoreau

Formatting Paragraphs

You can produce several different kinds of paragraphs with the **–ms** macro package. For example, standard paragraphs begin with an indented first sentence, and left block paragraphs don't indent the first sentence. The following section shows examples of how text would appear using **–ms** macros for formatting standard, left-block, indented, and quoted paragraphs.

Standard Paragraphs

The standard paragraph is an indented, left-aligned paragraph. Insert the **–ms** macro `.PP` to format the following text as a standard paragraph:

```
.PP
Because of the radiant properties of the sun, people
believe that it consists of an entirely different material
than earth. The sun burns because of its size. It consists
of the same cosmic matter from which all of the planets
are made.
```

When printed the paragraph appears with an indent as follows:

Because of the radiant properties of the sun, people believe that it consists of an entirely different material than earth. The sun burns because of its size. It consists of the same cosmic matter from which all of the planets are made.

Left-Block Paragraphs

A left-block paragraph is the same as a standard paragraph, only without an indent. Left block paragraphs are indicated by the macro `.LP`, as shown here:

```
.LP
The sun contains 99.8 percent mass of the solar system and
is a million times larger than the earth. The effect of its
size is to produce pressure at the center so great that
even atoms are crushed, exploding their nuclei, and
allowing them to smash into each other. These collisions
are actually nuclear reactions and are felt and seen by us
from 93 million miles away as heat and light.
```

When printed the paragraph appears left-aligned, without an indent, as follows:

> The sun contains 99.8 percent mass of the solar system and is a million times larger than the earth. The effect of its size is to produce pressure at the center so great that even atoms are crushed, exploding their nuclei, and allowing them to smash into each other. These collisions are actually nuclear reactions and are felt and seen by us from 93 million miles away as heat and light.

If you don't add an `.LP` or `.PP` request, all your paragraphs will be unindented with both the left and right margins aligned.

Block Quotes

The `.QP` (quoted paragraph) macro indents a paragraph on both sides, with blank lines above and below the paragraph.

```
.PP
The giant marlin has towed the old man's boat far off the
coast of Cuba. The old man is exhausted but has outlasted
the fish. He hoists a sail and begins heading for home.
Hemingway writes
.QP
They sailed well and the old man soaked his hands in the
salt water and tried to keep his head clear. There were
high cumulus clouds and enough cirrus above them so that
the old man knew the breeze would last all night. The old
man looked at the fish constantly to make sure it was true.
It was an hour before the first shark hit him.
.PP
```

The above example when printed appears as follows:

> The giant marlin has towed the old man's boat far off the coast of Cuba. The old man is exhausted but has outlasted the fish. He hoists a sail and begins heading for home. Hemingway writes
>
> > They sailed well and the old man soaked his hands in the salt water and tried to keep his head clear. There were high cumulus clouds and enough cirrus above them so that the old man knew the breeze would last all night. The old man looked at the fish constantly to make sure it was true. It was an hour before the first shark hit him.

Indented Paragraphs

Indented paragraphs are frequently used for creating bulleted or numbered lists. The syntax for creating an indented paragraph is as follows:

```
.IP label n
```

This command indents a paragraph **n** spaces after a "hanging" label. If a label is more than one word, the words must be enclosed in double quotation marks. If an indent isn't specified, an indent of five spaces is used. The following is an example of formatting indented paragraphs.

```
.IP (i) 3
Never use a metaphor, simile, or other figure of speech
which you are used to seeing in print.
.IP (ii) 3
Never use a long word where a short one will do.
.IP (iii) 3
If it is possible to cut a word out, always cut it out.
.IP (iv) 3
Never use the passive where you can use the active.
.IP (v) 3
Never use a foreign phrase, a scientific word, or a jargon
word if you think of an everyday English equivalent.
```

```
.IP (vi) 3
Break any of these rules sooner than say anything outright
barbarous.
```

When printed the above example appears as follows:

   (i)   Never use a metaphor, simile, or other figure of speech which you are used to seeing in print.

   (ii)   Never use a long word when a short one will do.

   (iii)   If it is possible to cut a word out, always cut it out.

   (iv)   Never use the passive where you can use the active.

   (v)   Never use a foreign phrase, a scientific word or a jargon word if you think of an everyday English equivalent.

   (vi)   Break any of these rules sooner than say anything outright barbarous.

Outline Paragraphs

To create an outline, use the **.IP** (indented) macro with the **.RS** (right-shift) and **.RE** (right-shift end) macros. Each time you use the **.RS** request, the indention moves in another five spaces. The **.RE** request moves the indention back five spaces.

```
.IP I.
Making the Most of Priorities
.RS
.IP A.
The To Do List
.RS
.IP 1.
Setting priorities
.IP 2.
Grouping Tasks
.RE
.RE
.IP II.
Tasks Better Left Undone
.RS
.IP B.
```

```
The 80/20 rule
.RS
.IP 1.
Skipping less important jobs
.IP 2.
Coping with information overload
.RE
.RE
```

The above example when printed appears as follows:

I. Making the Most of Priorities

    A. The To Do List

        1. Setting priorities

        2. Grouping tasks

II. Tasks Better Left Undone

    A. The 80/20 rule

        1. Skipping less important jobs

        2. Coping with information overload

Changing the Page Layout

You can change the layout of your document, such as margins or page sizing, if the default page-layout settings don't match your needs. Figure 6.1 shows the elements of page layout that you'll work with in this section.

Number Registers

In order to change the default page-layout settings, you need to use number registers. *Number registers* are memory locations that store values of page-layout settings. You usually use one or two letters to specify a number register, that is, to say which part of the layout you want to change. Table 6.1 lists a summary of **-ms** number registers.

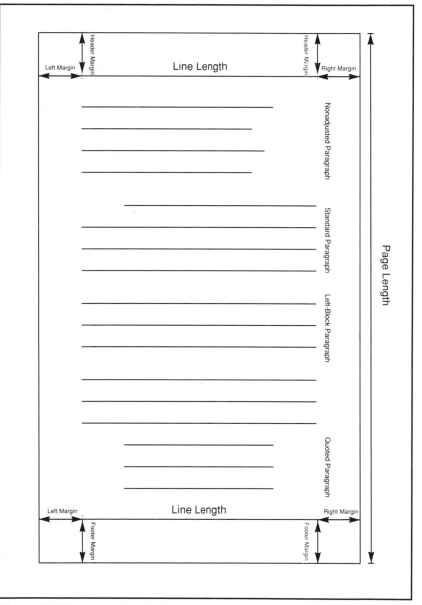

Figure 6.1: Elements of page layout

Table 6.1: -ms Number Registers

Register	Controls	Default
CW	Column width	7/15 of the set line length
FM	Footer margin	1 inch
GW	Gap width between columns	1/15 of the set line length
HM	Header margin	1 inch
LL	Line length	6 inches
PD	Paragraph spacing	0.3 of line spacing
PI	Paragraph indent	5 spaces
PO	Page offset	26/27 inch
PS	Point size	10 points
VS	Line spacing	12 points

Setting the Left and Right Margins

Margins are the white spaces at the top, bottom, left, and right of your printed document. By default the left margins are initially set to zero in **nroff** (in **troff** they are set at 1 inch). To specify a left margin 1-inch wide, at the beginning of your text insert the command

```
.nr PO 1i
```

The **nr** in this command stands for number register. The **PO** stands for Page Offset; the number **1** followed by the letter **i** will offset the page 1 inch.

The right margin is determined by the left margin setting and the line length setting. To discover how wide your right margin is, subtract the length of your text line and the width of the left margin from the total width of the page, which is normally 8.5 inches. The result is the size of the right margin. The default line length is 6 inches. If you want 1-inch margins on both sides of the printout of your document, you need to offset the left margin by 1 inch and change the line-length setting to 6.5 inches. To do this, you would insert these commands above the first line of the file you want to format:

```
.nr PO 1i
.nr LL 6.5:
```

LL is the number register that stores the line length, which is specified after the number register (here 6.5 inches).

Setting Top and Bottom Margins

The **.pl** (page length) request lets you change the number of lines on a page. This request actually specifies how many vertical inches of space the text should fill. At the top of the document, insert **.pl** *n*, where *n* indicates the number of inches the text should fill. The default page length is 11 inches. For example, to change the page length to 10 inches, use the following command:

```
.pl 10i
```

Determining Page Breaks

Sometimes it is necessary to begin printing information on a new page. The **.bp** (break page) request ends the text at the bottom of a page and begins it at the top of the next page.

Following is an example of using the **.bp** request to ensure that a list of paintings begins on a new page:

```
The following page lists the paintings that accompany this
document.
.bp
The List of Paintings

.nf
Old Woman
Old Guitarist
Les Demoiselles d'Avignon
The Three Musicians
Guernica
```

Keeping Text Together

nroff and **troff** break pages when the text reaches the bottom margin. You can prevent a page break from occurring in the middle of a block of text by using the **.KS** and **.KE** macros. Suppose you have a paragraph that appears at the bottom of a page and you want it to appear with a paragraph on the next page. Precede the first paragraph with **.KS** and end it with **.KE**, as shown in the following example:

```
.KS
People look for a reflection of their own personalities or
the person they dream of being in the eyes of an animal
companion. That is the reason I sometimes look into the
face of my dog Stan (I have two) and see wistful sadness
and existential angst, when all he is actually doing is
slowly scanning the ceiling for flies.
.KE
```

If you need to keep text together on the same page, try using the **.ne** *n* (need) request, where *n* is the number of lines to keep on the page. If there is room on the page, **.ne** places all the specified lines on that page.

Headers and Footers

Headers and footers are titles that appear at the top and bottom of a page. Titles that occur at the top of a page are called *headers*. Titles printed at the bottom of a page are called *footers*. If you want to use headers or footers, you must use **.pl** to create space at the top and bottom of your printed pages. These spaces are called the *header margin* and the *footer margin*.

Headers and footers begin printing on the second page of your document. When you use **-ms**, date and page number headers are added automatically. Add the **.ND** macro if you want to eliminate the date when using the **-ms** macro package. To create the header "Great Plays in Basketball," type the following request on the very first line of your file:

```
.ds CH "Great Plays in Basketball"
```

The **.ds CH** (define string Center Header) request clears the default setting of **CH**, which is the current page number surrounded by hyphens, and instructs **nroff** to instead center the text Great Plays in Basketball as the new header. Note that the quotes are not printed with your header. If you want to add a page number to your header, use the percent sign (**%**). The percent sign tells the automatic page counter to place page numbers in your header. To include page numbers in our previous example, insert

```
.ds CH "Great Plays in Basketball" %
```

at the top of the file.

You can create headers and footers and specify their location by using the requests listed below:

Command	Header and Footer Text Placement
.ds LH	Places header text at the left margin
.ds CH	Centers header text
.ds RH	Places header text at the right margin
.ds LF	Places footer text at the left margin

Command	Header and Footer Text Placement
`.ds CF`	Centers footer text
`.ds RF`	Places footer text at the right margin

Creating Multiple Columns

Use the following macros with the `col` command to create multiple columns.

Macro	Result
`.2C`	Begins the first column of two-column text
`.RC`	Begins the second column of two-column text
`.1C`	Returns to single-column text

The following excerpt from the *Virginia Pilot* shows how to create double columns with the `.2C` request.

The `.PP` request begins standard, indented paragraphs.

```
.2C
.PP
A group calling itself the Partiers League for Christmas
Cookie Liberation kidnapped a Ronald McDonald statue from a
Sacramento, California, McDonald's. They sent a ransom note
which read: "Mr. McDonald is safe, unharmed, and, I assure
you, entirely unable to escape." The note demanded that
McDonald's give a free box of cookies to any child under
eight who visited the restaurant on Christmas Eve.
.RC
.PP
"This is not a hoax," said the note. "If any qualified
child is refused cookies, Ronald dies."
.PP
The note came with a photo of a blindfolded Ronald
McDonald, a stick of dynamite hanging from his neck. A
note on the wall behind the statue read: "Do as they say
or I'm McHistory."
.1C
This is not the only case of a crime involving the theft of
a restaurant statue. In Iron Mountain, Michigan, someone
```

```
absconded with a Big Boy restaurant statue and whisked it
off to Niagara, Wisconsin.
```

Entering the command

```
nroff -ms filename | col | lpr
```

pipes the file name through the **col** filter to print this example as follows:

A group calling itself the Partiers League for Christmas Cookie Liberation kidnapped a Ronald McDonald statue from a Sacramento, California, McDonald's. They sent a ransom note which read: "Mr. McDonald is safe, unharmed, and, I assure you, entirely unable to escape." The note demanded that McDonald's give a free box of cookies to any child under eight who visited the restaurant on Christmas Eve.

"This is not a hoax," said the note. "If any qualified child is refused cookies, Ronald dies."

The note came with a photo of a blindfolded Ronald McDonald, a stick of dynamite hanging from his neck. A note on the wall behind the statue read: "Do as they say or I'm McHistory."

This is not the only case of a crime involving the theft of a restaurant statue. In Iron Mountain, Michigan, someone absconded with a Big Boy restaurant statue and whisked it off to Niagara, Wisconsin.

Creating Tables

It's easy to create simple tables in SunOS. Below is an example of a table that contains design elements you often use in tables.

Phone List

Names	*Phone Numbers*	*Contact*
Sun Support	800-872-4786	Ann
Bookware	415-493-1663	Steve
Sybex	415-523-8233	George

Here is the combination of formatting entries and text that was used to create this table.

```
.TS
tab(/);
c s s
l l l.
Phone List

Names/Phone Numbers/Contact

Sun Support/800-872-4786/Ann
Bookware/415-493-1663/Steve
Sybex/415-523-8233/George
.TE
```

The following list explains the formatting entries used to create the table.

Option or Macro	*Result*
.TS (table start)	Begins the table
tab (/)	Indicates that / will be used to delimit columns (the delimiting character will not be printed)

Option or Macro	Result
c s s	Specifies a table of three columns beginning with a centered header (**Phone List**) that spans all three columns. (Only the **Phone List** line will be created because it is the only one without column delimiters.) You cannot use the letter **s** in the first column because the **s** indicates entries from a previous column span the following column.
l l l .	Indicates that each column is left aligned (include period)
.TE	Ends the table

When you want to print a table, use the **tbl** command as follows:

```
tbl tablename | nroff | lpr
```

Below are some common formatting entries that were not used in the example table.

Option	Result
r	Right-adjusted column entry
n	Numerical column entry
s	Span previous column's text across this column

The following list contains options you can use to affect the whole table:

Option	Result
allbox	Boxes each entry in the table in a box
box	Frames the entire table with a box
center	Centers the table on the page
doublebox	Frames the table with a double line box

Option	*Result*
`linesize(n)`	Sets the table text to *n* point size
`tab(x)`	Uses *x* to separate table entries

You can combine these options on one line. For example, an option line added after the `.TS` request might be

```
center allbox tab(/) ;
```

Be sure to end your option line with a semicolon, otherwise the system will display an error message.

Running Print Jobs

An essential feature of SunOS is printing files. The following section teaches you how to print files, check the status of print jobs, and cancel print jobs. Printers are often in high demand in a networking environment because multiple terminals are often connected to a small number of printers. To keep things running smoothly, SunOS usually feeds printing jobs to printers on a first-come, first-served basis. A *printing job* is a term for a file sent to be printed as hard copy (on paper). Printing jobs are sent to a print *queue*, which stores the printing jobs in memory in the order they're received.

Most networks have multiple printers available for you to choose from. Each printer in a network has a unique name. The **printername** acts as an address for sending your printing jobs to a specific printer. Usually, your system also has a *default printer*. If you don't specify a particular printer when sending a print job, the print job is automatically sent to the default printer.

Sending Files To Be Printed

The general command syntax for printing a file is

```
lpr -Pprintername filename
```

The **lpr** (line printer) command instructs SunOS to send to the print queue a copy of the file to be printed. The **-P***printername* option requests the specific printer by its assigned name. For example, if you wanted to send a copy of the file **sports** to the printer named **laserwriter**, you would type the following:

```
lpr -Plaserwriter sports
```

If you want to send the printing job to the default printer, you don't need to add the **-P***printername* option to your command. Instead, simply type

```
lpr filename
```

Sending Multiple Files to the Printer

You can specify several files to be printed by separating file names with a space. For example, to print the files **junk1** and **junk2** on the default printer, type

```
lpr junk1 junk2
```

Remember, if you want to use a different printer than the default printer, you need to specify the printer after the **lpr** command using the **-P***printername* option.

Printing the Output of a Command

As with most SunOS utilities, you can connect the output of a command to the input of the print command using a pipe (|). For example, you can instruct SunOS to list the contents of a directory using the **ls** command, then redirect the output of the **ls** command to the printer as follows:

```
ls | lpr
```

Getting Notified When a Print Job Is Done

You can instruct the print command to let you know when the printer has finished printing your job. When your printing job is finished, at the next system prompt the message **You have mail** is displayed. To be notified that a print job is completed, type the command

```
lpr -m filename
```

The **-m** option instructs the print command to send you a mail message at the next system prompt after your printed job has been completed.

Checking the Printer Queue

To list your printing jobs waiting in the default print queue, enter the command

```
lpq username
```

To list your printing jobs waiting in another printer, add the **-Pprintername** option to the **lpq** command.

You can determine how busy a printer is by viewing how many print jobs are waiting in a printer queue. To view a printer queue's entries, enter

To see which printer will print your job first, use **lpg** to determine how many other print jobs are waiting on the available printers.

```
lpq -Pprintername
```

If you're checking the default printer, simply leave off the **-Pprintername** option. If the queue is empty, the **lpq** command responds with the message **no entries**. If there are entries in the queue, the **lpq** command lists for each print job the current position in the queue (rank), user's name, job number, name of input file, and the total size of the file in bytes. Such a list appears similar to the following:

```
Rank      Owner        Job   Files        Total Size
active    lbird        18    freethrows   39668 bytes
```

```
1st      mjordan      19    slamdunks      36994 bytes
2nd      mjohnson     20    assists        37678 bytes
```

Using the **-l** (long) option displays queue information in the long format, which includes the host computer from which a print job originated. The command to display queue information in the long format is **lpq -P***printername* **-l** *username*.

Removing Printer Jobs

If you decide not to print a job after sending it to the default printer, you can remove it from the queue by typing the command **lprm**, followed by the job number, as shown below:

```
lprm job_number
```

You can find out the job number by first typing the command **lpq** to list the print jobs and their assigned job numbers. If your printing job is already printing, the printing job isn't terminated. You can remove all your printing jobs from the default printer queue by typing the following:

```
lprm username
```

If you have only one print job in a print queue to remove, it's easier to use **lprm** *username* than having to find the job number, then using the command **lprm** *job_number*.

Printing troff Files

The **troff** formatting program is designed to format files for printing on typesetters or laser printers. To send a file formatted with **troff** formatting commands, you need to add the **-t** option to the **troff** and **lpr** commands as follows:

```
troff -t filename | lpr -Pprintername -t filename
```

Printing Multiple Copies of a File

You can easily print multiple copies of the same file adding the **-#***n* option to the **lpr** command, where *n* is the number of copies you want. For example, suppose you want to use the default printer to print 7 copies of the file **slamdunk**; type the following:

```
lpr -#7 slamdunk
```

Changing or Suppressing the Banner Page

Each printing job when printed is preceded by a single page called a banner page. The *banner page* contains information about the printer and the user issuing the print job. You can add a title line of up to eight characters to the banner page. Suppose you wanted to add the title "Celtics" to the banner page for the file **baskets**. Enter the command

```
lpr -J Celtics baskets
```

If you want your title to include more than one word (that is, if there is a space between characters), such as "f throws," you must place the title in quotes. For example, **lpr -J "f throws" baskets**.

Adding the **-h** option to the **lpr** command suppresses the printing of the banner page. For example,

```
lpr -h baskets
```

would print **baskets** without a banner page.

Printing Multiple-Page Files

For more sophisticated formatting tasks, use **nroff** or **troff** in combination with **lpr**.

Thus far, you've been using the **lpr** command to send printing jobs to the printer. If a file you send to the printer is longer than a page, the **lpr** command by itself doesn't separate text into pages or add header and footer margins. However, SunOS provides a handy page formatting and printing utility program called **pr**. Using the **pr** command, each page is identified by header and footer margins with the date, time, file name, and page number appearing as a left header. The general command syntax for the **pr** command is

```
pr filename | lpr -Pprintername
```

Remember, you can omit the **-Pprintername** option if you're using the default printer. The pipe symbol (|) instructs SunOS to take the output of the **pr** command (the formatted file) and send it to the printer. As with the **lpr** command, you can print multiple files using the **pr** command. For example, to format and print the files **junk1** and **junk2**, type

```
pr junk1 junk2 | lpr -Pprintername
```

You can connect the output of a command to the input of the **pr** command using a pipe symbol (|). For example, to instruct SunOS to first list the contents of a directory, use the **ls** command, then redirect the output of the command to the **pr** command to format the listing and then print it. The command for this task is

```
ls | pr | lpr -Pprintername
```

Customizing the pr Command

The **pr** command allows you to add options to customize the formatting and printing of your files. In this section you'll learn the most useful **pr** command options, which allow you to do the following:

- Change the default file name header
- Delete headers and footers
- Change the page length
- Begin printing on a specified page
- Change the page width

The **pr** command syntax is **pr *filename* | lpr**. To add an option to the **pr** command, type in the option after the **pr** command as follows:

```
pr option filename | lpr -Pprintername
```

As explained earlier, the default header produced by the **pr** command contains the date, time, file name, and page number as follows:

```
Feb 14 12:10 1999 sports Page 1
```

You can modify the **pr** command to add header text that replaces the file name by using the **-h** option. For example, typing

```
pr -h "Great Players" sports | lpr -Pprintername
```

creates the following left header when you print out the file **sports** with the **pr** command

```
Feb 14 12:10 1999 Great Players Page 1
```

The following list describes several useful options that can be used with the **pr** command

Option	Result
-h	Allows you to change the default file name header with header text of your own. For a single word replacement, the new header text follows **-h**, separated by a space. If the new header contains more than one word, it must be enclosed in quotes.
-t	Instructs the **pr** command not to print the headers or footers normally supplied for each page
-l*n*	Changes the length of the page to *n* lines. The default is 66 lines for an 8.5-by-11-inch page.

Don't confuse the **-h** option used with the **lpr** command to suppress the printing of the banner page with the **-h** option used with the **pr** command to add your own header text.

Option	Result
+n	Begins printing starting at the page number indicated by *n*
-wn	Changes the width of the print job by the number specified by *n*

Printing the Screen

If you want to capture an image of the screen and send it to the printer, use the following command:

```
screendump | rastrepl | lpr -Pprintername -v &
```

The **screendump** command captures the screen image, the **rastrepl** command increases its size, and the **-v** option of the **lpr** command prints the resulting image.

◉ Screen images take a long time to print.

This command takes a considerable amount of time to process. Adding the ampersand (**&**) at the end of the command line places the processing of this command in the background so you can continue to work on your terminal.

Summary

In this chapter, you learned basic **nroff**, **troff**, and **-ms** macro formatting requests to enhance your files for printing. In addition, you learned how to print your files using SunOS's printing commands. You now know how to

- use an editor of your choice to embed **nroff**, **troff**, and **-ms** formatting commands into your files.

- change your fonts to underline, italicize, and boldface text, and change the size of a font.

- fill and justify the lines of your file, change line spacing, and insert, indent, and center lines.

- format standard, left-block, block quote, indented, and outline paragraphs.

- change page layout options, including left and right margins, top and bottom margins, page breaks, and multiple columns.

- define your own headers and footers for multipage documents.

- send a file to be printed.

- check a printer queue using **lpq** and remove printing jobs using **lprm** commands.

- print multiple copies of a single file, suppress a banner page, and add a title line to a banner page.

- use the page formatting and printing command **pr** to format your printouts into pages with headers.

- customize **pr** to suit your printing needs.

Table 6.2 lists the commands and requests covered in this chapter.

Table 6.2: Commands and Requests Covered in Chapter 6

Command or Request	Result
.ad	Returns to justified right margin
.B	Boldfaces text
.bp	Ends text at the bottom of a page and begins it at the top of the next page
.ce	Centers a single line of text
.ds	Changes the default setting of headers and footers

Table 6.2: Commands and Requests Covered in Chapter 6 (continued)

Command or Request	Result
`.fi`	Restarts line filling
`.I`	Changes type to italic
`.in` *n*	Indents text *n* spaces
`.IP` *n*	Indents a paragraph *n* spaces after a hanging indent
`.KE`	Signifies end of text to keep on one page
`.KS`	Keeps a specified block of text on one page
`.LG`	Makes font two points larger
`.LP`	Formats text into left-block paragraphs
`lpq`	Lists your print jobs waiting in the default print queue
`lpr`	Sends a copy of the file to be printed to the print queue
`lprm`	Removes a print job from the print queue
`.ls` *n*	Inserts *n* spaces between each line
`-ms`	Indicates the **ms** macro package
`.na`	Produces a nonjustified margin
`.ND`	Eliminates date in headers when using the **-ms** macro package

Table 6.2: Commands and Requests Covered in Chapter 6 (continued)

Command or Request	Result
`.ne n`	Keeps *n* lines on one page
`.nf`	Stops the line-filling process
`.NL`	Returns font to normal size
`.nr PO ni`	Offsets left margin *n* inches
`nroff`	Text formatting command used with line printers
`.1C`	Returns from two-column to single-column text
`.pl n`	Changes the page length to **n** inches
`.PP`	Formats text into standard paragraphs
`pr`	Allows user to customize the formatting and printing of files
`.QP`	Formats text into block quotes
`.R`	Returns to normal typeface
`rastrepl`	Increases size of printed screen image
`.RC`	Begins the second column of two-column text
`.RE`	Moves indent to left five spaces
`.RS`	Shifts indent five spaces to the right
`screendump`	Captures the screen image

Table 6.2: Commands and Requests Covered in Chapter 6 (continued)

Command or Request	Result
`.SM`	Makes font two points smaller
`.sp n`	Inserts *n* line spaces in text
`.ta`	Sets tabs
`.TE`	Indicates the end of a table
`.ti n`	Temporarily indents a line *n* spaces
`troff`	Text formatting command used with typesetters and laser printers
`.TS`	Indicates the beginning of a table
`.2C`	Begins the first column of two-column text
`.UL`	Underlines text in a sentence
`.ul n`	Underlines *n* words

CHAPTER 7

Multitasking and Customizing SunOS

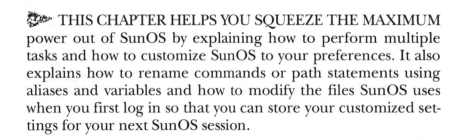

THIS CHAPTER HELPS YOU SQUEEZE THE MAXIMUM power out of SunOS by explaining how to perform multiple tasks and how to customize SunOS to your preferences. It also explains how to rename commands or path statements using aliases and variables and how to modify the files SunOS uses when you first log in so that you can store your customized settings for your next SunOS session.

Multitasking

SunOS is a multitasking operating system, which means you can run several commands simultaneously. SunOS's job control features allow you to manage multiple running commands, which are called jobs. The term *job* is simply another word for the processing of a command. For example, editing, sorting, or formatting a file are all jobs. One job may contain more than one process connected by pipes. SunOS provides you with a collection of commands for managing your jobs. Using these commands you can suspend, resume, list, terminate, or switch jobs between the foreground and background. Running SunOS jobs in the *foreground* means running them directly on your screen. Running jobs in the *background* allows you to run other commands on your screen while a job placed in the background is being processed. Each job you stop or place in the background is given a *job number*, but every job you run is assigned a *process ID* (PID) number. Job numbers are assigned by SunOS for jobs generated at your terminal. PID numbers are assigned by SunOS for all processes throughout the system.

Checking Job Status

You can check the status of jobs placed in the background using the **jobs** command, which indicates if a job is done, running, or stopped. Typing **jobs** displays a list similar to the following:

```
[2]        Stopped    troff -ms yearend report92
[3]    -   Stopped    find / -name a*
[4]    +   Stopped    vi program1.c
[5]        Running    screendump | rastrepl | lpr -v &
```

The first column identifies the job with a number in brackets. The current job is indicated by a plus sign (**+**), and the next job after that is indicated by a minus sign (**-**) to the right of the first column. The **-l** (long) option displays both job and PID numbers for all your background jobs, similar to the following:

```
[2]        194    Stopped    troff -ms yearend report92
[3]    -   207    Stopped    find / -name "a*"
[4]    +   211    Stopped    vi program1.c
[5]        243    Running    screendump | rastrepl | lpr -v &
```

Here the PID numbers are given in the third column.

Suspending and Restarting Jobs

You can suspend a job you're currently working on in the foreground by typing Control-Z. Using this command suspends the processing of the program, places the program in the background, and assigns the stopped program a job number. To resume the program in the background, enter **%n &**, where *n* is the job number you want to resume. You can also stop a background job by typing **stop %n**, where *n* is the job number you want to stop. The **stop** command, like Control-Z, suspends but doesn't terminate the command.

Logging Out of SunOS with Stopped Jobs

If you try to log out of SunOS while a job is stopped in the background, SunOS displays the warning message **There are stopped jobs**. Typing the **logout** command again will log you out and terminate any stopped jobs in the background. If you want to view which jobs are stopped before you log out, type **jobs**. Any commands running in the background continue to run even after you log out.

Creating a Background Job

Certain commands take a long time to run, such as the **nroff** program, which formats documents for printing or display. This type of time-consuming program is best run in the background so it doesn't tie up your screen and keep you from doing other work. To run a command as a background job, add the ampersand (**&**) at the end of the command line before you press Return. For example, typing

```
nroff -ms sports | lpr &
```

instructs SunOS to format the file **sports** using the **nroff** program and run the job in the background.

Redirecting Background Job Output

A background job normally sends the result of its processing to the screen unless you redirect its output. To ensure that a background job isn't written to your screen while you're working on another program, restrict writing to your terminal by entering the command **stty tostop**. When the **stty tostop** command is activated, SunOS suspends any background program that attempts to write to the screen. You can remove the screen output restriction by typing the command **stty -tostop**.

Switching Jobs between Foreground and Background

To move a running job from the background to the foreground, use the **fg** command followed by a percent sign and the job number. For example, typing **fg %2** moves job 2 into the foreground. Typing **fg** without a job number brings the current job (marked by the plus sign (**+**) in the **jobs** list) to the foreground.

Suppose you have a program running in the foreground and need to perform another task on your screen. You can quickly place the foreground command into the background. First press Control-Z, which automatically stops the program and places it in the background. Then type **bg** to resume running the program in the background. To resume a stopped job in the background, type **%n &**, or **bg %n**, where *n* is the job number. For example, typing **%4 &** instructs SunOS to resume running job number 4 in the background.

Remember, any time you need to know a job number, type **jobs** for a listing of background jobs and their respective numbers.

If you start a background job from a directory different from your working directory and bring that job to the foreground, SunOS changes your working directory to that directory. SunOS warns you when the system changes your working directory as a result of bringing a background job to the foreground.

Terminating Jobs

The **kill** command can only be used for terminating jobs running in the background.

Any time you accidentally execute a wrong command or realize you don't want a particular program to run, you can terminate the job using the **kill** command. To terminate a running program in the background, type **kill %n**, where **n** is the job number you want to terminate. For example, typing **kill %3** terminates job number three. Some programs need more than the **kill** command to be terminated. Strengthen the killing power of the **kill** command with this syntax:

```
kill -9 %n
```

To terminate a program running in the foreground, press Control-C. You can also terminate a foreground program by pressing Control-Z to suspend it and move it to the background. Then use the **kill** command to terminate the program.

Notification of Job Status Changes

If you have jobs running in the background, you may want to be notified when they're completed. SunOS normally notifies you when background jobs change status, such as when a job terminates, by displaying **done** before the next SunOS system prompt. You can instruct SunOS to notify you immediately after a background job changes status by typing **notify %n**, where **n** is the number of the job you want to be immediately notified of when its status changes. For example, typing **notify %5** instructs SunOS to notify you immediately after any status change in job number 5, such as when that job is done. SunOS then displays a message on your screen, regardless of what you're working on in the foreground. A more powerful version of the **notify** command, **set notify**, allows you to be notified immediately when any background job changes its status. However, if you have a lot of background jobs running, you may end up with a number of status change messages cluttering up your screen. Table 7.1 lists essential job control commands.

Table 7.1: Job Control Commands

Command	Description
command &	Creates a background job
Control-Z	Stops the job you're working on
jobs	Lists both stopped and background jobs, assigning them job numbers in brackets; for example, **[1]**. The current job is identified with a (**+**) and the next job with a (**−**). With the **−l** option, includes the PID number in the listing.
fg	Brings the current job marked with **+** from the jobs list into the foreground, starting the job if it's stopped
fg %n	Brings job **n** from the jobs list into the foreground, starting the job if it's stopped
%n	Suspends the current job in the background
%n &	Resumes job **n** in the background
bg	Puts the current job (marked with a **+** in the jobs list) into the background, starting the job if it's stopped
bg %n	Resumes job **n** in the background
stop %	Stops the current job in the background
stop %n	Stops background job **n**
notify	Notifies you when the current job changes status

Table 7.1: Job Control Commands (continued)

Command	Description
`notify %n`	Notifies you when job **n** changes status.
`set notify`	Notifies you when any job changes status
`kill %n`	Terminates background job **%n**
`stty tostop`	Suspends background jobs that write to the screen
`stty -tostop`	Allows background jobs to write to the screen

Managing Processes

As mentioned earlier, each command interpreted by SunOS is assigned a unique PID number. SunOS juggles its time and resources amongst the various processes currently running and uses the PID to track the progress, current status, amount of time, and percentage of available memory each process uses. PID numbers are different from job numbers. Job numbers are unique and relevant only to your work on the system, while PID numbers are assigned to processes throughout the system by SunOS regardless of their source.

Checking the Status of a Process

To see what processes you have running, type **ps** and press Return. SunOS displays a list of processes generated from your account during the current work session similar to the one below:

```
PID  TT   STAT TIME COMMAND
395  co   R    0:00 ps
397  060  T    0:04 csh
400  060  Z    0:13 nroff
```

In addition to showing the PID number for each process generated from your account, the ps command also lists the terminal where it originated, its current status, processing time used, and the command it's performing. Codes used in the **ps** listing are shown in Table 7.2.

Terminating a Process

You can use **kill** with PID numbers. First type the **ps** command to determine the PID number. Once you know the PID number, type **kill**, followed by the PID number. For example, typing **kill 3193** terminates the command running in the background with the assigned PID number **3193**. Use the command **kill -9 *PID number*** to terminate a process that won't terminate using the **kill** command alone. If the **slay** command is active on your system, you can use it to kill any process without having to look up the PID number. For example, typing **slay hefty** terminates the program **hefty** running in the background.

Table 7.2: The ps Command Codes

Column	Symbol	Meaning
PID		Process ID number
TT		Terminal:
	co	**/dev/console**
	mn	**/dev/ttymn**
STAT		State of the process:
	R	Runnable (running)

Table 7.2: The ps Command Codes (continued)

Column	Symbol	Meaning
STAT		State of the process:
	T	Stopped
	P	Paging
	D	Waiting on disk
	S	Sleeping (less than 20 seconds)
	I	Idle (more than 20 seconds)
	Z	Terminated, control passing to parent
	W	Swapped out
	>	Exceeded soft memory limit
	N	Priority was reduced
	<	Priority was raised
TIME		Processing time (so far)
COMMAND		Command being performed

Scheduling Processes

You can execute commands at a time and date you specify, regardless of whether you're at the terminal or not, using the **at** command. When SunOS executes commands at the time and date specified with the **at** command, it sends the results of the process via electronic mail to whomever you indicate. The syntax of the **at** command is

> **at** *time date increment*

You can specify the time for the **at** command as a one-, two-, or four-digit number. One- and two-digit numbers specify an hour, while four-digit numbers specify an hour and a minute. The **at** program assumes a 24-hour clock unless you place **am** or **pm** immediately after the number, in which case **at** uses a 12-hour clock. You can also use the word **now** in place of a time. If you do use **now**, you must also specify a date or an increment of time. An acceptable increment is a number followed by one of the following (plural or singular): minutes, hours, days, weeks, months, or years. For example, typing

> `at now + 30 minutes`

means execute the command 30 minutes from the time the command is entered. You can also use the word **next** to specify when a command will be executed. For example

> `now next week`

means excute the command at the current time one week from now.

You can specify the date on which you want **at** to execute the process. If you don't specify a date, **at** executes the job the same day if the hour you specify in time is greater than the current hour. If the hour is less than the current hour, **at** executes the process the next day. You can abbreviate the days of the week to the first three letters. You can use the name of the month followed by the number of the day in the month to specify a date. You can also follow the month and day with a year.

Performing a Process at a Later Time

Suppose you want to send the text file **fired.ltr** to a user named **buecker**, but you want to hold its release until 8 a.m.

the next morning. The following four steps demonstrate how to send the file at 8 a.m. the following day and let someone else know when the dirty deed has been done.

1. Type **at 8am** and press Return. If you are using the **at** command before 8 a.m. on the day before you're sending this file, you need to specify the day. SunOS displays the **at** command prompt, **at>**.

2. At the **at>** prompt, enter

   ```
   mail -s 'Greetings from Personnel' buecker < fired.let
   ```

   then press Return. This command instructs SunOS to mail the file **fired.let** to the user **buecker**.

3. At the **at>** prompt, enter

   ```
   echo 'Message sent' | mail -s Message ihangman
   ```

   then press Return. This command instructs SunOS to send a message to **ihangman**, confirming the file **fired.let** was sent to **buecker**.

4. At the **at>** prompt, press Control-D to end the **at** command session. SunOS displays **<EOT>** and ends the **at** command session, displays a job confirmation message, then returns to the SunOS prompt, as shown in the following example:

   ```
   % at 8am
   at>mail -s 'Greetings from Personnel' buecker <
    fired.let
   at>echo 'Message sent' | mail -s Message ihangman
   at><EOT>
   job 31629 at Thu Feb 22 08:00:00 1999
   %
   ```

You can remove an **at** command process using the **-r** (remove) option by typing **at -r n**, where **n** is the PID number of the process. To find out the PID of the process you want to remove, type **at -l**, which displays a list of all the processes you've indicated with the **at** command as well as their PID numbers. Typing **at -r** cancels the last process you submitted to the **at** command.

Aliases

Aliases give you the power to rename any SunOS command to a name you can more easily remember. For example, if you're new to SunOS but familiar with IBM's PC DOS operating system, you might frequently find yourself entering the DOS command **dir** instead of **ls** to list a directory's contents. Assigning an alias named **dir** to the command **ls** enables you to use the list command by typing either **dir** or **ls**. When SunOS processes your commands, the command line is scanned from left to right to see if it contains an alias. If a command line has an alias, the SunOS command that matches the alias is used. Aliases may already be available to you, depending on how your system administrator has set up your account. Typing the **alias** command by itself displays all defined aliases.

Creating an Alias

Both single and double quotation marks can be used to indicate multiword text.

To create an alias, type **alias** followed by the name you want to assign as the alias, then type the command you want to match the alias. For example, **alias dir ls** enables you to type either **dir** or **ls** to obtain a directory listing. Using the **alias** command, you can abbreviate long command lines. To create an alias for multiword strings, enclose the multiword string in quotes. For example, typing **alias lc "ls -l chap*"** causes the system to display a long listing of all the files in the working directory beginning with **chap** when you enter **lc**. Note that the asterisk (*****) wildcard character is enclosed *inside* the quotation marks.

Undoing an Alias

You remove an alias by entering the **unalias** command, followed by the alias name. For example, **unalias dir** removes the **dir** alias. You can also use wildcard characters to eliminate groups of aliases. For example, **unalias l?** removes all aliases that are two characters long and begin with the letter **l**.

Shortcuts Using Variables

A *variable* is a named memory location in which you store text you want to reuse. A set of *predefined variables* exists when you first begin using SunOS. Some of these variables are added by your system administrator. For example, **home** is a predefined variable that keeps track of your home directory. Another common predefined variable is **noclobber**. The **noclobber** variable ensures that you don't overwrite existing files when you use the **>** ("to") redirection symbol. By setting your own variables, you can avoid repeatedly typing long strings of characters.

Setting Variable Names and Values

To assign the name and value of a variable, use the **set** command followed by the variable name you want, an equal sign, and the string of characters you want to assign to the variable. An example of setting a variable is to assign an abbreviation to a long pathname. For example, the command

```
set benchmark = ~/test/results
```

allows you to type **$benchmark** to indicate the **results** subdirectory of **test** in your home directory. You can also use filename substitution in variables. In command lines you indicate a variable by preceding it with a **$**. For example, if you entered

```
set play = (/usr/games/{a,c,f}*)
```

and then entered the command **ls $play**, you would get a list of files in the **games** directory beginning with the letters **a**, **c**, and **f**, such as **arithmetic**, **canfield**, **chess**, **ching**, **craps**, **cribbage**, **factor**, **fish**, and **fortune**.

Displaying a Variable's Contents

The **set** command by itself prints a list of all existing variables and their current values. The **echo** command followed by a full variable name (including the **$**) displays the variable's contents. For example, using the **echo** command on the previous variable **benchmark**,

```
echo $benchmark
```

displays

```
~/test/results
```

Storing a List of Words as a Variable

Instead of typing out long, complicated commands or pathnames, you can store them as variables and use a simple variable name to refer to them. You can also store a list of words as a variable with the **set** command by enclosing the list of words in parentheses. For example, entering

```
set opus = (frame/chaps frame/notes frame/docs)
```

allows you to type **$opus** to indicate each subdirectory in the parentheses. For example,

```
ls -l $opus
```

lists the contents of the subdirectories **chaps**, **notes**, and **docs**.

Specifying Variables in a List

You can specify any word in a variable list by indicating the word number in brackets; for instance, using the **opus** variable example above and entering the command

```
echo $opus[2]
```

should display the second value in the list of variables, which in the previous example is the pathname

```
/frame/notes
```

You can also specify a range of words in a variable. For example,

```
echo $opus[2-3]
```

prints

```
frame/notes frame/docs
```

If you indicate a number larger than the number of words in a variable list, SunOS displays the message: **Subscript out of range**.

Running Commands Using a Variable List

With the **foreach** command, you can save time when you want to perform a set of commands on every word in a list. The **foreach** command applies a set of commands successively to every string separated by a space in a variable list. The syntax of the **foreach** command is

```
foreach index ($word_list_variable)
```

After you press Return, the **foreach** command prompts you for a command with a question mark. The **foreach** command continues to prompt you for other commands until you type the command **end** to signify the end of the list of commands. The commands you enter at the question mark are then repeated for each word in the variable list. The following shows an example of using the **foreach** command to copy the files contained in the directories listed in **opus** to a directory named **backup**.

```
foreach dir ($opus)
? cp $dir/* backup
? end
```

The index is simply a variable name that you choose. **foreach** uses this variable to refer to the individual words in the word-list variable. In the previous example, the index **dir** refers to each of the directories (that is, each word) listed in **opus**. You can think of **foreach dir ($opus)** as meaning "for each directory in opus" and **cp $dir/*** as meaning "copy all files in the directories." Because the index is a variable, you must precede it with a **$** when you reference it.

To see how the **foreach** command processes each word in a list, try using **foreach** and **echo** as follows:

```
foreach word (Sun Mercury Venus Earth Mars)
?echo $word
?end
```

Entering this example displays

```
Sun
Mercury
Venus
Earth
Mars
```

Suppose you have several files that contain names and phone numbers. You want to locate phone numbers for three people, but you are not sure which files contain the numbers. You can use the **foreach** and **grep** commands to perform a search for all three names. For example, entering

```
foreach search ("Biggs" "Baker" "Merry")
?grep  $search *
?end
```

executes the **grep** command and replaces the search variable (**$search**) with the names in the parentheses to locate lines containing these names in any of the files in the working directory (indicated by the asterisk). Here is sample output from this example:

```
phonelist: Sally Biggs 493-1663
blackbk: Norma Baker 878-4786
todolist: Call back Kim Merry at 244-0559
```

Output Substitution and Variables

Output substitution allows you to use the output of a command as an argument for another command. When you surround a command with single opening quotation marks (` ) anywhere in the command line, the command within the single opening quotation marks is executed and substitutes the resulting output for the text in single opening quotation marks. For example, suppose you have a list of file names stored in a file called **printlist**; entering **lpr `cat printlist`** prints each file listed in the file **printlist**. The following example uses output substitution and the **set** command to assign the current date to a word-list variable.

```
set day = `date`
echo $day
```

displays

```
(Wed Jan 22 12:00:00 PDT 1992)
```

The command

```
echo $day[4]
```

displays

```
12:00:00
```

Storing Aliases and Variables in the .cshrc File

Any aliases and variables you've created up to this point are lost when you log out of SunOS. In order to store your variables so that you don't have to recreate them each time you log in, add them to the **.cshrc** file, where SunOS stores your default settings.

The letters in **.cshrc** are short for the **c sh**ell **r**un **c**ommand. The C shell is the command interpreter that is the connection between you, the operating system, and your workstation. When you first log in, the `.cshrc` file is executed, and any settings in it are put into effect. Before changing your `.cshrc` file, copy it to a file named **cshrc.bkup** as a backup to ensure that you can return to your default settings. Once you have a backup of your original file, you can experiment with the settings and decide if you want to use the original. A sample `.cshrc` file with the file name **Cshrc** is also included in the **/usr/lib** directory.

The Default Permissions

One of the first lines in the `.cshrc` file contains the **umask** command, which disables the default file and directory permissions assigned to the files and directories you create. The syntax for the **umask** command is

```
umask nnn
```

where each **n** is a number that sets the permissions for files and directories for the owner, group, and public. The first number indicates the owner permissions; the second, group permissions; the last, public permissions. The **umask** command uses different values for permissions than the **chmod** command. Table 7.3 lists the file and directory permissions used with **umask**. The most common setting for the **umask** command is **022**, which assigns files with read and write permissions for the owner and read only to everyone else (**-rw-r--r--**). The 022 setting assigns directories with read, write, and execute permissions for the owner; execute and read permissions for groups; and execute permissions to the public (**drwxr-x--x**).

Changing .cshrc Variables

You can list the variables set in your `.cshrc` file using the **set** or **printenv** commands. The following lists some typical `.cshrc`

Table 7.3: The umask File and Directory Permission Values

Value	File Permissions	Directory Permissions
0	rw-	rwx
1	rw-	rw-
2	r—	r-x
3	r—	r—
4	-w-	-wx
5	-w-	-w-
6	—	—x
7	—	—

file entries with explanations. You can ignore commands in the `.cshrc` file by placing a pound sign (**#**) to the left of the line you want to ignore. You can also indicate multiple commands using the semicolon, just as you do when using the command line.

cwd	Stands for current working directory and is a built-in variable that can be accessed faster than the **pwd** command can be executed
history = 20	Sets the **history** mechanism to record the last 20 commands entered
set savehist = 10	Saves the last 10 commands in the **history** list when you log out

set noclobber	Safeguards against unintentionally over-writing (clobbering) a file when using the **>** ("to") redirection symbol. You can temporarily override **noclobber** protection by using an exclamation point **!** after the **>** redirection symbol.
set ignoreof	Prevents accidentally logging out when you type Control-D. If this variable is not set, pressing Control-D is the same as issuing the **logout** command.

The Path Statement

The **set path =** statement identifies directories that the system should look in for commands you enter at the command line. Regardless of your current directory, SunOS will search through the directories in your path variable for the command you are executing. The path statement needs to exist to allow access to SunOS commands. The default is typically **(./usr/ucb /usr/bin)**. Note that each pathname is separated by a space. If you need to access a program not in your home directory, add it to the path statement and then execute the program without changing directories. The following is an example of a typical path statement:

```
set path = ( . /usr/ucb /usr/bin /bin ~/bin /vol/local/bin \
/usr/local/bin /files/sundesk/bin /files/xnews)
```

Changing the Prompt

By default the prompt is set to a percent sign (**%**). Entering

```
set prompt="{`hostname`:\!} "
```

changes the prompt to display the hostname, a colon, and the last event number in the history list.

You can create a prompt that always displays the current directory by using the **alias** and **set prompt** commands, the **cwd** (current working directory) variable, and the special word designator **!***. When preceded by a backslash, the special characters **!*** act as a placeholder for arguments. The command

```
alias cd 'cd \!*;set prompt="$cwd> " '
```

assigns **cd** as the alias for two commands. The first command

```
cd \!*
```

simply changes the directory to the one you specify when you use the alias (**\!*** is a placeholder for the directories you specify). The second command

```
set prompt="$cwd> "
```

changes the prompt to display the pathname of the new working directory. Note that the complete command line

```
alias cd 'cd \!*;set prompt="$cwd> " '
```

uses single closing quotation marks to connect the aliased **cd** command with the **set prompt** command. Make sure you use a single closing quotation mark ('), not an opening quotation mark, or SunOS will interpret your entry as a command rather than a word. Also note that the argument to **set prompt** is enclosed in double quotation marks so that a space can be added at the end to separate the prompt from your commands. The result of entering the above example will be a prompt similar to the following:

```
home/reports>
```

Adding Aliases

Some aliases are already predefined by your system administrator. For example, the **cp** (copy) and **mv** (move) commands may have the interactive option (**-i**) added to prevent you from accidentally overwriting them, prompting you when existing files are going to be overwritten. The following is an example of aliases commonly found in a **.cshrc** file:

# user aliases	Adds a comment (notice the pound sign, #) identifying the user aliases section of the **.cshrc** file
alias cd 'cd \!*;echo $cwd'	Causes the **cd** command to display the current working directory using the **$cwd** variable
alias pwd 'echo $cwd'	Causes the **pwd** command to use the **$cwd** variable to display the current working directory
alias ls 'ls -F'	Adds the **-F** option to the **ls** command to mark which files are executable and which files are directories when listing directories
alias cp 'cp -i'	Adds the **-i** (interactive) option to the **cp** (copy) command to protect against accidentally overwriting files
alias mv 'mv -i'	Adds the **-i** (interactive) option to the **mv** (move) command to protect against accidentally overwriting files
alias rm 'rm -i'	Adds the **-i** (interactive) option to the **rm** (remove) command to protect against accidentally overwriting files
**alias print 'pr \!*	lpr'**	Creates an alias named **print** which allows you to enter **print** *filename* to automatically format *filename* with the **pr** command and send it to the printer

If you frequently use the **history** command, try adding the following to your **.cshrc** file:

```
alias h history
```

You can now get a **history** listing by simply typing the letter **h**.

The .login File

The **.login** file is located in your home directory and is the file read in directly after the **.cshrc** file. This file sets up your terminal and executes other files needed to set up your environment. The **.login** file uses special variables called *environment variables*. It is a popular convention to use all capital letters for names of environment variables. Normally you don't have to worry about changing environment variables. You can check to see what environment variables you're using by entering the **printenv** command. The following is a typical listing of environment variables set in a **.login** file:

```
HOME=/home/abozo
SHELL=/bin/csh
TERM=sun-cmd
USER=abozo
PATH=.:/usr/ucb:/usr/bin:/bin:/home/abozo/bin::/vol/local \
  /bin:/usr/local/bin
LOGNAME=abozo
PWD=/files/home/users/abozo
AUTOMOUNT_FIXNAMES=true
MAIL=/home/abozo/mbox
LANG=USA-English
TTY=/dev/console
```

Setting Environment Variables

Many commands need to know what type of terminal you're using or which printer to send output to. You can set environment variables using the **setenv** command. The syntax for the

setenv command is **setenv *NAME* value**. To unset an environment variable, use the **unsetenv** command. The following example changes the default printer from the printer named **lp** to a printer named **lw**:

```
unsetenv PRINTER
setenv PRINTER lw
```

Customizing the .mailrc file

The **.mailrc** file works similarly to the **.cshrc** file, only it stores aliases and variables relating to the mail program for sending and receiving electronic mail. The **.mailrc** file is usually stored in your home directory.

Adding an Alias for Sending Mail to a Group

You can add aliases to your **.mailrc** file to define a group of user names as a single name. For example, adding the following line to the **.mailrc** file

```
alias jazz lemon@polyphony duke@swing parker@bebob
```

allows you to send a letter to **lemon**, **duke**, and **parker** at their respective machines via the **mail** program using the alias name **jazz**.

Setting .mailrc Variables

The **.mailrc** file contains several predefined variables. You can turn default mail variable settings off by preceding the predefined variable with **no**. For example, to turn the variable **hold** off, add **no** to the **hold** variable as follows: **set nohold**. If a file is indicated by a variable, it's set with an equal sign; for example, **MBOX = mbox** sets the storage mailbox for your mail to the file named **mbox**. The following is a list of **.mailrc** variables and their default settings:

append	Adds letters to the end of **mbox**. Default is off.
askcc	Automatically displays the carbon copy prompt **Cc:** when writing a letter. Default is on.
asksub	Automatically prompts for a subject when writing a letter. Default is on.
autoprint	Automatically displays the next letter in the mailbox when one is deleted. Default is off.
DEAD	Stores partial letters in case of interruption, such as a power failure. The default sends the contents to a file called **dead.letter** in your home directory.
dot	Makes a single dot (period) act as the termination character to indicate the end of a letter. Default is off, but is set to on in the global start-up file.
EDITOR	Sets the editor to use when composing letters. The default is ex.
folder	The directory that contains your mail folders. Default is **mail**.
header	Causes the header list to be displayed when you enter the **mail** command. Default is on.
hold	Holds letters in your mailbox until you save or delete them. Default is off.
ignoreof	Sets the end-of-file character to a period on a line by itself or the tilde character rather than Control-D. Default is off.

keep   Retains your mailbox even if it's empty. When set to **nokeep** the mailbox is removed until you receive mail. Default is off.

keepsave   Prevents **mail** from deleting a letter from your mailbox when you save the letter in another file or folder. Default is off.

MBOX   The file where letters are stored after they've been read. Default is **mbox** in your home directory.

metoo   Sends letters to yourself when you send a letter to an alias group of which you're a member. Default is off.

outfolder   Keeps a record of every letter you send in a folder named **outfolder**. Default is off.

page   Ejects a page after each letter. Default is off.

prompt   Sets the mail prompt. The default is **&;**.

quiet   Suppresses the initial **mail** program display of its version number and a short sample letter. Default is off.

save   Saves partial letters into the file specified in the **DEAD** variable setting. Default is on.

SHELL   The name of the command interpreter. Set from the environment setting.

showto   When sending copies of letters to yourself or letters to a group of which you're a member, displays the letter's recipient rather than your name. Default is off.

Summary

In this chapter you learned how to manage and schedule jobs. You also learned how to customize SunOS using aliases and variables. You learned how to

- check on the status of a job using the **ps** (process status) command.

- start, stop, or suspend jobs.

- run jobs in the background or schedule a job to be processed later using the **at** command.

- rename commands using the **alias** command.

- create single word or lists of words as variables using the **set** command.

- display the contents of a variable using the **echo** command.

- modify your **.cshrc** file to save your aliases and variable settings for future SunOS sessions.

- change the default permission settings with the **umask** command.

- add directories to your path statement to access programs in other directories.

- modify the default **.mailrc** variables or create aliases to send letters automatically to members of a group you specify.

Table 7.4 lists the commands covered in this chapter that are not contained in the earlier tables.

Table 7.4: Miscellaneous Commands Covered in Chapter 7

alias	Allows user to rename a command
at	Executes commands at specified time and date

Table 7.4: Miscellaneous Commands Covered in Chapter 7 (continued)

`echo`	Displays a variable's contents
`foreach`	Applies a set of commands to each word in a variable word list
`logout`	Logs out and terminates any stopped jobs in the background
`ps`	Lists processes currently running
`set`	Allows user to create a variable, and prints a list of all existing variables
`setenv`	Allows user to set environment variables
`umask`	Sets the default file and directory permissions assigned to the files user creates
`unalias`	Allows user to remove an alias
`unsetenv`	Unsets an environment variable

CHAPTER 8

Getting Started
with the Deskset

THIS CHAPTER INTRODUCES THE OPENWINDOWS and SunView windowing environments and explains how to use the DeskSet in either environment. The *DeskSet* is a set of easy-to-use, integrated, graphics-based productivity tools provided by Sun Microsystems. These tools save time and make mastering SunOS easy because they enable you to use a mouse to select icons and menus as an alternative to typing a series of SunOS commands to navigate the file system, send and receive mail, edit files, and perform a variety of other functions. This chapter explains working with menus, icons, windows, and buttons and details the minor differences of the DeskSet in the Open-Windows and SunView environments.

About the OpenWindows and SunView Environments

SunView and OpenWindows are full-featured window environments that provide an interface rivaling the ease of a Macintosh, yet tapping the power of Unix. Sending and receiving mail, editing text, and running programs are as easy as pointing and clicking a mouse button.

The major difference between SunView and OpenWindows is that SunView is proprietary, meaning that it can only run on Sun Workstations. OpenWindows, however, can run on a variety of platforms, provided they follow the standard Unix System V Release 4 (SVR4) guidelines.

SunView is an acronym for Sun Visual/Integrated Environment for Workstations. SunView was one of the first products that provided a graphical interface with Unix. Because SunView is not a standard and only runs on Sun Workstations it is being replaced by OpenWindows as the default interface.

OpenWindows is an improved windowing environment based on the X Window standard, a standard network windowing environment, and the Network extensible Windowing System (NeWS). NeWS supports Postscript, a page description language that describes text fonts and graphics images; Multimedia, which supports concurrent processing of voice, video, and data; Integrated Services Digital Network (ISDN), an international telecommunications standard that allows a communications channel to simultaneously support voice, video, and data; and thin wire connection support for hooking up networks. OpenWindows allows you to run applications that take advantage of these standards. Another feature of OpenWindows is the integration of OpenFonts technology. Using OpenFonts, OpenWindows only needs to store a single outline font for each typeface, which is quickly scaled to size when needed. OpenFonts provides applications with 627 scalable, rotatable fonts.

Some applications have not been upgraded to work under OpenWindows and must run under SunView; however, virtually all applications are being modified to support OpenWindows.

Starting SunView or OpenWindows

On some systems, SunView comes up when you log in. If the system prompt (**%**) is displayed, you can start SunView from the command line by entering the command **sunview**. When you start SunView, it displays tools in black and white. If you are using a gray-scale or color monitor, you can start the three dimensional tools by entering

```
sunview -3D
```

A special version of SunView is required in order to use the SunView DeskSet. This version of SunView is shipped with the DeskSet. If the DeskSet does not appear as described in this chapter, see your system administrator or see Appendix B, which explains installing the SunView DeskSet and OpenWindows.

If OpenWindows is on your system, you can start OpenWindows by entering

```
openwin
```

If you are using the default settings and enter one of these commands, the screen turns gray and two windows appear on your screen: a **Console** window, which displays system messages, and the **File Manager Tool** window, used to manage your files, as shown in Figure 8.1. If a **Console** window does not appear in the upper-left corner of your screen, system messages are displayed at random on your screen. You can open a **Console** window if one is not displayed, as explained later in this chapter.

If you are using Sunview, you can easily determine whether or not you are using the DeskSet. Move the mouse so that the pointer is in the top border of the **Console** (or systems message) window. If you are *not* using the SunView DeskSet, the pointer changes to a target—a circle with a dot in the middle—representing an older SunView window that is not a part of the SunView DeskSet.

If you want to conserve memory, don't use the **-3D** option.

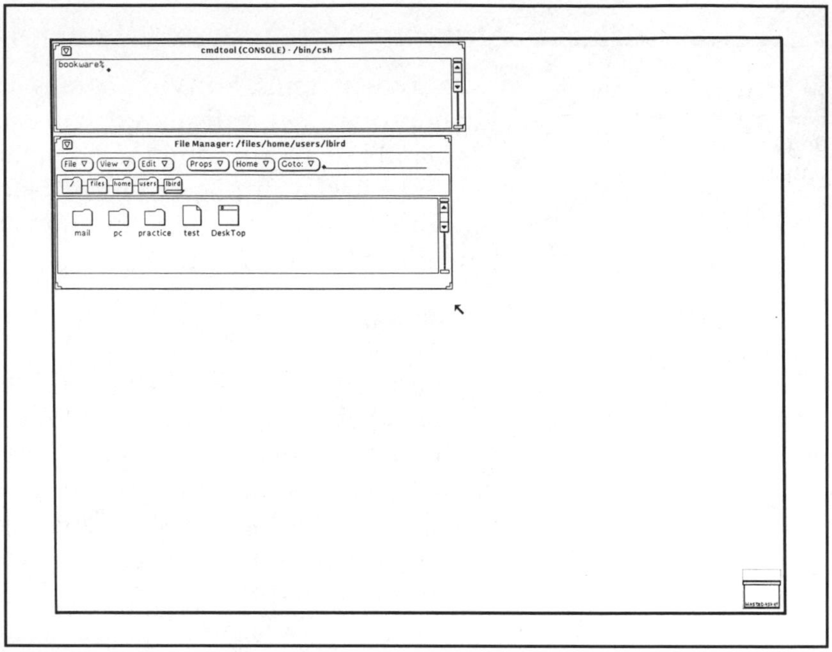

Figure 8.1: A sample screen

An Overview of the DeskSet

Sun now bundles
the DeskSet with
all its systems. If you
don't have the DeskSet,
it can be purchased for
the price of the docu-
mentation and media
and can be freely
copied.

The DeskSet works virtually the same in either Open Windows or SunView. If a difference does exist, it is noted. The following is a general overview of the DeskSet's main features.

- The DeskSet has three-dimensional menus and enhanced windowing features that make working with
windows exceptionally easy. The DeskSet also allows
you to keep important menus posted anywhere on
your screen by providing menus that can be moved
and pinned to the new location.

- Consistency in the DeskSet tools reduces learning
time, providing you with tools which work exactly the
same on different workstations.

- The DeskSet lets you drag icons representing files and drop them in other windows or icons to transfer files between applications. This drag-and-drop action in addition lets you effortlessly start applications. You can also easily drag and drop unwanted files in a wastebasket icon to quickly move them off the workspace.

- The DeskSet enables you to use a visual file management tool to copy, move, rename, and delete files and perform other file management tasks.

- The DeskSet's Mail Tool offers enhanced mail features previously not available.

- The DeskSet includes a scientific calculator so you can readily perform both simple and complex calculations.

- The Calendar Manager feature allows you to create an appointment calendar with reminders for upcoming appointments or sending mail.

- The DeskSet's Snapshot program allows you to easily take a picture of part of the screen or the entire screen.

- The DeskSet also provides you with a Print Tool to simplify printing.

- The DeskSet's Tape Tool provides a convenient way to back up and retrieve files using a tape drive.

Using the Mouse

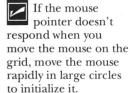 If the mouse pointer doesn't respond when you move the mouse on the grid, move the mouse rapidly in large circles to initialize it.

Sun's three-button mouse allows you to perform a variety of operations with the DeskSet by simply pressing a mouse button. The arrow that appears in the middle of your screen pointing towards the upper-left is the *pointer*, which changes locations when you move the mouse. To move the pointer, you must move the mouse on the silver plate with the blue grid that accompanies your system. Try moving the mouse in a circle; notice the pointer moves in a corresponding motion. You use the mouse to select an object on the screen by moving the pointer to the object and pressing the left mouse button to select or activate the object. The next section explains the mouse button actions you use with the DeskSet.

Mouse Button Actions

The crux of mastering the DeskSet depends on knowing where to move the mouse pointer and which mouse button to push. Figure 8.2 shows the effects of each mouse button when used on the DeskSet.

The following describes each mouse button and its related function:

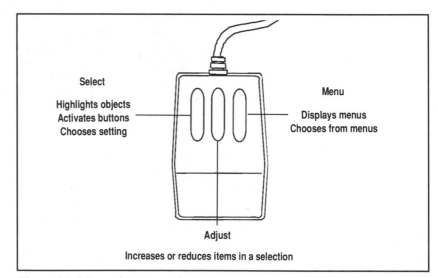

Figure 8.2: Mouse button actions

Mouse Button	Function
Left	Selects objects or moves icons or windows. The left mouse button is also referred to as *Select*.

Mouse Button	*Function*
Middle	Extends or reduces selected objects. The middle mouse button is also referred to as *Adjust*.
Right	Displays or chooses options from menus. The right mouse button is also referred to as *Menu*.

The mouse pointer also acts as an indicator of different actions occurring in the system. For example, when an application is busy, the mouse pointer changes to a stopwatch or an hourglass to indicate that the application is busy and cannot accept input.

The following describes the six actions performed with a mouse:

Action	*Description*
Click	Quickly press and release a mouse button
Double Click	Quickly press and release a mouse button twice (without moving the mouse)
Press	Hold down a mouse button without moving the mouse
Drag	Hold a mouse button down while moving the mouse
Control-drag	Press the Control key on the keyboard and drag the mouse
Point	Move the mouse to change the location of the pointer

Dragging and Dropping Files in Windows

To load or move a file into an application window, select a file using the left mouse button, drag the file inside the window's pane, and release the left mouse button. Releasing this button is known as dropping a file. The file is loaded or moved or a message appears in the window footer explaining why the drag and drop action was unsuccessful. For example, selecting a file's icon and dragging and dropping it into the File Manager moves the file to the current directory. Dragging and dropping text file icons in the pane of the **Text Editor** or **Mail Compose** window loads the file for editing. Dragging a text file icon on the Print Tool sends the file to the printer. To drag and drop a file into a window, follow these three steps:

1. Move the pointer onto the icon you want to drag and drop.

2. Press the left mouse button.

3. Drag the icon to its destination and release the left mouse button.

The Workspace Menu

The gray area that surrounds the window and icons is known as the *workspace*. The workspace is analogous to a desktop on which you create, change, and store documents.

The DeskSet is structured around pop-up menus that are associated with the general location of the mouse. The **Workspace** menu is a pop-up menu sometimes called the root menu because it is the primary menu you use to access the DeskSet programs and utilities. To display the **Workspace** menu, move the pointer to the gray area of your screen and press the right mouse button. In most cases the choices displayed are similar to those in Figure 8.3. To quit displaying the **Workspace** menu, move the pointer off the **Workspace** menu and release the left mouse button.

The following describes the options displayed in the **Workspace** menu in Figure 8.3.

⊙ Be careful when displaying the **Workspace** menu. If you release the right mouse button with a menu option highlighted, the option is activated. To ensure you don't mistakenly activate a **Workspace** menu option, move the pointer off the **Workspace** menu before releasing the right mouse button.

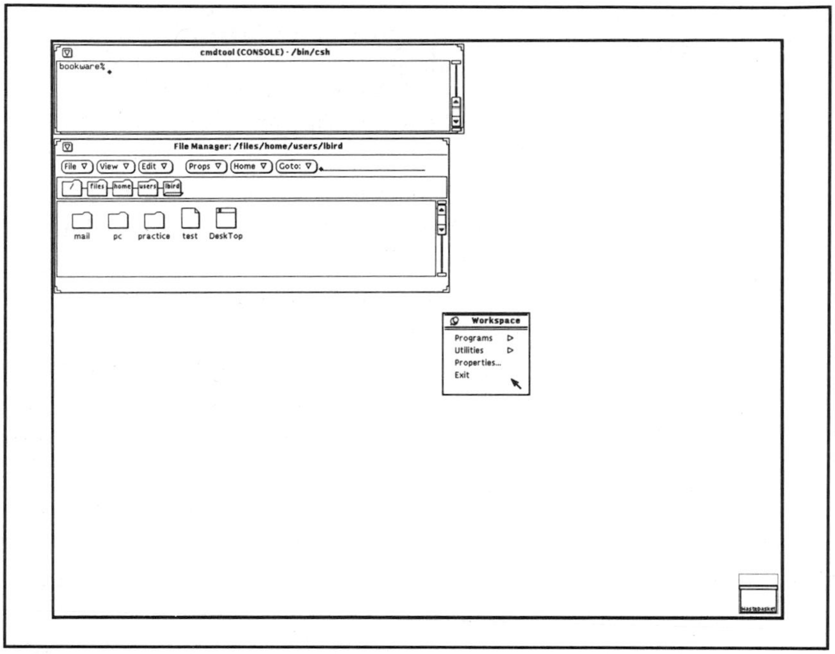

Figure 8.3: The Workspace menu

Option	Result
Programs	Displays a submenu of tools
Utilities	Displays a submenu of services for redisplaying (refreshing) or locking the screen, resetting the input point, saving the workspace layout, or opening a new console command window
Properties...	Displays a window containing options for customizing your workspace environment
Exits	Exits OpenWindows or SunView

Using the Workspace Menu

The **Workspace** menu displays right-facing triangles following the menu items **Programs** and **Utilities**. These triangles act as arrows; moving the pointer to the right with the highlight on this option will display a submenu. With the pointer on the **Workspace** menu and the highlight on the **Programs** option, move the mouse to the right. The **Programs** submenu is displayed. The **Programs** submenu lists the tools available. The selections available in the **Workspace** menu depend on whether you are using the SunView DeskSet or OpenWindows. Notice that the program option appears circled in the **Workspace** menu. This indicates the default option so that quickly clicking the right mouse button selects this option. Figures 8.4a and 8.4b display the OpenWindows and the SunView DeskSet **Program** menus. To close the menus, move the pointer off the **Workspace** menus so that the highlight disappears and then release the right mouse button.

When you select an option from the **Program** submenu, you are actually loading the tool on the workspace. You can load and

It is a common mistake not to move the pointer off the **Workspace** menu before releasing the right mouse button. This causes the File Manager icon to appear because it is the default option of the **Programs** submenu.

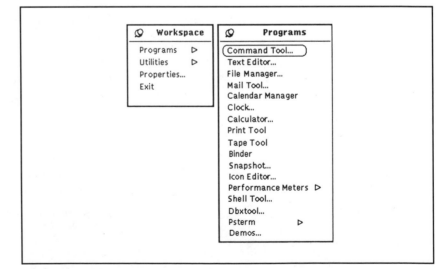

Figure 8.4a: The OpenWindows Workspace Program menu

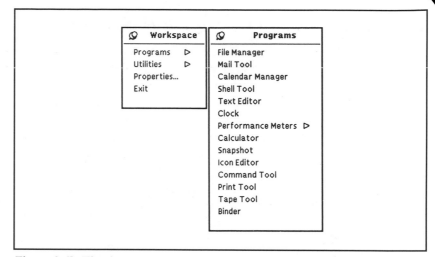

Figure 8.4b: The SunView DeskSet Workspace Program menu

open more than one of the same tool. For example, you can open two or three Shell Tools at one time.

Pinning and Unpinning the Workspace Menus

You can keep the **Workspace** menu and submenus displayed by pressing the right button and placing the pointer on top of the push pin in the upper-left corner of the menu, then moving the push pin into the hole in the upper-left corner. When you release the button the menu is posted on the workspace. The **Workspace** menu remains pinned until you unpin it or select the **Dismiss** option from the **Window** menu by clicking the right mouse button with the pointer on the menu's header, the area above the line at the top of the menu. You can also access the **Window** menu by moving the pointer on any part of the menu's border and pressing the right mouse button. The **Window** menu is explained in detail later in this chapter.

You can move a pinned menu anywhere on the workspace by moving the pointer to the menu header, pressing the left mouse button, then dragging the menu to its new location.

Loading a DeskSet Tool

To load a DeskSet tool you first need to display the **Workspace** menu. Press the right mouse button with the pointer on the workspace. The **Workspace** menu appears. Move the pointer to the right with the highlight on the **Programs** option. Move the mouse pointer to highlight the tool option in the **Programs** submenu you want to load. When you release the right mouse button, the program is loaded. The icon which represents the program appears on your screen.

The icons for tools shown in Figure 8.5 may not exactly match the icons on your screen. When a tool is closed, it cannot accept input from the keyboard and displays an icon. To open a tool, move the pointer onto an icon and double click the left mouse

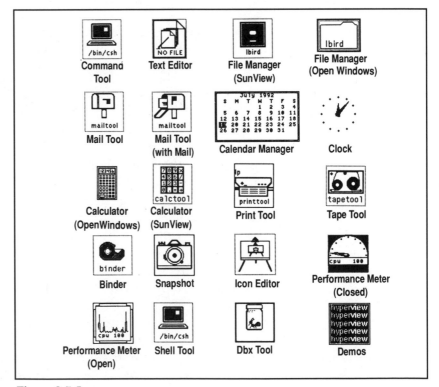

Figure 8.5: Icons

button. Open tools display one (or more) windows. For example, the open rectangle in the upper-left corner of the screen is a **Command Tool** window labeled **Console**, which displays messages.

An Overview of the DeskSet Tools

Figure 8.5 shows the icons displayed for each of the programs. The following gives a brief description of each application available in the **Workspace Programs** submenu.

Application	*Description*
Command Tool	A computer icon represents the Command Tool. The Command Tool gives you text editing features so you can search and replace, copy, or move text, or save the contents of the window to a file.
Text Editor Tool	An icon containing a pen and papers represents the DeskSet text editor. This text editor is covered in Chapter 11.
File Manager Tool	The file cabinet or file folder indicates the File Manager Tool, which is used to manage your files. Some of the features of the File Manager Tool allow you to quickly list, delete, copy, move, sort, or print files, or change permissions of files.
Mail Tool	A mailbox indicates the **mail** program, which allows you to exchange messages with other users. If your icon displays an open mailbox with the flag in the up position and an envelope in the front, you have mail.

Application	*Description*
Calendar Manager	The calendar indicates the Calendar Manager, an easy-to-use appointment scheduler. It includes a daily, weekly, bimonthly, monthly, and yearly scheduler and alarm features for appointments and mail.
Clock	The clock icon opens to a small rectangular window that displays the current time, using either a digital or analog clock face. You also have the option of displaying the clock with or without a second hand and the date.
Calculator	The calculator icon (labeled as **Calctool** in the SunView DeskSet) represents a scientific calculator that emulates a Texas Instruments TI-3 or Hewlett-Packard HP-10C, or a slide rule. You can use the left mouse button to press the calculator buttons.
Print Tool	The Print Tool is indicated by a picture of a Sun LaserWriter with the name of the default printer above it. The Print Tool lets you conveniently print files and display printing information such as how many print jobs are before yours.
Tape Tool	The streaming tape cartridge indicates the Tape Tool. The Tape Tool is primarily used by a system administrator to backup or load files on the system.

Application	*Description*
Binder	The Binder Tool is represented by a tape dispenser. This tool is designed to be used by a system administrator to bind applications, icons, colors, and scripts (such as a series of commands to print a file in a special format) to files.
Snapshot	The camera icon indicates the Snapshot program, which allows you to save screen images into a file, then view or print them. You can take a picture of a portion of a screen or the entire screen.
Icon Editor	The easel icon with pictures of two smaller easels represents the Icon Editor, which allows you to create and edit small images to generate your own icons, buttons, cursors, and panel items.
Performance Meters	When opened the Performance Meter is displayed as an icon-size graph. When closed it is displayed as a meter. This icon displays a system performance meter for a variety of system features. For example, the default value displays the percentage of the central processing unit (CPU) being used.
Shell Tool	A computer (identical to the Command Tool icon) represents a C Shell window which contains a command-line interface so you can issue SunOS commands.

Application	*Description*
Dbx Tool	The Dbx Tool icon is a picture of a bug in a bottle. This is a programming tool to debug programs. This tool supports programs written in C, Pascal, or FORTRAN 77. The Dbx Tool is not covered in this book.
Psterm	The **Psterm** option is available in Open-Windows. This option is not represented by an icon but by a menu that presents options for different-size Sun terminal emulators. You can choose 24, 36, or 56 lines. Each terminal emulator maintains 80 columns.
demos	The **demos** option is only available in OpenWindows. When selected, **demos** displays an icon with the word Hyper-view in a variety of colors. The Hyperview demo allows you to activate a variety of impressive X Window and NeWS pro-grams, including PostScript demos, and several image and animation demos, a calculator, and a journaling accessory that records and plays back keystrokes and mouse actions.

Working with Windows

The DeskSet tools provide a consistent way to use the mouse with windows regardless of the tool you are using. In other

⊞ You can get online help for any part of a window by moving the pointer to the part of the window you want explained and pressing the Help Accelerator key, located at the bottom left of your keyboard if you are using a type 4 keyboard. If you are using another type of keyboard, press F1.

words, you open, close, move, and resize windows the same way regardless of the environment you are using or the tool the window contains. Once you know how to change one window you can change any other window. Figure 8.6 uses a **Text Editor** window to illustrate the parts of a window.

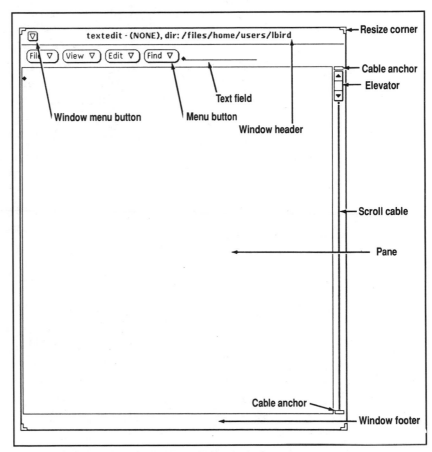

Figure 8.6: The parts of the Text Editor window

The following describes each part of the DeskSet's **Text Editor** window:

Window header	The wide stripe at the top of the window is called the window header. The contents of the header depend on the application you are using. The header typically tells you the name of the tool associated with the window. If the window is a text file, the pathname for the file is usually included. You can access the **Window** menu, described later in this chapter, by pressing the right mouse button in the window header.
Scrollbar elevator	The scrollbar elevator allows you to move (scroll) through the contents of a window using a mouse. You can move the pointer to any part of the scrollbar and press the right mouse button to display a **Scrollbar** menu. The boxes at the ends of the scrollbar are cable anchors that allow you to move quickly to the beginning or end of a file by moving the pointer to a cable anchor and clicking the left mouse button.
Pane	The area containing the window's workspace.
Menu button	Each application with a menu button has menus that pop up when you press the right mouse button. The button labels are command names. Menu buttons with a triangular arrow beside the button label always have additional menus layered underneath. Three dots (...) on a button indicates that a window will pop up when you click on it with the left mouse button.

Text field	This window area accepts text. The text field is usually associated with the menu button to its direct left. To enter text in a text field, move the pointer next to the dimmed diamond and click the left mouse button. The diamond changes to a black triangle, indicating you can enter text.
Resize corner	By moving the mouse pointer on any of the four resize corners, you can press the left mouse button and stretch the window to a new size, larger or smaller.
Window menu button	The window menu button activates the default item from the **Window** menu without displaying the menu. Typically the default is the **Close** option, which allows you to easily close a window by moving the pointer on top of it and pressing the left mouse button.
Window footer	This area of the window displays messages and status information.

If you are using the first version of the SunView Desk-Set, the **Properties** option, which is used to customize a window's color or default location, appears dimmed because the original release did not support this menu option.

Moving the pointer on top of an icon, a window header, or the border of a window and pressing the right mouse button displays the **Window** menu. The **Window** menu provides you with options to open, close, or resize a window to take up the full screen. You can also move windows to the background behind another window. If a window is not displayed correctly, you can also use the **Window** menu to redisplay it. The following sections explain how to work with windows using the **Window** menu and other alternative methods. Figure 8.7 shows the **Window** menu.

Opening and Closing a Tool

You open a DeskSet tool by placing the pointer on top of the icon and double clicking the left mouse button. You close a DeskSet tool by moving the mouse pointer to the **Window** menu button and clicking the left mouse button. You can also close a tool by moving the pointer to any part of the window header or

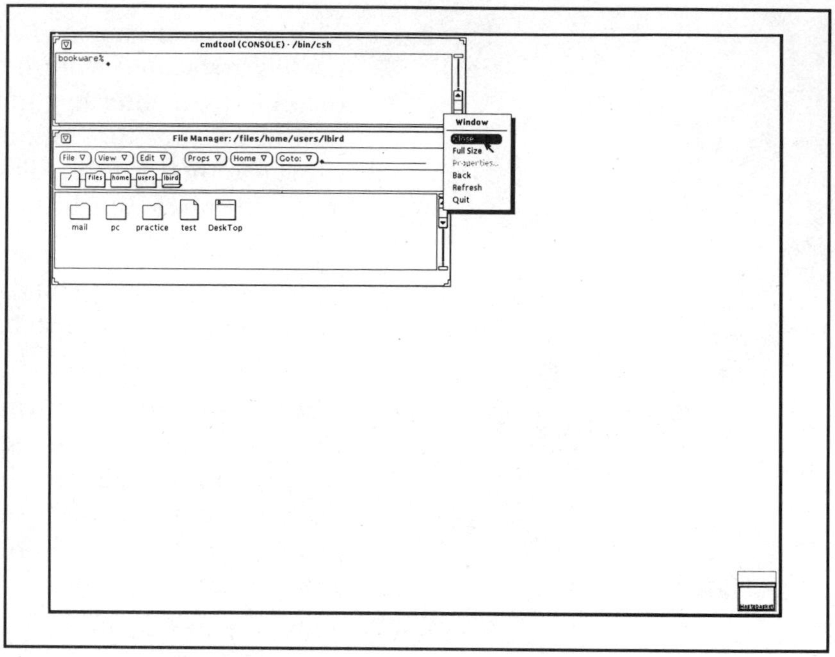

Figure 8.7: The Window menu

the outside border of the window, pressing the right mouse button, and selecting (moving the highlight to) the **Close** option if it is not already highlighted, as shown in Figure 8.7. When you release the mouse button, the window shrinks back to an icon, as shown in Figure 8.8.

If you are using a type 4 keyboard or have redefined your keyboard to include *accelerator* keys, they can be used in conjunction with or in place of the mouse.

An alternative to using the mouse to open or close a window (after moving the pointer to the window border or icon) is to press the Open key (or L7 on older Sun keyboards) located on the left side of the keyboard. The Open key is a toggle key, which means it opens a closed window or closes an opened window. Remember, the pointer must be located on the icon or window you want to affect in order to use the Open key.

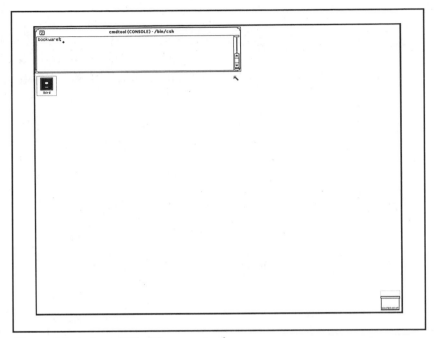

Figure 8.8: A closed File Manager tool

You can enter commands in the **Console** (system messages) window, but it is recommended you use a **Command Tool** window and reserve the **Console** window for system messages.

Entering Commands in a Window

You can enter commands in either a **Command Tool** or **Shell Tool** window. If a Command Tool or Shell Tool icon or window is not displayed on your screen, you can open one by selecting the **Command Tool** or **Shell Tool** option from the **Workspace Programs** submenu. Figure 8.9 shows an open Command Tool. Once a **Command Tool** window is open, the system prompt appears near the top of the window. Next to the system prompt is a symbol indicating the point where text will be inserted. If the symbol next to thc command prompt is a nonblinking diamond displayed in a light shade of gray, it indicates that the pointer is outside the command window and the window is inactive. When the window is active, the symbol appears as a black, blinking triangle, which indicates it is ready for you to enter a command. If you open a Shell Tool, a rectangle indicates the insertion point. If a solid rectangle is displayed, it indicates that it is ready for you to enter a command. A hollow rectangle indicates that the pointer is outside the Shell Tool and the window is inactive.

Try entering the cal command to display the calendar for the current month. If no characters appear in the window, move the pointer next to the system prompt and click the left mouse button.

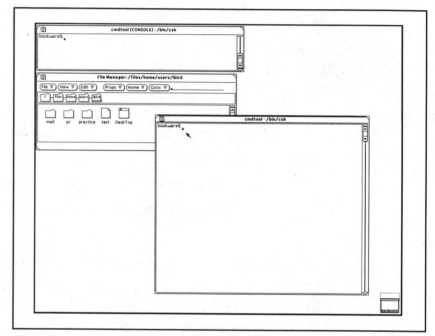

Figure 8.9: An open Command Tool window

Scrolling through the Contents of a Window

In most cases, the right side of a window displays a scrollbar. The *scrollbar* is made up of five major components: cable anchors, Up arrow, drag box, Down arrow, and the cable. Figure 8.10 identifies each of these parts of a scrollbar.

Pressing the left mouse button and dragging the mouse with the pointer on the drag box moves the contents up or down

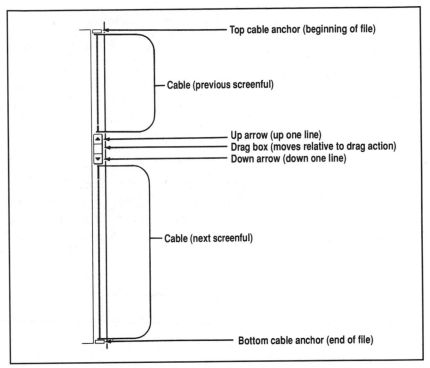

Figure 8.10: The parts of the scrollbar

relative to the direction you drag the drag box. The following explains how to use a scrollbar to move through a file:

Movement	*Action*
Beginning of a file	Click the left mouse button with the pointer on the top cable anchor.
Bottom of a file	Click the left mouse button with the pointer on the bottom cable anchor.
Up a screenful	Click the left mouse button with the pointer located on the cable between the top cable anchor and the Up arrow.
Down a screenful	Click the left mouse button with the pointer located on the cable between the bottom cable anchor and the Down arrow.

Movement	*Action*
Up one line	Click the left mouse button with the pointer on the Up arrow.
Down one line	Click the left mouse button with the pointer on the Down arrow.

The Scrollbar Menu

You can also use the **Scrollbar** menu to move to one of three locations in a window. To display the **Scrollbar** menu, move the pointer anywhere on the scrollbar and press the right mouse button. A **Scrollbar** menu is displayed as shown in Figure 8.11.

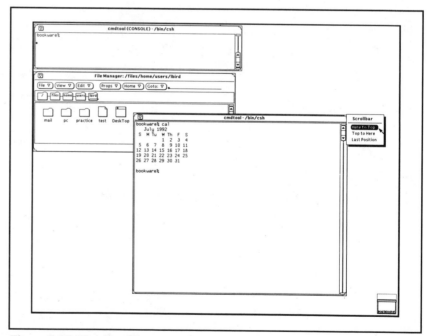

Figure 8.11: The Scrollbar menu

You select a **Scrollbar** menu option by moving the pointer to highlight the option you want. The following explains the three scrollbar options:

Option	Result
Here to Top	Moves the line in which the pointer is located to the top of the window
Top to Here	Moves towards the top of the file an amount relative to the position of the pointer in the scrollbar
Last Position	Moves to the last position you were located when you pressed a mouse button

Moving a Window

You can rearrange windows or icons anywhere on your screen, even on top of other windows or icons. You can move the window in any direction. When you move a window, an outline of it moves as you drag the pointer. This outline is known as a *bounding box*. To move a window, move the pointer to the window header of the window you want to move. Press the left mouse button, and drag the bounding box to its new location. When you release the left mouse button, the window is moved to the location of the bounding box.

Moving Windows to the Background

 To quickly move a window from the background to the foreground, move the pointer to the window header or window border and click the left mouse button.

Opening windows is similar to stacking papers on your desk. Adding too many windows clutters your screen, causing windows to overlap. To move a window covered by another window, move the pointer to the window header or the border of the window you want to move to the background, click the right mouse button, and select the **Back** option from the **Window** menu. You can also use the Front accelerator key on the left side of your keyboard or L5 on older Sun system keyboards to move a window to the foreground (the top window). This key acts as a toggle, so clicking it again sends the frame to the background. Figures 8.12a and 8.12b show a **Calendar** window before and after using the **Back** option from the **Window** menu.

Resizing a Window

Moving the pointer to any of the resize corners of a window, pressing the left mouse button, and then dragging the mouse allows you to stretch a window's height and width. The bounding box changes size when you drag the pointer, and the window changes to the size of the bounding box when you release the mouse button.

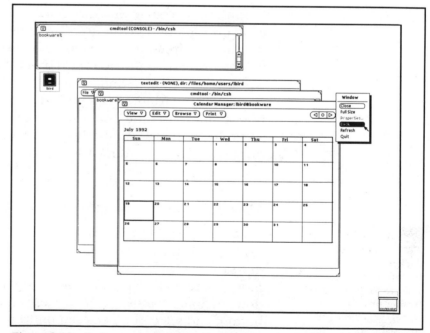

Figure 8.12a: Before selecting the Back option in the Window menu

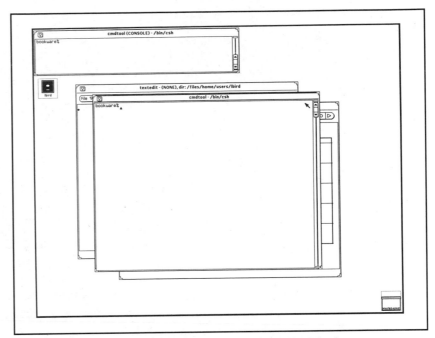

Figure 8.12b: After selecting the Back option in the Window menu

Resizing a Window to Take Up the Full Screen

An easy method of resizing a window so that it takes up the full height and width of the screen is to move the pointer to the window header or border, press the right mouse button, and select the `Full Size` option from the `Window` menu, as shown in Figure 8.13a. Once you release the left mouse button, the window is resized to the size of your screen, and the `Full Size` option in the `Window` menu changes to `Restore Size`, as shown in Figure 8.13b. To return to the normal size of the window, select the `Restore Size` option from the `Window` menu.

Redisplaying a Window

Sometimes fragments of previous work appear in a window, or a portion of the window appears to have a section missing.

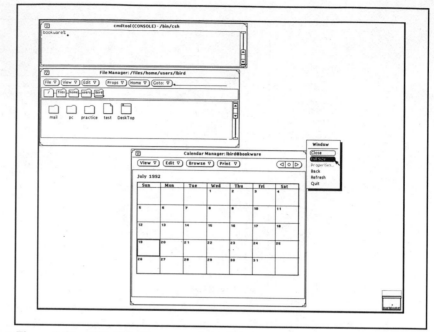

Figure 8.13a: The Window menu's Full Size option

You can redisplay the window using the **Refresh** option in the **Window** menu to clear the deranged portions of your window. Choosing the **Refresh** option redraws the window.

Quitting a Window

The last menu selection in the **Window** menu is the **Quit** option. Quitting is different from closing a window because the tool is actually removed from the desktop. In some cases, highlighting **Quit** and clicking the right mouse button displays a confirmation dialog box. A confirmation dialog box usually contains two *buttons* (outlined choices): **Confirm** and **Cancel**. If the button outline is shown in bold face or a double outline surrounds the button, you can press Return to select that choice; otherwise, you must move the pointer directly below the

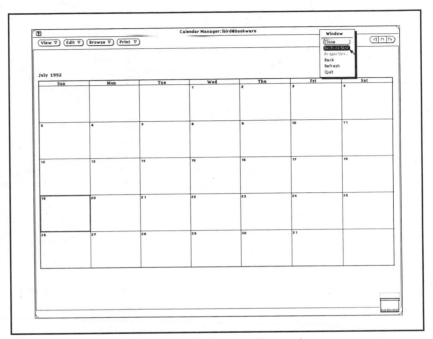

Figure 8.13b: The Window menu's Restore Size option

button you want to select and click the left mouse button. If you want to quit using the tool and remove the icon or window from the workspace, click the left mouse button or press Return, and the icon or window disappears. Otherwise you can cancel the **Quit** selection by moving the pointer to the **Cancel** button and clicking the left mouse button.

Working with Pop-Up Windows

Pop-up windows provide controls to conveniently change specific attributes of an application, such as which directory to save files in, the color of windows, or how often to check for mail. Each button or option in a menu that displays a pop-up window is followed by three dots (...). Figure 8.14 shows a typical

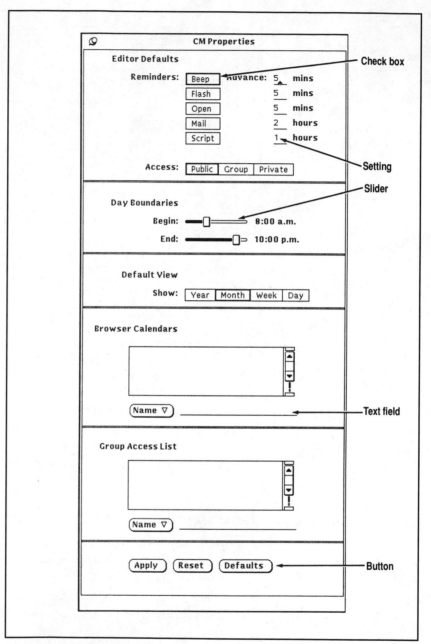

Figure 8.14: A pop-up window

pop-up window. The following list explains the pop-up window controls:

Buttons	These display menus or perform commands by moving the mouse pointer onto them and clicking the left button.
Check Boxes	Settings activated or deactivated by moving the pointer inside the check box and clicking the left mouse button
Text Fields	Text input areas for entering text, such as specifying directories, files, or numeric settings
Scrolling Lists	Lists of settings that include a scrollbar. Most scrolling lists allow you to edit the list.
Settings	Characteristics or attributes you choose or enter
Sliders	These set a value for a range of values and display a visual indicator of where the value is within the range.

The Pop-Up Window Menu

Pop-up windows have an associated menu that you get by clicking the right mouse button with the pointer in the window header. Figure 8.15 shows an example pop-up window menu. The following explains the pop-up window menu options:

Option	Result
Dismiss	Provides you with options for dismissing (terminating) the current pop-up window or dismissing all pop-up windows
Back	Moves the current window to the back of the screen

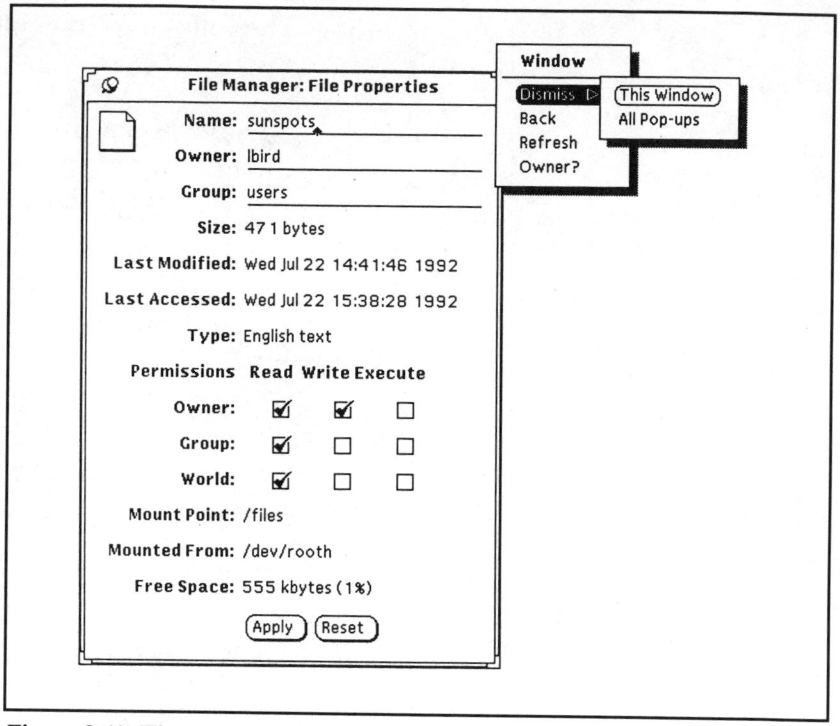

Figure 8.15: The pop-up window menu

Option	Result
Refresh	Redisplays the contents of the pop-up window
Owner?	Flashes the window header of the window that the pop-up window was started from and moves the application window of the associated application to the front of the screen

The Screen Saver

If you leave your terminal unattended or do not press a key within a certain period of time, an image, such as the Sun Microsystems logo, bounces around your screen. This bouncing image protects your screen so that the characters are not burned into it. To return to your original screen, simply press any key or move the mouse.

Protecting Your Terminal

If you want to leave your terminal for an extended length of time, you can lock your screen to protect your work and implement the bouncing images to protect your screen. The **Lock Screen** option is found in the **Utilities** menu of the **Workspace** menu. To unlock your screen, press any key (other than F1 or Caps) or move the mouse. SunOS displays a message instructing you to enter your password to unlock your screen, as shown in Figure 8.16. After you enter your password the message **validating login** appears. If you entered your password correctly, you are returned to your original screen.

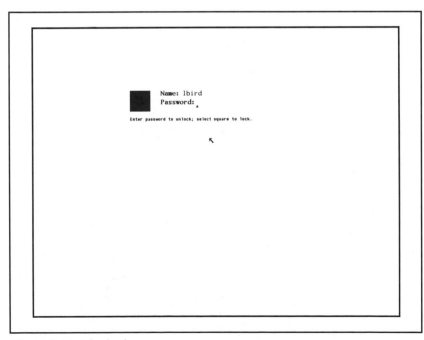

Name: lbird
Password:

Enter password to unlock; select square to lock.

Figure 8.16: A locked screen

Exiting

If you have finished using the DeskSet, you can exit the Open-Windows or SunView environment using the **Exit** option of the **Workspace** menu. To exit, select the **Exit** option from the **Workspace** menu. SunOS displays a dialog box asking you to confirm that you want to exit, as shown in Figure 8.17. The pointer automatically appears below the **Confirm** button. Click the left mouse button. In most cases you are returned to a system prompt.

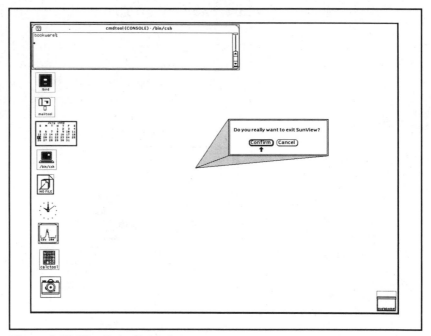

Figure 8.17: The Exit dialog box

Summary

In this chapter you learned

- what the OpenWindows and SunView environments are and which one you should use.

- what tools are available in the DeskSet.

- how to use the mouse to display and select options from pop-up menus and select and work with windows.

- how to display the **Workspace** menu by pressing the right mouse button with the pointer on the workspace, as well as how to select and display the default menu option.

- how to open and close a DeskSet window using the **Window** menu and the **Window** menu button.

- how to enter commands in a **Command** or **Shell Tool** window.

- how to use the scrollbar, including the scrollbar's cable and cable anchors, to move through a file.

- how to move or resize a window using the resize corners of a window or the **Window** menu.

- how to uncover a window and send a window to the background using the **Window** menu or the accelerator button.

- how to quit a window using the **Quit** option in the **Window** menu.

- how to protect your terminal so that you can leave your terminal without exiting and others cannot tamper with your work.

- how to exit OpenWindows or SunView using the **Exit** option of the **Workspace** menu.

CHAPTER 9

Using the
File Manager

▶ ONE OF THE MOST BENEFICIAL AND ESSENTIAL tools in the DeskSet is the File Manager, which simplifies working with files. A *file* is a storage place for data or executable programs. Special files called *directories* contain indexes that are used to group and locate files. This chapter explains how to navigate, create, name, find, copy, move, delete, and print files using the File Manager. This chapter also explains how to protect and share files by setting access permissions and linking files. For more information on the SunOS file system, see Chapter 3.

The File Manager Icon

The File Manager uses a file cabinet metaphor to help you work with directories and files; when closed, the File Manager displays a folder icon in the OpenWindows environment or a file cabinet icon when using the SunView DeskSet. The icon also displays the name of the current directory. To close the File Manager, click the left mouse button on the window menu button (the upside down triangle in the upper-left corner).

The Parts of the File Manager Window

The **File Manager** window is made up of three main parts: a path pane, a control panel, and a folder pane, as shown in Figure 9.1. Each of the parts of the **File Manager** window is described in this section.

The Path Pane

Folders represent directories.

The path pane displays your current location in the file system. You can view the path pane either as a path of connected

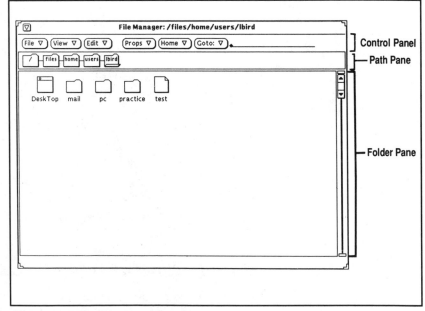

Figure 9.1: The File Manager window

folders or as a tree that shows all or part of your file system structure. By default the File Manager displays the path where you started OpenWindows or SunView. If you started the File Manager using the **Programs** option from the **Workspace** menu, it displays your home directory. To change the path to a tree display, move the pointer to the **View** menu, press the right mouse button, and move the highlight to the **Tree** option. When you release the right mouse button, the path pane displays a tree representation of the file system with your home directory at the bottom. Figure 9.2 shows the File Manager displaying directories using the **Tree** option of the **View** menu.

The path pane also provides a **Path Commands** pop-up menu, which contains commands similar to those of the menus in the control panel described in the following section. You can display the **Path Commands** pop-up menu by moving the pointer to any area in the path pane that is not displaying a directory

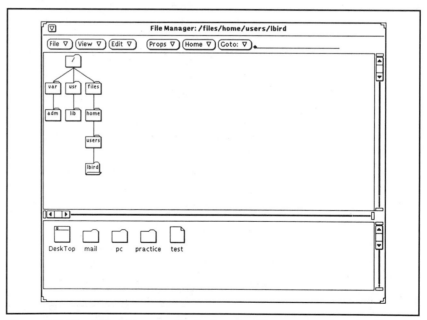

Figure 9.2: The File Manager displaying the file system using the Tree option

folder and pressing the right mouse button. The **Path Commands** pop-up menu appears as shown in Figure 9.3.

The Control Panel

The control panel of the File Manager has six menu buttons: **File**, **View**, **Edit**, **Props**, **Home**, and **Goto**. (To the right of the **Goto** button is a field in which you can enter pathnames for directories and files.) These buttons display menus that allow

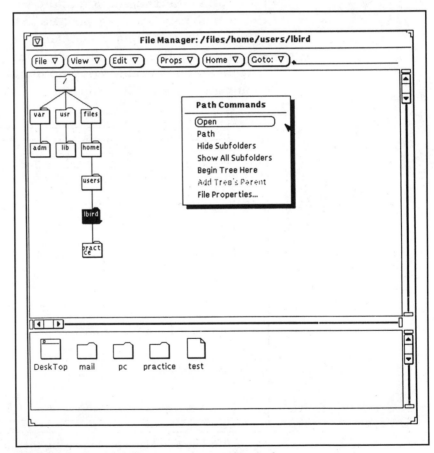

Figure 9.3: The Path Commands pop-up window

you to perform a variety of operations on one or more selected files. You can display any of one of these menus by moving the pointer to a menu button and pressing the right mouse button. You select a menu option from the displayed menu by keeping the right mouse button pressed and moving the pointer down the menu, highlighting the menu option you want, and then releasing the right mouse button. If a menu option is dimmed, it is unavailable. In most cases you must select a file, as explained later in this chapter, before certain menu options are made available. To stop displaying the menu, move the pointer off the menu and release the right mouse button. Figure 9.4 shows the `File Manager` window's control panel.

Figure 9.4: The File Manager window's control panel

The Folder Pane

The last folder in the chain displayed in the path pane is your current directory, and its contents are displayed in the folder pane. The folder pane is located directly below the horizontal scrollbar. When you first start the File Manager, the folder displays files and directories as icons with their names beneath them. You can use the folder pane's elevator scrollbar to move up or down and display the icons. Files are represented by three kinds of icons:

File Type	Icon
Directory	Folder
Data file	Sheet of paper with the upper-right corners bent
Executable file	Small window or application icon

The folder pane provides a **Folder Commands** pop-up menu, which contains commands related to files and folders. These menu options are a subset of the commands you access from the File Manager control panel. To display the **Folder Commands** pop-up menu, move the pointer anywhere in the folder pane that is not displaying a file, folder, or application icon and press the right mouse button. Figure 9.5 shows the **Folder Commands** pop-menu. Remember to move the pointer off the menu before releasing the right mouse button so you do not accidentally select an option from this menu.

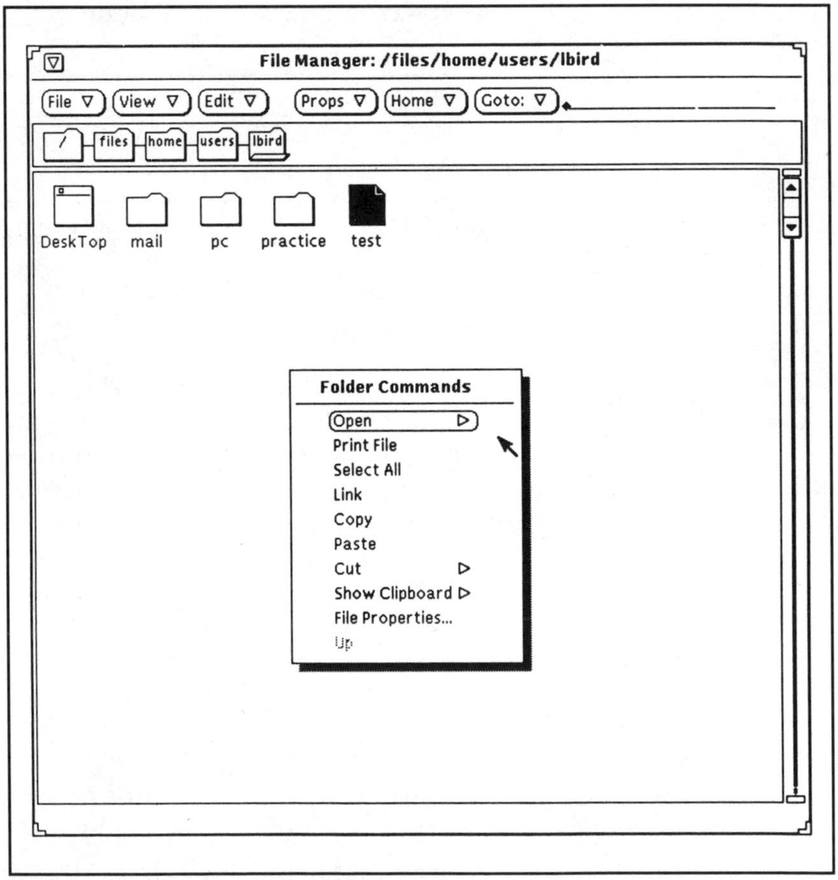

Figure 9.5: The Folder Commands pop-up menu

Getting Online Help in the File Manager

Online help is available for most of the buttons and parts of the **File Manager** window. To view help, move the mouse pointer to the button or window part you want information on and press the Help key on your keyboard. A help box is displayed. If the information takes up more than the box space, a scrollbar appears in the box, which you can use to scroll through the help text. To remove the help box from your screen, click the left mouse button with the pointer on the pin in the upper-left corner of the help box.

Viewing Files, Folders, and Applications

The **View** menu in the control panel provides options to change the display of your file system in the path pane. For example, you can change the way icons are displayed by using the **Folder Display** submenu of the **View** menu, as shown in Figure 9.6.

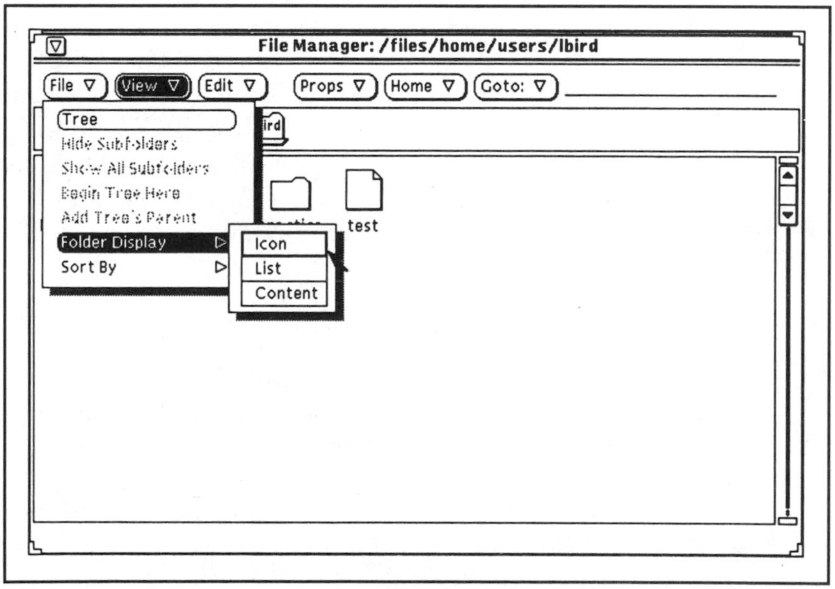

Figure 9.6: The View Folder Display submenu

The following describes each of the **Folder Display** menu options:

Option	Result
Icon	Displays a list of standard-size icons with the name of the icon centered below it
List	Displays miniature icons with the icons' names to their direct right. The **List** option is helpful if you want to show the maximum number of files, folders, and applications in a minimal amount of space. You select miniature icons the same way you select regular-size icons. You can customize the amount of information displayed using the **Tool Properties** window explained later in this chapter.

Option	Result
Content	Displays the picture contained in raster files (files that contain images, such as icons or screendumps), in addition to the name of the file. The images are not displayed to scale. Using this option slows scrolling because the File Manager must perform additional processing to display each image. (This option is only available in the Sun-View DeskSet.)

Sorting Files

The **View** menu's **Sort By** submenu, as shown in Figure 9.7, allows you to arrange files in the folder pane in one of the following orders:

Name	Arranges files alphabetically by name
Date	Displays files in reverse chronological order by date

Size   Displays files by descending file size

Type   Displays directories first, then files, and lastly
By Name   application programs

Selecting Files

Before you can perform an operation on a file such as copying or moving, you need to select the file or folder by moving
the pointer on the file or folder you want and clicking the left
mouse button. The icon turns black, indicating it has been
selected. After selecting one file or folder, you can select additional files and folders by moving the pointer on the next file or
folder you want to select and clicking the middle mouse button.
There are several types of operations you can perform on
selected files, folders, and executable programs. For example,
you can open, copy, move, delete, or print files or change the

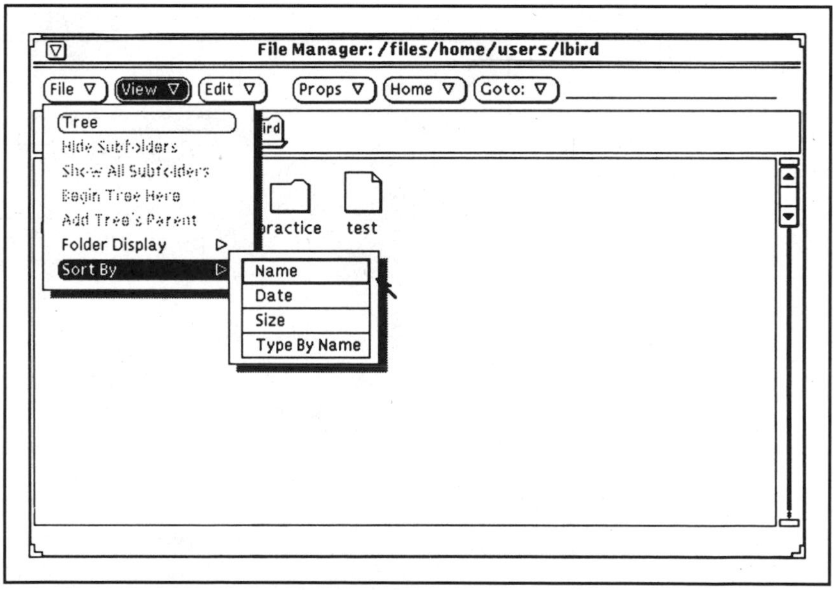

Figure 9.7: The View menu's Sort By submenu

file or folder's properties such as its name, ownership, and access permissions.

Opening and Loading
Files and Starting Applications

You can open a data file or execute a program file by moving the pointer to the file icon you want to open or start, and then double clicking the left mouse button. The File Manager connects each data file with the application it is related to so when you open a data file by moving the pointer on the icon and double clicking the left mouse button the application is automatically started and the data file loaded. For example, double clicking on a text file starts the text editor with the text file in the text editor window. If you choose a file not bound to a specific application, you may see a dialog box asking if you want to open the executable file in a shell tool, as shown in Figure 9.8.

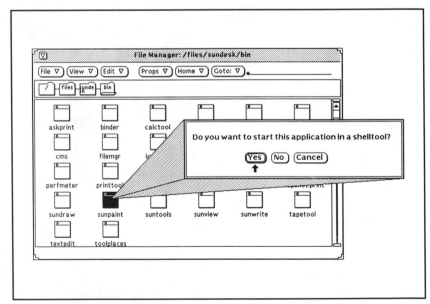

Figure 9.8: A notice asking whether or not to start an application in a shell tool

If you have a specific reason for wanting to use a shell tool, choose **Yes**.

Performing Operations on Files

You can perform many operations such as copying, moving, deleting, and printing a file (all described in detail later in this chapter) by using one of the following methods:

- Selecting the file and choosing a command from the Control panel. For example, you can open selected files or folders by moving the pointer to the **File** menu, pressing the right mouse button, and choosing the **Open** option. This displays a menu with three options: **File**, which opens the selected file, **With 'Goto' Arguments**, which opens a file selected in the **Goto** text field, and **In Document Editor**, which opens the file in the text editor.

- Placing the pointer on the file and using the accelerator keys on the left side of the keyboard. For example, pointing to a text file icon and pressing the Open accelerator key starts the text editor and displays the file in a window.

- Dragging (while pressing the left mouse button) and then dropping (by releasing the left mouse button) the file on other windows, icons, or the workspace. For example, dragging a text file icon onto an open text editor window loads the selected file into the text editor.

If you drop an icon on an application with an inappropriate format, for example, if you drop a file created with the Snapshot application on the text editor, the move is not performed. A message appears in the window footer telling you that the file is in an incorrect file format.

The results of dragging and dropping a file onto another application outside the File Manager depend on whether the file is dropped on a window or an icon. When you drop a file onto a window of an application, it is loaded into the application. When you drop a file onto an icon, it is loaded into the application, but it is not displayed until you open the application. If you drop an icon on an application with an inappropriate format, the move is not performed, and a message telling you that the file is in an incorrect file format appears in the window footer. Even though you can start an application by dragging it from the File Manager onto the workspace, you cannot quit the application by dragging it back onto the File Manager. You need to use the **Window** menu's **Quit** option.

Opening folders (directories) is as easy as dragging and dropping them on the workspace; the contents of the folders you drop are displayed in pop-up windows. You can then perform operations on the files by dragging and dropping them. Text files dropped on the workspace are displayed in Text Editor pop-up windows.

Navigating the File System

You can use the path or folder pane to move to and display another directory by double clicking on the folder that indicates the directory you want to move to. You can use this method regardless of the type of view you are displaying. The **Open** option is provided in both the **Path Commands** and the **Folder Commands** menus. Choosing this option makes a selected file or folder the current file or directory.

Returning to Your Home Directory

After moving through the file system, you can quickly return to your home directory using the **Home** menu button in the control panel. This menu provides you with options that allow you to return quickly to your home directory from anywhere in the file system or to one of the last nine directories you changed to. Your home directory is the default item on the directory. The other options that appear on the menu show you up to nine of the most recently accessed folders. You can change to any of these directories by pressing the right mouse button and highlighting the directory you want to move to. Figure 9.9 shows an example of the **Home** menu.

Moving and Searching with the Goto Button

When you know the path of the folder you want to open, or when you know the path and file name of a specific file you want to select, you can type the path or path and file name in the `Goto` text field and either press Return or move the pointer on the `Goto` button and click the left mouse button.

Using the Goto Text Field

When you enter a path, the directory you specify becomes the current directory, and its contents are displayed in the folder pane. When you enter a path and a file name, the file is located and is selected in the folder pane. If you change your location in the file system, you can click the left mouse button with the pointer on the `Goto` button, and the directory is changed to the directory entered in the text field.

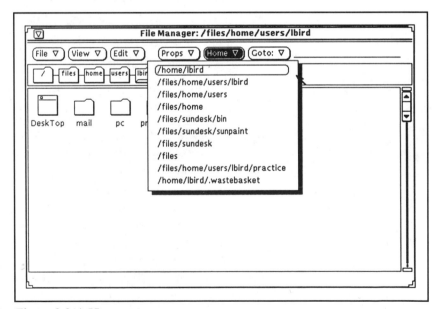

Figure 9.9: A Home menu

You can use wildcard characters in the **Goto** text field to select groups of related files. For example, entering

```
practice/*.c
```

finds and highlights all files in the practice directory ending in `.c`.

Using the Find Pop-Up Window

If you do not remember the exact name of the file or directory you want to find, use the **Find** option in the **Goto** menu to locate the file or directory. Choosing the **Find** option displays a pop-up window with controls that allow you to perform searches for

- File names that include or exclude a specific string of characters
- Files that include or exclude a specific owner
- Files modified before or after a date you specify
- Specific file types, such as data directories, data files, or application files
- Files containing a specific text string, word or phrase

The **Find** pop-up window also allows you to choose whether or not to ignore the case of the search for files and folders to locate files, for example, to locate files named **Document** or **document**. Figure 9.10 shows the **Find** pop-up window.

After filling in the fields to restrict the search, move the pointer to the **Find** button and click the left mouse button. If you want to cancel the search, move the pointer to the **Stop** button and click the left mouse button. When files that match the search criteria are found, their full pathnames are displayed in the bottom of the **Find** window. If more than one file is found,

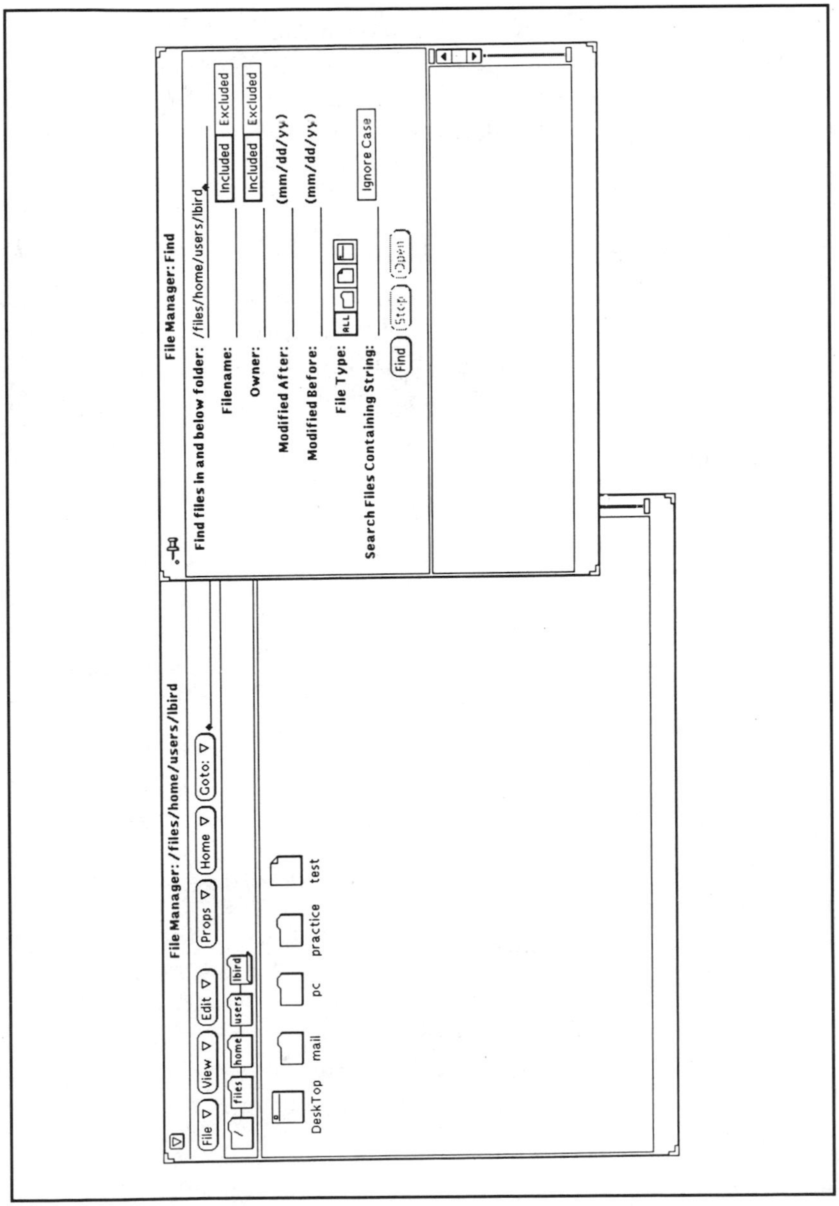

Figure 9.10: The Find pop-up window

you can move the pointer onto the correct file's icon and click the left mouse button to select the file. In order to open the file you must then move the pointer to the **Open** button and click the left mouse button.

Creating Folders and Documents

The **File** menu in the control panel provides you with options to create folders (directories) or documents. A SunOS document is a text file. When you create a new file or folder, they are automatically added to your path or folder pane.

Creating a Folder

To create a folder, make sure you are located in the directory where you want to create a subdirectory. Press the right mouse button with the mouse pointer on the **File** menu button, move the highlight to the **Create Folder** option, and release the right mouse button. An empty directory named **NewFolder** appears, underlined with a dimmed diamond at the end of the line.

Creating a Document

You create a document similar to the way you create a folder only instead you use the **Create Document** option of the **File** menu. When you create a document a file icon appears with the name **NewDocument** underlined with a dimmed diamond at the end of the line. Figure 9.11 shows a new document displayed in **lbird**'s home directory.

Naming Folders and Documents

To change the name of a folder or file, move the mouse pointer to the folder document and click the left mouse button.

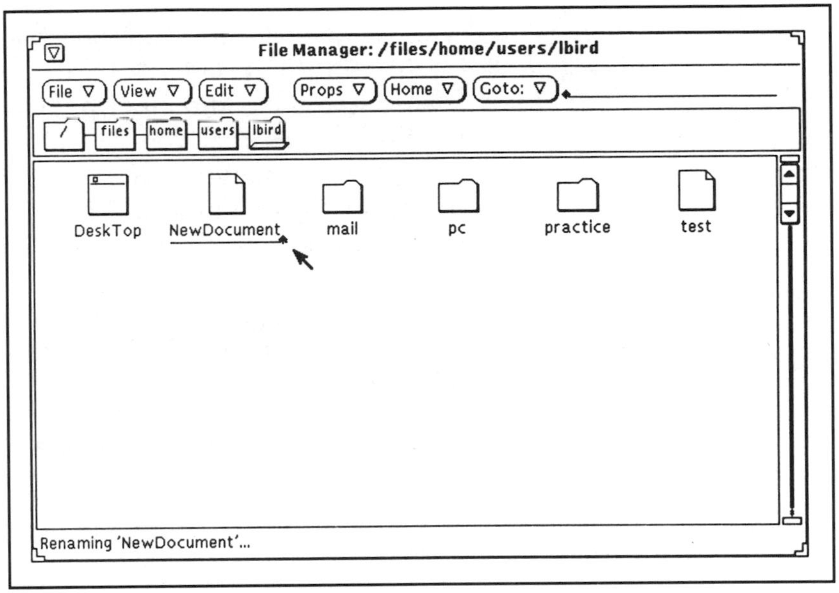

Figure 9.11: A new document in lbird's home directory

Then move the pointer onto the file name and click the left mouse button. This selects the icon and displays the file or folder name underlined with a caret at the end, which indicates the insertion point. You can backspace and delete the previous file or folder name, **NewDocument** or **NewFolder**, and then rename it by typing in a new name. When you are finished renaming the file or folder, press Return, and the file or folder is sorted and displayed with its new name.

Deleting Files and Folders

The wastebasket is a type of holding tank for files you want to remove from the folder and permanently remove at a later time. You can easily store a file in the wastebasket by moving the pointer on the icon of the file you want to discard, pressing the left mouse button, dragging the file, and dropping it onto the wastebasket. When you drag and drop a file or folder icon onto the wastebasket, papers appear in the wastebasket. You can store up to 100 files in the wastebasket. Files you discard in the wastebasket are stored in a directory named `.wastebasket` in your home directory so that you can move them back to the File Manager if you change your mind. Files remain in `.wastebasket` (even if you quit the File Manager) until you select the **Really Delete** option from the **Edit** menu or **Folder Commands** pop-up menu.

If the wastebasket becomes full, a message warns you that you must empty it before adding additional files. To empty the wastebasket,

1. Open the **Wastebasket** by double clicking on the icon.

2. Place the pointer in the blank area of the folder pane.

3. Press the right button to bring up the **Folder Commands** pop-up menu.

4. Highlight the **Select All** option and release the right mouse button. All the folders and files are then selected.

5. Press the right mouse button to again display the **Folder Commands** menu and display the **Cut** menu by moving the highlight to the **Cut** option and dragging the pointer to the right.

6. Move the highlight to the **Really Delete** option and release the right mouse button. A dialog box appears, which asks

   ```
   Are sure you want to remove these file(s)?
   ```

   Clicking the left button with the pointer under the **Yes** option permanently removes all the files in the wastebasket.

To selectively delete files stored in the wastebasket

1. Open the **Wastebasket** window by double clicking on the wastebasket icon.

2. Select the files you want to delete. Use the left mouse button to select the first file and the middle button for additional files.

3. Move the pointer into the blank area of the folder pane.

4. Press the right button to bring up the **Folder Commands** pop-up menu.

5. Highlight the **Cut** option and drag the pointer to the right.

6. Highlight the **Really Delete** option and release the right mouse button. A dialog box appears and asks

   `Are you sure you want to remove these file(s)?`

7. If you want to permanently remove the selected files, click the left button with the pointer under the **Yes** option.

The **Cut** menu's options are explained below:

 The **Really Delete** option permanently deletes files. When you delete files using either the **Cut to Wastebasket** or **Move to Clipboard** options, your files are still accessible.

Option	Result
Cut to Wastebasket	Moves selected files to the **Wastebasket** window. If you have quit the wastebasket, creates a new one and moves the selected files.
Move to Clipboard	Stores the files in the clipboard buffer till you either paste them to a folder or perform another cut action. (The clipboard and associated operations are explained shortly under "Using the Clipboard.")
Really Delete	Permanently removes files

Copying and Moving Files

There are two ways you can copy and move files. The easiest is the drag and drop method. The other method uses a clipboard which is a storage place in memory.

To use the drag and drop method to move files, simply select the file(s), drag the file(s) to the directory you want to move the file(s) to, and release the left mouse button to finish the operation. Remember, you can drag and drop folders (directories) on the workspace to copy and move files between directories.

To copy one or more files so that the file(s) are not removed from their original directory

1. Select the file(s) to copy

2. Hold down the Control key

3. Press the left mouse button

4. Drag the file(s) to the directory you want to copy the file(s) to

5. Release the left button to finish the copy operation

Whenever you perform a move or copy operation, a message appears in the window footer stating whether or not the copy or move action was successful.

Using the Clipboard

Only one item or group of items is stored on the clipboard at a time. If you choose the **Cut** or **Copy** option and anything is already stored on the clipboard, the previous information is lost. If you quit the File Manager or exit SunView or OpenWindows, the contents of the clipboard are lost.

The *clipboard* is a buffer, a storage place in memory that temporarily holds files during copy and move operations. The clipboard options are available in both the **Edit** menu and the pop-up **Folder Commands** menu. You can *cut* or *copy* files to the clipboard and *paste* them into other folders or applications.

- *Cutting text*: a specified section of text is taken out of the document and placed in the clipboard.

- *Copying text*: a specified section of text is copied into the clipboard (this text also remains in its original position).

- *Pasting text:* text is removed from the clipboard and placed in a specified location.

To copy a file, select the files you want to copy and then select the **Copy** option from the **Edit** menu, the **Folder Commands** pop-up menu, or use the accelerator keys on the left side of your keyboard.

If you want to see what is on the clipboard, you can view its contents at any time by using the **Show Clipboard** option in the **Edit** or the **Folder Commands** pop-up menu. This option displays the first 30 characters of the contents of the clipboard.

The following steps explain how to copy or move a group of files:

1. Use the right mouse button to select the first file and the middle button to select additional files you want to copy or move. The files selected are highlighted in black.

2. With the mouse pointer on the **Edit** menu, press the right mouse button and move the highlight to either the **Copy** option from the **Edit** menu to copy the files or the **Move to Clipboard** option of the **Cut** submenu if you want to move the files, as shown in Figure 9.12.

3. Change to the folder where you want to copy or move the files to.

4. Move the pointer to the **Edit** menu, press the right mouse button, and move the highlight to the **Paste** option in the **Edit** menu.

⊙ If the mouse pointer is not in a File Manager window when you choose **Paste**, only the name of the file is pasted.

When you move the pointer to the directory you want to copy or move the files to and you choose the **Paste** option, the directory is automatically opened. If a folder cannot accept the files, it displays a lock. This lock lets you know you do not have permission to move the file to the new directory.

Copying Files to Other Systems

You can use the **Remote Copy** option in the **File** menu to transfer copies of files between systems. You can copy between

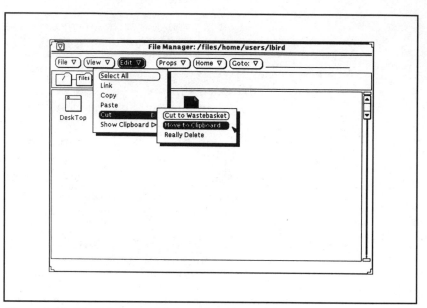

Figure 9.12: The Move to Clipboard option of the Edit menu's Cut
submenu

systems only if the permissions and ownership of directories and
files allow you to perform the operation.

When you select the **Remote Copy** option, a pop-up window
is displayed, prompting you for the source machine, source
path, and the destination machine and path. After you fill in
these fields, move the pointer to the **Copy** button and press the
left mouse button to perform the remote copy.

Printing Files

There are sure to be times you want a printed copy of a data
file. Using the File Manager, you can print text files in two ways:

- Select the files in the folder pane and then choose the
  Print File option from the **File** menu. When you
  select a file, the **Print** option becomes available; the
  Print option appears dimmed in the menu otherwise.

When you select the **Print** option, an information message is displayed in the footer.

- Selcct the files in the folder pane, then drag and drop them onto the Print Tool icon. Files are printed using the default print instructions, which are bound to the icon.

File and Folder Permissions

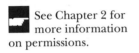 See Chapter 2 for more information on permissions.

The SunOS security system is structured around permissions. Permissions determine which users can read, write, or execute files. You can only change the permissions for any file or folder you own. Each folder and file in the file system has permissions assigned to it that can be changed to allow or restrict access.

To display the **File Properties** pop-up window so you can change the permissions of files and folders, first select the file or folder you want to change permissions for and move the pointer to the menu button labeled **Props** in the control panel. Press the right mouse button, and two menu options are displayed, **File Properties** and **Tool Properties**, as shown in Figure 9.13. Move the highlight to the **File Properties** option and release the right mouse button.

Changing File and Folder Permissions

The **File Properties** pop-up window allows you to change the permissions of a file or folder. If you have write permission for a file, you can change the permissions for three types of users:

Owner   The owner of the file or folder (usually the person who created the file or folder)

Group   The name of a specified group that can access the file

World   All others users on your network

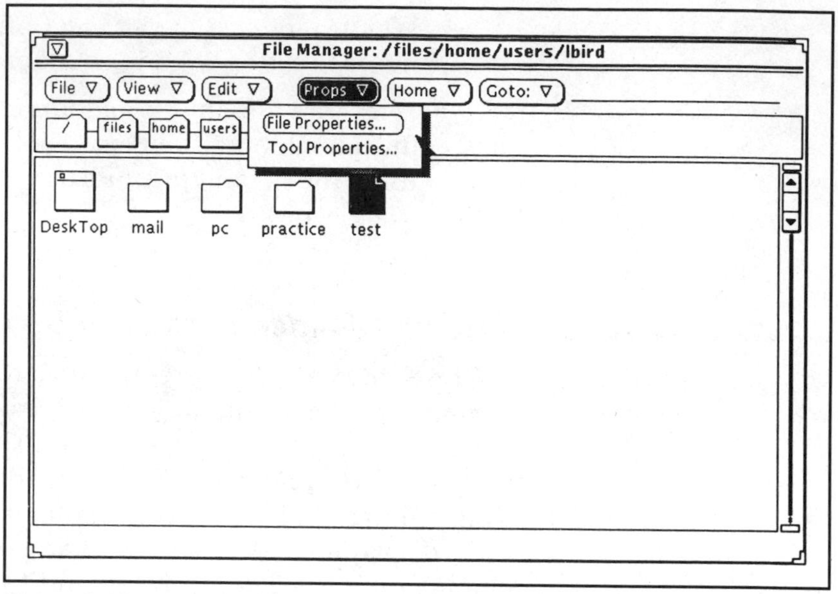

Figure 9.13: The File and Tool Properties options

To change file or folder permissions, click the left mouse button on the boxes representing the permissions you want to change. The **Read**, **Write**, and **Execute** permission boxes are toggles which turn permissions on or off. If a box appears checked and you press the left mouse button with the pointer in the box, it then appears unchecked.

Changing Permissions for Groups of Files

You can select more than one file to change the permissions of several files at the same time. If you select more than one file, the file properties window shows those properties the selected files have in common. File or directory names and individual file or directory information are not displayed. You can change the permissions for the group of selected files the same way you change a single file: move the pointer to the check boxes representing the permissions you want to change and click the left mouse button on the permissions to add or subtract.

Linking Files

A link is a symbolic connection or pointer to a single file that allows acccss from more than one directory without having to move to the original directory where the file resides. The **Link** command on the **Edit** menu allows you to create a link to a file. When a file is linked, an icon appears in the directory where it is linked as though the file resides in that directory. Any editing changes you make to a file with links are reflected in all of the directories because there is really only one file.

Creating a Link

To link a file to a directory, select the file or files you want to link and perform the following steps:

1. Choose the **Link** command from the **Edit** menu.

2. Open the folder you want to link the file to.

3. Choose the **Paste** option from the **Edit** submenu of the pop-up **Folders Commands** menu or use the Paste accelerator key.

If the display produced by your **List** option differs from Figure 9.14, activate the **Links** setting in the **Tool Properties** window (which is explained shortly).

Once a link is established, the file's link information can be displayed using the **File Properties** option of the **Props** menu. If you use the **List** option in the **View** menu's **Folder Display** submenu, the linked file appears with an arrow pointing to the directory name that contains the file with which the file is linked. Figure 9.14 shows a linked file in **lbird**'s home directory that is linked to a file named **file1** in **dquayle**'s home directory.

Removing a Link

You can remove a link by selecting the file and choosing the **Really Delete** option from the **Cut** submenu. Removing a link does not remove the original file. If you remove the original file without also deleting the link, the icon for the link changes to display a broken chain, as shown in Figure 9.15.

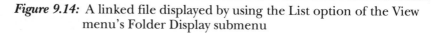

Figure 9.14: A linked file displayed by using the List option of the View menu's Folder Display submenu

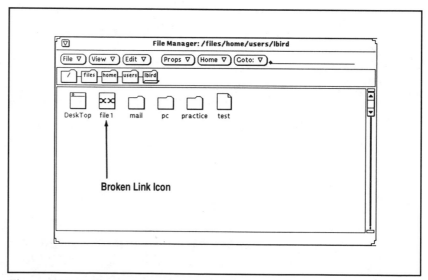

Figure 9.15: A file icon representing a broken link

Customizing Files and Tools

You can customize the way the file system is displayed in the path pane using the **View** menu. You can also change many of the File Manager's properties using the **Tool Properties** window. For example, you can cause the folder pane to display only files matching specified criteria. If you are using a color monitor, you can change the colors of the file, folder, and application icons. The File Manager also allows you to create your own commands submenu so that you can easily access frequently used commands that suit your needs.

Customizing the Tree Display in the Path Pane

To display the **Path Commands** menu, place the pointer in an empty area of the path pane and click the right mouse button.

The **View** menu and the **Path Commands** pop-up menu (shown in Figure 9.16) display options to selectively show all or part of the file system. For example, you can display sections of the file system you want access to and hide unwanted directories. The second option is a toggle which switches between displaying the folder pane as a tree or a single path. The other options relating to the path pane display allow you to

- Hide or display subdirectories using the **Hide Subfolders** or **Show All Subfolders** options.

- Begin the directory tree at a selected directory using the **Begin Tree Here** option.

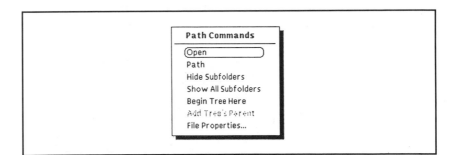

Figure 9.16: The Path Commands pop-up menu

- Display the parent directory of a subdirectory using the **Show Parent** option.

Using the Tool Properties Window

Selecting the **Tool Properties** option from the **Props** menu displays a pop-up window that provides you with options to customize how the File Manager displays and works with files, directories, and applications. Figure 9.17 shows the **Tool Properties** pop-up menu. The following list explains each of the options available in the **Tool Properties** pop-up window.

Option	Description
List Options	Allows you to choose how much information is displayed when you use the **List** option in the **View** menu **Folder Display** submenu. You can select one or all of the **List** options. To select an option, move the pointer to the option you want and click the left mouse button to toggle the setting on or off. When a setting is on, it appears with a bold border.
Hidden Files	Files that begin with a dot (a period) are hidden files and by default are not displayed. You can choose to display hidden files by selecting the visible option.
Deletions	Allows you to choose whether confirmation notices are displayed when you perform delete operations.
Default Document Editor	Specifies which default editor the File Manager uses to display data files not specifically bound to another application. If you specify a different text editor which does not display its own window, such as the emacs editor, you must type **shelltool**, followed by the name of the editor.

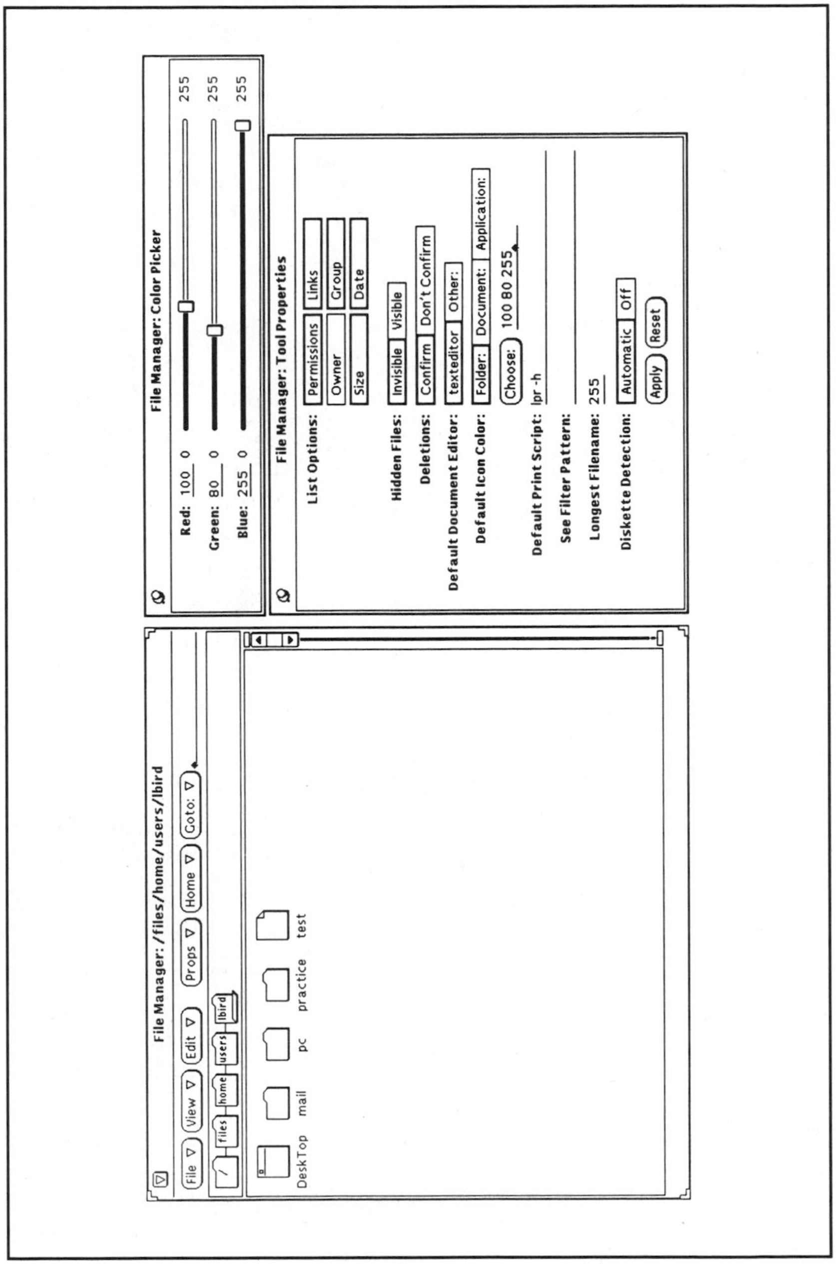

Figure 9.17: The Tool Properties pop-up window

Option	*Description*
`Default Icon Color`	If you have a color monitor, this option specifies a default icon color for folders, documents, or applications in the File Manager. (This option is available in the SunView DeskSet.) The red, green, and blue (RGB) values for the color are displayed in the text field in that order. To adjust the red, green, and blue values, click the left mouse button with the pointer on the **Choose** button. The slider drag box appears, as shown in Figure 9.16. Moving the pointer to a handle and dragging the handle of the slider bar changes the color and automatically updates the values in the text field. You can adjust the color values one unit at a time by clicking the right mouse button with the pointer on either side of the slider bar. All settings set to 0 display black; all set to 255 display white.
`Default Print Script`	This text field allows you to specify a different print script for files printed using the **Print File** option in the File Manager. The default is the standard `lpr` print command. If you want to print a file using the **nroff** program without a header page, type **nroff $FILE \| lpr -h**. The variable name **$FILE** acts as a placeholder for a file you select.

Option	*Description*
See Filter Pattern	This text field allows you to specify that only files of a certain type are displayed in the folder pane of the File Manager. For example, entering ***.c** lists all files ending with a **.c**. The filter pattern used to filter files is always listed in the header of the window.
Longest Filename	You can type any number from 0 to 999 in this numeric field to choose how many characters of each file name are displayed in the folder pane of the File Manager. The default is 255. In the Open-Windows environment, names that do not fit within the specified length are followed by a greater than sign (**>**), indicating that the complete name is not displayed.
Diskette Detection	Allows you to choose whether or not the File Manager checks periodically to see if there is a diskette in the drive. The default setting is **Off**. (This option is available only in the SunView DeskSet.)

Once you have changed the properties you want to change, move the pointer onto the **Apply** button at the bottom of the **Tool Properties** pop-up menu and click the left mouse button. The new properties are applied to your files, folders, and applications.

Creating Your Own Commands Menu

The **Your Commands** option in the **File** menu allows you to create and store commonly used operating system commands. Use the **Enter Command** option to display the **Enter Command** pop-up window, which allows you to enter commands to be included on the menu. Figure 9.18 shows an example of the **Your Commands** menu.

The **Shell** option opens a pop-up **Shell Tool** window. This **Shell Tool** window is different from the Shell Tool in the **Workspace Programs** submenu—it is pinnable and is linked directly to the File Manager. If you quit or close the File Manager this Shell Tool is also removed or closed.

You can type any SunOS command or series of commands (separated by semicolons) in the text area of this pop-up window. If a command requires a window in which to display its information, be sure to include a window-based tool (such as **shelltool**) at the beginning of the command.

The **Your Commands** option supports a default variable named **$FILE**. This variable allows you to perform your command on any file you select. For example, assume you have added the command **shelltool vi $File** to the **Your Commands** menu. Selecting a file named **testfile** and choosing this command opens a shell tool, replaces the variable **$File** with the selected file **testfile**, and loads it into the vi editor.

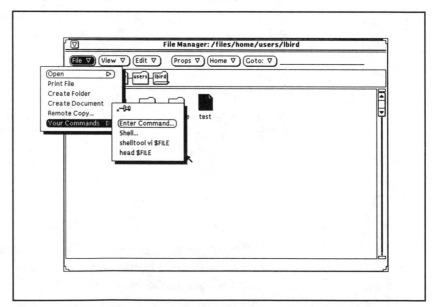

Figure 9.18: Sample command options in Your Commands submenu

Once you have added the commands to the menu, you can use them at any time by pressing the right mouse button and displaying the **Your Commands** submenu and highlighting the command you want to perform.

Commands for the **Your Commands** menu are stored in a file named **.fvcmd** located in your home directory. If you enter a command you later want to delete, simply delete the command from this file using the text editor. Don't be concerned if the command appears on the menu after you have deleted the command from the **.fvcmd**. The next time you log in the command is deleted from the menu.

Summary

In this chapter you learned how to use the File Manager to perform the following:

- Select a file or folder or a group of files and folders
- Navigate SunOS directories by double clicking on folder icons
- View and sort files and directories using the **View** menu
- Open and load files using the **File** menu or double clicking with the pointer on the file you want to open
- Create and delete a directory or file using the **File** menu
- Copy and move a file or directory by either dragging or dropping the icon or using the **Edit** menu
- Locate files using the **Goto** test field or the **Find** pop-up menu
- Protect your files and directories by changing the read, write, and execute permissions
- Create and remove links to access and share files in different directories

- Customize the File Manager to list files that match your preferences, match a color scheme you select, and use any editor you choose

- Create your own menu of commands using the `Your Commands` menu

CHAPTER 10

The Mail Tool
Makes Mail Easy

COMMUNICATING WITH OTHERS ON THE SYSTEM IS an integral part of working with SunOS. The Mail Tool makes communicating with other users convenient. In the Mail Tool's friendly graphical environment, you can easily receive, write, send, and manage your electronic mail. This chapter explains all the Mail Tool fundamentals, as well as other helpful features, such as using templates (premade mail message formats), sending files with mail messages, informing other users you are away on vacation, forwarding mail, or locating users' addresses with the Name Finder.

Starting the Mail Tool

You can open the Mail Tool by selecting the **Mail Tool** option from the **Workspace Programs** submenu. Press the right mouse button anywhere in the workspace to display the **Workspace** menu. Drag the mouse pointer to the right of **Programs** option. The **Programs** submenu is displayed. Drag the pointer to highlight the **Mail Tool** option, then release the right mouse button. The Mail Tool icon appears on the workspace. The icon for the Mail Tool looks like a rural-style mailbox with the door closed and the flag down. When new mail arrives, the flag goes up and the door of the mailbox opens to indicate you have new mail messages. Double click the Mail Tool icon to display the primary **Mail Tool** window.

The Mail Tool

The Mail Tool application is made up of two windows: the primary **Mail Tool** window and the **Compose Message** window. When you double click the left mouse button with the pointer on the Mail Tool icon, the primary **Mail Tool** window is displayed.

The primary **Mail Tool** window provides you with a set of controls for sending, sorting, and receiving mail as well as accessing other parts of the Mail Tool, such as the **Compose Message** window. The primary **Mail Tool** pane displays the list and status of your mail messages. The primary **Mail Tool** window usually displays the list of mail messages in your **In Tray** file. The **In Tray** file is where you receive your electronic mail, as explained later in this chapter.

The **Compose Message** window, accessed by clicking the left mouse button on the **Compose Message** button in the primary **Mail Tool** window, is used to compose and send mail messages. Once you have opened a **Compose Message** window, as shown in Figure 10.1, you can use it to write and send electronic mail letters without reopening the primary **Mail Tool** window. When you close the **Compose Message** window without sending the message you are composing, the Compose icon displays an envelope and a pencil.

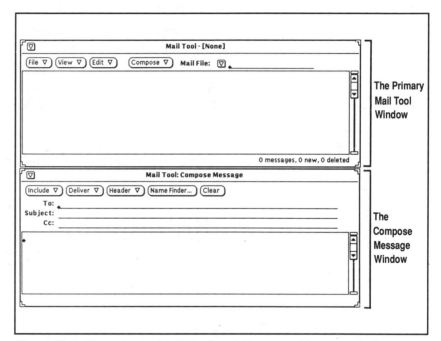

Figure 10.1: The primary Mail Tool and Compose Message windows

The Primary Mail Tool Control Panel

The control panel of the **Mail Tool** window has four main menu buttons: **File**, **View**, **Edit**, and **Compose**. In addition, the control panel has a **Mail File** text field. The following list provides a brief description of these menu buttons and the **Mail File** text field.

- The **File** menu is used to open a mail file, copy and move mail messages into a mail file, print messages, and save your changes.

- The **View** menu allows you to view your mail messages with either abbreviated or full headers, select the mail messages to view, and sort mail messages.

- The **Edit** menu provides options to edit mail messages, such as copying, cutting, and deleting mail messages.

- The **Compose** menu provides options to write and send mail messages.

- The **Mail File** text field and menu button are used to retrieve and create mail files. Mail files are special files used by the Mail Tool to store your mail messages.

The Message Functions Pop-Up Window

Some of the most often used options in the primary Mail Tool's control panel menus are also available using the **Message Functions** pop-up window. To display the **Message Functions** pop-up window, move the pointer anywhere in the primary **Mail Tool** window's pane and press the right mouse button. The **Message Functions** pop-up window is displayed, as shown in Figure 10.2.

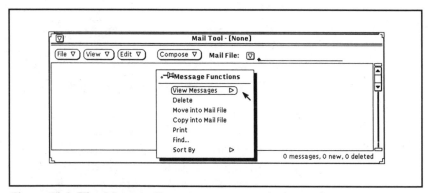

Figure 10.2: The Message Functions pop-up window

Getting Online Help in the Mail Tool

Online help is available for most of the buttons and windows in the Mail Tool. To view online help for the part of the Mail Tool you are working with, move the mouse pointer to the button or part of the window you want information on and press the Help key on your keyboard. A help box is then displayed. If the information takes up more than the box space, a scrollbar appears in the box, which allows you to scroll through the help text. To remove the help box from your screen, click the left mouse button with the pointer on the push pin in the upper-left corner of the help box.

Receiving Mail

When new mail is received in your electronic mailbox, the flag goes up and the mailbox door opens to show an envelope on the Mail Tool icon. The Mail Tool automatically checks and incorporates new mail messages in a time period specified from the **Mail Tool Properties** window, explained later in this chapter. To manually check your mail messages, double click the left mouse button with the pointer on the Mail Tool icon to open the primary **Mail Tool** window and perform the following steps:

1. Move the mouse pointer to the **File** button and press the right mouse button.

2. Drag the mouse button to the right of the **Open** option and move the highlight onto the **In Tray** option.

3. Release the right mouse button.

Mail messages stored in the **In Tray** mail file, the default mail file for all incoming mail messages, are retrieved and their headers displayed in the primary **Mail Tool** window. Status messages are displayed at the right side of the window footer telling you how many messages are in your **In Tray**, the number of new messages, and how many you have deleted.

Receiving Mail Using Mail Files

If you have a problem receiving mail, it may be that your mail-box is set up so that mail is sent to a mail file rather than to the **In Tray**. If you know the name of the mail file used to receive incoming mail, enter it into the **Mail File** text field before you choose the **Mail File** option from the **Open** submenu in the **File** menu.

How mail is received depends on how your Mail Tool is set up by your system administrator. Normally, your incoming mail is sent directly to your **In Tray**. However, mail may be sent to a mail file other than to your **In Tray**. This file is usually named **+inbox**. If this is not the mail file used for incoming messages, check with your system administrator to find out which mail file is.

To check your incoming mail messages in a mail file other than **In Tray**, do the following:

1. Move the pointer to the **Mail File** menu button and press the right mouse button.

2. With the highlight on the **Mail Files** option, drag the pointer to the direct right. This action displays a selection of mail files.

3. Move the pointer to the mail file you want to retrieve your incoming mail messages from (in most cases this will be the file named **+inbox**).

4. Release the right mouse button, and the highlighted file name is displayed in the **Mail File** text area.

5. Move the pointer to the **File** menu button and press the right mouse button

6. Drag the pointer to highlight the **Open** option and drag the pointer to the direct right. The **Open** sub-menu appears.

7. Drag the pointer to highlight the **Mail File** option.

8. Release the right mouse button and the **Mail File**

name appears in the window header. Any mail stored in the highlighted mail file is retrieved.

Mail Message Headers

The mail message headers displayed in the header pane in the primary **Mail Tool** window, as shown in Figure 10.3, list information about the mail message. Each header has nine columns of information.

The following explains each of these columns from left to right:

- The status of the mail message: An arrow points to the current message; an N shows you that the message is new; a U shows the message is unread; and a blank indicates you have viewed the message.

- A message number automatically assigned to messages by the Mail Tool in the order in which each arrives.

- The electronic mail address of the sender of the message.

- The day of the week the message was sent.

- The month the message was sent.

- The date the message was sent.

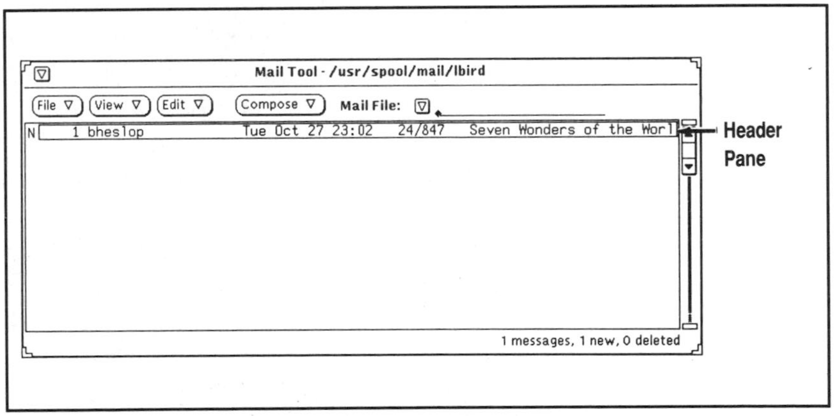

Figure 10.3: A mail message header

- The time the message was sent.

- The size of the message. The first number tells how many lines are in the message, and the second number tells the number of characters in the message.

- The subject of the message if the person who sent the message provided a subject line.

Selecting and Viewing Mail Messages

You can select each message header from the primary **Mail Tool** window by moving the pointer into the header line and clicking the left mouse button. A selected message header is surrounded by a box. You can select additional messages by moving the pointer into the line and clicking the middle mouse button. If the message is already selected, clicking the middle button unselects it.

After you've selected one or more messages, you can view them using the **View Message** pop-up window, as shown in Figure 10.4. In addition to displaying the mail messages you selected in the headers pane, the **View Messages** pop-up window allows you to perform text editing functions. The number of the mail message is displayed in the window header of the **View Messages** pop-up window. Figure 10.4 shows the number 1 mail message in the window header.

To view mail messages, move the mouse pointer to the **View** button and then press the right mouse button. The **View** menu is displayed. Drag the pointer to highlight the **Messages** option. Release the right mouse button. If you selected multiple mail messages, the **View Messages** pop-up windows are laid on top of one another in the numerical order of the messages listed, as shown in Figure 10.5. You can move the windows so they do not overlap one another, or you can click the left mouse button on the header to bring an individual message window to the front of the screen, or dismiss each window individually after you have read the message.

To display a **View Message** window without using a menu, double click the left mouse button on the mail message header.

Figure 10.4: The View Message pop-up window

Once you have displayed a message in a **View Message** window, its **New** status is changed whether or not you actually have read the message.

Viewing the Next or Previous Mail Message

When the **View Message** pop-up window is displayed, you can view the next selected message in the same window by moving the pointer to the **View** menu button and clicking the left button. The next message is displayed using the existing **View Message** window. If you prefer, you can double click the left button on the header of the next message to display it in the **View Message** window. When the last message in your **In Tray** is displayed in the **View Message** window, choosing **Next** displays the previous message. To otherwise display the previous message, move the pointer to the **View** menu button, press the

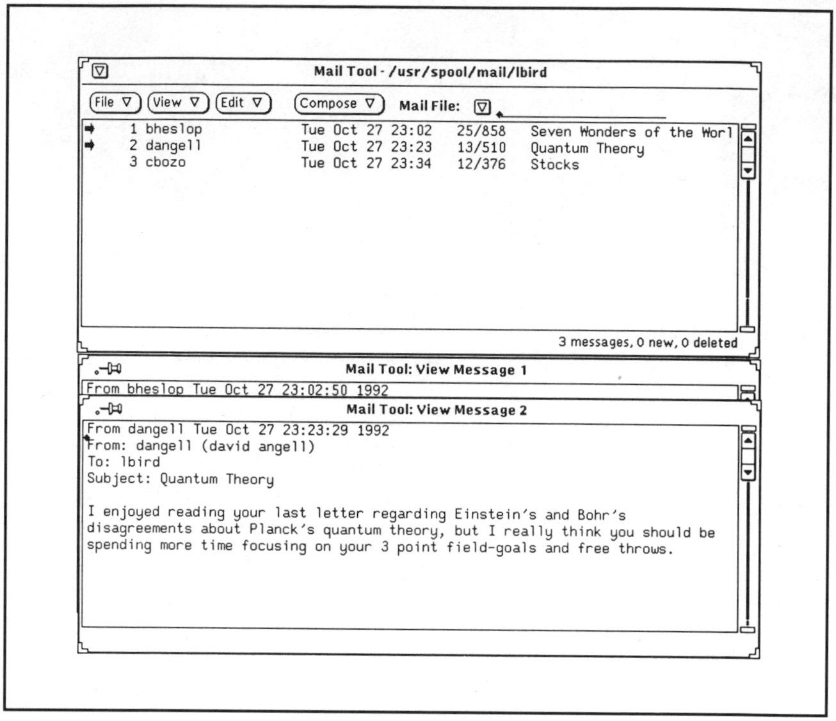

Figure 10.5: Multiple mail messages displayed

right mouse button, highlight **Previous**, and release the right mouse button.

Viewing Mail Messages with Full Headers

You can view messages with the full mail message header, as shown in Figure 10.6, instead of the default abbreviated header setting. To display a message with the full message header, first select a mail message. Move the pointer to the **View** menu button and press the right mouse button. With the highlight on the **Messages** option, drag the pointer to the right to display the **Messages** submenu, and highlight **Full Header** option. When you release the right mouse button, the full header is displayed.

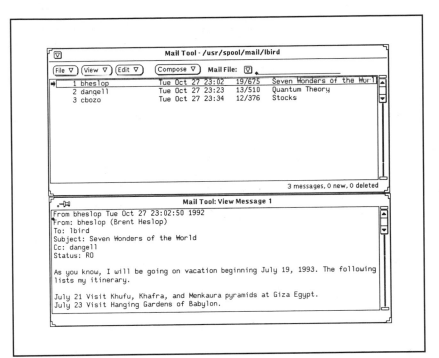

Figure 10.6: A full mail message header

Deleting Mail Messages

If you don't want to save a mail message, delete it from the primary **Mail Tool** window. To delete mail messages, follow the steps below:

1. Select the message headers for messages you want to delete. Remember that you click the left button to select the first message, then click the middle button on each subsequent message to either add it to the group or remove it if it is already selected.

2. Move the pointer to the **Edit** menu and press the right mouse button. Drag the pointer to the **Delete** option.

3. Release the right button. The selected mail messages are deleted, and the status message in the footer reflects the current state of your **Mail Tool** window.

Undeleting Messages

As long as you do not switch to another mail file or choose either **Save Changes** or **Done** from the **File** menu (explained in the following section), the deleted messages remain available, and you can undelete them. When no deleted messages are available, the **Undelete** option in the **File** menu appears in gray, indicating it is inactive. To undelete a message, follow these steps:

1. Move the pointer to the **Edit** menu button and press the right mouse button.

2. Drag the pointer to highlight the **Undelete** option.

3. Drag the pointer to the right to display the **Undelete** submenu.

4. Move the pointer to the **Last** option to undelete the last message you deleted.

5. Release the right mouse button.

You can also choose the **From List** option in the **Undelete** submenu to display a pop-up window with a list of messages you have deleted since you last saved changes in the Mail Tool. Select the headers you want to undelete and click the left mouse button on the **Undelete** button in the bottom of the **Undelete** pop-up window, which is shown in Figure 10.7.

Saving Mail Tool Changes

The Mail Tool does not automatically save changes you have made in the **Mail Tool** window. You can save changes using either the **Save Changes** or **Done** options in the **File** menu. Using the **Save Changes** option saves changes made in the

Mail Tool without closing the **Mail Tool** window. The **Done** option closes the **Mail Tool** window and saves any changes.

If you quit the Mail Tool using the **Quit** option in the **Window** menu (accessed by pressing the right mouse button on the window header), a notice is displayed, as shown in Figure 10.8, listing these options:

Options	*Results*
Save Changes	Saves any changes you have made and quits the Mail Tool, removing the icon from the workspace

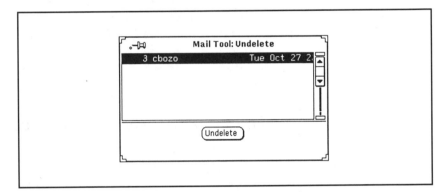

Figure 10.7: The Mail Tool Undelete pop-up window

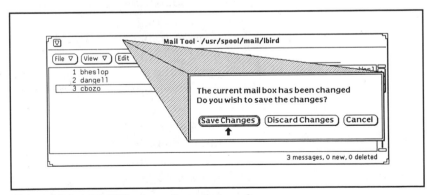

Figure 10.8: A Mail Tool confirmation notice

Options	Results
Discard Changes	Disregards changes you've made, restoring any deleted messages, and quits the Mail Tool, removing the icon from the workspace
Cancel	Aborts your request to quit the Mail Tool

Printing Mail Messages

You can print your electronic mail messages directly from the Mail Tool using the **Print** option from the **File** menu. To print messages, first select the headers for the messages you want to print. Then press the right mouse button on the **File** menu button. Drag the mouse pointer to highlight the **Print** option and then release the right mouse button. Customizing the way your messages are printed is covered later in this chapter.

The Compose Message Window

The **Compose Message** window is used for composing and sending your mail messages. To display a **Compose Message** window, move the pointer to the **Compose** menu in the primary **Mail Tool** window and click the left mouse button. The pane of the **Compose Message** window is where you type the contents of the message you want to send. The **Compose Message** window provides you with the **Text Pane** pop-up menu, which contains text editing options. To display the **Text Pane** pop-up menu, move the pointer anywhere in the text pane and press the right mouse button. This menu provides you with the standard text editing features available from the Text Editor Tool.

The **Compose Message** window operates independently from the primary **Mail Tool** window. You can close an opened **Compose Message** window to an icon for later use or keep the **Compose Message** window open while the primary **Mail Tool** window is closed to an icon. You can open several **Compose Message** windows at one time to reply to or compose several messages concurrently. The **Compose Message** window is shown in Figure 10.9.

The Compose Window Control Panel

The **Compose Message** window has its own set of controls, which are displayed as five buttons in its control panel: **Include**, **Deliver**, **Header**, **Name Finder**, and **Clear**.

- The **Include** menu button provides choices that allow you to include selected messages as part of the message you are composing and also provides you with a set of templates for creating different types of messages.

- The **Deliver** menu button provides choices for how the **Compose Message** window behaves once the message is delivered.

- The **Header** menu button provides choices for the number and type of text fields provided to create the message header.

- The **Name Finder** window button displays a pop-up window that you can use to search your system for user names and electronic mail addresses.

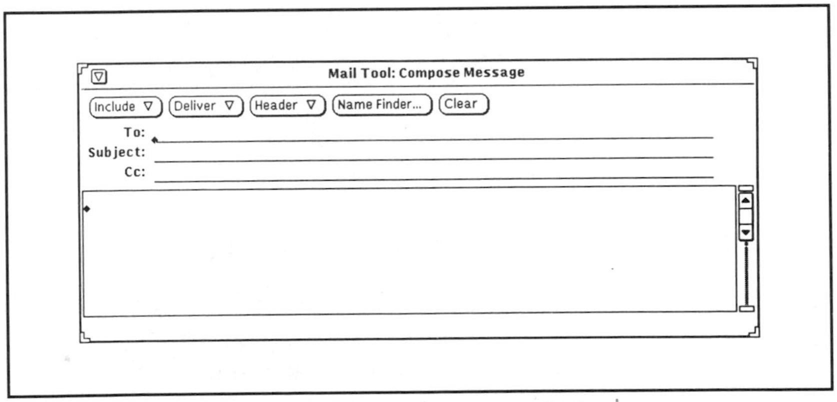

Figure 10.9: The Mail Tool Compose Message window

- The **Clear** button clears the contents of the **Compose** window.

Just below the control panel are three text fields: **To**, **Subject**, and **Cc**. These text fields allow you to include the address of the user(s) you want to send your mail message to, the subject of the message, and any optional addresses of users you want to send carbon copies of the mail message to.

Composing and Sending Mail Messages

The following steps illustrate how to compose a mail message and send it to one or more users.

Watch the mouse pointer. You may find yourself entering text without realizing you are in the wrong area. Remember that the flashing black triangle indicates the insert point.

1. Move the mouse pointer to the **Compose** menu button on the primary **Mail Tool** window and press the right mouse button. Make sure the pointer is on the **New** option then release the button. The **Compose Message** window is displayed.

2. Move the pointer into the **To** text field and click the left mouse button to set the insert point. Type the address or series of addresses you want to send your mail message to. If you type more than one address, separate each one with a comma or space.

3. Press Tab or Return to move the insert pointer to the **Subject** field and type the subject of your message. You can also move the mouse pointer and click the left mouse button to reposition the insert point.

4. Press Tab or Return to move the insert point to the **Cc** field. Type the addresses of all those you want to receive a carbon copy of the message.

5. Press Tab or Return or move the pointer into the **Compose Message** window's text pane or click the left mouse button to set the insert point in the pane.

6. Type in your mail message. Pressing the right mouse button in the text pane displays the standard **Text Pane** pop-up menu.

7. When you have finished composing the message, click the left mouse button on the **Deliver** button. The message is delivered and the **Compose Message** window is closed.

Replying to Mail Messages

You can easily reply to any mail message listed in the primary **Mail Tool** window. Using the **Reply** option in the **Compose** menu automatically places the senders address in the **To** text field and places the subject of the mail message sent to you in the **Subject** text field of your reply message. The **Reply** submenu offers four choices for sending replies.

Option	*Result*
To Sender	Adds the name of the originator (sender) of the selected message to the To field and the subject from the selected message **Subject** field to the **Subject** text field
To All	Fills in the **To** and **Cc** fields with all the names in the selected message's text fields, including the originator of the message, and fills in the **Subject** field with the subject of the selected message
To Sender, Include	Fills in the **To** and **Subject** text fields and puts a copy of the text of the message into the **Compose Message** window pane
To All, Include	Adds all the names from the selected message to the **To**, **Subject**, and **Cc** text fields, and puts a copy of the text of the message into the **Compose Message** window pane

To reply to an individual message or to a group of messages, follow these steps:

1. Select the message header or headers that you want to answer by pressing the left mouse button for the first header and the middle mouse button for other headers.

2. Move the pointer to the **Compose** menu.

3. Press the right mouse button and drag the pointer to the right of the **Reply** option.

4. Drag the pointer to highlight one of the four options from the **Reply** submenu and release the right mouse button.

A **Compose Message** window is opened for each selected header.

Finding Other Users' Addresses

When you do not know the address of a person, or a mail message is returned as undeliverable because the address is incorrect, use the **Name Finder** pop-up window to locate the correct address. To use the **Name Finder** feature, move the pointer to the **Name Finder** button in the **Compose Message** window. Click the left mouse button, and the **Name Finder** pop-up window is displayed, as shown in Figure 10.10. Type in the first name, last name, or a fragment of a name. The **Name Finder** is case insensitive, so you do not need to use exact capitalization. If you are not certain of the spelling of the last name of a person, you can search by the first name. The **Name Finder** displays the full name, login name, mail alias, and address for each matching name. Use the scrollbar to view multiple names. If you are uncertain of the spelling of a name, click the left mouse button on the **Sounds Like** box in the **Name Finder** to broaden the scope of the search to match names that sound like your entry

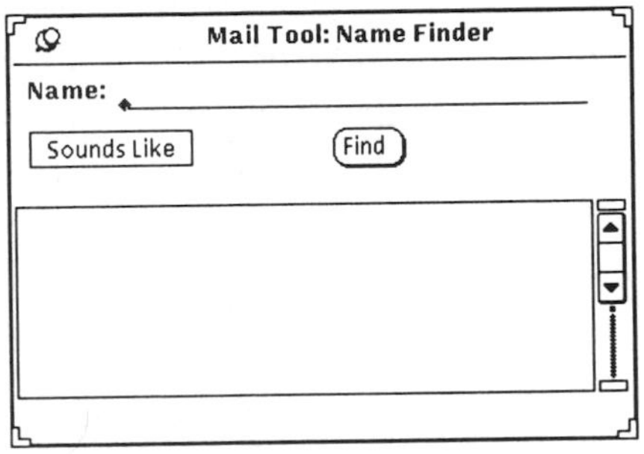

Figure 10.10: The Name Finder pop-up window

in the **Name** text field. When you click the left mouse button on the **Find** button, names similar to your entry are displayed.

Managing Your Mail Messages

When you checked your new mail messages, you selected the **Open** option from the **File** menu. The Mail Tool allows you to create additional mail files for storing and organizing your mail messages.

Creating a New Mail File

To create a mail file and store multiple mail messages, follow the steps below:

1. Type **+*filename*** in the **Mail File** text field. The **+** sign tells Mail Tool to put your mail file in the **Mail File** directory specified using the **Mail Tool Properties** window, as explained later in this chapter. For example, typing **+*epistles*** will create a storage file named **+epistles**.

2. Select the mail message headers from the primary **Mail Tool** window to move or copy to the new mail file by

clicking the left mouse button on the first item and then clicking the middle button on subsequent items.

3. Press the right mouse button on the **File** menu and drag the pointer to highlight the **Move to Mail File** option.

4. Release the right mouse button; the message is moved to the new file, and an information message is displayed in the footer of the **Mail Tool** window.

Adding Messages to a Mail File

To add subsequent mail messages to a mail file, first type the file name of the mail file you want to add messages to in the **Mail File** field or select the file name from the **Mail Files** submenu. Then select the additional mail messages and choose the **Copy into Mail File** or **Move into Mail File** options from the **File** menu to append the additional messages to those already in the mail file. The **Copy into Mail File** option copies the mail message leaving the original intact. The **Move into Mail File** copies the mail message and deletes the original mail message.

Sorting the Contents of a Mail File

You can sort items in your mail files by time and date of receipt, name of sender, or subject in ascending alphabetical (A–Z) or numeric (0–9) order. To sort your mail files:

1. Enter the name of the mail file in the **Mail File** text field.

2. Choose **Mail File** Option from the **Open** submenu in the **File** menu.

3. Move the pointer onto the **View** menu button and press the right mouse button.

4. Drag the pointer to highlight the **Sort By** option and drag the pointer to the right to display the **Sort By** submenu.

5. Drag the pointer to highlight the sorting option you want—**Time and Date**, **Sender**, or **Subject**—and release the right mouse button. The message headers are redisplayed, sorted according to your selection.

Finding Specific Messages

To help you find messages, you can search your **In Tray** or mail files for messages sent to you by a specific person, subject, or person and subject. To find a message, display the **Find** pop-up window, as shown in Figure 10.11, by choosing **Find** from the **Edit** menu. The **Search** text fields are case insensitive and match partial words and phrases. You don't need to type a complete sender name; you can use keywords to match subjects. For example, typing the name **bird** in the **Sender** text field locates files sent by **bird@aviary** as well as **lbird**.

To search for messages by sender, type the sender name in the **Sender** text field. Clicking the left mouse button on the **Find Forward** button selects the next message header with the sender name you specify. Clicking the left mouse button on the **Find Backward** button selects the previous message header with the sender name you specify. Clicking the left mouse button on the **Select All** button selects all message headers with the sender name. An information message is displayed in the footer

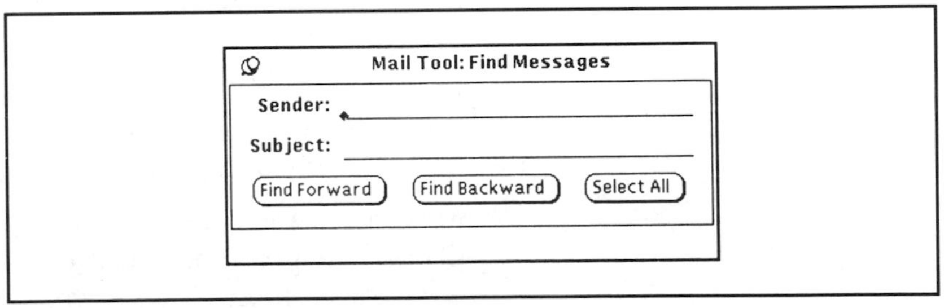

Figure 10.11: The Find pop-up window

of the **Find Messages** window that tells you how many messages are selected.

To search for messages by subject, type a word or phrase in the **Subject** text field. To search for messages by sender and by subject, type the appropriate information in each text field and click the left mouse button on one of the **Find** buttons. SunOS will search for messages that match both the sender and subject you specify.

Creating Mail Tool Templates

The Mail Tool allows you to use timesaving template files containing text you frequently use to create boilerplate mail messages, such as a mail message in a memo format. You can create a template using the **Compose Message** pane or a text editor. The DeskSet provides an easy-to-use text editor which you can access from the **Workspace Programs** submenu. See Chapter 11 for further information on using the Text Editor.

After you create a template file, you need to add it to a menu list in the **Template Properties** pop-up window, as shown in Figure 10.12, so it can be displayed as an item on the **Include Templates** submenu, as shown in Figure 10.13. The following steps explain how to add a template file to the **Compose Message** window's **Include Templates** submenu. If at any time you decide you want to cancel creating the template, move the pointer on the **Reset** button and click the left mouse button.

1. In the primary **Mail Tool** window move the mouse pointer to the **Edit** button and press the right mouse button to display the **Edit** menu. Drag the mouse pointer to the **Properties** option and release the right mouse button. The **Mail Arrival Properties** pop-up window is displayed.

2. Move the mouse pointer to the **Display** button and press the right mouse button. The **Mail Tool Properties** submenu is displayed. Drag the mouse pointer to the **Template Properties** option and release the

right mouse button. The **Template Properties** pop-up window is displayed.

3. Move the mouse pointer to the **Name** field and type the name you want to give to the template file. (It can be the same name as the original mail file.) This name is displayed when you select a template from the **Compose Message** window.

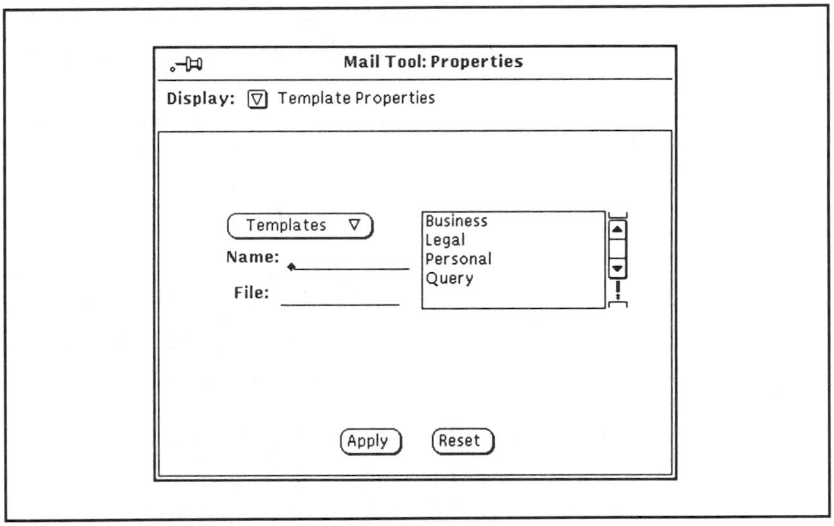

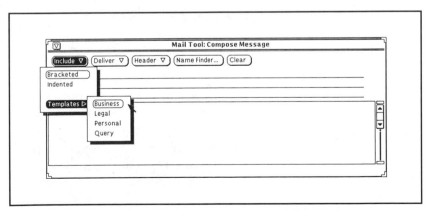

Figure 10.12: The Template Properties pop-up window

Figure 10.13: The Include Templates submenu with added options

4. Press Tab or Return to move the insert point to the **File** field. Type the path and name of the file you created in the text editor. If the file is in your home directory, you can just enter the file name.

5. Move the pointer to the **Templates Name** menu button and press the right mouse button. The list of existing template names is displayed in the scrolling box to the right of the **Templates** button. Choose the **Add Before** option or the **Add After** option from the **Templates** menu to determine where your new template is to be displayed in the templates list. If you select the **Add Before** option, the template name is inserted at the beginning of the templates list. If you select the **Add After** option, the template name is appended to the end of the templates list.

6. Click the left mouse button on the **Apply** button. The new template is placed in the scrolling list and added to the **Include Templates** submenu. The **Properties** pop-up window is cleared from your screen.

To delete a template, click the left mouse button on the **template** in the scrolling list, choose **Delete** from the **Templates** menu, and click the left mouse button on **Apply**.

Using a Template

To use a template, move the mouse pointer to the **Include** menu in the **Compose Message** window. Press the right mouse button to display the menu. Drag the mouse to the right of the **Templates** option. A submenu of template names is displayed. Drag the mouse pointer to the template you want and release the right mouse button. The template is inserted into the **Compose Message** window pane at the location of the insertion point. Figure 10.14 shows a sample template.

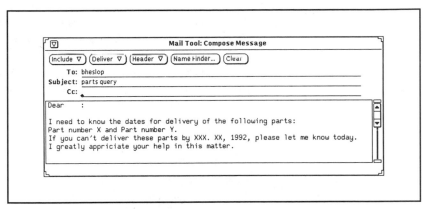

Figure 10.14: A sample template

Forwarding Mail

If you receive mail that needs to be sent to another user, you can forward it by selecting the mail message or messages and using the **Forward** option in the **Compose** menu of the primary **Mail Tool** window. When you forward a mail message, a **Compose Message** window is opened with the selected message included in the text pane. You can then forward the mail message by specifying the user you want to receive the mail message in the **To** text field.

Using the Vacation Notifier

When you are away from your terminal for an extended period of time, you can use the Vacation Notifier to notify anyone sending you mail that you are not available to read it. The Vacation Notifier is accessed from the **Compose** menu. Move the mouse pointer to the **Compose** menu in the primary **Mail Tool** window and press the left mouse button. Drag the mouse pointer to the right of the **Vacation** option, and then drag the mouse

pointer to the **Start/Change** option and release the mouse button. The **Vacation Setup** pop-up window is displayed with a
generic message form you can edit and customize to suit your
needs, as shown in Figure 10.15. You can edit the message in the
same way you edit messages in the **Compose Message** window.
The **"$SUBJECT"** variable of the message automatically extracts
the subject from the message sent by the sender and includes it
as part of the Vacation Notifier's reply message.

To start the reply message, click the left mouse button on the
Start button located in the window footer. The word **Vacation** is displayed in the header of the **Mail Tool** window to
remind you that the Vacation Notifier is turned on. Incoming
messages are stored in your **In Tray** and are readily available
when you return to the office. Once you've activated the Vacation Notifier, the **Stop** item on the **Vacation** submenu is also
activated. To stop the Vacation Notifier, choose the **Stop** option
from the **Vacation** submenu. If you decide you don't want to
activate the Vacation Notifier, move the pointer to the window
header and press the right mouse button to dismiss the pop-up
window.

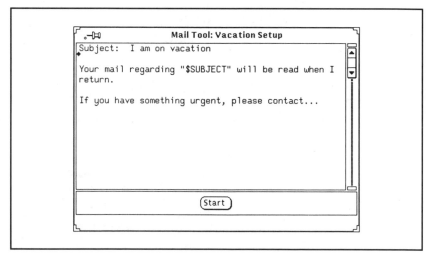

Figure 10.15: The Vacation Setup pop-up window

Customizing the Mail Tool

You can customize several properties of the Mail Tool program using the **Mail Tool Properties** pop-up window. To display the **Mail Tool Properties** window, choose the **Properties** option from the **Edit** menu. To show the menu that lists the types of properties you can customize, move the pointer to the **Display** menu button and press the right mouse button. The **Display** menu lists four options: **Mail Arrival Properties**, **Composition Header Properties**, **Template Properties**, and **General Properties**. Move the highlight to the option you want and release the right mouse button. Each of these menu options displays a pop-up window containing buttons and text fields to set the properties associated with them. These options are explained in the following sections. Changing template properties was covered earlier in this chapter.

The Mail Arrival Properties Pop-Up Window

The **Mail Arrival Properties** pop-up window, shown in Figure 10.16, allows you to change how often the Mail Tool checks for new mail, how you are notified of incoming mail, and whether headers are automatically displayed. You can type a number in the numeric fields or click the left mouse button on the appropriate arrow button to the left of the field to either increase or decrease the number of seconds between mail checks and the number of beeps and flashes SunOS will use to indicate the arrival of new mail. The values for each numeric field can be any number from 0 to 9999. If you want the Mail Tool to automatically display the headers for incoming mail messages, set the **Automatically Display Headers** option to **Yes**. If set to **No**, Mail Tool does not display headers for incoming messages unless you specifically request them by choosing **Open** or **Save Changes** from the **File** menu.

After you have changed any mail arrival properties, click the left mouse button on the **Apply** button to apply them to the Mail

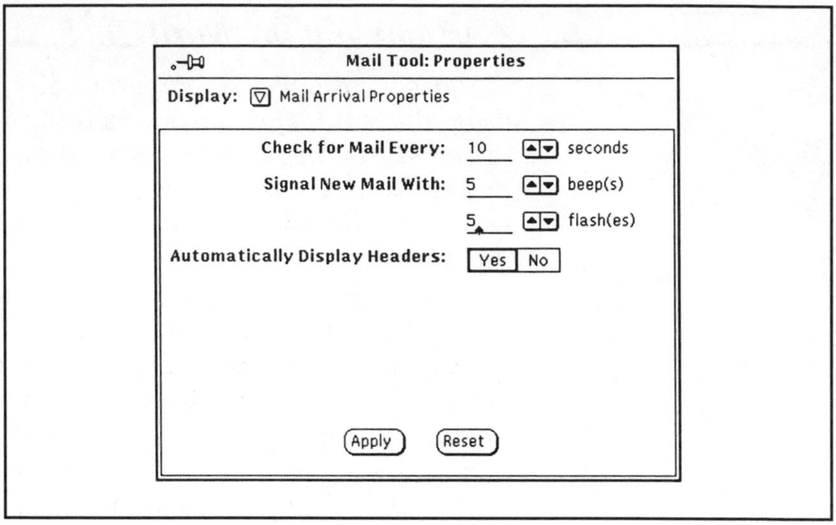

Figure 10.16: The Mail Arrival Properties pop-up window

Tool program. These mail arrival properties become effective immediately. If you want to cancel any changes you made, move the pointer to the **Reset** button and click the left mouse button. The mail arrival properties return to their previous settings.

The Composition Header Properties Pop-Up Window

You can customize the text fields at the top of the **Compose Message** window using the **Composition Header Properties** pop-up window, as shown in Figure 10.17. To automatically include a **Subject**, **Cc** (carbon copy), or **Bcc** (blind carbon copy) line, move the pointer to the **Yes** setting and click the left mouse button. To exclude a **Subject**, **Cc**, or **Bcc** line, click the left mouse button with the pointer on the **No** setting. **Bcc** is the same as **Cc** except that the list of users you send copies of the mail message to doesn't appear in the mail message header. This allows you to send a copy of the mail message to another user without alerting the addressee. By default, the **Bcc**

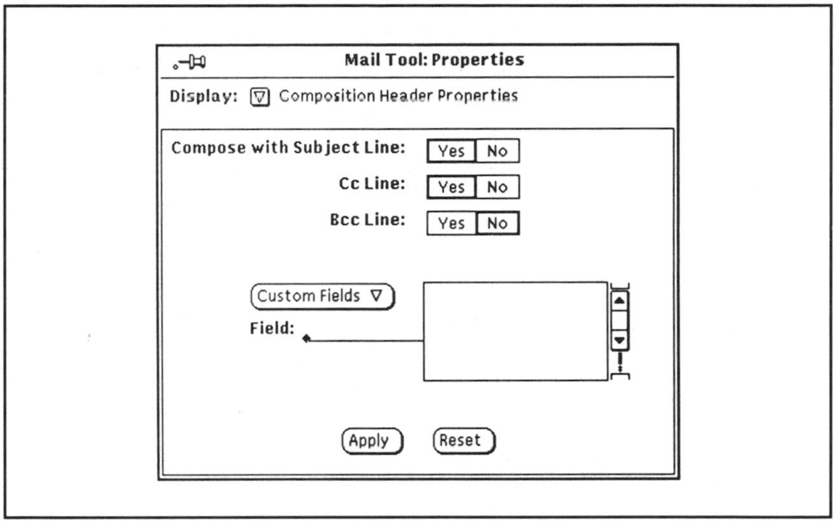

Figure 10.17: The Composition Header Properties pop-up window

line is not displayed. You can also create a custom header line of your own by following the steps below:

1. Move the pointer to the **Field** insert point and click the left mouse button.

2. Type the label for the text field to add in the field line. A colon is automatically added to the end of the added text field.

3. Move the pointer to the **Custom Fields** menu button and press the right mouse button.

4. Move the highlight to either the **Add Before** or **Add After** option from the **Custom Fields** menu.

5. Release the right mouse button. The item is added to the scrolling list.

6. Click the left mouse button on the **Apply** button to apply the change to the Mail Tool. The changes become effective immediately, adding the custom field to the **Add Custom** option in the **Header** menu of the **Compose Message** window.

To delete a custom field, click the left mouse button on the item in the scrolling list, choose **Delete** from the **Custom Fields** menu, and click the left mouse button on **Apply**. To change back to the previous composition header settings, move the pointer to the **Reset** button and click the left mouse button.

To include a customized field for a mail message you are creating, move the mouse pointer to the **Header** button and press the right mouse button. Drag the mouse pointer to the right of the **Add Custom** option to display a submenu of available custom headers. Drag the mouse pointer to the custom header you want and release the right mouse button. The custom header is displayed in the header area of the **Compose Message** window.

The General Properties Pop-Up Window

The **General Properties** option, as shown in Figure 10.18, allows you to specify general properties such as the size of the panes, print scripts (a series of printing and formatting commands), the directory for mail files, and whether confirmation

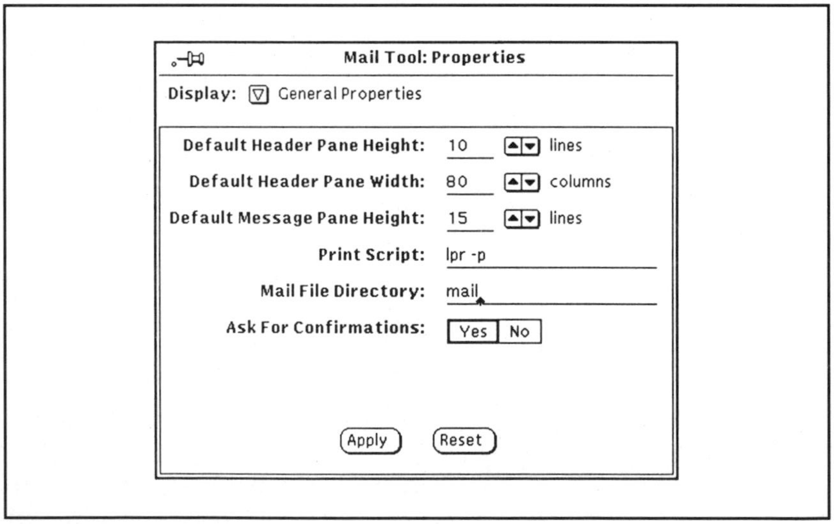

Figure 10.18: The General Properties pop-up window

The changes to **Mail Tool** window sizes made with the **General Properties** pop-up window become effective the next time you start Mail Tool. **Print Script** and **Mail File Directory** properties become effective immediately.

notices are displayed when you make changes to a mail file.

You can specify the number of lines displayed in the Mail Tool message header pane, the number of columns in the panes for all windows, and the number of lines in the pane of the **View Message** pop-up window. When you change the size of the Header or Message panes, the changes do not take effect until you apply them and open a new Mail Tool.

You can also specify a different print script and a file for mail file messages. The print script is effective as soon as you use the **Apply** button to save your changes.

Use the **Mail File Directory** text field to specify the directory where mail files are stored when you move or copy them. If the directory name you specify does not exist, when you click the left mouse button on the **Apply** button a notice is displayed asking you if you want to create the directory.

To be prompted for confirmation before performing an irreversible action with the Mail Tool, set the **Ask For Confirmations** option to **Yes**. A dialog box is displayed when you have made editing changes to a message in the **View** window, when you display a new message, or when you receive new incoming mail. If you choose **No**, any editing changes are automatically incorporated when you display a new message or receive new incoming mail without notifying you of the changes. Remember that after changing any of the general properties, you need to click the left mouse button on the **Apply** button to save your changes or the **Reset** button to cancel your new settings.

Encoding Files

Files other than ASCII text, such as raster or PostScript files, can be sent with a mail message by selecting the file icons representing the file you want to send from the File Manager and dragging and dropping them into the **Compose Message** window. When you drop a file onto the **Compose Message** window, a dialog box is displayed, as shown in Figure 10.19, asking how you want Mail Tool to process the contents of the file.

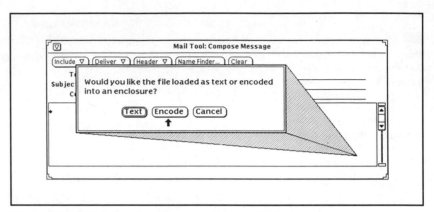

Figure 10.19: A dialog box for encoding mail files

Choosing the **Text** option inserts the file at the end of the message and inserts **(E)** at the beginning of the subject line to show that the mail message contains encoded data. Choosing the **Cancel** option stops the operation.

Decoding Encoded Files

To decode an encoded file, select the header and drag and drop it onto the **File Manager** folder pane. To copy and decode the encoded file, simply open both the File Manager and the Mail Tool windows and follow these four steps:

1. Move to the directory in the File Manager where you want to store the encoded mail message.

2. Select the encoded file in the Mail Tool by placing the pointer on the header of the mail message that contains the name of the encoded file and press the left mouse button.

3. Press Control and drag the header to the File Manager using the left mouse button to copy the message. A small envelope is displayed.

4. Release the Control key and the left mouse button; the file is decoded, and icons representing the encoded files are displayed and highlighted in the folder pane.

If you want to move and decode the message, rather than copy and decode the message, do not press the Control key; simply drag and drop the header.

If you drop a header into a folder that contains identical file names, the **Console** window displays a message asking if you want to overwrite the existing files (those in the folder). If you choose no, the files are displayed with a compress icon and a **.Z** extension.

Summary

In this chapter you learned how to use the DeskSet Mail Tool to receive, write, send, and manage electronic mail messages. You learned how to

- navigate the Mail Tool's environment and get on-line help.

- retrieve and view your new mail messages from the **In Tray** mail file.

- delete or print your mail messages.

- compose and send a mail message.

- find a user's mailing address.

- manage your mail messages using mail files you create to store mail messages after reading them from your **In Tray**.

- retrieve, view, sort, and add messages to mail files.

- create Mail Tool templates to quickly add frequently used formats or text to your mail messages.

- use the Vacation Notifier to alert users sending you mail that you are away from your terminal.

- customize the Mail Tool using the **Properties** option to affect mail arrival, the composition header, and general properties.

CHAPTER 11

Using the Shell Tool,
Command Tool,
and Text Editor

THIS CHAPTER EXPLAINS THE DESKSET TOOLS USED to enter commands and text. The Shell Tool, the Command Tool, and the Console allow you to enter and edit SunOS commands. The Text Editor allows you to create, edit, and save text files.

The Shell Tool

The Shell Tool is a command interpreter that accepts, interprets, and executes your SunOS commands. Figure 11.1 shows an open **Shell Tool** window. The pane of the **Shell Tool** window is referred to as a *terminal emulator* pane, meaning that working in it is the same as working from a command prompt at a terminal. The point of text insertion of the Shell Tool is indicated by a rectangle that appears as an outline when inactive and as a solid black block when active. To activate the insert point, move the pointer inside the **Shell Tool** window. If the insert point does not change to a solid block, click the left mouse button. After typing a SunOS command and pressing Return, the command is executed. For example, type the **ls** command and press Return while in the **Shell Tool** window to list the files in the current directory.

The Shell Tool Pop-Up Menu

When pressing the right mouse button with the pointer in the pane of the Shell Tool, a pop-up menu appears, as shown in Figure 11.2. The **Shell Tool** pop-up menu has three options:

- **Stuff** allows you to select and insert text in a Shell Tool.

- **Enable Page Mode** allows you to view one pane of text at a time.

- **Copy then Paste** allows you to store text in memory and paste it in the same Shell Tool or another Shell Tool.

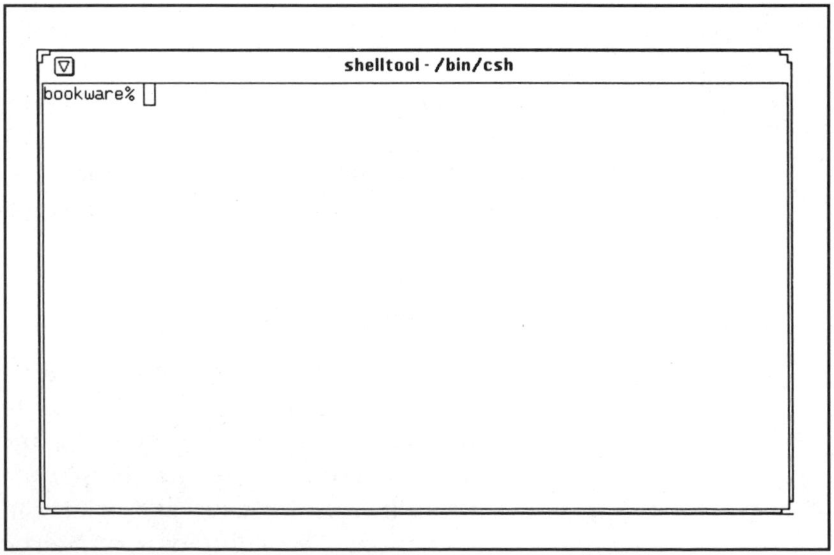

Figure 11.1: The Shell Tool window

Each of these options is described below.

Selecting and Inserting Text in a Shell Tool

The **Stuff** option in the **Shell Tool** pop-up menu enables you to insert (stuff) text at the insert point of another Shell Tool. Before you can use the **Stuff** option you need to select text to insert. You select text by moving the pointer to the beginning of the text you want and pressing the left mouse button. Then move to the end of the text and press the middle mouse button. (Selecting text is covered in greater detail later in this chapter.) Once you have selected a group of text in a Shell Tool, you can use the **Stuff** option to move the selected text to the insert point in the same window or another window. For example, move the pointer to the beginning of the **ls** command, click the left mouse button, then move to the end of the command and click the middle mouse button. The command is now selected. Press the right mouse button in the text pane the same Shell Tool or another Shell Tool and drag the pointer to highlight the

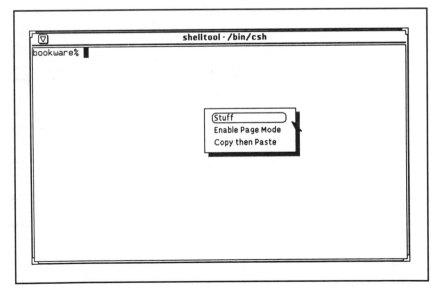

Figure 11.2: The Shell Tool pop-up menu

Stuff option. The selection is then inserted at the insert point, issuing the **ls** command again.

Viewing Text

The **Enable Page Mode** option of the **Shell Tool** pop-up menu allows you to show only one paneful of text at a time so that text does not scroll past the window without allowing you to see it. For example, if you have a long directory listing that takes two panefuls to display and you enter the **ls** command, the first paneful is displayed, and the pointer turns to a stop sign, as shown in Figure 11.3, indicating that the pane has stopped scrolling. To resume scrolling the contents of the Shell Tool, press any key except F1 or Help. The **Enable Page Mode** option is replaced with the **Disable Page Mode** option when activated. If the **Disable Page Mode** option is activated, text

```
┌─────────────────────────────────────────────────────┐
│  ┌─────────────────────────────────────────────────┐ │
│  │ ▽          shelltool - /bin/csh                  │ │
│  ├─────────────────────────────────────────────────┤ │
│  │total 40                                          │ │
│  │drwxrwsrwx  6 lbird      1024 Oct 19 21:11 ./     │ │
│  │drwxr-sr-x 11 users       512 Jan  5  1990 ../    │ │
│  │-rw-r--r--  1 lbird         63 Oct 21  1992 .callog│ │
│  │-rw-r--r--  1 lbird          6 Oct 19 20:11 .clockrc│ │
│  │-rw-r--r--  1 lbird        780 Jan 26  1990 .cshrc │ │
│  │-rw-r--r--  1 lbird       4546 Oct 20 11:35 .defaults│ │
│  │-rw-r--r--  1 lbird         70 Oct 21  1992 .filemgrrc│ │
│  │-rw-r--r--  1 lbird         30 Oct 20 00:10 .fvcmd │ │
│  │-rw-r--r--  1 lbird         42 Oct 20 00:10 .fvcmd%│ │
│  │-rw-------  1 root        1106 Mar  7  1990 .login │ │  ❢
│  │-rw-r--r--  1 lbird       1178 Oct 19 21:11 .mailrc│ │
│  │-rw-r--r--  1 lbird        547 Nov 15  1988 .oldcshrc│ │
│  │-rw-r--r--  1 lbird       1069 Nov 15  1988 .oldlogin│ │
│  │-rw-r--r--  1 lbird       1351 Jan 17  1990 .orgrc │ │
│  │-rw-r--r--  1 lbird       1186 Jul 20 04:31 .rootmenu│ │
│  │-rw-r--r--  1 lbird       1218 Jul 20 04:31 .rootmenu%│ │
│  │-rw-r--r--  1 lbird        847 Jan 26  1990 .sunview│ │
│  │-rw-r--r--  1 lbird        847 Jan 26  1990 .sunview%│ │
│  │■rw-r--r--  1 lbird        847 Jan 26  1990 .sunview-│ │
│  └─────────────────────────────────────────────────┘ │
└─────────────────────────────────────────────────────┘
```

Figure 11.3: A partially scrolled Shell Tool pane

scrolls without stopping until it reaches the end of the text to be displayed.

Copying and Pasting Text in a Shell Tool

The **Copy then Paste** option of the **Shell Tool** pop-up menu is similar to the **Stuff** option in that it allows you to insert selected text. Unlike the **Stuff** option, the **Copy then Paste** option allows you to select text to copy then paste in any window rather than just a Shell tool. The text you select using this option is stored in a special memory buffer known as the clipboard. (The clipboard is covered in greater detail later in this chapter.)

The Command Tool

The Command Tool acts as a command interpreter and provides you with all the features of the standard Text Editor pane, discussed later in this chapter. The **Command Tool** icon looks the same as the **Shell Tool** icon. When opened, however, the **Command Tool** window displays a scrollbar and a different pop-up menu than the Shell Tool, as shown in Figures 11.4 and 11.5.

Switching between Command Modes

You can disable the editing capabilities of the Command Tool so it appears and acts like a **Shell Tool** window by displaying the **Command Tool** pop-up menu and selecting the **Disable Scrolling** option from the **Cmd Modes** submenu, as shown in Figure 11.5. This option nearly doubles the performance of a **Command Tool**; when the scrolling feature is disabled, the window doesn't demand the overhead processing required to store commands. Selecting the **Disable Scrolling** option causes the **Command Tool** pop-up menu to appear as the **Shell Tool** window with one additional option labeled **Enable Scrolling**, which allows you to return to the original **Command Tool** window.

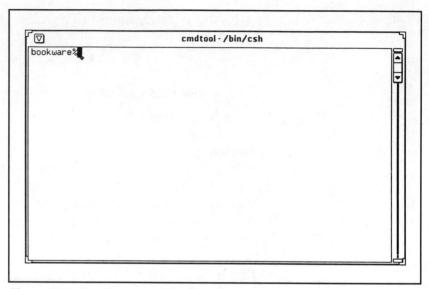

Figure 11.4: The Command Tool window

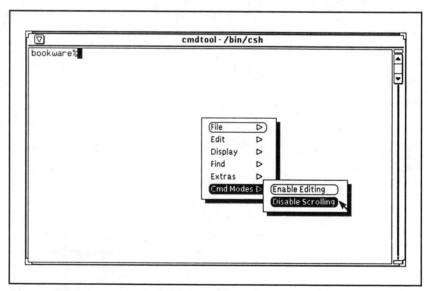

Figure 11.5: The Cmd Modes submenu

Saving the Contents of a Command Tool Window to a File

Using the **Command Tool** window, you can save a series of commands as a file by doing the following:

1. At the prompt, type a file name. Be sure to include a pathname if you want to save the file to a directory other than the current directory.

2. Move the pointer to the beginning of the file name and press the left mouse button.

3. Move the pointer to the end of the file name and press the middle mouse button. The text appears highlighted in reverse video.

4. With the pointer inside the **Command Tool** pane, press the right mouse button. The **Command Tool** pop-up menu is displayed.

5. Make sure the **File** option is highlighted and drag the pointer to the direct right. The **File** submenu is displayed.

6. Move the mouse pointer to highlight the **Store as New File** option and release the right mouse button. The **Store File** pop-up window is displayed with your highlighted file name in the **File Name** text field. Move the pointer to the **Apply** button and click the left mouse button. The text is stored in the file with the name you typed in step 1.

The Console

A **Console** window is opened automatically whenever you use the OpenWindows or SunView environments. The **Console** window is used to display system or application messages. You can clear these messages using the **Redisplay All** option from the **Workspace Utilities** submenu. If you accidentally quit a **Console** window, you can also use the **Console** option from the **Workspace Utilities** submenu to open a **Console** window. Messages are displayed in the newest **Console** window if you have more than one **Console** window open.

Opening more than one **Console window** at a time is not recommended because it is easy to miss important messages if you do not pay attention to which **Console** window was opened last.

The Text Editor Window

The Text Editor simplifies editing operations. You can easily cut and paste text directly between the Text Editor and any other text pane in the DeskSet.

The **Text Editor** window has a control panel and a text pane where you compose and edit text. The header of the **Text Editor** window always displays the path and the name of the file you are editing or the word **None** if you have not yet named your file. When you have made editing changes or have not yet saved a file, the word **edited** is displayed in parentheses following the file name.

The Control Panel

The control panel of the Text Editor has four menu buttons: **File**, **View**, **Edit**, and **Find**.

- The **File** menu provides you with options to save, clear, or merge files.

- The **View** menu provides you with options to change the position of the cursor and change the portion of the file in the text pane.

- The **Edit** menu provides you with editing options to copy, move, delete, or undelete text.

- The **Find** menu provides you with options to locate any text selection in the text pane or in a special storage area known as the clipboard.

Using the **Find** menu, you can also locate a string of text and replace it with another. The line containing the dimmed diamond next to the **Find** menu button is the **Find** text field, used to enter and select text.

The Text Editor Pane and Text Editor Pop-Up Menu

The text pane is the area in which you compose and edit your text. Placing the pointer inside the text pane and pressing the right mouse button displays the **Text Editor** pop-up menu. The **Text Editor** pop-up menu is the same as the pop-up menus displayed in the editing panes of the **Console**, **Command Tool**, and **Mail Tool Compose** windows. The options for these pop-up menus operate in the same way as the menus in the control panel except for the **Extras** submenu. The **Extras** submenu's options are covered later in this chapter. Figure 11.6 shows the Text Editor and the **Text Editor** pop-up menu.

Starting the Text Editor and Loading Files

To start the Text Editor, press the right mouse button with the pointer anywhere in the SunView or Open Windows workspace. Place the pointer on the **Programs** option and drag it to the direct right to display the **Programs** submenu. Move the pointer to highlight the **Text Editor** option and release the right mouse button. A **Text Editor** icon appears on the workspace. To open the **Text Editor** window, move the pointer on the **Text Editor** icon and double click the left mouse button. Once the **Text Editor** window is opened, move the pointer inside the text pane and begin entering your text. If no characters appear, move the pointer to the dimmed diamond and click the left mouse button.

If you want to load an already existing file into a **Text Editor** pop-up window, move the pointer on the file's icon in the File Manager and double click the left mouse button. A **Text Editor**

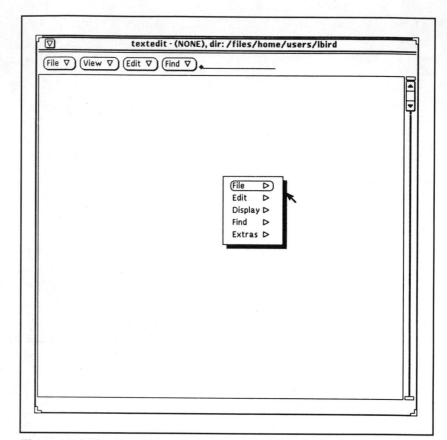

Figure 11.6: The Text Editor and Text Editor pop-up menu.

pop-up window is opened and the file is automatically loaded. Note that a **Text Editor** pop-up window does not provide a control panel. You must use the **Text Pane** pop-up window. To load a file with the Text Editor, use the **File** menu's **Load File** option to display the **Load File** pop-up window, as shown in Figures 11.7a and 11.7b.

To load a file using the **File** menu's **Load File** option:

1. Move the pointer to the **File** menu button and press the right mouse button.

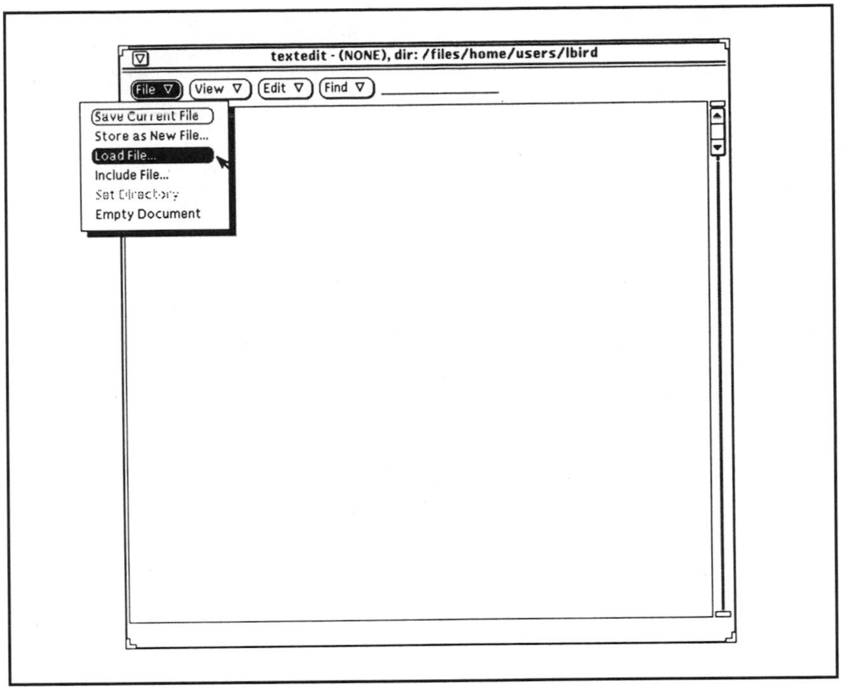

Figure 11.7a: The Load File option

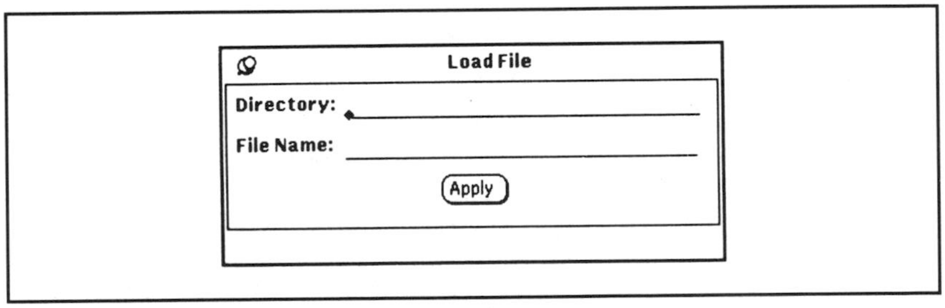

Figure 11.7b: The Load File pop-up window

2. Drag the pointer to the **Load File** option and release the right mouse button. The **Load File** pop-up window appears.

3. Type the directory and press Return.

4. Type the name of the file you want to load.

5. Click the left mouse button on the **Apply** button. The file is loaded in the **Text Editor** window, replacing any existing text.

Loading Files into the Text Editor

You can drag and drop file icons into the **Text Editor** window to load the files. The following describes how to drag a copy of a file from the File Manager into the **Text Editor** window.

1. Move the pointer on the icon in the File Manager that represents the file you want to load.

2. Press and hold the Control key and simultaneously press the left mouse button.

3. Release the Control key and drag the file onto an open Text Editor.

4. Release the left mouse button, and the file is loaded in the text pane.

Saving a New File

When you have created a new file but have not saved it, the icon displays the words **No File**. If **NONE** is shown as the file name, use the **File** menu's **Store as New File** option to display a **Store File** pop-up window, as shown in Figures 11.8a and 11.8b. The **Store File** pop-up window automatically displays the selection in the **File** text field. If you do not specify a directory, the Text Editor uses the current directory. You can also use the Store File pop-up window to save the current file when you type the directory and file name of the current file in the appropriate text fields. Move the pointer onto the **Apply** button and click the left mouse button to save the contents of the Text Editor pane.

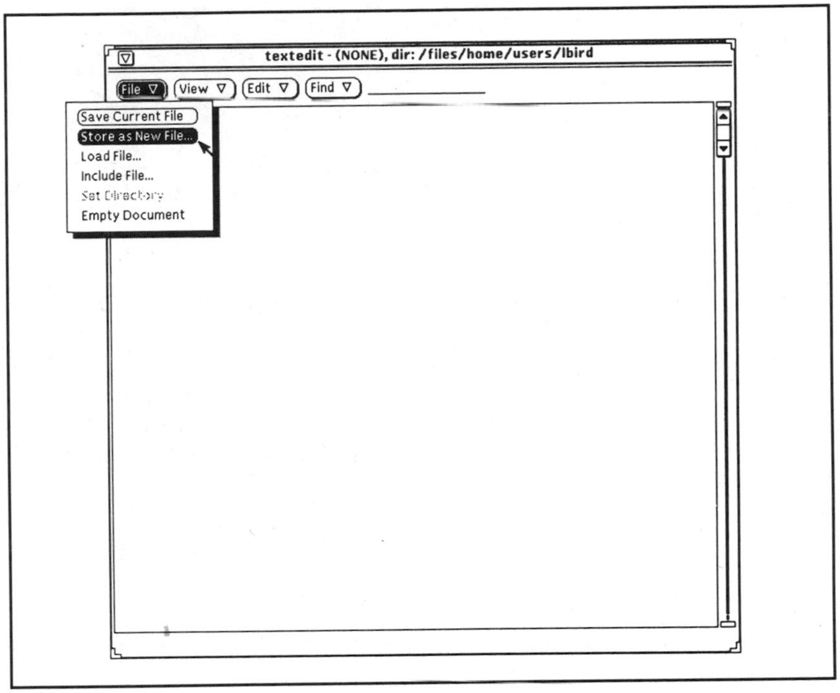

Figure 11.8a: The Store as New File option

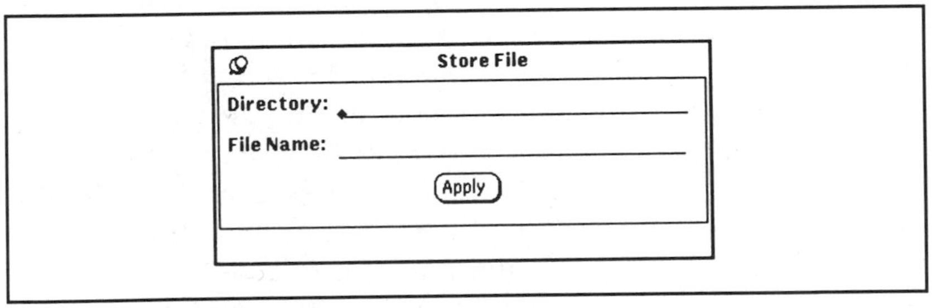

Figure 11.8b: The Store File pop-up Window

Once you have named your file, the Text Editor icon shows the beginning six characters of the file name. When the file has been edited and you have not saved changes, the file name is preceded by a **>** symbol. Figure 11.9 shows an example of a Text Editor icon of a named but edited file.

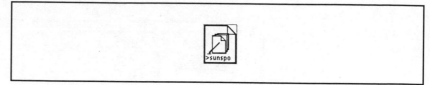

Figure 11.9: Text Editor icon of an edited file

Saving a Named File

The **File** menu also contains the **Save Current File** option, which saves the contents of a named file. Use the **Save Current File** option to save the contents of the Text Editor pane that has previously been saved. Remember the name of the file is always displayed in the Text Editor's window header following the directory name.

Changing Directories in the Text Editor

Use the **Set Directory** option to change to a different directory. First type a directory in the **Find** text field. Remember the text field is the line with the dimmed diamond in the control panel. Select the directory name by moving the mouse pointer before the first character of the file name, clicking the left mouse button, then moving the pointer directly after the last character of the directory name and clicking the middle mouse button. The directory name appears highlighted. Choose the **Set Directory** option from the **File** menu and the directory is changed to the selected directory. Notice the new directory name appears in the window header.

Controlling the Position of the Cursor

The **View** menu provides you with options you can select to control the position of the cursor (insert point). The following explains the **View** menu options to move the insert point.

Option	*Result*
Show Caret at Top	Moves the insert point to the beginning of the **Find** text field in the Text Editor control panel
Move Caret to Start	Moves the insert point to the beginning of the text file
Move Caret to End	Moves the insert point to the end of the text file

Moving to Specific Lines

Perform the following steps to move to a specific line number in a document:

1. Enter the line number in the **Find** text field.

2. Select the number, using the left and middle mouse button.

3. Move the pointer to the **View** menu button or the **Display** option in the **Text Pane** pop-up menu and press the right mouse button.

4. Drag the highlight to the **Select Line at Number** option. The text on the specified line number is highlighted, and the insert point is moved to the end of the selected text.

When there is no number as the current selection, the **Select Line Number** option is inactive.

Use the **What Line Number?** option in the **View** menu or the **Display** option of the **Text Pane** pop-up menu to locate the line number where the selected text begins. The line number is displayed in the window footer. If there is not a current selection in the **Text Editor** window, the **What Line Number?** option is inactive.

Entering and Selecting Text

Entering text is as easy as moving the pointer to the text pane where you want to add text and typing. If no text appears, make sure the pointer is in the text pane and click the left mouse button.

The left mouse button is also used to mark the beginning of a text selection, and the middle mouse button ends a text selection. Selected text is highlighted in reverse video. Once text is selected, it is awaiting deletion or an operation using the clipboard. If you type a character, the highlighted text is deleted and replaced with the typed character.

The following list explains different methods of selecting text in a text pane:

The *clipboard* is a storage place in memory for selected text to be copied, moved, or deleted.

Selection	*Operation*
Word	Move the pointer onto the word and double click the left mouse button.
Paragraph	Move the pointer onto the paragraph and click the left mouse button three times.
Block of text	Click the left mouse button to set the insert point, move the pointer to the end of the selection, and then click the middle mouse button.
Entire document	Click the left mouse button four times anywhere in the document.

You can add to the beginning or the end of the selected text by moving the pointer to the beginning (to add at the front) or end (to add at the end) of the text you want to add to and clicking the middle mouse button.

You can also make a selection smaller by moving the pointer into the highlighted text and clicking the middle mouse button. Highlighting is removed from part of the selection. Reducing a selection may not work exactly as you expect because the adjustment depends on the method of the original selection and the starting position of the insert point.

Copying, Moving, and Deleting Text Using the Clipboard

The **Edit** menu and the **Text Pane** pop-up menu, shown in Figures 11.10a and 11.10b, provide you with standard editing functions to copy, move, and delete text. You can also perform any of these operations using the accelerator keys on the left side of your keyboard. Remember, when you cut or copy text, it is stored on the clipboard (in memory).

Using the Clipboard to Copy a Text Selection

Only one selection can be stored on the clipboard at a time. If something is already on the clipboard and you do a copy or cut, the contents of the clipboard are overwritten with the new information.

You need to select the text you want to copy, otherwise the **Copy** option is dimmed in the **Edit** menu, indicating it is unavailable. After you select the text you want to copy, move the pointer onto the **Edit** menu button and press the right mouse

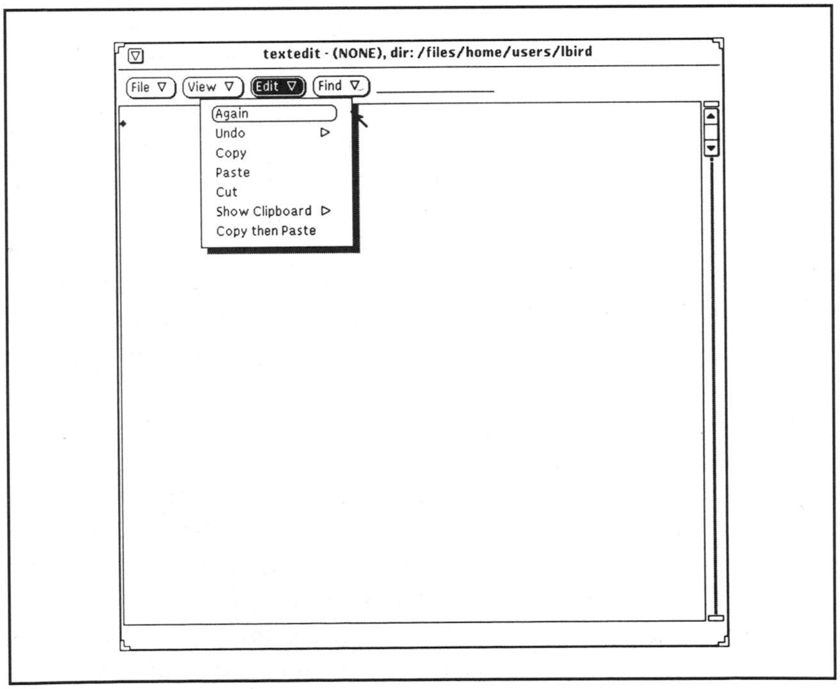

Figure 11.10a: The Edit menu

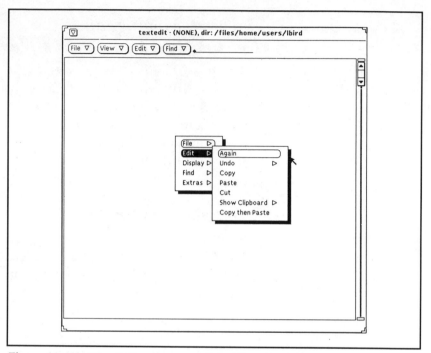

Figure 11.10b: The Edit submenu of the Text Pane pop-up menu

button. Drag the pointer to highlight the **Copy** option. When you release the right mouse button, a copy of the selected text is stored on the clipboard.

Once a selection is copied, the **Paste** option becomes active so that you can select it to paste the contents of the clipboard at the insertion point. You can copy and paste text selected in another window by simply choosing the **Copy then Paste** option from the **Edit** menu.

The **Text Pane** pop-up menu and accelerator keys (on the left side of your keyboard) allow you to perform the same copy operations. The **Text Pane**'s pop-up **Edit** submenu provides the **Copy** and **Copy then Paste** options, which work in the same way as the **Edit** menu's **Copy** and **Copy then Paste** options. The Copy accelerator key on a type 4 keyboard is identical to choosing the **Copy** option from an **Edit** menu option. If you are using another type of keyboard, the Copy key is labeled L6.

Pressing one of the meta keys (the diamond keys on both sides of the space bar) in conjunction with the letter P is the keyboard equivalent to using the **Copy then Paste** option.

Using the Clipboard to Move a Text Selection

The process of moving a selection is similar to the copying process, only instead of using the **Copy** option, you choose the **Cut** option from the **Edit** menu. The **Cut** option removes the selected text and stores it on the clipboard. Once text is stored on the clipboard, you can select the **Paste** option to move the text from the clipboard to its new location.

The **Text Pane** pop-up menu and the accelerator keys (on the left side of your keyboard) allow you to perform the same move operation. The **Text Pane**'s pop-up **Edit** menu also provides **Cut** and **Paste** options, which work identically to the **Cut and Paste** options in the control panel's **Edit** menu. The Cut and Paste accelerator keys on a type 4 keyboard are identical to choosing the **Cut** and **Paste** options from an **Edit** menu. If you are using another type of keyboard, the Cut key is labeled L10 and the Paste key is labeled L8.

Displaying the Contents of the Clipboard

Use the **Show Clipboard** option in the **Edit** or **Text Pane** pop-up menu to display the current contents of the clipboard. The **Show Clipboard** option displays up to thirty characters of the last string cut or copied. Figure 11.11 shows the results of selecting the word **Sunspots**, copying it to the clipboard, and choosing the **Show Clipboard** option from the **Edit** menu.

Repeating or Undoing Edits

You can repeat the last editing action that changed your text by selecting the **Again** option from the **Edit** menu or the **Text Pane** pop-up menu.

Figure 11.11: The results of choosing the Show Clipboard option

If you make a mistake and want to undo either the last editing action or all editing actions since you last saved your file, use either the **Edit** menu or the **Text Pane** pop-up menu as follows: press the right mouse button and move the pointer to highlight the menu's **Undo** option, and then move the pointer to the direct right. You can undo the last editing action or all editing actions by selecting the **Undo Last Edit** or **Undo All Edits** options from the **Undo** submenu, as shown in Figure 11.12.

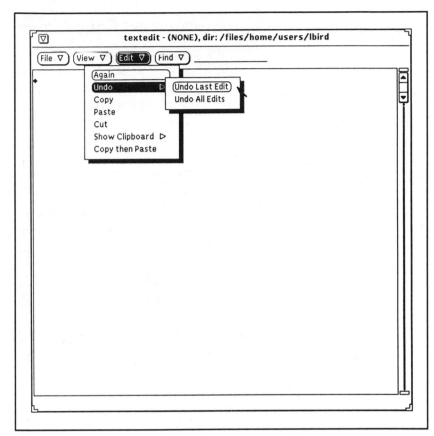

Figure 11.12: The Undo submenu of the Edit menu.

Emptying the Contents of a Text Pane

If you want to clear the text pane of a window, use the **File** menu's **Empty Document** option. This clears the contents of the current text pane. If you have made editing changes and have not saved them, a dialog box is displayed, asking you to confirm or cancel the operation.

Splitting the Text Editor Pane

Use the **Split View** option to split the view in the Text Editor pane so that you can view and edit two (or more) parts of the text in the same window. Because the document itself is not split, any editing changes you make in one view are reflected in other views as well. You can split the view in a pane following the steps below:

1. Choose the **Split View** option from the **View** menu. A message is displayed that tells you how to split the pane.

2. Move the pointer to the place in the text where you want to create the split.

3. Click the left mouse button. The pane is split into two independently scrollable panes, and the message is cleared, as shown in Figure 11.13.

After splitting a text pane, the **Destroy View** option is automatically added to the **View** menu. To remove a split text pane, move the pointer into the portion of the text pane you want to remove and choose the **Destroy View** option from the **View** menu.

Merging Files

The **File** menu displays the **Include File** option shown in Figure 11.14a. When selected, this option displays the **Include File** pop-up window, as shown in Figure 11.14b. This option allows you to merge two or more text files by typing the directory and name of the file you want to include and clicking the left mouse button on the **Apply** button. The file is inserted at the insert point in the text pane.

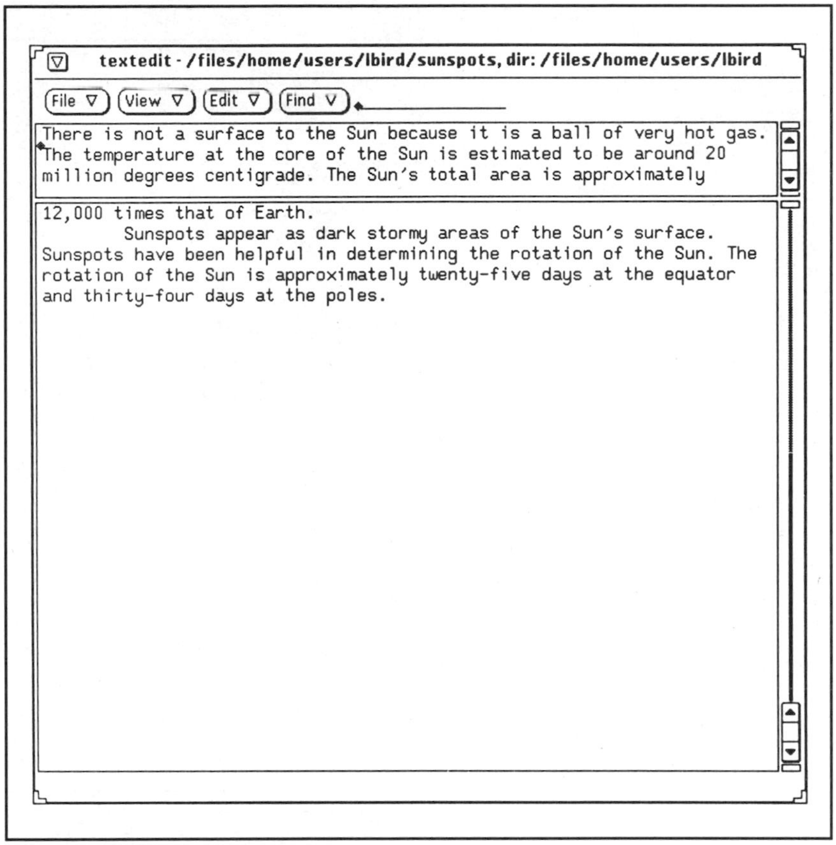

Figure 11.13: A split Text Editor pane

Changing the Line Wrap Mode

The **View** menu contains the **Change Line Wrap** option, which provides you with a submenu listing three choices for line wrapping: **Wrap at Character**, **Wrap at Word**, and **Clip Lines**. The option that is current is always inactive. The most commonly used wrapping method is to wrap at the end of words. If you choose **Clip lines**, the beginning of each line that ends with a Return is displayed. If you use the **character** option, lines wrap at the closest character before the window's border.

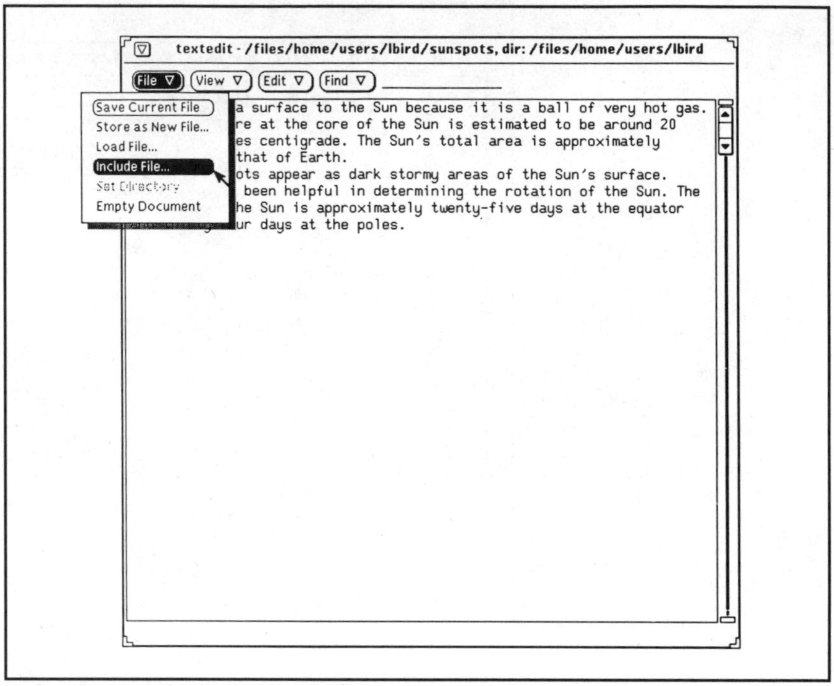

Figure 11.14a: The Include File option

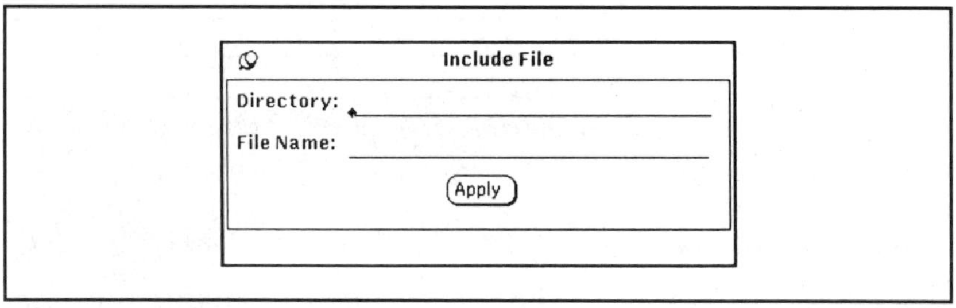

Figure 11.14b: The Include File pop-up window

Finding and Replacing Text in a Text Pane

The **Find** menu allows you to search for specific text strings, special characters, and delimiters. You can also use the **Find** menu to locate a specific text string and replace it with another.

To locate text, you must first select it using the left and middle mouse button. If the text you want to find already exists in the window, you can simply select it. Otherwise you must type it into the window of the **Find** text field and then select it. Then move the pointer to the **Find** menu button, press the right mouse button, and drag the pointer to choose the direction to search from the **Find Selection** submenu, as shown in Figure 11.15. The **Find Selection** option always searches for the text string that is highlighted. Click the left mouse button on the **Find** button again to find and select the next occurrence of the text string.

Figure 11.15: The Find Selection submenu

Replacing Text in the Text Editor

The **Find and Replace** option is similar to the **Find Selection** option, but choosing this option causes a pop-up window to automatically display the current selection in the **Find** text field as the text to be located. You can then enter the text you want to replace the **Find** text field by entering text in the **Replace** text field of the pop-up window, as shown in Figure 11.16.

To replace the current selection with a text string, type the text in the **Replace** text field and click the left mouse button on the **Replace** button. You can use the **Replace** button and the **Find** button to locate a string and then replace it with another. You can replace a string with nothing by leaving the **Replace** text field blank.

The buttons at the bottom of the **Find and Replace** pop-up window combine these find and replace operations: **Find then Replace**, **Replace then Find**, and **Replace All**. The following explains each of the **Find and Replace** pop-up window buttons:

Option	*Result*
Find then Replace	Searches for the next occurence of the text string entered in the Find text field of the **Find and Replace** pop-up window, shown in Figure 11.16, and replaces the matching text with the text entered in the **Replace** text field of the **Find and Replace** pop-up window
Replace then Find	Replaces currently selected text (even if the text is different than the text in the **Find** text field) with the text in the **Replace** text field and then searches for the next occurence of the text in the **Find** text field

Option	*Result*
`Replace All`	Replaces every occurence of the text in the **Find** text field with the text in thc **Replace** text field

Restricting the Find and Replace Operation

You can specify whether you want the find and replace operations to apply to all of the text or restricted to the text between the insert point and the end of the document by clicking the left mouse button on either the **All Text** or **To End** options.

Finding Text in the Clipboard

The **Find Clipboard** option matches the text string that is currently stored in the clipboard with occurrences of the same string in the Text Editor pane. You can search forward or backward from the insert point by choosing **Forward** or **Backward** from the **Find Clipboard** pop-up menu. For example, if the clipboard contains the text string **SPARC**, you can search for **SPARC** either forward or backward from the insert point in the

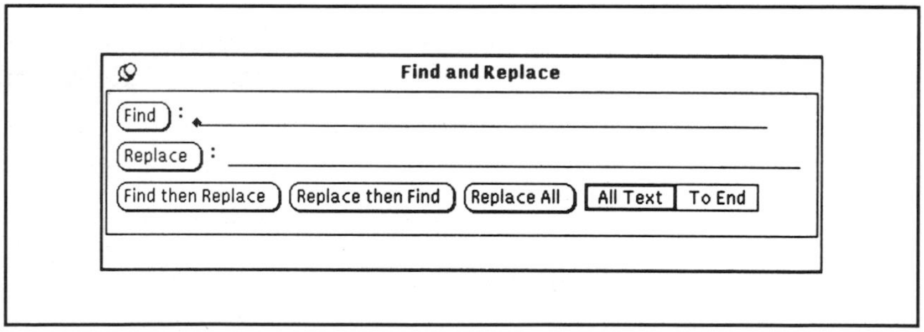

Figure 11.16: The Find and Replace pop-up window

Text Editor pane by choosing either the **Forward** or **Backward** option from the **Find Clipboard** submenu.

Searching for Delimiters

A *delimiter* is any character or combination of characters used to separate one item or set of data from another. For example, many databases use commas to delimit one field from another. You might think of a period as a type of delimiter used to separate sentences. The **Find Marked Text** option in the **Find** menu searches for and highlights text between a matched set of delimiters. Eight types of delimiters are provided as options in the **Find Marked Text** pop-up window, as shown in Figure 11.17.

The **Backward**, **Forward**, and **Expand** buttons in the **Find Marked Text** pop-up window allow you to search for text between two or more sets of matched delimiters, such as two sets of matched parentheses (**( )**). When one or more matched sets of delimiters are placed within another set of delimiters, they are referred to as *nested delimiters*. To select text within a set of nested delimiters, make sure the insert point is before the delimiters you want to locate and do the following:

1. Move the pointer on the Text Editor's **Find** menu button.

2. Press the right mouse button and drag the pointer to highlight the **Find Marked Text** option.

3. Release the right mouse button and the **Find Marked Text** pop-up window is displayed.

4. Move the pointer to the type of nested delimiters that surround the text you want to select and click the left mouse button.

5. Move the pointer to the **Forward** button and click the left mouse button.

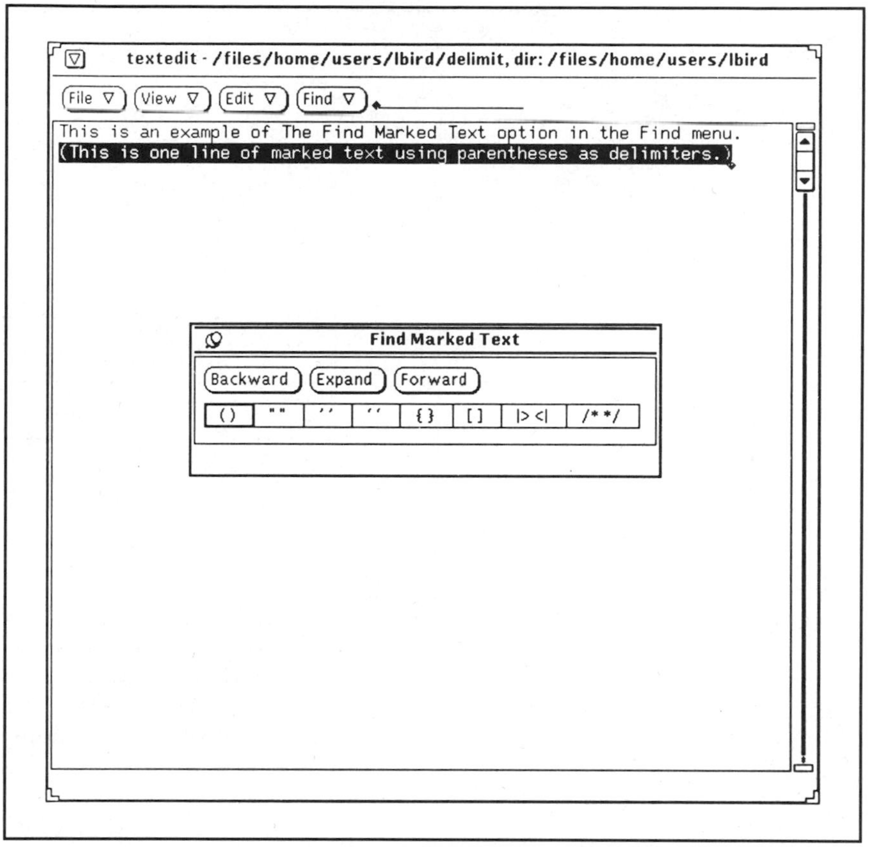

Figure 11.17: The Find Marked Text pop-up window

6. With the pointer still on the **Forward** button, click the left mouse button again.

To expand the matching delimiter selection in the previous example, move the pointer to the **Expand** button and press the left mouse button. Figure 11.18a shows the results of pressing the **Forward** button three times to select text within two nested sets of matching delimiters, and Figure 11.18b shows the results of then pressing the **Expand** button.

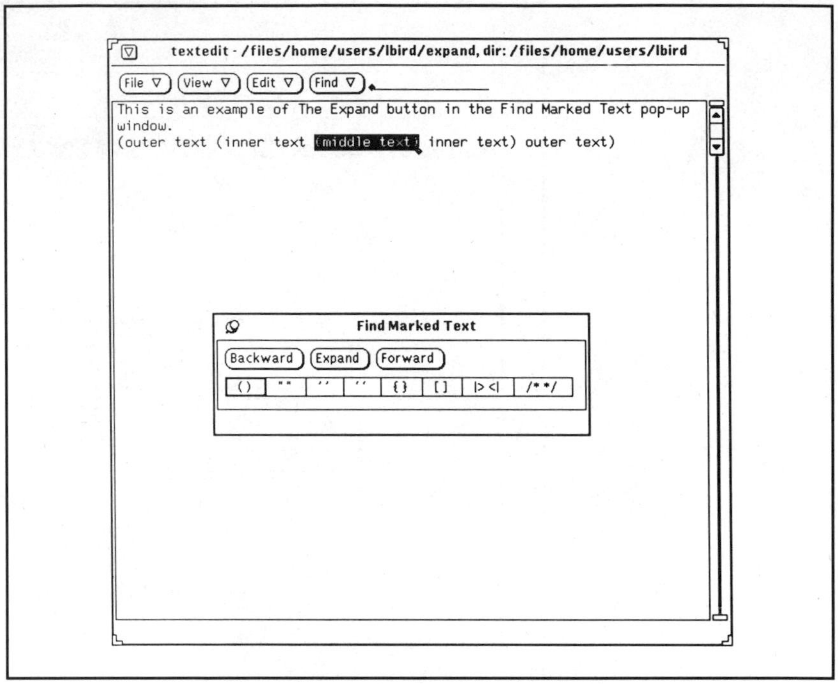

Figure 11.18a: Using the Forward button to select text and delimiters within two sets of nested delimiters

Matching Delimiters

You can quickly select matching delimiters and the text within them by selecting the first delimiter and choosing the **Match Delimiter** option in the **Find** menu. This automatically extends the selection to include the text and matching end delimiter. The delimiters recognized by the **Match Delimiter** option are the same as those provided in the **Find Marked Text** pop-up window, as shown in Figure 11.13. When the beginning and ending delimiters are a matched set (for example, brackets, braces, and parentheses), the **Match Delimiter** option searches forward if the character you select is a beginning delimiter and backward if the character you select is an ending delimiter. If there is no difference between the beginning and the ending delimiter, **Match Delimiter** searches forward.

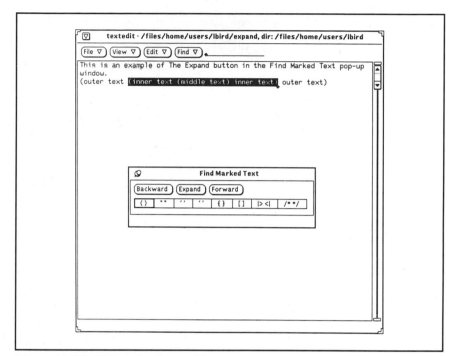

Figure 11.18b: Using the Expand button to expand text and delimiter
selection

Finding and Replacing Fields

The characters **|>** and **<|** act as text field delimiters, used to
indicate fields in a SunOS file. You can search forward through
text from the insert point to find the text of each field and select
them using the **Replace |>field<|** option. Displaying the
Replace |>field<| submenu provides you with three options
explained below:

Option	*Result*
Expand	Searches in both directions and selects the entire field and its delimiters
Next	Searches forward from the insert point and selects the next field

Option	Result
Previous	Searches backward from the insert point and selects the previous field

The Text Pane's Extras Pop-Up Submenu

The Text Pane's **Extras** pop-up submenu provides you with six options that allow you to format, indent, and change the case of text, sort specified fields, insert brackets, or replace slashes. Figure 11.19 shows the **Extras** submenu, and the following briefly describes each of these options:

Options	Results
Format	Divides text into lines of not more than 72 characters. The **Format** option fills and joins lines, but it does not split words between lines. For more information on formatting lines, see Chapter 6.
Shift Lines	Inserts or removes a tab character at the beginning of each line in a selection. Choosing the **Right** option moves the selected lines to the right one tab. Selecting the **Left** option moves the selected lines one tab to the left.

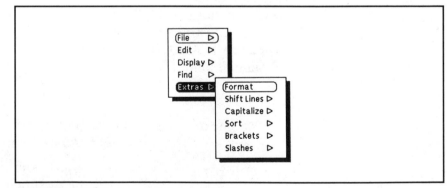

Figure 11.19: The Extras submenu options

Options	*Results*
Capitalize	Changes the case of selected text from lowercase to uppercase (**abcd -> ABCD**), uppercase to lowercase (**ABCD -> abcd**), or capitalizes the first letter of every word in selected text (**abcd -> Abcd**).
Sort	Sorts one of five columns you specify in alphabetical (**Text**) or numerical (**Numeric**) order. The **Text** or **Numeric** submenus display the **Forward** and **Reverse** options to sort the columns in ascending or descending order.
Brackets	Inserts or removes matched parentheses, brackets, curly brackets, or quotation marks (**()**, **[]**, **{}**, or **" "**).
Slashes	The **/to** option changes forward slashes (**/**) to back slashes (****) in selected text. The **\to/** option changes back (**/**) slashes to forward slashes (****) in selected text.

Keyboard Equivalents

The following tables list key combinations and function keys that are keyboard equivalents for mouse operations to erase text, reset the insert point, and perform various editing operations in text panes.

Table 11.1: Erasing Text

Key	**Erases**
Backspace	Character to the left of the insert point
Control-W	Word to the left of the insert point

Table 11.1: Erasing Text (continued)

Key	Erases
Shift-Control-W	Word to the right of the insert point
Control-U	To the beginning of the line
Shift-Control-U	To the end of the line

Table 11.2: Resetting the Insert Point

Key	Movement of Insert Point
Control-B	One character to the left
Control-F	One character to the right
Control-, (comma)	One word to the left
Control-. (period)	To the end of a word
Control-A	To the start of a line
Control-E	To the end of the line
Control-P	Up one line
Control-N	Down one line
Shift-Control-Return	To beginning of text
Control-Return	To end of text

Table 11.3: Stopping, Repeating, or Undoing an Editing Operation

Key	Result
Stop (L1)	Stops current operation
Again (L2)	Repeats previous operation
Undo (L4)	Undoes previous operation

Table 11.4: Copying or Moving Selected Text

Key	Result
Copy (L5)	Copics selected text to the clipboard
Paste (L8)	Copies the clipboard contents beginning at the insert point
Cut (L10)	Cuts selected text and stores it on the clipboard

Table 11.5: Finding and Replacing Selected Text

Key	Result
Find (L9)	Locates selected text to right of insert point
Shift-Find (L9)	Locates selected text to the left of insert point
Control-Find (L9)	Displays the **Find and Replace** pop-up window

Summary

In this chapter you learned how to

- work with the **Shell Tool**, **Command Tool**, and **Console** windows.

- select and save text in a text pane of a **Command Tool**, **Text Editor**, or **Mail Compose** window.

- start and load files in a Text Editor.

- move to a specific line of text in a file.

- create, name, and save text files.

- control the position of the insert point.

- select a word, paragraph, block of text or the entire document.

- copy, move, and delete a text selection.

- split a text pane.

- merge two or more files.

- locate text using the **Find** menu.

- search and replace text.

- search for text between matching delimiters and fields.

CHAPTER 12

Get Organized with the Calendar Manager

THE CALENDAR MANAGER IS A HANDY APPOINTMENT scheduler and reminder application. It allows you to organize and plan your activities on a daily, weekly, monthly, or yearly basis. The Calendar Manager reminds you of upcoming appointments you've entered into it. You can browse through other users' appointment calendars or allow other users to browse through your appointment calendar. The Calendar Manager can automatically notify other users of an upcoming event using SunOS mail features or execute SunOS scripts or commands automatically at a time you specify. This chapter teaches you how to harness the features of this powerful time-management application.

Starting the Calendar Manager

The Calendar Manager is opened by selecting it from the **Workspace Programs** submenu. To display the **Workspace** menu, move the pointer anywhere on the workspace not displaying a window or icon and press the right mouse button. Drag the pointer to the right of the **Programs** option; the **Programs** submenu is displayed. Drag the pointer to highlight the **Calendar Manager** option, then release the right mouse button. The Calendar Manager icon appears, displaying the calendar for the current month with the current date highlighted. Double click the left mouse button on the Calendar Manager icon to display the **Calendar Manager** window, as shown in Figure 12.1.

The Calendar Manager Window

The **Calendar Manager** window's default display is the calendar view of the current month. You can change the default display to show views for the day, week, or year, as explained later in this chapter. When you first display the Calendar Manager, a double-line border surrounds the current day of the month, indicating that it is selected. Appointment information is displayed in the appropriate date box area; this information is usually clipped to accommodate the size of the date box. Each line in a date box is used for separate appointment text. To see additional appointment text, use one of the resize corners to stretch the window vertically or horizontally. Selecting the **Full Size** option from the **Window** menu expands the calendar view to the full size of your screen.

The Calendar Manager Window Control Panel

The control panel of the **Calendar Manager** window displays four menu buttons: **View**, **Edit**, **Browse**, and **Print**.

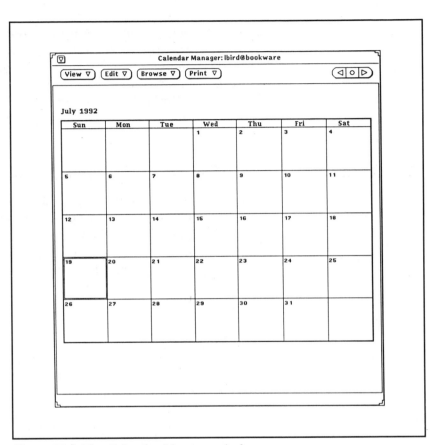

Figure 12.1: The Calendar Manager window

- The **View** menu lets you view the calendar by year, month, week, or day.

- The **Edit** menu contains commands for editing your appointments and customizing your Calendar Manager.

- The **Browse** menu contains commands to access other calendars, such as other users' calendars.

- The **Print** menu allows you to print calendar information for any day, week, month, or year.

In the upper-right corner of the control panel are three navigational buttons that allow you to quickly browse through the preceding or following unit of the calendar view type currently displayed. For example, with the **Month** view displayed, clicking the left mouse button on the left arrow displays the previous month's calendar. Clicking the left mouse button on the right arrow displays the next month's calendar. Clicking the left mouse button on the circle returns you to the current month.

The Four Views of the Calendar Manager

Four different calendar views, **Day**, **Week**, **Month**, and **Year**, are available with the Calendar Manager. The **Day** view, as shown in Figure 12.2, is useful for viewing in detail any appointment information scheduled for a particular day. The **Week** view, as shown in Figure 12.3, displays a weekly calendar that is determined by the date you've selected or the default, which is the calendar for the current week. The **Week** view displays an hourly box schedule with appointment times shaded. The **Month** view (the default) displays appointments from a monthly perspective. The **Year** view, as shown in Figure 12.4, displays a yearly calendar for any year from 1970 through 1999; it doesn't display any appointment information. Appointments entered into any of the calendar views are integrated and displayed into the other calendar views. Entering appointments is done in the same way, regardless of the view you're working with.

Navigating the Views

Several methods are available to navigate calendar views. The following steps explain changing the calendar view using the **View** menu button.

1. Move the pointer onto the **View** menu button and press the right mouse button. The **View** menu is displayed.

2. Drag the pointer to highlight the view you want.

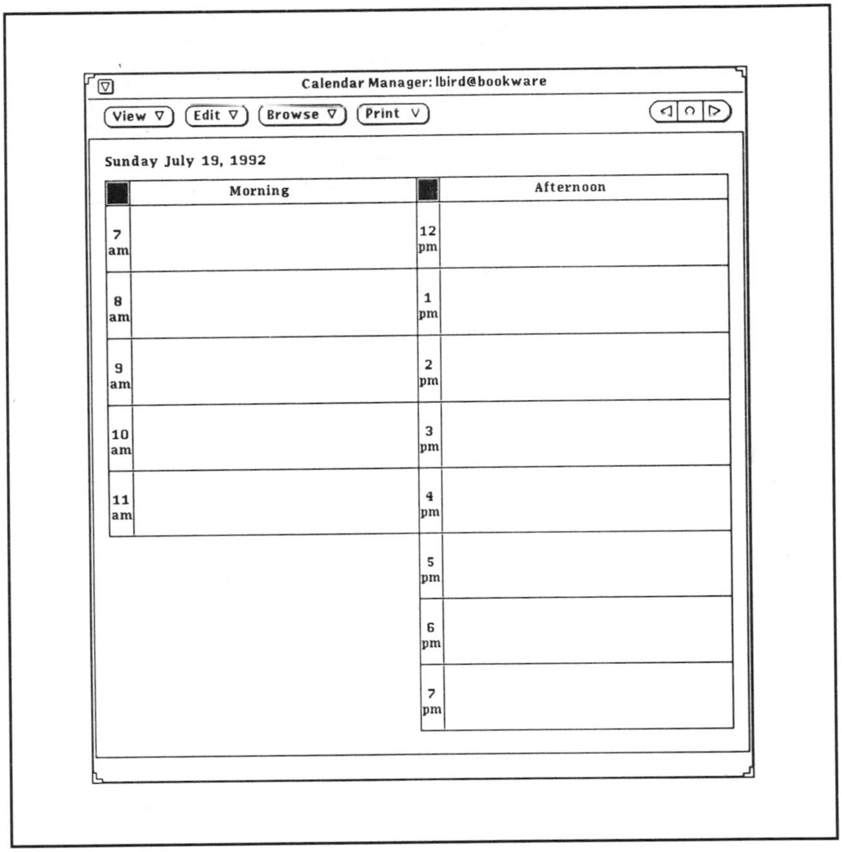

Figure 12.2: The Day view display

3. Release the right mouse button. The view you selected is displayed.

The Calendar Manager provides several shortcuts for quickly accessing the **Week** and **Day** views from the default **Month** view. To access the **Week** view from the **Month** view, move the pointer to any day of the week you want in the **Month** view and click the left mouse button. Now move the pointer to the **View** menu button, press the right mouse button, and drag the pointer to the **Week** option. When you release the right mouse button, the **Week** view is displayed with the day you selected outlined with a double line.

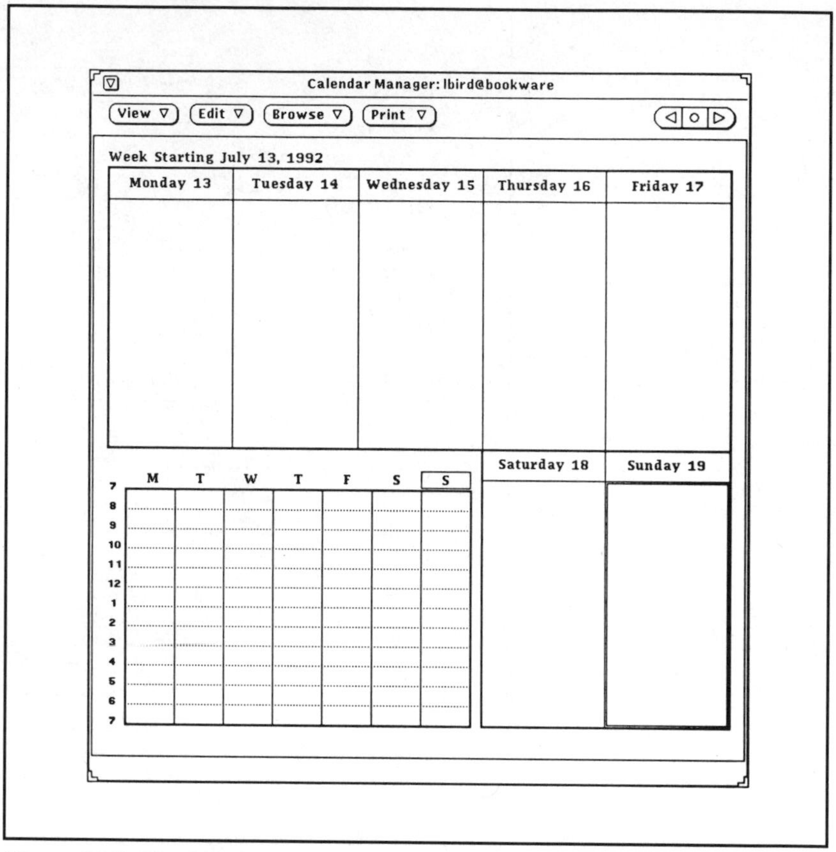

Figure 12.3: The Week view display

To access the **Day** view from the **Month** view, move the pointer to the date you want in the **Month** view, then click the left mouse button to select the date. The date box is now outlined with a double line. Now move the pointer to the **View** menu button and click the left mouse button. The **Day** view is displayed.

To move quickly from the **Year** view to the **Month** view, double click the left mouse button with the pointer on the month you want.

Clicking the left mouse button on the **View** menu button, regardless of the view you're displaying, shows the selected **Day** view.

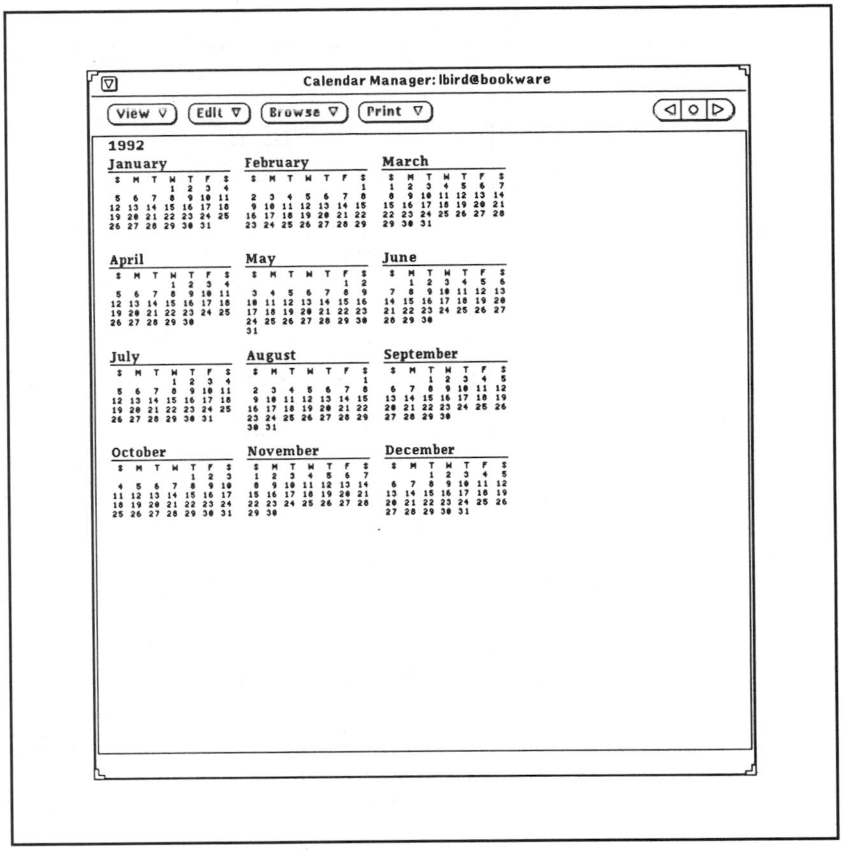

Figure 12.4: The Year view display

Entering Appointments into the Calendar Manager

The **Appointment Editor** pop-up window, as shown in Figure 12.5, is used to enter appointments into the Calendar Manager. Any appointment entered using the Appointment Editor is available in all calendar views. To display the **Appointment Editor** pop-up window, double click the left mouse button on the day you want in either the **Week** or **Month** view. For the **Day** view, double click the left mouse button on the hour you want

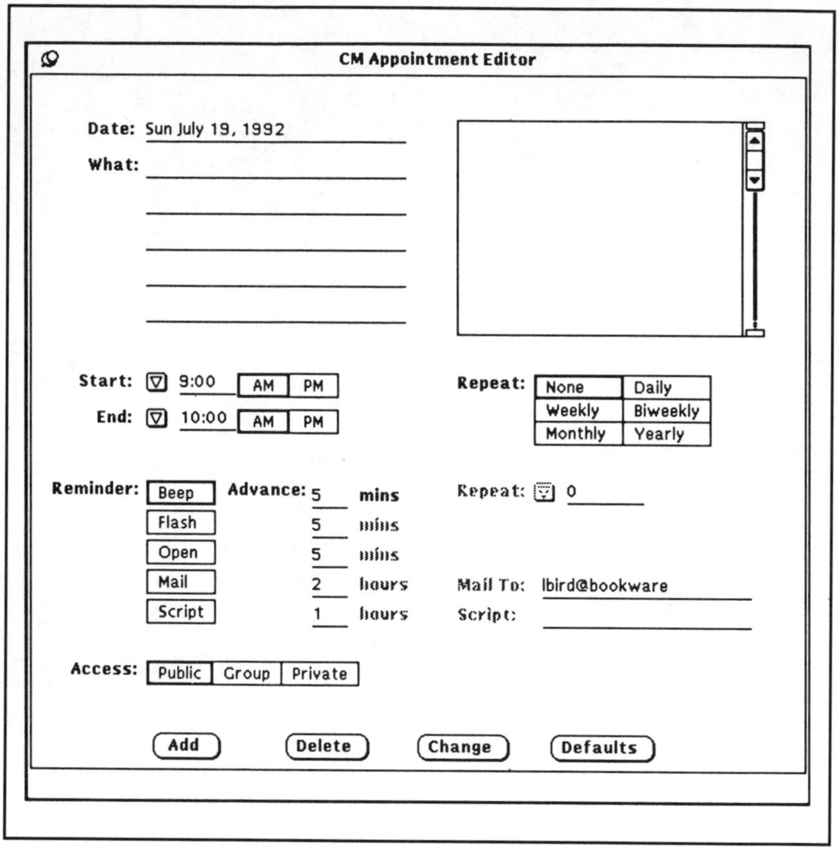

Figure 12.5: The Appointment Editor pop-up window

for the start of your appointment. Moving the pointer to the **Edit** menu button and clicking the left mouse button also displays the **Appointment Editor** pop-up window for the day you selected in either the **Week** or **Month** view or the hour for the **Day** view.

The Appointment Editor Pop-Up Window

The Appointment Editor allows you to enter and set various parameters for your appointments; for example, you can choose the method the Calendar Manager uses to remind you of an appointment. The Appointment Editor includes these features:

- All appointments previously scheduled for the day displayed in the **Appointment Editor** are listed in a scrolling list in the upper-right corner of the window.

- The date you selected is displayed in the **Date** text field. Changing this date adds an appointment for the date you specify.

- You type information about an appointment in the **What** text field. Each line in the **What** text field represents a separate appointment. You are not limited to the displayed space in these fields. If you type in more text than can be displayed in the **What** text field, an arrow button appears on the left side of the text field to indicate there is hidden text. Moving the pointer to the arrow button and clicking the left mouse button scrolls through the hidden text, moving it to the right. As the text moves to the right, another arrow button is displayed on the right side of the **What** text field to indicate there is hidden text to the right.

- The **Start** and **End** text fields allow you to set the time of the appointment. When you set the start time, the Appointment Editor automatically changes the end time to one hour later.

- **Reminder** and **Advance** fields let you determine when and how you will be reminded of an appointment. Use as many of the reminder controls as you like for each appointment.

- The **Mail** reminder allows you to notify yourself or other users of upcoming appointments using SunOS's mail features.

- The **Script** setting lets you run shell scripts or SunOS commands at a specified time.

- The **Repeat** field allows you to determine the frequency of the appointment reminders. If the appointment is a regularly scheduled event, you can be reminded on a regular basis using the parameters you define.

- The **Access** settings let you control accessibility to appointment information for other users allowed to browse through your appointment calendar.

- The **Add**, **Delete**, **Change**, and **Defaults** buttons located at the bottom of the **Appointment Editor** pop-up window allow you to save, delete, or edit existing appointments, or return the Appointment Editor settings to their defaults. Appointments are added using the **Add** button and edits made using the **Change** button.

Changing the Date Field

Appointments can be added for any date you want by entering a new date in the **Date** field. To delete the date in the **Date** field, move the pointer to the beginning of the date text and click the left mouse button to set the insert point. Move the pointer to the end of the date text and press the middle mouse button to select the date. Press the Cut (L10) accelerator key, and the date is deleted from the **Date** text field. Enter the date for which you want to create the new appointment. You can type in a date in any of the following formats:

Format	Example
MM/DD/YY	11/22/90
M/D/Y	1/4/91
Mon. Day, Yr.	Nov 4, 90
Month Day, Year	November 4, 1990
Day, Mon. Day, Year	Sat Nov 4, 1990

You can also enter any of the following in the **Date** text field:

Today

Tomorrow

Yesterday

Next *Weekday*

Last *Weekday*

Next *Month*

Last *Month*

Reminder Setting Options

The **Appointment Editor** provides five reminder settings: **Beep**, **Flash**, **Open**, **Mail**, and **Scripts**.

- The **Beep** setting reminds you of an upcoming appointment with a beeping alarm sound

- The **Flash** setting causes your screen to flash to remind you of an upcoming appointment.

- The **Open** setting displays a **Reminder** pop-up window, as shown in Figure 12.6, to remind you of your upcoming appointment.

- The **Mail** reminder setting allows you to send the appointment reminder via E-mail to yourself or any users on the system.

- The **Script** setting allows you to automatically run a file containing a shell script (a series of commands) or execute a SunOS command line at a specified time.

When you click the left mouse button on the **Mail** reminder setting, the **Mail To** text field located to the right appears in boldface, indicating the field is activated. You then enter the user name or user's E-mail address you want an appointment reminder sent to.

When you select the **Script** setting, the **Script** text field appears in boldface, indicating it is activated, so you can type the name of a file containing an executable script or a SunOS command in the **Script** text field. For example, you could use a script to generate a status report at a fixed time before a regularly scheduled status meeting. The **Script** text field allows you to enter up to 255 characters.

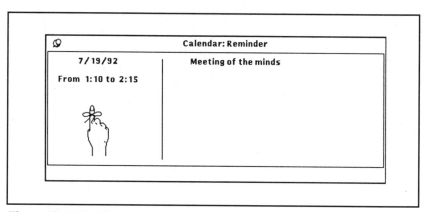

Figure 12.6: The Reminder pop-up window

You can combine reminder settings; for example, the Calendar Manager can remind you of an appointment by beeping, flashing the screen, and sending you a mail message reminder at the same time.

Access Settings

Any time you create or change an appointment reminder, you can specify the accessibility of that appointment information to other users browsing through your Calendar Manager. (Browsing through appointment calendars is explained later in this chapter.) The Appointment Editor provides three access levels.

- The **Public** option allows any user who has browsing access to your calendar to view the appointment information.

- The **Group** option allows any user in a group you specify using the **Calendar Manager Properties** window to access appointment information. Anyone not in the group cannot view appointment information, but instead will see only the word **appointment** and the specified appointment time.

- The **Private** option suppresses all information about an appointment to any user browsing through your Calendar Manager.

The security access settings **Public**, **Group**, and **Private** do not correlate directly with other SunOS file security mechanisms.

These access levels only affect other users' ability to read the contents of your appointments. Regardless of what security you assign to each appointment, any user can enter new or edit existing appointments for your calendar. If somebody has edited or altered an appointment, display the Appointment Editor and select the appointment in the scrolling list; the name of the person who changed the appointment is displayed in the footer of the **Appointment Editor** window.

Creating an Appointment Reminder

To create an appointment reminder, first select the day you want the appointment set for in the **Week** or **Month** view or select the **Hour** in the **Day** view. You can also select a day by simply entering the exact date you want for your appointment in the **Date** text field of the Appointment Editor. With the **Appointment Editor** pop-up window displayed, follow these steps to enter a new appointment:

Remember, each line displayed in the **What** text field is used for a separate appointment entry.

1. In the **What** text field, click the left mouse button to set the insert point. Type the appointment information; you can use up to eighty characters in length. If the text is longer than the space in the **What** text field, an arrow

button appears to the right and/or left of the text field to indicate there is hidden text in the direction of the arrow button. Click the left mouse button on either arrow button to move the line of text in the direction of the arrow button.

2. Move the pointer to the **Start** text field and press the right mouse button on the menu button to display a menu of hour options, as shown in Figure 12.7. Each hour has a submenu with **00**, **15**, **30**, and **45** minute options, which you can use by dragging the pointer to the right of the hour setting you want. After highlighting the start of your appointment, release the right mouse button. You also need to choose the correct a.m. or p.m. setting for your appointment. When you set a start time, the end time is automatically set one hour later. If the appointment is longer than an hour, set a different end time by pressing the right mouse button on the menu button in the **End** field, dragging the highlight to the time you want, and releasing the right mouse button.

The choice of times on the **Time Setting** menu is determined by the **Day Boundaries** settings from the **Properties** window, which can be changed, as explained later in this chapter.

3. Select the reminders for this appointment. You can set as many as you like by clicking the left mouse button with the pointer on the **Reminder** option you want to add. The selected settings and the corresponding **Advance** text field appear in boldface. Move the pointer to the **Advance** setting and click the left mouse button to set the insert point. Enter the amount of advance time for your reminder. If you select either the **Mail To** or **Script** setting, the appropriate text field is activated. In the **Mail To** text field, enter your name or the name of the user you want to send the appointment reminder to. In the **Script** text field, enter the name of the script file containing the commands you want to run.

4. If the appointment is repeated regularly, move the pointer onto the appropriate **Repeat** option (located below the scrollbox) and click the left mouse button.

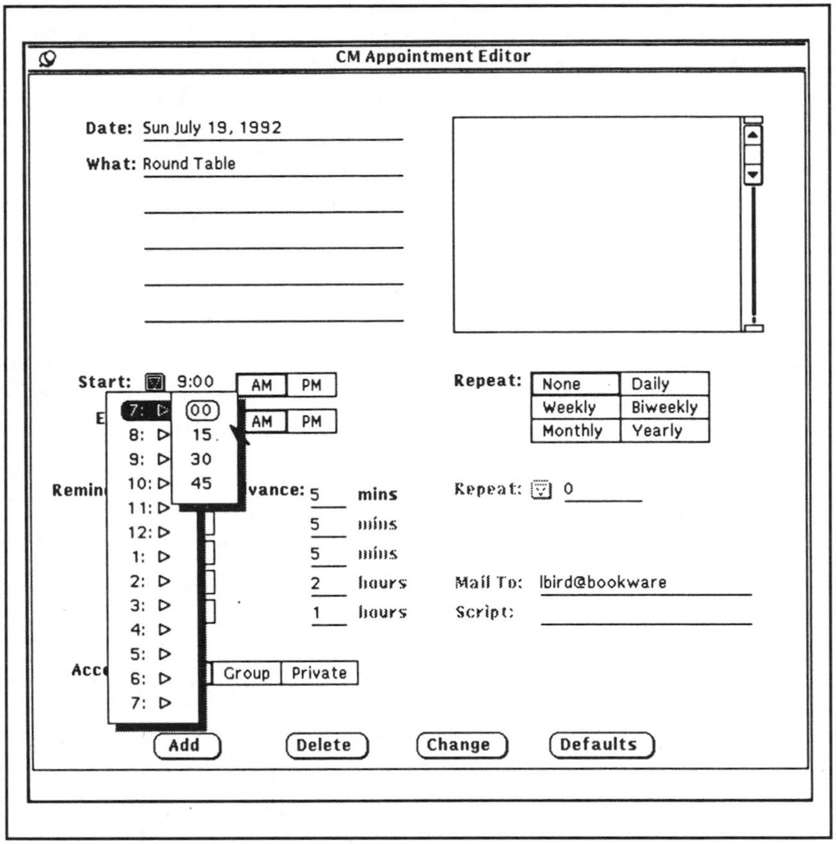

Figure 12.7: The Time Setting menu

When you select a **Repeat** option (other than the default **None**), the **Repeat** text field and menu button are activated. Move the pointer to the **Repeat** menu button and press the right mouse button. Drag the pointer to highlight the reminder frequency setting you want and release the right mouse button; the repeat rate is entered in the **Repeat** text field. For example, to be reminded of a regular weekly meeting for the next four weeks, select the **4** option. The default setting is **forever**.

Remember, **Public** allows everyone access to your appointment information. **Group** allows those in a group you specify access and **Private** allows only your access.

5. Move the pointer to the **Access** settings and select the setting you want. (Browsing through other user's appointment calendars is explained later in this chapter.)

6. When you have entered all the information for the appointment, click the left mouse button with the pointer on the **Add** button. The appointment is added to the scrolling list in the **Appointment Editor** pop-up window as well as to the current calendar view. The **Appointment Editor** pop-up window remains displayed, allowing you to enter another appointment by entering a new date in the **Date** field or adding additional appointments to the current date.

7. When you are finished with the **Appointment Editor** pop-up window, click the left mouse button with the pointer on the push pin or choose the **Dismiss** option from the **Window** menu.

Deleting Existing Appointments

Appointments are constantly being changed or cancelled, so the Calendar Manager makes it easy to remove a scheduled appointment from your calendar. To delete an existing appointment from your Calendar Manager, follow these simple steps:

1. Move the pointer to the date containing the appointment you want to delete. Double click the left mouse button; the **Appointment Editor** pop-up window is displayed.

2. Move the pointer onto the appointment in the scrolling list you want to delete and click the left mouse button. The appointment is highlighted and the appointment information is displayed in the **What** text field. The user name of the person who created the appointment is displayed in the window footer.

3. Move the pointer onto the **Delete** button and click the left mouse button. The appointment is deleted

from both the scrolling list and the calendar view in the **Calendar Manager** window. If you select an appointment with a **Repeat** setting, when you click the left mouse button on the **Delete** button, a dialog box is displayed, as shown in Figure 12.8, asking you if you want to delete the appointment for one or all dates or cancel the operation. Move the pointer to the option you want and press the left mouse button. The appointment is deleted accordingly.

Changing Existing Appointments

If an existing appointment is changed, or you want to edit your appointment information, you update your calendar using

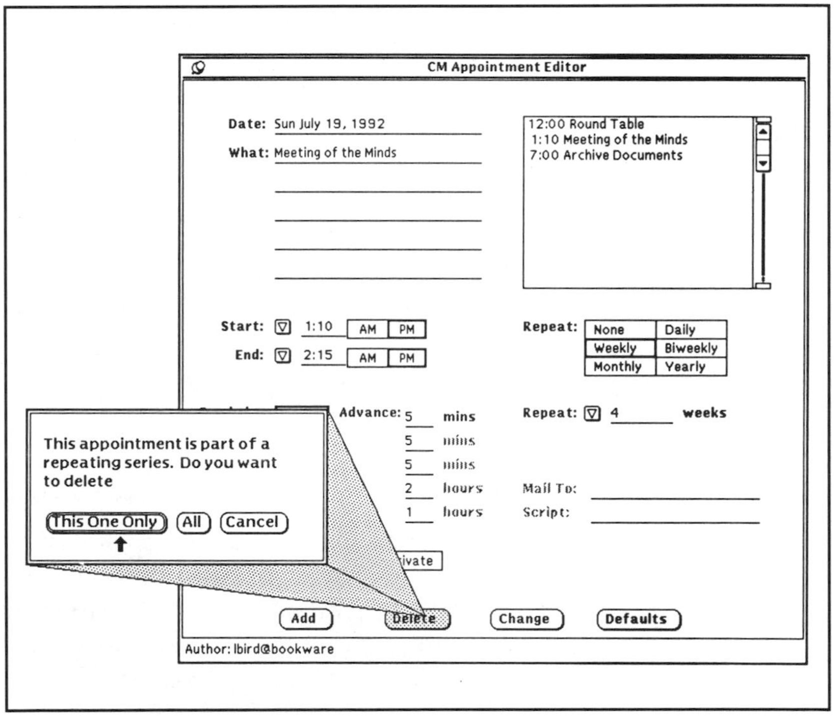

Figure 12.8: The Delete Appointment dialog box

the **Appointment Editor** pop-up window. The following steps explain how to use the Appointment Editor to change existing appointment information:

1. Select an hour from a **Day** view or a day from a **Week** or **Month** view and display the **Appointment Editor** pop-up window. When you have not made a selection, the Appointment Editor displays appointments for the current date.

2. Move the pointer onto the appointment in the scrolling list you want to edit and click the left mouse button. The appointment is highlighted, the appointment information is displayed in the **What** text field, and the author of the appointment is displayed in the window footer.

3. Edit the information describing the appointment or change the time or reminder controls to reflect the new information for the appointment.

4. Move the pointer onto the **Change** button and click the left mouse button. If you made changes to an appointment with **Repeat** settings, a dialog box is displayed asking if you want to change the appointment for the selected date only or for all dates, or cancel the operation. Move the pointer to the option you want and press the left mouse button. The appointment is changed accordingly.

Printing Calendar Views

The Calendar Manager provides you with high-quality printed output for day, week, month, and year views. You set the printer name and options from the **Printer Options** pop-up window, accessed from the **Print** menu, as shown in Figure 12.9. To print the Calendar Manager, choose the view you want to print from the **Print** menu by pressing the right mouse button on the **Print** menu button and highlighting the appropriate option. To change your print options, highlight the **Options** item in the **Print** menu. The **Printer Options** pop-up window is displayed. This pop-up window allows you to specify the destination of the printed output: **Printer** or **File**, the printer name or directory and file name, the width and height of the printed image, and the left and bottom margin position settings. In addition, you can specify the number of time units (day, week, month, year) to print. For example, entering **3** in the **Months** field prints the calendars for the month currently displayed and the next two months. The **Print Options** pop-up window displays the time unit for the view being displayed; for example, Figure 12.9 displays the units as months. Subsequent units print according to the number you enter in this field. The last option is the **Copies** text field, which is accompanied by arrow buttons

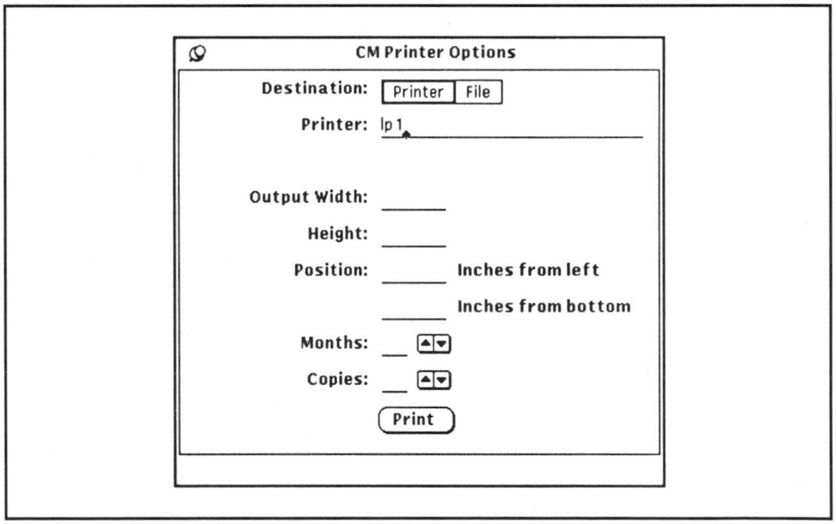

Figure 12.9: The Print Options pop-up window

that allow you to use the left mouse button to specify the number of copies to print.

Clicking the left mouse button with the pointer on the **Print** button in the **Print Options** window prints the view displayed in the **Calendar Manager** window. For example, if you are displaying appointments for a day, choosing **Print** prints a day view. When you change the settings from the **Printer Options** pop-up window, they become the new default printer settings until you quit the Calendar Manager.

Printing any of the four Calendar Manager views is done in the same way. You simply need to specify the calendar view you want. The printed appointment calendars match their screen counterparts. The following explains printing appointment calendars for a day, week, month, or year:

Day Choose the **Day** option from the **Print** menu. To print appointments for a day other than the current one, move the pointer onto the day you want to print and click the left mouse button. Then choose the **Day** option from the **Print** menu.

Week Choose the **Week** option from the **Print** menu. To print appointments for a week other than the current one, move the pointer onto the week you want to print and click the left mouse button. Then choose the **Week** option from the **Print** menu.

Month Choose the **Month** option from the **Print** menu. To print appointments for a week other than the current one, move the pointer onto the month you want to print and click the left mouse button. Then choose the **Month** option from the **Print** menu.

Year   Choose the **Year** option from the **Print** menu. To print a year other than the current one, select the **Year** view and use the arrow buttons in the upper-right corner to change to the year you want to print. Then choose the **Year** option from the **Print** menu. The **Year** option allows you to print two different calendars, the standard and alternate calendars. The standard year option, labeled **(Std)**, is similar to the on-screen version, as shown in Figure 12.10. The alternate year option, labeled **(Alt)**, prints the year calendar with each day denoted by a small box, as shown in Figure 12.11.

Browsing through Other Users' Calendars

Anyone can add appointments to another user's Calendar Manager the same way appointments are added to their own calendar, regardless of the user's access settings.

The Calendar Manager gives you access to the appointment schedules of other users as well as allowing other users to view your appointments. This convenient feature enables users to coordinate scheduling of appointments. For example, individual users can access an appointment calendar to coordinate scheduling of conference rooms. Remember, you can view specific appointment information only if the owner has granted access permission.

You browse through other users' calendars by first moving the pointer to the **Browse** button and pressing the right mouse button to display the **Browse** menu. Initially the **Browse** menu options include a **Browse** pop-up window and your login and machine name. You can add additional user names to the **Browse** menu temporarily or permanently.

1992

7/19/92 1:43 am   lbird@bookware

				January			
S	M	T	W	T	F	S
				1	2	3	4
5	6	7	8	9	10	11
12	13	14	15	16	17	18
19	20	21	22	23	24	25
26	27	28	29	30	31	

February

S M T W T F S
                        1
2 3 4 5 6 7 8
9 10 11 12 13 14 15
16 17 18 19 20 21 22
23 24 25 26 27 28 29

March

S M T W T F S
1 2 3 4 5 6 7
8 9 10 11 12 13 14
15 16 17 18 19 20 21
22 23 24 25 26 27 28
29 30 31

April

S M T W T F S
            1 2 3 4
5 6 7 8 9 10 11
12 13 14 15 16 17 18
19 20 21 22 23 24 25
26 27 28 29 30

May

S M T W T F S
                  1 2
3 4 5 6 7 8 9
10 11 12 13 14 15 16
17 18 19 20 21 22 23
24 25 26 27 28 29 30
31

June

S M T W T F S
      1 2 3 4 5 6
7 8 9 10 11 12 13
14 15 16 17 18 19 20
21 22 23 24 25 26 27
28 29 30

July

S M T W T F S
            1 2 3 4
5 6 7 8 9 10 11
12 13 14 15 16 17 18
19 20 21 22 23 24 25
26 27 28 29 30 31

August

S M T W T F S
                        1
2 3 4 5 6 7 8
9 10 11 12 13 14 15
16 17 18 19 20 21 22
23 24 25 26 27 28 29
30 31

September

S M T W T F S
            1 2 3 4 5
6 7 8 9 10 11 12
13 14 15 16 17 18 19
20 21 22 23 24 25 26
27 28 29 30

October

S M T W T F S
                  1 2 3
4 5 6 7 8 9 10
11 12 13 14 15 16 17
18 19 20 21 22 23 24
25 26 27 28 29 30 31

November

S M T W T F S
1 2 3 4 5 6 7
8 9 10 11 12 13 14
15 16 17 18 19 20 21
22 23 24 25 26 27 28
29 30

December

S M T W T F S
            1 2 3 4 5
6 7 8 9 10 11 12
13 14 15 16 17 18 19
20 21 22 23 24 25 26
27 28 29 30 31

Year view by **Calendar Manager**

Figure 12.10: Printed standard year view

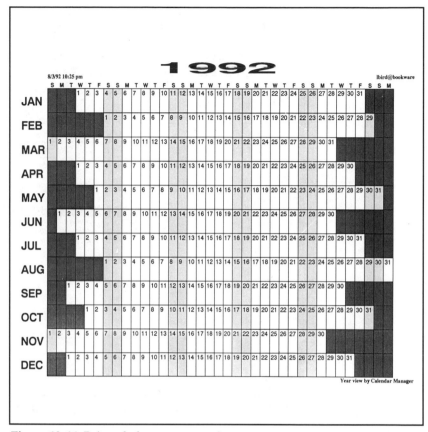

Figure 12.11: Printed alternate year view

Temporarily Adding Other Users to the Browse Menu

Temporarily adding another user's appointment calendar to the **Browse** menu is accomplished using the **Browser** pop-up window. User names you add using the **Browser** pop-up window remain on the **Browse** menu until you quit the Calendar Manager or delete them using the **Delete** button in the **Browser** pop-up window. To display the **Browser** pop-up window, move the pointer to the **Browse** menu button and click the left mouse button. The **Browser** pop-up window is displayed as shown in

Figure 12.12. The Browser scrolling list shows all the user names from the **Browse** menu, whether you added them from the **Properties** window or the **Browse** window. To temporarily add a user's calendar to the **Browser** menu, select the **Browse** option from the **Browse** menu and follow the steps below.

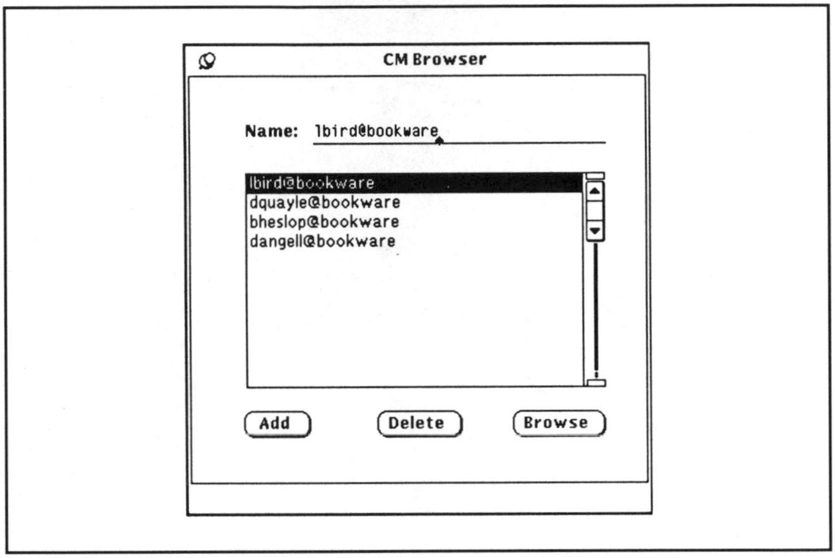

Figure 12.12: The Browser pop-up menu

1. With the **Browser** pop-up window displayed, move the pointer to the **Name** text field and click the left mouse button to set the insert point.

2. Type the user name you want to add to the **Browse** menu.

3. Move the pointer onto the **Add** button and click the left mouse button or press Return. The user name is added to the scrolling list and to the **Browse** menu.

By highlighting a user name in the scrolling list, then clicking the left mouse button on the **Delete** button, you can delete user names you have added in the **Browser** pop-up window. The user name is also removed from the **Browse** menu.

Browsing through Another User's Calendar

Once a user name has been added to the **Browse** menu, you can display another user's Calendar Manager and view his or her appointment information, depending on the access settings the user set. The following explains how to view another user's Calendar Manager:

1. Move the pointer to the **Browse** menu button. Click the left mouse button with the pointer on the **Browse** menu button to display the **Browse** pop-up window.

2. Move the pointer onto the **Browse** menu button and click the left mouse button to display the **Browser** pop-up window and select the name of the user whose calendar you want to browse. You can also press the right mouse button on the **Browse** menu button and drag the pointer to highlight the user name you want and release the right mouse button. In either case, the Calendar Manager for the user you requested is displayed.

If the Calendar Manager cannot find the user name or access the appointments for that user, an error message is displayed in the window footer. Otherwise the Calendar Manager displays the user name in the header of the **Calendar Manager** window. To change back to your own calendar, choose your user name from the **Browse** menu.

Customizing the Calendar Manager

You can customize your Calendar Manager settings by changing the Appointment Reminder default settings, defining day boundaries, changing the default calendar view, permanently adding user names to the **Browse** menu, and defining the group access using the Calendar Manager's **Properties** pop-up window, as shown in Figure 12.13. To display the **Properties** pop-up window, first move the pointer to the **Edit** menu and

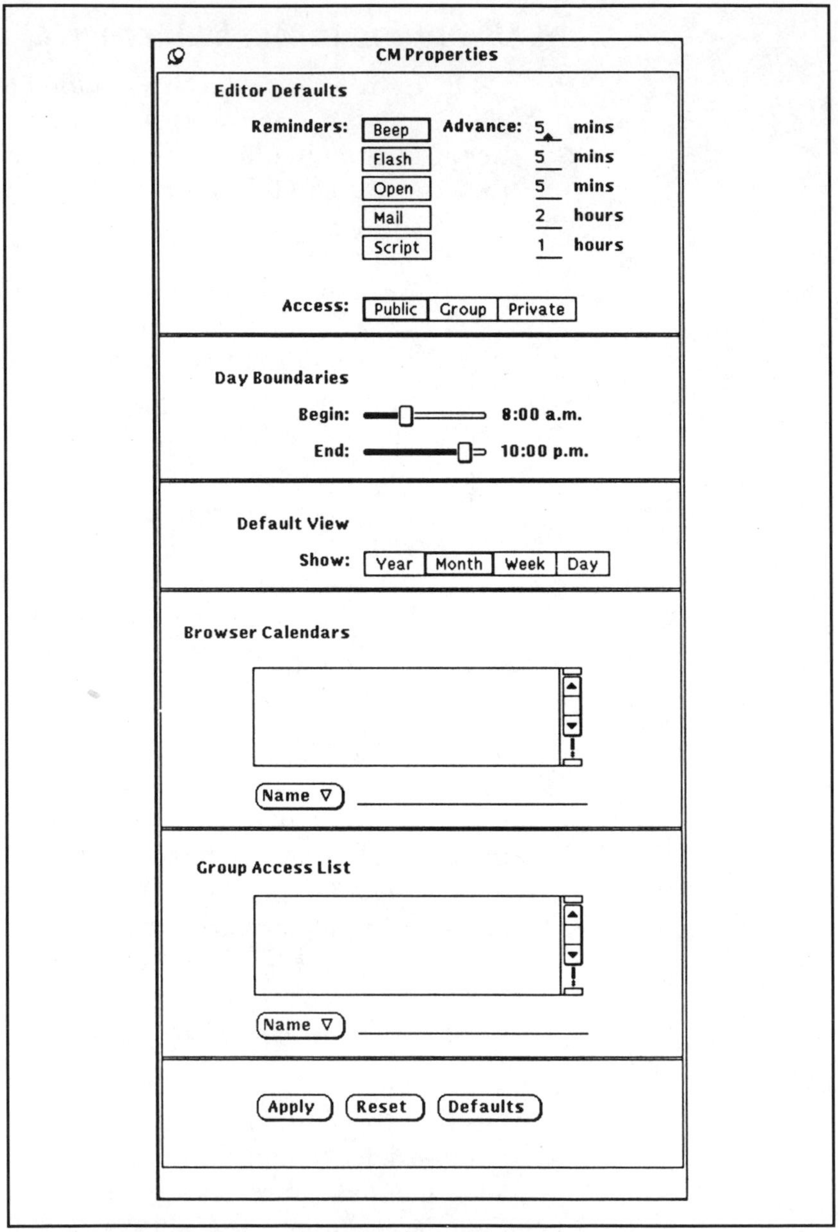

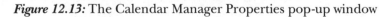

Figure 12.13: The Calendar Manager Properties pop-up window

press the right mouse button. Drag the pointer to highlight the **Properties** option and release the right mouse button.

There are three buttons at the bottom of the **Properties** window.

- The **Apply** button is used to save current changes made to the **Properties** window.

- The **Reset** button restores the original properties settings you had before you made changes in the current session.

- The **Defaults** button restores all your Calendar Manager property settings to default settings.

Changing Appointment Reminder Defaults

Changing the **Reminders** settings in the **Editor Defaults** box does not affect any appointments already scheduled using the previous default choices.

The **Properties** pop-up window allows you to specify which of the five available **Reminders** options are selected automatically when you activate the **Appointment Editor** pop-up window. To select one or more **Reminders** setting(s), move the pointer to the **Reminders** option(s) you want and click the left mouse button. Note that the corresponding **Advance** text field(s) appears in boldface, indicating that you can change the default advance time for that **Reminders** option(s). To enter a new time, move the pointer to the appropriate **Advance** text field and click the left mouse button to set the insert point. Type in a new number. After making changes to the **Editor Defaults**, click the left mouse button on the **Apply** button, and the new defaults are saved and become effective immediately. Make sure you always click the left mouse button on the **Apply** button before leaving the **Properties** window and quitting to save your changes.

Changing Appointment Access Defaults

To change the default **Access** setting from **Public** to either **Group** or **Private**, move the pointer to the appropriate setting and click the left mouse button. As explained earlier in this chapter, this setting affects which users can view your appointment information. Choosing the **Private** option restricts anyone from viewing your appointment information. The **Group** option allows only users designated in the **Group Access List** setting in the **Properties** window. Any user not designated in the **Group Access List** sees only a message that an appointment exists, but cannot view the specific appointment information when browsing through your Calendar Manager. Choosing the **Public** option allows any user who has access to your Calendar Manager to view your appointment information.

Changing Day Boundaries

To specify the range of hours for both the **Day** view and the **Start** and **End** time setting options in the **Appointment Editor** pop-up window, use the **Day Boundaries** option in the **Properties** pop-up window. This option allows you to define your working hours for appointments. For example, if your normal working hours are 9 a.m. to 5 p.m., you would select 9 a.m. as your **Start** boundary and 5 p.m. as your **End** boundary. To change the **Day Boundaries** setting, follow these steps:

1. Move the pointer to the slider drag box and press the left mouse button.

2. Drag the pointer to the left or to the right. Note the time changes as you drag the slider. The pointer is locked onto the drag box as long as you keep the left mouse button pressed.

3. When the time you want is displayed, release the left mouse button. You can add or subtract an hour by moving the pointer to the right of the drag box to increase the time and the left of the drag box to decrease the time and clicking the left mouse button.

You cannot set a day boundary that ends before it begins. For example, you can't enter 9:00 a.m. in the **Start** time text field and 8:00 a.m. in the **End** time text field. If the values overlap, the **Start** and **End** drag boxes move together in the direction that otherwise would create an impossible set of values.

4. Once the **Day Boundaries** have been set, click the left mouse button with the pointer on the **Apply** button to save your settings. The changes take effect immediately.

Changing the Default Calendar View

As explained earlier in the chapter, the **Month** view is displayed by default when you open the Calendar Manager. You can change this default view to **Day**, **Week**, or **Year**. To change the default view, click the left mouse button with the pointer on the **Default View** setting you want and then click the left mouse button on the **Apply** button. The change takes effect immediately.

Permanently Adding User Names to the Browse Menu

Using the **Browser** pop-up window in the Calendar Manager allows you to temporarily enter user names to the **Browse** menu to access other users' Calendar Managers. Using the **Browser Calendars** option in the **Properties** pop-up window, you can enter user names to the **Browse** menu permanently (unless you delete them). New user names are displayed in both the **Browse** menu and the **Browser** pop-up window in the order entered. To add user names, perform the following steps:

1. Move the pointer to the **Name** text field and click the left mouse button to set the insert point.

2. Type the user name you want to add to your **Browse** menu.

3. Move the pointer to the **Name** button and click the left mouse button to add the name. The user name is added to the scrolling list.

4. To add additional user names, delete the previous text and type in another user name. Then click the left mouse button on the **Name** menu button.

To delete a user name, move the pointer to the user name you want to delete in the scrolling list and click the left mouse button to select it. Move the pointer to the **Name** menu button and press the right mouse button. Drag the pointer to the **Delete** option and release the right mouse button. The user name is not deleted from the **Browse** menu until you quit the Calendar Manager and start it again.

User names you add or delete using the **Browser Calendars** option are not automatically displayed in the **Browse** menu because the Calendar Manager only looks at the list when you start it. To display your changes as part of the Calendar Manager, quit and restart the application. In addition, the Calendar Manager does *not* check to be sure the user name entered in the **Properties** window is valid or that appointment information is available for that user name. The Calendar Manager checks this when you choose the user name from the **Browse** menu.

Creating a Group Access List

Restricting access to appointment information to a specific group of users is a simple operation. You specify the users that you want to grant access to by entering their user names in the **Group Access List** option in the **Properties** pop-up window. When you choose the **Group** setting in the **Access** field in the Appointment Editor, any users included on the Group Access List can view all of the information about that appointment. Users who are not included on the Group Access List can see that you have an appointment scheduled for a specific block of time, but cannot see the specific information about the appointment. Adding and deleting user names in the Group Access List is done in the same way you added names in the **Browser** and **Properties** pop-up windows.

Summary

In this chapter you learned how to manage your appointments using the Calendar Manager, including how to:

- Navigate the Calendar Manager views for **Day**, **Week**, **Month**, and **Year**

- Enter, edit, or delete appointments in the Calendar Manager using the **Appointment Editor** pop-up window

- Print your appointment calendar for the day, week, month, or year

- Browse through other users' appointment calendars and allow other users access to your appointment calendar

- Change appointment reminders, such as sending yourself a mail message to notify you of an upcoming appointment

- Set the day boundaries to match your work schedule

- Add users to your **Browse** menu

- Add or delete users to a group access list to determine which users can browse through your appointment information

CHAPTER 13

More DeskSet Applications

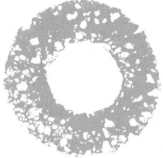

TO EXTEND YOUR MASTERY OF THE DESKSET, THIS chapter covers these DeskSet applications:

- The Print Tool, which prints your files

- The Snapshot application, which allows you to take pictures of part of or the entire screen

- The Clock, which displays the current time and date

- The Performance Meter, which allows you to monitor the performance of your system

- The Calculator, which enables you to perform mathematical calculations

- The Icon Editor, which allows you to create your own file icons

All the applications in this chapter can be started in the same manner as tools you have used previously—display the **Work-space** menu, press the right mouse button, and drag the pointer to highlight the name of the application in the **Workspace Programs** submenu. When you release the right mouse button, the application is started.

The Print Tool

The Print Tool makes printing easy by providing you with a friendly user interface that lets you send files to the printer. The Print Tool allows you to print files by either typing the file name of the file to be printed in the **File** text field or by dragging and dropping files from the File Manager. You can also drag and drop a mail message header from the Mail Tool or the contents of a **Text Editor** window into the Print Tool for printing. The Print Tool allows you to specify the printer you want to use, the number of copies you want to print, and the file format of the file you want to print. The status of your print jobs in the print queue can be quickly displayed and specific or all printing jobs stopped. The **Print Tool** window is shown in Figure 13.1. Clicking the right mouse button on the window menu button in the upper-left corner of the **Print Tool** window closes it to an icon.

Printing a File

To print an ASCII file using the default settings in the **Print Tool** window, first type the complete pathname of the file in the **File** text field. The default **None** option in the **Filter** setting is for ASCII file formats. Move the pointer to the **Copies** text field, press the left mouse button to set the insert point, and enter the number of copies you want to print by typing a number in or clicking the left mouse button on the arrow (increment/ decrement) buttons. Moving the pointer to the **Print** button and clicking the left mouse button sends your file to the printer queue. One of the following printing status messages is displayed in the window footer; **Printing** *filename*, which indicates that your print request is printing, or **(n) Print Job(s) Submitted**, which indicates your print request is waiting in a queue to be printed.

To print a file using the drag and drop method, follow the steps below:

1. Select one or more files from the File Manager or one or more mail message headers from the Mail Tool header pane.

2. Press the Control key on the keyboard, and then press the left mouse button. Release the Control key.

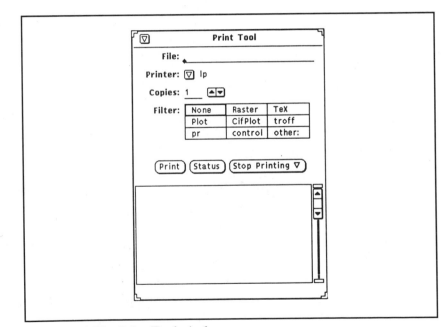

Figure 13.1: The Print Tool window

3. Drag the selected file(s) or mail message header(s) onto the **Print Tool** window and release the left mouse button to drop the file(s). The file name(s) is automatically entered in the **File** text field, and a message indicating the status of your print request is displayed in the footer of the window.

Choosing Another Printer

The Print Tool automatically displays the default printer indicated by the **/etc/printcap** file. Other printers available to you in the **/etc/printcap** file are listed on the **Printer** menu. To choose another printer, follow the steps below:

1. Move the pointer to the **Menu** button next to the **Printer** label.

2. Press the right mouse button. The **Printer** menu is displayed.

3. Drag the pointer to highlight the name of the printer you want to choose.

4. Release the right mouse button. The name of the new printer you choose is displayed to the right of the **Printer** menu button.

Checking the Print Queue Status

Clicking the left mouse button on the **Status** button lets you view a list of print jobs in the print queue. When there are no entries, the message **No Entries** is displayed in the footer. When there are entries in the print queue, the list of all the jobs for that printer (not just your jobs) is displayed in the scrolling list in the lower part of the **Print Tool** window, as shown in Figure 13.2.

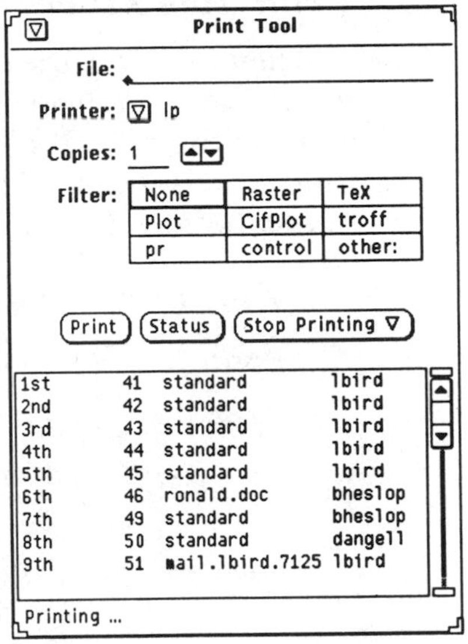

Figure 13.2: Jobs in the Print Queue

Stopping Printing Jobs

When you stop printing one or more print jobs, the Print Tool does not accept further input until the printer acknowledges the request. Depending on the number of jobs selected and the status of the printer queue, it may take several minutes for the printer to respond to your request.

The Print Tool allows you to stop printing all your jobs in the job queue by choosing the **All Print Jobs** option from the **Stop Printing** menu. To stop specific printing jobs, follow the steps below:

1. Click the left mouse button with the pointer on the **Status** button to display jobs in the print queue.

2. Move the pointer to the job in the scrolling list you want to stop and click the left mouse button. To stop more than one job at a time, move the pointer to the additional jobs you want to stop and click the middle mouse button.

3. When you have selected the jobs you want to stop, move the pointer to the **Stop Printing** button and press the left mouse button.

Print Tool Filters

When the file you are printing has a print filter added, the filter format is automatically chosen and displayed when you drop a file on the Print Tool or type its file name in the **Print Tool** window and click the left mouse button with the pointer on the **Print** button. The filters are explained below:

The **None** and **troff** settings are provided as part of the standard SunOS installation. The other filters shown here may be provided as part of other printer installations.

Filter Option	Description
None	Default filter setting for ASCII file formats
Plot	For files produced by plot
pr	Prints pages headed by date, file name, and page number
Raster	For raster images, such as screen dump or SunPaint files
CifPlot	For files produced using CifPlot
control	Interprets the first character of each line as a standard FORTRAN carriage control character
TeX	For documents formatted using the TeX formatting utility
troff	For files containing **troff** commands
other:	For printing a file with another print method. Displays a text field for typing any command line print method, including SunOS pipes. This text field accepts three variables. The **$FILE** variable substitutes the name of the specified file in the print script. The **$PRINTER** variable substitutes the name of the printer currently selected in the Print Tool. The **$COPIES** variable substitutes the number of copies currently specified in the **Copies** text field.

The Snapshot Application

The Snapshot application allows you to take black-and-white, gray-scale, and color snapshots of a region (a section of the screen), a window, or the entire screen. These snapshots are created and stored as raster files. *Raster files* represent a picture as a matrix of dots. When you use Snapshot on a monochrome monitor, the snapshots created are always black and white. When you take snapshots on a color monitor, the snapshots are always in color. Some applications can handle black-and-white snapshots but cannot handle gray-scale or color snapshots. For example, using the SunView DeskSet File Manager, the **Content** option in the **Folder Display** submenu of the **View** menu allows you to preview contents of black-and-white raster files in the folder pane. It cannot, however, preview the contents of gray-scale or color raster files. The **Snapshot** window is shown in Figure 13.3. Clicking the right mouse button with the printer on the window menu button in the upper-left corner of the **Snapshot** window closes it to an icon.

The Snapshot Window

The Snapshot application stores the files it creates in the directory specified in the **Directory** text field and gives them

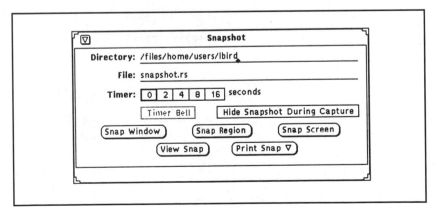

Figure 13.3: The Snapshot window

the names specified in the **File** text field. It uses your current working directory and a file named **snapshot.rs** as defaults. (It is a good idea to use a common suffix for raster file names to make it easier for you to manage them as a group.)

Snapshot has a timer to set the time period between initiating the snapshot and taking it. The timer is especially useful if you are taking snapshots of menus that you must display after you start the snapshot, or if you want to be sure the pointer is at a specific location when the snapshot is taken. When the **Timer** is set to 0 seconds, the snapshot is taken immediately. When the timer is set for more than 0 seconds, the **Timer Bell** option is activated and can be set. By clicking the left mouse button with the pointer on a **Timer Bell** setting, a bell beeps each second between the time when you initiate the snapshot and when it is taken. Clicking the left mouse button on the **Timer Bell** setting acts as a toggle, setting it on or off.

The **Hide Snapshot During Capture** setting allows you to hide the **Snapshot** window when you're taking a snapshot of the screen. The **View Snap** button allows you to view your snapshots after they are taken. The **Print Snap** button lets you print your snapshots and provides a pop-up window to customize your printer settings. Snapshot also provides three buttons for creating snapshots:

- **Snap Window** takes a snapshot of a single window.
- **Snap Region** takes a snapshot of part of the screen.
- **Snap Screen** takes a snapshot of the entire screen.

Taking a Snapshot of a Window

To take a snapshot of a window, make sure the window or icon you want to capture is completely visible and not partly obscured by overlapping windows (unless you want to include them in the snapshot) and follow the steps below:

1. Type the name of the directory in which you want to save the file and the file name you want to use for the snapshot in the **Directory** and **File** text fields at the top of the **Snapshot** window.

2. Set the **Timer** and **Timer Bell** settings if you want to use them. When you have the timer set and are taking snapshots of windows or icons, Snapshot records the window position when the snap is initiated. However, if you move the window before the snapshot is completed, you may not get all the information you wanted in the window snapshot.

3. Click the left mouse button with the pointer on the **Snap Window** button. If a file with the name you have specified already exists in that directory, a dialog box is displayed, asking for confirmation before overwriting the file. The **Snap Window** button appears shaded, indicating it is working, and an information message is displayed in the footer.

4. Move the pointer into the header of the window you want to snap and click the left mouse button to start the snapshot. To cancel the operation, click either the middle mouse button or the right mouse buttons. When the snapshot is complete, a message is displayed in the footer of the snapshot window, revealing whether the snapshot succeeded or not. If the snapshot was successful, it also displays the size of the raster file. You can view the snapshot using the **View Snap** button, as explained later.

Taking a Snapshot of a Region

Snapshots of any rectangular area of the screen you specify can be taken using the **Snap Region** button. Before taking a snapshot of a region of the screen, make sure the screen is displaying the windows or icons you want to capture, and perform the following steps:

1. Type the path of the directory and the file name you want to use for the snapshot in the **Directory** and **File** text fields at the top of the Snapshot base window.

2. Set the **Timer** and **Timer Bell** settings if you want to use them.

3. Click the left mouse button on the **Hide Snapshot During Capture** option if you need to.

4. Click the left mouse button on the **Snap Region** button. A message appears in the window footer: **Select: Draw Box. Adjust: Snap. Menu: Cancel. Select** means to click the left mouse button. **Adjust** means to click the middle mouse button. **Menu** means to click the right mouse button.

5. Move the pointer to the corner of the region you want to define and press the left mouse button. Drag the pointer to define the rectangular region to be included. A bounding box is displayed. Release the left mouse button. An outline of the snapshot region is displayed.

6. Click the middle mouse button. Snapshot takes the snapshot of the boxed region of the screen and displays a message in the Snapshot window footer indicating whether the snapshot was successful. If the snapshot succeeded, the size of the raster file is also displayed. If you want to cancel the snapshot, click the right mouse button.

Taking a Snapshot of the Screen

Taking a snapshot of the entire screen is the easiest type of snapshot to take; however, it takes longer and takes more disk space to store. If you don't need the entire screen, it is recommended you use the **Snap Window** or **Snap Region** option. To take a snapshot of the entire screen, make sure the screen is set up in the configuration you want and follow these steps:

1. Type the path of the directory and the file name you want to use for the snapshot in the **Directory** and **File** text fields at the top of the **Snapshot** window.

2. Set the **Timer** and **Timer Bell** settings if you want to use them.

3. Click the left mouse button on **Hide Snapshot During Capture** unless you want the **Snapshot** window in the screen shot.

4. Click the left mouse button with the pointer on the **Snap Screen** button. After the snapshot is taken an information message telling you whether the snapshot was successful or not is displayed in the window footer. If the snapshot was successful, the size of the raster file is also displayed.

Hiding the Snapshot Window during Capture

When taking a snapshot, the Snapshot application allows you to hide the **Snapshot** window so that it is not included in the screen shot. To hide the **Snapshot** window, click the left mouse button with the pointer on the **Hide Snapshot During Capture** setting before taking the snapshot.

Viewing a Snapshot

The Snapshot application allows you to view a snapshot (raster) file at any time by typing the directory and the name of the file in the **Directory** and **File** text fields and clicking the left mouse button with the pointer on the **View Snap** button. A pop-up window is displayed, as shown in Figure 13.4, showing the contents of the snapshot file. To view a snapshot immediately after taking it, simply click the left mouse button on the **View Snap** button. Snapshot automatically converts a copy of gray-scale or color images to black and white so that gray-scale or color snapshots can be displayed on a black-and-white monitor. The file itself is not changed.

Only one snapshot at a time can be viewed, unless you load and use multiple snapshot applications. When the **View Snap** pop-up window is displayed, and you type a new snapshot file name in the **File** text field and click the left mouse button with the pointer on the **View Snap** button, the **View** window is reused and automatically resizes to match the size of the second snapshot file.

Printing a Snapshot

Snapshot files can be printed by clicking the left mouse button on the **Print Snap** button. If you want to change the default printing settings, press the right mouse button with the pointer

Figure 13.4: View of a snapshot using the **View Snap** button

on the **Print Snap** button and drag the pointer to the **Options** option. The **Print Options** pop-up window is displayed, as shown in Figure 13.5, allowing you to change your printer settings for Snapshot. You can designate whether a snapshot is sent to a printer or to a file. When the **Printer** option is selected, use the text field to specify which printer you want to use. When the **File** option is selected, the **Directory** and **File** text fields are displayed.

Choose the orientation of the printed image on the page by clicking the left mouse button with the pointer on the **Upright** setting to print a portrait image, or click the left mouse button with the pointer on the **Sideways** setting to print a landscape image.

Margins for the printed image can be changed from ¼ inch at the left and bottom by typing new values in the **Position** text fields. The width of the printed image on the page can be specified by choosing **Scale** and typing a value, either whole number or decimal, in the **Width** text field. The image is automatically scaled proportionate to the width you select. When you click the left mouse button on the **Size** setting, a **Height**

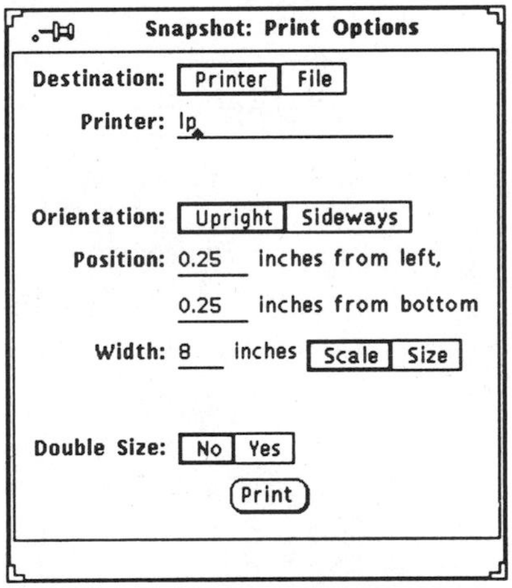

Figure 13.5: The Print Options pop-up window

text field is displayed, allowing you to specify an absolute height for the image to fit into. A file can be printed in the size you specify or printed in a doubled size using the **Double Size** option.

Clicking the left mouse button on the **Print** button prints the file specified in the **File** field of the **Snapshot** window. Once you change the settings in the **Print Options** pop-up window, they are recorded and used each time you click the left mouse button on the **Print Snap** button until you exit or quit the **Snapshot** window.

Pixels are the smallest display element on a video screen. A pixel is made up of one or more dots. On a color monitor the dots that make up a pixel are energized to different intensities. The intensity of gray-scale and color raster files are commonly referred to as being "eight-bits deep" and black-and-white raster files as being "one-bit deep."

Only black-and-white raster files can be filtered and printed on a standard laser printer. Eight-bit images can be converted to one-bit images using the **rasfilter8to1** command. To convert a raster file, open a Command Tool and at the system prompt enter

```
rasfilter8to1 input_filename output_filename
```

For example, to convert **snapshots.rs** to a one-bit deep raster file named **snapshot.81**, enter

```
rasfilter8to1 snapshot.rs snapshot.81
```

Both files can be viewed using the **View Snap** button, but only the **snapshot.81** file can then be sent to a filter (such as the PostScript filter, **pssun**) and be printed using a PostScript laser printer.

The Clock Application

The Clock application displays an analog clock icon that shows the current time of day, as shown in Figure 13.6. When you open the Clock icon, the same clock is displayed in the pane of a window. The **Clock** window has a header and resize corners to make the clock image larger or smaller.

Customizing the Clock

The Clock can be customized using the settings in the **Clock Properties** window. To display the **Clock Properties** window, move the mouse pointer into the Clock pane and press the right mouse button. The **Clock Properties** pop-up window is displayed, as shown in Figure 13.7.

Choosing the **Digital** option and clicking the left mouse button with the pointer on the **Apply** button changes the display in the window to a digital clock, as shown in Figure 13.8. (The icon always displays an analog clock, regardless of the

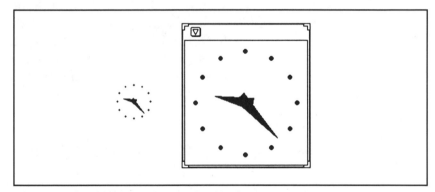

Figure 13.6: A Clock window and a Clock icon

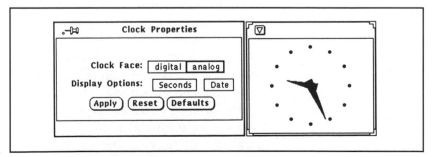

Figure 13.7: The Clock Properties pop-up window

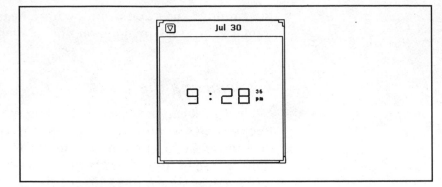

Figure 13.8: The Digital Clock display

Clock Face property setting.) Choosing the **Seconds** option displays a seconds hand on the analog clock or numbers indicating seconds on the digital clock.

Choosing the **Date** option displays the date in the header of the **Clock** window but does not affect the icon display. Clicking the left mouse button on the **Reset** button returns the clock properties to their previous settings. Clicking the left mouse button with the pointer on the **Defaults** button returns the settings to the system default settings.

The Performance Meters

The DeskSet environment provides ten different Performance Meters that can be used to monitor the various aspects of your system. One or a combination of these meters can be run (displayed) at the same time.

The **Performance Meters** option in the **Workspace** menu has a submenu of the four most frequently used Performance Meter options, as shown in Figure 13.9. If you want to display a Performance Meter, select the **Performance Meters** option from the **Programs** submenu of the **Workspace** menu.

The default **CPU Performance Meter** window is displayed at the size of a typical icon. Moving the pointer to the window header and clicking the right mouse button closes the meter window to display an active speedometer-like gauge. Figure 13.10 shows both a closed and open Performance Meter.

The needles in the Performance Meter icon move as system conditions change. The short needle, referred to as an hour hand, tracks average performance over a 20-second interval, and the long one, referred to as the second hand, tracks current performance over a 2-second interval. To change these default times, use the **Performance Meter Properties** pop-up window described later in this chapter. The performance option being measured is shown in the lower-left corner of the icon and its maximum value is shown in the lower-right corner.

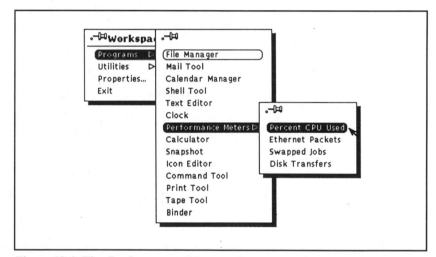

Figure 13.9: The Performance Meters submenu options

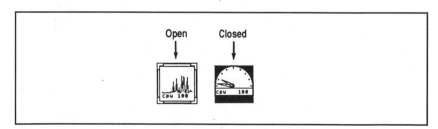

Figure 13.10: An open and closed Performance Meter

The Performance Meter Pop-Up Menu

You can quickly change the performance value to be monitored from any **Performance Meter** window using a **Performance Meter** pop-up menu. First move the pointer to an open **Performance Meter** window and press the right mouse button to display a pop-up menu of the ten available Performance Meter options, as well as a **Properties** option for customizing the Performance Meter. Drag the pointer to select the option you want to change to, then release the right mouse button. The **Performance Meter** pop-up menu is displayed as shown in Figure 13.11. The following is a brief description of what each of the ten options on this menu monitors:

Option	*Monitors*
Show CPU	Percent of CPU being used
Show Packets	Number of ethernet packets per second (*Ethernet packets* are units for transmitting messages over a network.)
Show Page	Paging activity in pages per second
Show Swap	Number of jobs swapped per second

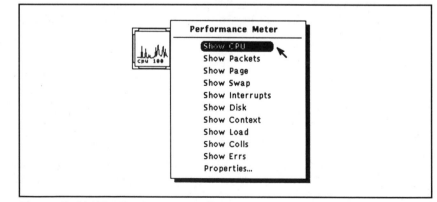

Figure 13.11: The Performance Meter pop-up menu

Option	*Monitors*
Show Interrupts	Number of job interrupts per second
Show Disk	Disk traffic in transfers per second
Show Context	Number of context switches per second
Show Colls	Number of collisions per second detected on the ethernet
Show Errs	Number of errors per second on receiving packets

Customizing Performance Meters

The last option in the **Performance Meters** pop-up menu, labeled **Properties**, allows you to customize the features of a particular Performance Meter option. Selecting the **Properties** pop-up window displays a **Perfmeter: Properties** pop-up window, as shown in Figure 13.12.

Choosing one of the **Monitor** settings and clicking the left mouse button with the pointer on the **Apply** button is the same as choosing one of the same options from the **Performance**

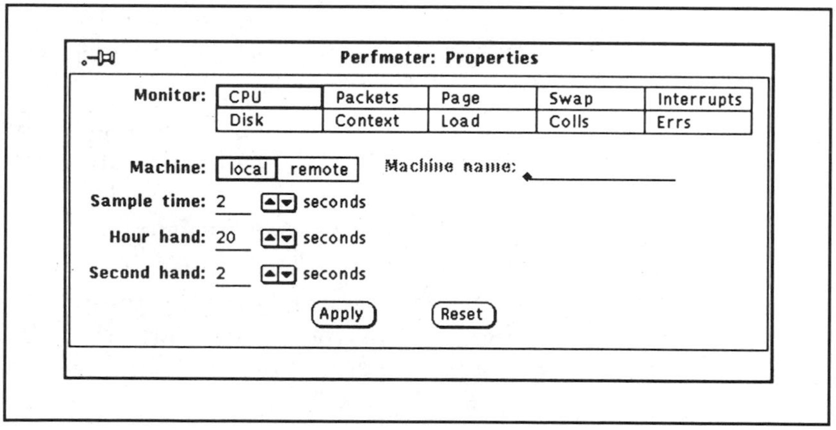

Figure 13.12: The Perfmeter: Properties pop-up window

Meter pop-up menu. The **Machine** setting allows you to monitor the performance for your own machine (**local**, which is the default) or for another machine (**remote**) on the network. If you select the **remote** setting, a **Machine name** text field is activated to enter the name of the machine you want to monitor. The **Sample Time** setting allows you to change the frequency with which the meters are updated and the units measured by the hour hand and the second hand on the icon speedometer.

If you change the values of any of the performance meter properties, you need to click the left mouse button with the pointer on the **Apply** button to record the changes. Pressing the left mouse button with the pointer on the **Reset** button returns all settings to the system defaults.

The Calculator

The Calculator is a powerful scientific calculator designed to perform a variety of mathematical functions. It looks and works in much the same way as many hand-held calculators. The Calculator allows you to use decimal, binary, octal, or hexadecimal numbers as well as scientific notation. Numbers can be stored in ten different memory registers and easily retrieved and replaced. In addition, functions you create can be stored in a menu.

The Calculator window is shown in Figure 13.13. Clicking the right mouse button on the window menu button on the upper-left corner of the **Calculator** window closes it to an icon.

Notice that the **Calculator** window does not have resize corners or a control area—this is because the buttons of the calculator are the controls that activate its functions. It has twelve rows of buttons, some arranged as buttons within other buttons, to emulate a typical calculator. The top and bottom of each button activates a particular function or feature when you click the left mouse button with the pointer on it. Buttons that have a menu mark (the upside-down triangle) display menus when you move the pointer on them and press the right mouse button.

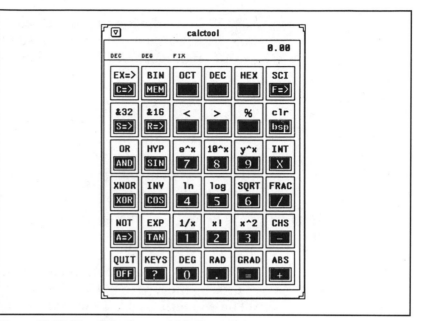

Figure 13.13: The Calculator window

Performing Simple Calculations

While the DeskSet Calculator is a powerful, scientific calculator, it allows you to perform simple arithmetic operations, such as addition, subtraction, division, and multiplication. To perform a numerical operation, such as adding two numbers together, follow the steps below:

1. Move the pointer to the number you want to enter first and click the left mouse button. Numbers can also be entered using the keyboard. The number is entered in the calculator's display in the upper-right corner.

2. Move the pointer to the operation button you want and click the left mouse button; for example, move the pointer to the plus sign (+) to add a number.

3. Move the pointer to the next number you want and click the left mouse button.

4. Move the pointer to the equal sign (=) and click the left mouse button. The result is displayed in the upper-right corner, below the window header.

Modes of Operation

The Calculator has three modes of operation: number bases, trigonometric bases, and notation (fixed point or scientific). The area below the header of the Calculator displays the current mode.

Number Bases

Binary, octal, decimal, and hexadecimal number bases can be set using the keys in the top row labeled **BIN**, **OCT**, **DEC**, and **HEX**. The numeric keypad changes to display those numbers appropriate to the number base mode you choose. To choose a number base, move the pointer to the appropriate Calculator key and click the left mouse button. The keypad layout changes accordingly. The following list gives a brief description of each of the number bases using the calculator. Figure 13.14 identifies the binary, octal, decimal, and hexadecimal keypads.

Number Base	Displays
BIN	Binary (base 2) displays the digits 0 and 1
OCT	Octal (base 8) displays the digits 0 through 7
DEC	Decimal (base 10) displays the digits 0 through 9 keypad
HEX	Hexadecimal (base 16) displays the digits 0 through F

Trigonometric and Notation Bases

Trigonometric bases for degrees, radians, and gradients can be set using the keys **DEG**, **RAD**, and **GRAD** in the bottom row of the keypad.

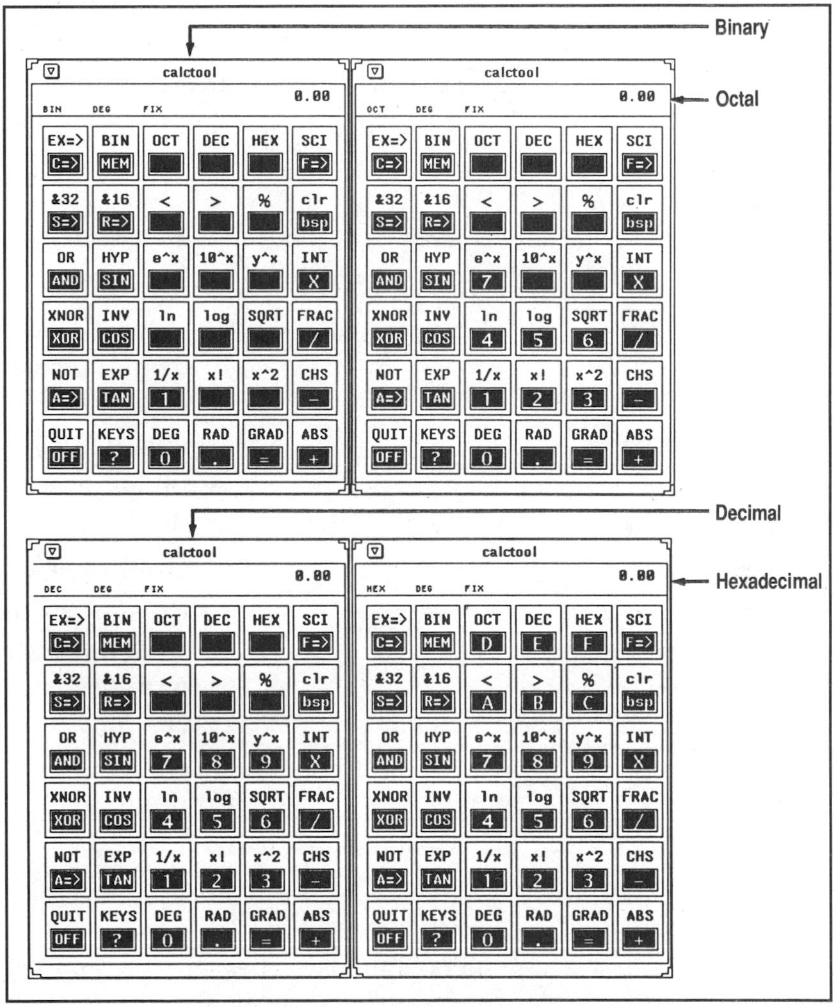

Figure 13.14: The binary, octal, decimal, and hexadecimal keypads

The results can also be displayed in either fixed point or scientific notation using the toggle keys labeled **SCI** or **FIX** in the upper-right corner. When the notation is fixed, the label on the key is **SCI**. When the notation is scientific, the label on the key is **FIX**.

Miscellaneous Functions

The following list describes additional Calculator function keys:

Key	Description
CLR (Clear)	Clears the value from the display
BSP (Backspace)	Removes the rightmost character from the current display and recalculates its value
AC (Accuracy)	Chooses the number of digits of precision used in the Calculator display
QUIT	Quits the Calculator
KEYS	Changes the display of the keys to show the keyboard equivalents for mouseless operation of the Calculator
ASCII	Displays the ASCII value of the character in the appropriate numeric base

Memory Registers

The Calculator has ten memory registers that can store and retrieve values for calculations. Registers are a handy way of storing calculation results for future computations. These memory registers can be accessed using the following keys:

Memory Register	Description
EX (Exchange registers)	Exchanges the value shown in the current display with a selected register number from the pop-up menu
MEM (Memory)	Displays a pop-up window showing values of the ten memory registers in the current base to the current accuracy
ST (Store)	Stores the current value in the memory register number you choose from the pop-up menu
RT (Restore)	Retrieves a value from the memory register number you choose from the pop-up menu

The following steps take you through storing and retrieving register values.

1. Move the pointer to the number you want to store as a register value and press the left mouse button. The number appears in the Calculator's display area.

2. Move the mouse pointer to the **ST** (store) button at the beginning of the second row of keys. Press the right mouse button and drag the pointer to highlight the register you want to store the number in.

3. Release the right mouse button. The number is now stored as the register value you selected. To view the stored register value, move the pointer to the **M** (memory) key, the second key in the top row, and press the left mouse button.

4. To retrieve the register value you just stored, move the pointer to the **RT** (retrieve) key and press the right mouse button. Drag the pointer to highlight the register value to retrieve and release the right mouse button.

User-Defined Functions

The Calculator allows you to enter your own set of constants and define your own functions using the **CN** (constant) and **FN** (function) keys. Each of these keys contains a menu. Choosing the first item on the menu displays a pop-up window that lets you enter the name of a constant or a function and its value. Once you enter the number by clicking the left mouse button at the bottom of the pop-up window, the number and its name are displayed as an item on the pop-up menu. To use the constant or the function, choose the appropriate item from the pop-up menu. The numbers you enter are stored in a **.calc-toolrc** file in your home directory. To edit or delete items from the **Constant** or **Functions** menus, you must edit the **.calctoolrc** file using vi or any other text editor. The following example describes how to create and use a function which, when chosen, determines the circumference of a circle.

1. Move the pointer onto the **FN** key (in the upper-right corner) and press the right mouse button.

2. Highlight **Enter Function** and release the right mouse button. The **Enter Function** pop-up window is displayed.

3. Place the pointer in the **Name** text field and press the left mouse button to set the insert point. Type a function name in the **Name** field, for example, **circum**.

4. Press Return to move the insert point to the **Value** field.

5. Type a function into the **Value** field. To create a function to determine the circumference of a circle, for example, enter **3.14159 d ***.

6. Move the pointer on the **New Function** button and click the left mouse button to store the new function in your **.calctoolrc** file and add it to the **Functions** menu.

7. Move the pointer on the **FN** (Function) key and press the right mouse button. Move the pointer to highlight the function **3.14159 d * [circum]** option. Releasing the mouse button displays **3.14** with a multiplication sign below it, indicating the next number you enter will be applied to the function.

8. Enter a number using the mouse or the keyboard to indicate the diameter of the circle you want to determine the circumference of and either press Return or move the pointer to the **=** (equals) key and click the left mouse button.

Number Manipulation Functions

The Calculator provides the following number manipulation functions:

%	Calculates the percentage of the last number entered and the next number given
INT	Returns the integer portion of the currently displayed value
FRAC	Returns the fractional portion of the currently displayed value
CHS	Changes the arithmetic sign of the currently displayed value or the exponent being entered
ABS	Returns the absolute value of the currently displayed value

Logical Functions

The Calculator provides the following logical functions:

Logical Function	Description
OR	Performs a logical OR operation on the last number and the next number entered, treating both numbers as unsigned long integers
AND	Performs a logical AND operation on the last number and the next number entered, treating both numbers as unsigned long integers
XNOR	Performs a logical XNOR operation on the last number and the next number entered, treating both numbers as unsigned long integers
XOR	Performs a logical XOR operation on the last number and the next number entered, treating both numbers as unsigned long integers
NOT	Performs a logical NOT operation on the current displayed value

Trigonometric Functions

The Calculator provides the following trigonometric functions:

Key	Description
HYP	Sets or unsets the hyperbolic function flag. This flag affects SIN, COS, and TAN trigonometric functions.

Key	Description
SIN	Returns the trigonometric sine, arc sine, hyperbolic sine, or inverse hyperbolic sine of the current value, depending on the setting of the **HYP** and **INV** flags. The result is displayed in the current units (degrees, radians, or gradients).
INV	Sets and unsets the inverse function flag. This flag affects **SIN**, **COS**, and **TAN** trigonometric functions.
COS	Returns the trigonometric cosine, arc cosine, hyperbolic cosine, or inverse hyperbolic cosine of the current value, depending on the settings of the HYP and **INV** flags. The result is displayed in the current units (degrees, radians, or gradients).
TAN	Returns the trigonometric tangent, arc tangent, hyperbolic tangent, or inverse hyperbolic tangent of the current value, depending on the setting of the **HYP** and **INV** flags. The result is displayed in the current units (degrees, radians, or gradients).

Logarithmic and Exponential Functions

The Calculator provides the following logarithmic and exponential functions:

Key	Description
e^x	Returns e raised to the power of the currently displayed value
10^x	Returns 10 raised to the power of the currently displayed value
yx	Raises the last number entered to the power of the next number entered

Key	Description
`ln`	Returns the natural logarithm of the currently displayed value
`log`	Returns the base 10 logarithm of the currently displayed value
`EXP`	Starts exponential input. Any numbers entered after you choose **EXP** are displayed exponentially. If no numerical input has occurred, a mantissa of 1.0 is assumed.
`SQRT`	Returns the square root value of the currently displayed value
`1/x`	Returns the current value of 1 divided by the currently displayed value
`x!`	Returns the factorial of the currently displayed value
`x2`	Returns the square of the currently displayed value

Bit-Masking and Shifting Functions

The Calculator provides the following bit-masking and shifting functions:

Key	Description
`&32`	Truncates the number displayed to return a 32-bit, unsigned integer
`&16`	Truncates the number displayed to return a 16-bit, unsigned integer
`<` (followed by a digit between 0 and 9)	Shifts the displayed binary value the designated number of places to the left

Key	Description
> (followed by a digit between 0 and 9)	Shifts the displayed binary value the designated number of places to the right

The Icon Editor

The Icon Editor allows you to create your own icon images. Your icons can be displayed in the File Manager by binding them to applications and data files using the Binder application.

The **Draw** pop-up window feature, which appears when you first start the Icon Editor, is explained later. The **Icon Editor** window, as shown in Figure 13.15, has a control panel containing **File**, **View**, and **Edit** menu buttons, a preview area that displays the final image size of the icon you are creating in the pane, and the canvas area you use to create your icon. Clicking the right mouse button with the pointer on the window menu button in the upper-left corner of the **Icon Editor** window closes it to an icon.

The **Draw** pop-up window is automatically displayed when you start the Icon Editor.

The Edit Menu

The **Edit** menu button provides you with the four editing options: **Undo**, **Draw**, **Invert**, and **Clear**, as shown in Figure 13.16. To display the **Edit** menu, press the right mouse button with the pointer in the icon canvas area, or place the pointer on the **Edit** button and press the right button. Drag the pointer to the option you want and release the right mouse button. To keep the menu displayed, press the right mouse button and drag the pointer over the push pin towards the hole to the direct left of the push pin.

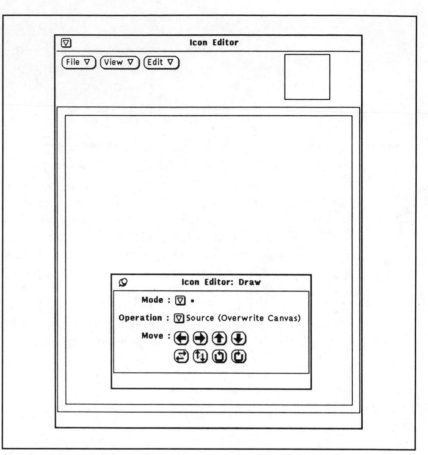

Figure 13.15: The Icon Editor window

The Undo Option

The **Undo** option in the **Edit** menu allows you to undo the last editing action performed on the canvas. Choosing **Undo** a second time undoes the undo, restoring the canvas to its condition before you chose **Undo**.

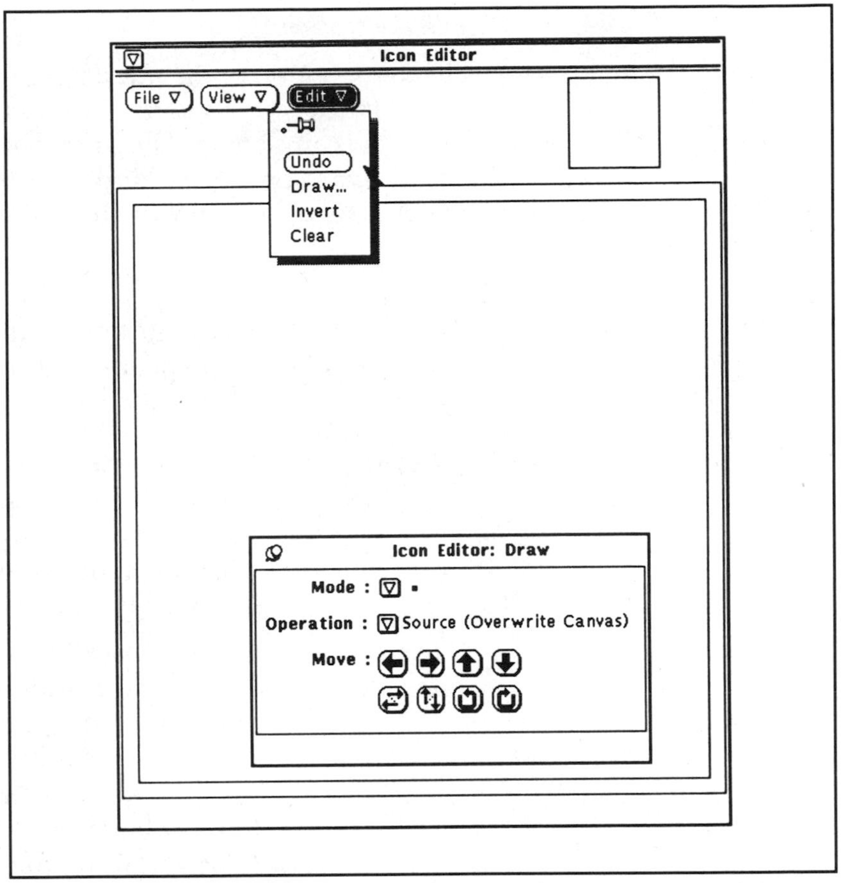

Figure 13.16: The Edit Menu

The Invert and Clear Options

Choosing the **Invert** option from the **Edit** menu allows you to display a reverse video image of an icon image. All pixels (picture elements) turned off are turned on, and all pixels turned on are turned off. The image can be deleted by choosing the **Clear** option from the **Edit** menu. No confirmation dialog box is displayed. If you change your mind, immediately choose the **Undo** option from the **Edit** menu.

The Draw Option

The **Draw** option of the **Edit** menu button displays the **Draw** pop-up window, which contains controls for drawing an icon image in the canvas area. The **Draw** pop-up window includes the **Mode**, **Operation**, **Move**, and possibly **Fill** menu buttons, which provide options for the Icon Editor's drawing tools.

The Mode Menu   Pressing the right mouse button with the pointer on the **Mode** menu button displays available drawing modes. The following explains each mode option and how to use it:

Point	Click the left mouse button to insert one black pixel at the spot of the pointer on the canvas. Point to a black pixel and click the middle mouse button to turn the pixel from black to white.
Line	Draws a black line one pixel wide. To draw a line, position the pointer at one end of the line, press the left mouse button, drag the pointer to the other end of the line, and release the left mouse button. A white line can be drawn in the same way using the middle mouse button.
Square	Draws open or filled squares (or rectangles) using any of the fill patterns from the **Fill** menu. Position the pointer at one of the squares, press the left mouse button, drag the pointer to the opposite corner of the square or rectangle, and release the left mouse button. A white rectangle can be drawn in the same way using the middle mouse button.

Circle	Draws open or filled circles using any of the fill patterns from the **Fill** menu. Position the pointer at the center of the circle and press the left mouse button, drag the pointer to the outside radius of the circle, and release the left mouse button. A white line circle can be drawn in the same way using the middle mouse button.
Ellipse	Draws open or filled ellipses using any of the fill patterns from the **Fill** menu. Position the pointer at the center of the ellipse and press the left mouse button, drag the pointer to the outside radius of the ellipse, and release the left mouse button. If you define a horizontal or vertical line, the ellipse is interpreted as a straight line. A white line ellipse can be drawn in the same way using the middle mouse button.
Region (rectangle outlines)	Defines a rectangular region on the canvas that you can move, flip, or rotate by clicking the left mouse button on any of the **Move** buttons
Text	Displays a pop-up window that allows you to type text to be displayed in your icon

You cannot fill previously drawn squares, circles, and ellipses.

The Fill Menu The **Fill** menu is only displayed when you select a square, circle, or ellipse from the **Mode** menu. The **Fill** menu, shown in Figure 13.17, allows you to choose one of ten fill patterns for squares, circles, ellipses, or irregular shapes. To create and fill squares, circles, or ellipses, first select a **Fill** option from the **Fill** menu *before* using the draw mode. You cannot fill previously drawn squares, circles, and ellipses.

The first option in the **Fill** menu, an open square, allows you to create an outline (unfilled) of the shape selected in the mode menu. You define the area of the square, circle, or ellipse by pressing the left mouse button and dragging it. When you

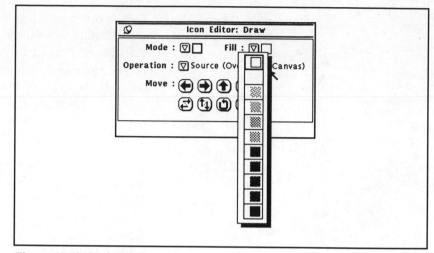

Figure 13.17: The Fill menu

release the left button, a border appears. The other options represent patterns, from white to black, that create filled squares, circles, or ellipses. Remember, you can click the middle mouse button to erase a black pixel in any area you have filled.

Adding Text to an Icon

Adding text to an icon is a simple operation. First choose the **Text** option from the **Mode** menu and a **Text** pop-up window is displayed. To add text to the canvas, do the following:

1. Move the pointer to the **Font** button, press the right mouse button, and drag the pointer to the font you want to use. Figure 13.18 shows the **Font** options in the Text pop-up window.

2. Move the pointer to the **Size** button, press the right mouse button, and drag the pointer to the font size you want.

3. Move the pointer to **Text** text field and type the text you want to add to your icon.

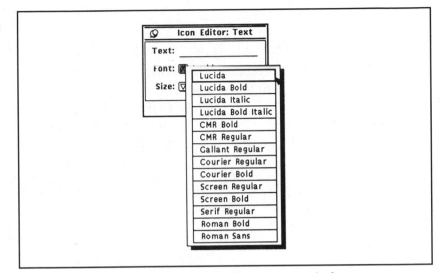

Figure 13.18: The Font options of the Text pop-up window

4. To insert your text in the icon, move the pointer onto the canvas, and press the left mouse button. A rectangle is displayed that shows the size of the text to be inserted. You can move the rectangle anywhere within the canvas to position it as long as you continue to press the left mouse button.

5. When the pointer is positioned correctly, release the left mouse button. The text is added to the canvas. White text can be typed on a dark background in the same way using the middle mouse button. Once you have added text to the canvas, it can be edited as you would any other part of the image.

The View Menu

The **Grid** option of the **View** menu allows you to display a grid background for your canvas. Figure 13.19 shows an example of the canvas with the grid turned on and set to the default grid setting.

The **Size** option provides four canvas sizing options based on pixel measurements. The standard canvas size is 64-by-64 pixels. The other canvas size options are 48-by-48 pixels, 32-by-32 pixels (the default size for icons that can be used with File Manager data file icons), and 16-by-16 pixels. The canvas size is centered in the **Icon Editor** window.

If you change the size of the canvas when an icon file is loaded, or load an icon into a different canvas size, the file is read from the upper-left corner. Larger images are cropped to fit the existing size of the canvas, but the full image is still available. The canvas

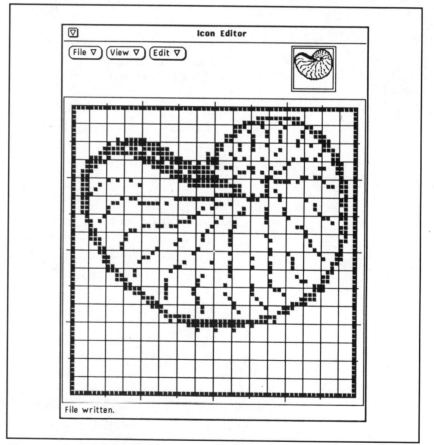

Figure 13.19: The Icon Editor with the Grid option turned on

can be changed to a larger size without losing data as long as you do not move the image. If you move the image, data outside the canvas is lost.

The **Preview Window** option from the **View** menu button displays a pop-up window, as shown in Figure 13.20. This window allows you to preview how your icon will look on different workspace background patterns. To choose a different pattern, move the pointer onto the pattern and click the left mouse button. The icon image displayed in the **Preview** window is determined by the canvas size you have selected.

The **Fill** menu button provides four fill options that allow you to determine how the surrounding area of your icon will look relative to the workspace background. These are the same options used in the **Operation** menu of the **Draw** pop-up window and are explained in the following section.

The Operation Menu

The **Operation** menu button in the **Draw** pop-up window provides four options that allow you to determine how the surrounding area of your icon will look relative to the workspace background: **Source (Overwrite Canvas)**, **Or (Union)**, **XOR (Exclusive Or)**, and the **And (Intersection)** options. Use the **Preview** pop-up window to determine which of these options you want to use to display your icon. The figures in this

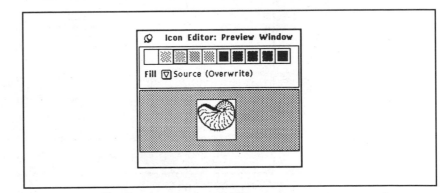

Figure 13.20: The Preview pop-up window

section show a sample icon as displayed in the **Preview** pop-up window of each of these options.

The **Source (Overwrite Canvas)** option displays the icon on top of the specified workspace background, as shown in Figure 13.21.

The **Or (Union)** option displays the icon area transparently, allowing the workspace background pattern to show through the icon area, as shown in Figure 13.22.

The **Xor (Exclusive Or)** option displays the icon transparently over the workspace background pattern, turning bits that are on in both images off and leaving the other bits unchanged, as shown in Figure 13.23.

Figure 13.21: The Source icon area option

Figure 13.22: The Or icon area option

The **And (Intersection)** option displays the icon area transparently over the workspace background pattern, retaining only the bits that are on in both images and turning all other bits off, as shown in Figure 13.24.

The Move Buttons

If you move part of the image off the canvas, the pixels are cropped from the image and are not restored if you move the image in the opposite direction.

The top four **Move** buttons (left, right, up, and down arrows) in the **Draw** pop-up window adjust the position of the entire drawing or a region of the drawing in the canvas one pixel in the direction indicated. To move a defined region of your image, select the **Region** option from the mode menu, indicated by

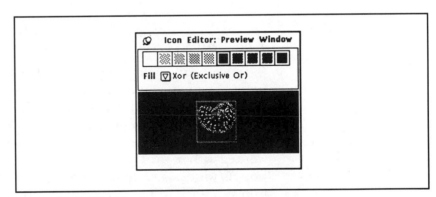

Figure 13.23: The Xor icon area option

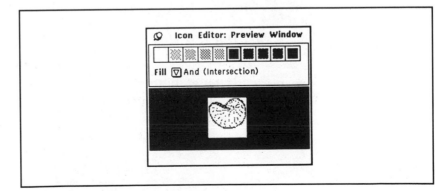

Figure 13.24: The And icon area option

intersecting dimmed rectangles. To select a region, move the pointer to the left corner of the region you want to move, press the left mouse button, and drag the pointer to the bottom-right of the region you want to affect. A bounding box indicates the selected region. Release the left mouse button and the region is selected.

To move the selected region or the entire drawing, click the left mouse button on one of the arrow buttons to move the drawing one pixel in the designated direction. The left two buttons in the bottom row of the **Move** buttons flip the image on the canvas or a defined region from left to right or top to bottom. The right two buttons rotate the image or a defined region 90 degrees in the direction of the arrow.

Loading a File

To load a file, click the left mouse button with the pointer on the **File** menu button and type the directory in the **Directory** text field and the file name in the **File** text field. You can specify the operation used to load the file with the **Load Operations** menu. The available options are the same options you worked with in the **Operation** menu of the **Preview** and **Draw** pop-up windows earlier. When you have chosen the load operation you want to use, click the left mouse button on the **Load** button to load the file into the canvas.

Saving a File

To save a file, type the directory in the **Directory** text field, the file name in the **File** text field, and click the left mouse button on the **Save** button. If a file of the same name already exists, a dialog box is displayed, asking if you want to overwrite the existing file or cancel the operation.

Browsing for Icon Files

The **Browse** button allows you to browse a specific directory for icon files. To browse a directory, type the name of the directory in the **Directory** text field and click the left mouse button with the pointer on the **Browse** button. The Icon Editor browses the specified directory and displays a message in the footer showing how many icon files are found. In addition, a pop-up window is displayed showing the icon files available in the directory.

To load one of the browse files, press the left mouse button on one of the icon images in the **Browse** window. The image is highlighted. When you release the left mouse button, the image is loaded and the **Browse** window is dismissed (unless you have already pinned the **Browse** window by clicking the left mouse button on the push pin). When there is an existing image on the canvas, a dialog box is displayed, asking you to confirm the overwrite. If you have directories with a large number of files, reduce browsing time by using wildcard characters in the **File** text field to narrow the search. For example, typing ***.icon** searches for only files with an **.icon** suffix.

Binding an Icon to a File

The DeskSet provides an application called the Binder that allows you to bind applications, icons, colors, and scripts to files. Because the Binder is designed to be used primarily by a system administrator, the focus of this section is only to bind an icon to a file. The Binder application is opened by selecting it from the **Workspace Programs** submenu. The **Binder** window is shown in Figure 13.25. Clicking the right mouse button on the window menu button on the upper-left corner of the **Binder** window closes it to an icon.

The **Binder** window has a control panel and a scrolling list. The control panel contains controls you use to add a new binding or modify or delete an existing binding. The scrolling list displays a list of existing bindings.

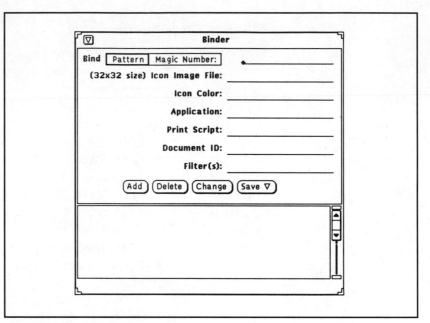

Figure 13.25: The Binder window

DeskSet environment installation creates an **/etc/filetype** file that contains the default bindings for the DeskSet environment. You can customize bindings and store them in a **.filetype** file in your home directory using the Binder. The scrolling pane displays your current bindings from **/etc/filetype** if you have not created a **.filetype** file. If you have a **.filetype** file in your home directory, the bindings from that file are displayed in the Binder pane.

To bind an icon to a file, follow the steps below:

1. If the icon does not exist, use the Icon Editor to create a 32-by-32 pixel icon.

2. Click the left mouse button with the pointer on **Pattern** (if necessary) and type the application name in the **Bind** text field.

3. Press Return or click the left mouse button in the **Icon Image File** text field to change the insert point.

4. Type the path and file name of the icon image.

5. Click the left mouse button with the pointer on the **Add** button.

6. Click the left mouse button on the **Save** button to save the current bindings in your **.filetype** file. The binding is saved and displayed in the scrolling list.

You can also choose from a selection of file formats to which you can bind your icon. In place of step 2, follow these directions: Move the pointer to the **Magic Number** setting of the **Bind** option and press the left mouse button. A menu button appears. By moving the pointer to the menu button and pressing the right mouse button, you can then drag the pointer to choose one of many predefined file formats; the selected format appears in the **Bind** text field. Then continue with the rest of the steps previously outlined to bind your icon to the selected file format.

Both the Binder and the File Manager read the **.filetype** file when you start them. An information message in the footer of the Binder reminds you that you must quit the File Manager and start it again before the changes you made are displayed.

Summary

In this chapter you learned how to work with several useful DeskSet applications. You learned how to

- print one or more files using the Print Tool.

- check the status of printing jobs using the **Status** button in the Print Tool.

- stop specific or all print jobs sent to the print queue.

- select or enter a print filter to ensure your files are printed correctly.

- use the Snapshot application to take a picture of a window, a region, or the entire screen.

- use the Snapshot application to view snapshot (raster) files and send them to the printer.

- convert a snapshot from an eight-bit raster file to a one-bit raster file to be printed on a standard laser printer.

- display and customize a digital or analog clock.

- display one or more performance meters to monitor the activity of your system.

- use the Calculator to perform calculations

- create your own icons using the Icon Editor.

- browse through existing icons using the Icon Editor.

- bind an icon to a file.

CHAPTER 14

SunOS
Command Reference

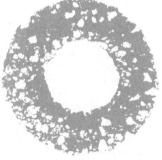

alias

Syntax

```
alias [name] [definition]
```

Description

The **alias** command lets you define shorthand ways to enter commands.

Options

The **alias** command takes no options.

Example

If you want to always be prompted before copying over files that are already existing, enter

```
alias cp 'cp -i'
```

into your `.cshrc`. This makes **cp** run **cp -i** instead, which prompts before overwriting files.
Entering

```
alias cp
```

displays any definition in effect for **cp**.
Entering

```
alias
```

displays all **alias** definitions in effect.

See Also

unalias, set

at

Syntax

```
at [options] time [date] [+increment] [script_file]
```

Description

The command **at** runs a command or program from a file at some later time. By using **at**, it is possible to print long files after working hours or send reminders to yourself or others. It is also possible to set up a job to run and reschedule itself every day, week, month, and so on.

When scheduling a job to run at a later time, you have a great deal of latitude in specifying when it is to run. The time may be specified as either 1, 2, or 4 digits. One or two digits specifies hours, while four digits specifies hours and minutes. The time may also be specified with a colon separating hours and minutes (hour:minute). Either a 24-hour clock or an appended **a.m.** or **p.m.** may be used. The special times **noon**, **midnight**, **now**, and **next** are also recognized. If no date is specified, the job runs at the next occurrence of *time,* the same day if *time* is after the current time, or the next day if *time* has already passed that day.

If *date* is included, it may take the form of either a month name followed by a day number or a day of the week. If a day of the week is used, it may be either fully spelled out or abbreviated with three letters. If the month given is before the current month, the next year is assumed.

An increment is a number followed by *minutes*, *hours*, *days*, *weeks*, *months*, or *years* (the singular form is used if appropriate). Thus, *at now + 15 minutes* means 15 minutes from the time the command is entered.

If no script file is specified (a script file is a file which contains SunOS commands, or programs, to be run together), **at** will take its input from the keyboard or standard input. If a script file is specified, it should contain the commands you would enter from the keyboard for **at** to run. If the script file named **run.at** contains

```
at 1500 today run.ps
at 0800 tomorrow run.at
```

and the file **run.ps** contains commands that print out memos which need to be routed every evening, then the system will automatically print out the memos every evening at 3:00p.m. and reschedule the job the next morning.

Options

-m	Sends mail after the job has been run, even if the job is successful
-r *[jobs]*	Removes jobs previously scheduled. The job number is determined by **at -l**.
-l *[jobs]*	Lists any jobs **at** has waiting to run

Example

Entering

```
at -m now + 15 minutes at_file
```

runs commands from the file **at_file** in 15 minutes and displays

```
job 36983 at Sat Oct 5 17:42:00 1992
```

where 36983 is the job queue entry number and will be a different number on your system. Because the **-m** option was specified, this command sends mail when completed. Entering

```
at 1:00pm Friday at_print
```

runs commands from the file **at_print** on the next Friday at 1:00p.m. and displays

```
job 36984 at Fri Oct 18 13:00:00 1992
```

Again, 36984 is the job queue entry number and will be a different number on your system. To delete Friday's job, enter

```
at -r 36984
```

Had you not been sure of the queue entry number, you could have entered

```
at -l
```

which would have displayed

```
job 36983 at Sat Oct 5 17:42:00 1992
job 36984 at Fri Oct 18 13:00:00 1992
```

from which you could determine the job queue entry.

biff

Syntax

```
biff [y|n]
```

Description

The **biff** command turns mail notification on or off. The **biff** command, without **y** or **n**, displays the current status. If notification is enabled, **biff** rings the terminal bell and displays the header and first few lines of arriving mail messages.

To always allow mail notification, enter **biff y** into your **.login** file.

Options

y Enables mail notification

n Disables mail notification

Example

Entering

```
biff y
```

enables notification of incoming mail. Entering

```
biff n
```

disables notification. Entering

```
biff
```

with notification disabled, displays

```
is n
```

which indicates notification is disabled.

cal

Syntax

```
cal [[month] year]
```

Description

The **cal** command by itself displays a calendar for the current month. The **cal** command followed by *month* and *year* gives a calendar for the month of the year specified. The **cal** command followed by *year* displays a calendar for the entire year. Note that entering **cal 11** displays the year 11 a.d., not November of the current year.

Options

The **cal** command takes no options.

Example

If today's date is Saturday, October 5, 1999, then entering

```
cal
```

displays

```
October 1999
S   M Tu  W Th  F   S
                1   2
3   4   5   6   7   8   9
10  11  12  13  14  15  16
24  25  26  27  28  29  30
31
```

For the more historically minded, entering

```
cal 9 1752
```

displays

```
September 1752
S   M Tu  W Th  F   S
        1   2  14  15  16
17  18  19  20  21  22  23
24  25  26  27  28  29  30
```

This displays the month of September for the year the calendar changed from Gregorian to Julian.

See Also

`calendar`

calendar

Syntax

```
calendar
```

Description

The **calendar** command is a reminder service. It looks for the file **calendar** in the current directory and displays lines that have today's or tomorrow's date. The **calendar** command recognizes **Aug. 31**, **august 31**, and **8/31** as valid dates, but not **31 August** or **31/8**. Designating the month as an asterisk (*) in the file **calendar** indicates all months.

Example

Entering *** 15 PAYDAY!** in the file **calendar** causes the **calendar** command to display *** 15 PAYDAY!** if the command is run on the fifteenth (or the day before) of any month. On Fridays the **calendar** command considers tomorrow to be Monday.

See Also

`cal`

cat

Syntax

```
cat [options] [filenames]
```

Description

The **cat** command creates, displays, and joins files.

Options

-n   Precedes each output line with a line number and counts lines

-b   Numbers the output lines (as -n), but omits line numbers from blank lines

-v   Makes control characters visible (for instance, Control-Z as ^Z, Control-D as ^D, and so on). The Delete character (hex 0FF) prints as ^?. Non-ASCII characters (high-bit set) are displayed as M-x, with M- as Meta and x as the character. Does not print tabs or newlines visibly (see -t and -e).

-t   Outputs control characters visibly (as -v), and displays tabs visually (^I)

-e   Outputs control characters visibly (as -v) and displays newlines visually (as $)

-s   Substitutes a single blank line for any multiple, sequential blank lines

Example

Entering

```
cat file1
```

displays the contents of *file1* to the screen. Entering

```
cat file1 file2
```

displays the contents of *file1* followed by the contents of *file2*. Entering

```
cat file1 file2 > file3
```

sends the contents of *file1* followed by *file2* to a new file called *file3*. Entering

```
cat > file1
```

takes input from the keyboard and sends the input to a new file called *file1*. Entering

```
cat file1 file2 >> file3
```

appends the contents of *file1* and *file2* to the already existing *file3*. Entering

```
cat
```

takes input from the keyboard (until a Control-D, end-of-file, is entered) and sends its output to the screen. Entering any of these commands:

```
cat file1 file2 > file1
cat file1 file2 > file2
cat file1 file2 >> file1
cat file1 file2 >> file2
```

will not work and results in

```
cat: input file4 is output
```

where *file4* is the specified output file.

See Also

```
cp, rm, more, pr, head, tail
```

cd

Syntax

```
cd [directoryname]
```

Description

The **cd** command changes the working directory to either your home directory, if no directory name is included, or to the directory indicated by *directoryname*. The main purpose of directories is to keep things organized. When working on multiple projects, you might make separate directories for each; thus, if two projects need a document called **description**, they will not conflict. By changing to the appropriate directory, you can avoid conflicting file names.

A directory is indicated by a relative or absolute path. A relative path references a subdirectory from the current directory when you type in the subdirectory's name, whereas an absolute directory always starts from the root directory. An absolute directory begins with a forward slash (**/**). A relative path can also use the dot(**.**) for the current directory or two dots (**..**) for the parent of the current directory.

Options

The **cd** command takes no options.

Example

Entering

```
cd
```

changes the current working directory to your home directory. Entering

```
cd /etc
```

changes the current working directory to the directory **/etc**. If your current directory is **/games/scores**, then entering

```
cd ..
```

changes the current working directory to the directory **/games**.

If you are a DOS user who has gotten used to seeing your current path as part of your prompt, place

```
alias cd 'cd \!*;set prompt="$cwd> "'
```

into your **.cshrc** file. This will replace the system's **cd** command with a new one, which resets the prompt to display the current directory every time **cd** is used.

See Also

pwd

chgrp

Syntax

```
chgrp [options] group filename(s)
```

Description

The **chgrp** command changes the *group* association of a file (or files in the case of the **-R** option). Since SunOS is a multi-user system, built-in safeguards keep users from accidentally (or even deliberately) deleting one another's files. These safeguards protect against unauthorized reading, writing, copying, and deleting of files (also executing of executable files). See your system administrator about setting up groups.

Each file has a set of permissions associated with it—read, write, and execute. These three permissions may be applied to the owner of the file (usually the creator of the file); everyone else on the system; and to specific groups of users. Entering the command **ls -lg** displays file names and information about their permission and group settings. The permissions are listed, then the number of links, the owner, the group ownership, the block size, the creation date, and finally the file's name.

```
drwxrwxrwx    8 lgoodman cntrct   4096 Feb  4 16:40 ./
drwxr-xr-x   12 root     authrs   4122 Aug  7 17:00 ../
-rwxrwxrwx    1 lgoodman cntrct 159360 Nov  5 11:40 file1
-rwxr-----    1 lgoodman cntrct    658 Dec  1 15:30 file2
-r-xr-xr-x    1 lgoodman cntrct  12555 Aug 13 08:30 archive
drwxrwxrwx   20 lgoodman cntrct   1536 Oct 15 11:11 public/
drwx------   11 lgoodman cntrct    385 Jul  5 02:40 private/
drwx-w--w-    2 lgoodman cntrct     10 Oct  4 10:01 incoming/
drwxr-xr-x    2 lgoodman cntrct     10 Jul 21 17:32 outgoing/
drwxrwx---   17 lgoodman proj1    3072 Feb 17 09:48 project1/
drwxrwx---   04 lgoodman proj2    4096 May 21 08:45 project2/
```

The **chgrp** command sets or changes the groups associated with a file's group permissions. To make the change you must be the owner of the file as well as a member of the group to which you change the file.

Options

-**f**   Inhibits the reporting of error messages.

-**R**   Causes **chgrp** to recursively descend through the
directory (that is, into the subdirectories)

Example

Entering

```
chgrp groupname filename
```

changes the group associated with **filename** to **groupname**.

See Also

chown, ls, chmod

chmod

Syntax

```
chmod [options] mode filename(s)
```

Description

The **chmod** command changes the permissions (**mode**) associated with the file **filename(s)** (or files in the case of the -**R** option). Because SunOS is a multiuser system, built in safeguards keep users from accidentally (or even deliberately) deleting one another's files. These safeguards prevent unauthorized reading, writing, copying, and deleting of files (also executing of executable files).

Each file has a set of permissions associated with it—read, write, and execute. These three permissions may be applied to the owner of the file (usually the creator of the file); everyone else on the system; and groups of people defined by entries in the file **/etc/passwd**.

Entering the command **ls -l** displays file names and information about their permissions. The permissions are listed first, then the number of links, the owner, the block size, the creation date, and finally the file's name.

```
drwxrwxrwx   8 lgoodman   4096 Feb  4 16:40 ./
drwxr-xr-x  12 root       4122 Aug  7 17:00 ../
-rwxrwxrwx   1 lgoodman 159360 Nov  5 11:40 file1
-rwx------   1 lgoodman    658 Dec  1 15:30 file2
-r--r--r--   1 lgoodman  12555 Aug 13 08:30 archive
drwxrwxrwx  20 lgoodman   1536 Oct 15 11:11 public/
drwx------  11 lgoodman    385 Jul  5 02:40 private/
drwx-w--w-   2 lgoodman     10 Oct  4 10:01 incoming/
drwxr-xr-x   2 lgoodman     10 Jul 21 17:32 outgoing/
drwxrwx---  17 lgoodman   3072 Feb 17 09:48 project1/
drwxrwx---  04 lgoodman   4096 May 21 08:45 project2/
```

The first letter indicates the listing is for a directory (**d**) or a file (**-**). The next three letters are the permissions given the owner of the file (**r**: read or copy permission; **w**: write or delete permission; **x**: execute or search permission). The next three letters are the permissions for the groups assigned. The last three letters are the permissions for everyone on the system. The listing shows that **file1** may be read, written, or executed by anyone on the system. **file2** may be read, written, or executed only by the owner, lgoodman. The file **archive** may be read by anyone, but no one (not even the owner) may overwrite the file. The directory **public** may have files read from, written to, or searched by anyone on the system. The directory **private** may only be written to, read from, or searched by the owner. The directory **incoming** may be written to by anyone, while no one but the owner may read or search it. The directory **outgoing** may be searched or copied from by anyone, but may only be written to by the owner. The directories **project1** and **project2** may be accessed only by members of the respective groups **proj1** and **proj2**.

The modes are given in either of two formats for this command. An absolute mode is an octal number formed by summing the following octal numbers representing the enabled permissions.

400   Read by owner allowed

200   Write by owner allowed

100   Execute (search in directory) by owner allowed

040   Read by associated group allowed

020   Write by associated group allowed

010   Execute (search in directory) by associated group allowed

004   Read by everyone allowed

002   Write by everyone allowed

001   Execute (search in directory) by everyone allowed

Thus, a permission mode of **777** enables all to read, write, and execute. A permission of **744** enables the owner to read, write, and execute while allowing everyone else only read permission.

The other format uses letter symbols instead of numbers. The symbolic mode looks like this:

`[who] operation permission`

where **who** is

u   User's permissions

g   Group's permissions

o   Other's permissions

a   Permissions for everyone (equivalent to **ugo**)

The **operation** is

+   Adds the permission

–   Removes the permission

=   Explicitly assigns the permission (Any permissions not listed will be disallowed.)

and the ***permission*** is a combination of

    r   Read

    w   Write

    x   Execute

Options

    -f   Causes **chmod** to complete without issuing any error messages

    -R   Sets the mode for all specified files in the current and any other appropriate subdirectories

Example

Entering

```
chmod o-w file1
```

denies write permission to others not in your group on the file named **file1**. Entering

```
chmod a+r file1
```

gives everyone (the owner, members of your group, and everyone else) read permission on the file named **file1**. Entering

```
chmod 700 file1
```

gives the owner of **file1** read, write, and execute permission while denying members of the owner's group and the rest of the users any permissions. Entering

```
chmod 222 file1
```

gives everyone write permission only.

See Also

  chgrp, chown, ls

chown

Syntax

```
chown [options] owner[group] filename
```

Description

The **chown** command (loacted in **\usr\etc**) changes the owner of the file named ***filename*** to the user named ***owner***. The user ***owner*** is specified by either the login name or the user identification number (UID). The ***group*** may likewise be specified as either a group name or group identification number (GID).

Since SunOS is a multiuser system, built-in safeguards keep users from accidentally (or even deliberately) deleting another's files. These safeguards protect against unauthorized reading, writing, copying, and deleting of files (also executing of executable files). Another safeguard is that only someone logged in as root (usually the system administrator) can execute **chown**.

Each file has a set of permissions associated with it—read, write, and execute. These three permissions may be applied to the owner of the file (usually the creator of the file); everyone else on the system; and specific groups of users.

Entering the command **ls -l** displays file names and information about their permissions. The permissions are listed first, then the number of links, the owner, the block size, the creation date, and finally the file's name.

```
drwxrwxrwx   8 lgoodman    4096 Feb  4 16:40 ./
drwxr-xr-x  12 root        4122 Aug  7 17:00 ../
-rwxrwxrwx   1 lgoodman  159360 Nov  5 11:40 file1
-rwx------   1 lgoodman     658 Dec  1 15:30 file2
-r--r--r--   1 lgoodman   12555 Aug 13 08:30 archive
drwxrwxrwx  20 lgoodman    1536 Oct 15 11:11 public/
drwx------  11 lgoodman     385 Jul  5 02:40 private/
drwx-w--w-   2 lgoodman      10 Oct  4 10:01 incoming/
drwxr-xr-x   2 lgoodman      10 Jul 21 17:32 outgoing/
drwxrwx---  17 lgoodman    3072 Feb 17 09:48 project1/
drwxrwx---  04 lgoodman    4096 May 21 08:45 project2/
```

The first letter indicates the listing is for a directory (**d**) or a file (**-**). The next three letters are the permissions given the owner of the file (**r**: read or copy permission; **w**: write or delete permission; **x**: execute or search permission). The next three letters are the permissions for the groups assigned. The last three letters are the permissions for everyone on the system. The listing shows **file1** may be read, written, or executed by anyone on the system. **file2** may be read, written, or executed only by the owner, lgoodman. The file **archive** may be read by anyone, but no one (not even the owner) may overwrite the file. The directory **public** may have files read from, written to, or searched by anyone on the system. The directory **private** may only be written to, read from, or searched by the owner. The directory **incoming** may be written to by anyone, while no one but the owner may read or search it. The directory **outgoing** may be searched or copied from by anyone, but may only be written to by the owner. The directories **project1** and **project2** may be accessed only by members of the respective groups and proj2.

Options

-f   Causes completion without issuing any error messages

-R   Sets the mode for all specified files in the current and any other appropriate subdirectories

Example

Entering

```
chown bheslop chap14
```

causes bheslop to become the owner of the file called **chap14**.

See Also

```
chgrp, chmod, ls
```

clear

Syntax

```
clear
```

Description

The **clear** command clears the screen and returns the cursor to the upper-left corner. This is useful for clearing clutter from the screen.

Options

The **clear** command takes no options.

Examples

Entering

```
clear
```

clears the screen.

compress

Syntax

```
compress [options] [filename]
```

Description

The **compress** command reduces the storage size of the file *filename* by use of a compression algorithm (Lempel-Ziv). The file *filename* is replaced by a file with a **.Z** extension. The **.Z** file is about half the size of the source file. The compression depends greatly upon the contents of the input file. To restore a compressed file, use the command **uncompress**. To view a file without changing the **.Z** file, use the command **zcat**.

Options

-c Writes to the screen (or standard output); does not change any files. The **zcat** command is equivalent to the **-c** option.

-f Forces compression regardless of whether the file actually shrinks (not all files shrink from **compress**) or the **.Z** file already exists

-v Displays the percentage of reduction attained by running **compress**

Example

Given a file, **report.text**, with a size of 4608 bytes, entering:

```
compress report.text
```

results in a file **report.text.Z** with a size of 2696 bytes. To uncompress **report.text.Z**, enter:

```
uncompress report.text
```

Note that with the **uncompress** command the **.Z** extension is optional.

See Also

uncompress

cp

Syntax

```
cp [options] filename1 filename2
cp [options] directory1 directory2
cp [options] filenames directory
```

Description

Entering **cp *filename1 filename2*** copies *filename1* to *filename2*. If *filename2* already exists, it is overwritten and the old file is lost. You might want to enter **alias cp 'cp -i'** into your `.cshrc` file. The **cp -i** command asks for confirmation before overwriting a file.

Entering **cp -r** *directory1 directory2* copies all the files of *directory1* and any files in any subdirectories of *directory1* into *directory2*, creating *directory2*, if it does not already exist, and any subdirectories of *directory2*.

Entering **cp** *filenames directory* copies all of the files specified by *filenames* into *directory*. The destination directory must already exist.

For those who are familiar with links (**ln**), **cp** copies the contents pointed to by a link, not the link itself; files that are linked will not have their copies linked.

Options

-i   Prompts for confirmation before overwriting an existing file. Pressing **y** confirms the copy should proceed; any other key aborts the **cp** operation.

-p   Copies the source file(s) and keeps the same modification time and permission modes

-r and **-R**   If any of the source files are directories, copies the directory, all its files, any subdirectories, and any files in the subdirectories.

Example

Entering

```
cp file1 file2
```

copies the contents of **file1** to **file2**. If **file2** does not already exist, it is created; if it does exist, the old contents are replaced and lost.

Here is an example of using **cp** to copy directories:

```
cp -r lgoodman/chap14 lgoodman/archive
```

This copies all of the directory **chap14** into the directory **archive**, creating **archive** if necessary.

See Also

> mv, ln, rename, mkdir

crypt

Syntax

> crypt [password]

Description

The **crypt** command encrypts and decrypts a file using *password* as a key. A file transformed using **crypt** will not be readable without the key. The technique used for **crypt** is well known and is not truly secure against an educated attempt to decrypt, but it should provide minimal security against casual reading.

Options

The **crypt** command takes no options.

Example

Entering

> crypt Scherbius <infile> outfile

encypts the file **infile**, sending the encrypted information to **outfile**, using **Scherbius** as the encryption key.

date

Syntax

> date [+format]

Description

The **date** command displays this information: *day month date hour:minute:second time-zone year*, thus giving you access to current time and date information at your work-station. The **date** command is also used by the system administrator to set the system date and time.

Options

%n	Newline character inserted
%t	Tab character inserted
%m	Month of year as two digits (*01* to *12*)
%d	Day of month as two digits (*01* to *31*)
%y	Last two digits of the year (*00* to *99*)
%D	Date in *mm/dd/yy* format
%H	Hour in 24-hour clock format
%M	Minute (*00* to *59*)
%S	Second (*00* to *59*)
%T	Time as *hour:minute:second*
%j	Day of the year (*000–366*)
%w	Day of the week (Sunday = *0*)
%a	Weekday abbreviated to three letters (*SUN*, *MON*, *TUE* ...)
%h	Month abbreviated to three letters (*MAY*, *JUN*, *JUL*...)
%r	Hour in 12-hour format (*AM/PM*)

Example

If today's date is Saturday, the 5th of October, 1999, and the time is 11:15 a.m., then entering

```
date
```

displays

```
Sat Oct 05 11:15:01 PDT 1999
```

For a gentle reminder every morning, you might add this into the `.login` file in your home directory

```
date +'Good Morning! Today is %a %h %d%nThe time is: %r.'
```

which displays

```
Good Morning! Today is Fri Aug 13
The time is 09:00:00 PM.
```

To change the date to Dec. 25, 1999, 12:01 a.m., become a super-user and enter

```
date 991225001
```

See Also

`time`

df

Syntax

```
df [options] [filesystem] [filename]
```

Description

The **df** command reports the amount of occupied disk space, the amount of used and available space, and how much of the file system's storage space has been used. **filename** may be either a file name or a pathname. If it is included, **df** reports on the system containing the file or path.

Options

-a	Reports on all file systems (all attached disk drives)
-t *type*	Reports on file systems of the type specified (for example, nfs or 4.2)

Example

Entering

```
df
```

displays

```
Filesystem   kbytes   used    avail   capacity   Mounted on
/dev/local   396884   341321  15874   96%        /a
/dev/share   15519    652     13315   5%         /b
```

Because the file system reserves space, the values under the **used** and **avail** columns do not add up to the total amount of file system space (the **kbytes** column).

See Also

```
du
```

diff

Syntax

```
diff [options] filename1 filename2
```

Description

The **diff** command compares *filename1* to *filename2* and identifies which lines to change to make the files identical. All differing lines are displayed as are commands needed to convert *filename1* into *filename2*. The commands are **a**, **d**, and **c**. An **a** means that lines are added to *filename1* to match *filename2*; a **d** means that lines are deleted from *filename1* to match *filename2*; a **c** means that lines have changed from *filename1* to *filename2*.

Options

-b   Ignores trailing blanks (spaces and tabs) and treats all other strings of blanks as equals

-i   Ignores the case of letters. Treats **A** as equivalent to **a**.

-w   Ignores all blanks (spaces and tabs). Treats **3 + 5 = 8** as equivalent to **3+5=8**.

Example

Given two files, **file1**, which contains

```
Anne  Addams        111 N 1st St        555-1111
Bill  Browne        222 S 2nd St        555-2222
Cher  Clarke        333 E 3rd Av        555-3333
Dave  Durham        444 W 4th Av        555-4444
```

and **file2**, which contains

```
Anne  Smythe        111 N 1st St        555-1111
Bill  Browne        222 S 2nd St        555-2222
Carl  Change        777 E 7th Av        555-7777
Dave  Durham        444 W 4th Av        555-4444
Eddy  Elliot        555 Park Pl         555-5555
```

Entering

```
diff file1 file2
```

yields

```
1c1
< Anne Addams        111 N 1st St        555-1111
---
> Anne Smythe        111 N 1st St        555-1111
3c3
< Cher Clarke        333 E 3rd Av        555-3333
---
> Carl Change        777 E 7th Av        555-7777
4a5
> Eddy Elliot        555 Park Pl         555-5555
```

This shows that lines one and three have been changed and line five has been added.

du

Syntax

```
du [options] [name]
```

Description

The **du** command gives the number of kilobytes used by a directory and all of its subdirectories. If no directory or file **name** is specified, reports on the current directory; otherwise reports on **name**, which may be either a file or a directory. If it is a directory, all subdirectories are included; if it is a file, either the **-s** or **-a** must be used, then only the file **name** is reported upon.

Options

-s   Displays the total disk usage for each specified **name** or the total for the current directory if **name** is not specified

-a   Reports on every file instead of just each directory

Example

Entering

```
du -a
```

displays disk usage information on all files in the current directory and all files in each subdirectory. Entering

```
du -s file*
```

displays disk usage information only on any file whose name starts with **file** (for example, **file1**, **file2**, and so on).

See Also

df

echo

Syntax

```
echo [options] arguments
```

Description

The **echo** command displays arguments on the screen (or standard output). This command is often used within a script file to display the progress of the file or to request some user input. (A script file is a file which contains SunOS commands, or programs, to be run together.)

Options

    -n   Does not output newline characters (carriage return characters)

Example

Entering

```
echo Hi Mom
```

displays

```
Hi Mom
```

expand

Syntax

```
expand [-n] [-tab1,tab2,...,tabn] [filename]
```

Description

The **expand** command copies the file specified by *filename* to the standard output, converting tab characters to spaces. This is useful before sorting, looking at specific columns, or printing on some printers (those which have no tab capability for instance).

Specifying *-n* sets the tab width. The default is eight spaces. The -**tab1,tab2...tabn** arguments indicate numbers used to set tabs at columns.

Options

The **expand** command takes no options.

Example

Enter

```
expand -2,10,18,30 report > report.notab
```

to make a copy of the file report with the tab stops set to the second, tenth, eighteenth, and thirtieth columns (just like setting tab stops on a typewriter).

Enter

```
expand -5 phonelist > phonelist.notab
```

to make a copy of **phonelist** (named **phonelist.notab**) with tabs converted to five spaces.

See Also

unexpand

file

Syntax

```
file [ -f namesfile] filename(s)
```

Description

The **file** command determines what kind of information a file contains, whether the file is executable, a text file, a C program, and so on. The **file** command sometimes mistakenly identifies files, such as confusing command files for C programs.

Options

-f *namesfile*   *namesfile* is a file containing a list of files to identify. *namesfile* must contain only names of files.

Example

Entering

```
file old.docs mygrep test.*
```

displays

```
old.docs:       directory
mygrep:         executable shell script
test.c:         c program text
test:           mc68020 demand paged executable
```

find

Syntax

```
find pathname_list expression
```

Description

The **find** command is an extremely powerful, useful, and adaptable tool. Although it is one of the more difficult commands to master, it is worth the effort. The **find** command searches all files and sub-directories of the directories in *pathname_list* and checks for files that meet the criteria described by *expression*.

pathname_list is a list of directories to be searched. **find** searches all files and subdirectories in *pathname_list*. *expression* is a list of selection criteria or actions to be taken. The selection criteria in *expression* are checked for each of the files in *pathname_list*. The criteria are checked until one of them fails, at which point the next file is checked.

It is possible to use **find** to perform such tasks as these:

- Check all files under a directory for the occurrence of a word, such as a group member's name
- Check each file's creation date and only list those files created after or before a date
- List only those files modified between two dates.

The ***expression*** list is traversed left to right. As long as the test in ***expression*** evaluates true, the next test is performed. In other words, the expresion is evaluated as if the items are connected with logical ANDs. If a test is not met, the processing of the current file is ended, and the next file is checked. It is - possible to cause a logical OR to be performed by using the **-o** argument; just because one check fails does not mean the termination of all further checking on the file. The criteria to be checked are separated by spaces.

Any action (as opposed to a test or check) in ***expression*** always counts as a test which is met; an action never causes an end to checking of the current file unless the action is the last item in the expression list.

Options

The **find** command takes no options.

Expressions

!	Negates the next argument. **!-name *filename*** checks true for files whose name is *not* **filename**.
-atime *n*	True if the file has been accessed in ***n*** days. Note: The **find** command itself changes the access time of files in ***pathname-list***.

-ctime *n*	True if the file has been changed in **n** days. That is, either the file has been modified or the file's attributes (its owner, group, permissions, and so on) have changed.
-depth	Always yields true. This is an action to be performed, not a check to be made. The **depth** argument causes the **find** command to check the contents of subdirectories before any other files in the directory containing the subdirectories.
-exec *command*	True if the executed *command* returns a zero value as an exit status. This usually means a requested command has occurred. (For instance, **grep** returns a zero if the requested string of characters was found and returns a nonzero if the requested string of characters was not found.) The specified command must be followed by an escaped semicolon (**\;**). To specify the current file, use curly braces (**{ }**).
\(expression \)	True if the parenthesized expression is true. Used for grouping expressions, usually with the **-o** operator. Parentheses must be preceded by backslashes, and the expression must be separated from the parentheses by spaces.
-group *groupname*	True if the file belongs to *groupname*

-links *n*	True if the file has *n* links
-ls	Always yields true. This is an action to be performed, not a check to be made. Prints the current pathname along with the following: inode number (the inode number is used by SunOS internally to identify where a file's contents are physically located), size in kilobytes, protection mode, number of hard links, user, group, size in bytes, and modification time.
-mtime *n*	True if the file has been modified (that is, written to) in the last *n* days
-name *filename*	True if filename matches the current file name. An *****, **?**, or **[** and **]** can be used, but must be escaped (that is, put within quotes or proceeded by a backslash).
-newer *filename*	True if the current file has been modified more recently than the file *filename*.
-nogroup	True if the file belongs to a group not in an assigned group in the /etc/group file
-nouser	True if the file belongs to a user not in the /etc/passwd file

-o	If two criteria are separated by spaces, they must both be true to continue checking; that is, both must be true to proceed because as soon as a check fails, the next file is checked. Using -o between two arguments causes a logical OR to be performed. Thus (**-name larry -o -name brent**) will evaluate to true if the current file has a name of either **larry** or **brent**.
-ok *command*	Like **-exec**, except *command* is written to the screen (**<** *command* ... *arguments***>?**); input from the keyboard is then expected, and *command* is executed only if a **y** is input.
-perm *octal-number*	True if the octal number matches the file permissions of the current file
-print	Always yields true. This is an action to be performed, not a check to be made. Prints the current pathname.
-prune	Always yields true. This is an action to be performed, not a check to be made. This is used to keep find from checking into directories—it prunes the search tree.
-size *n*	True if the file is *n* blocks long (there are typically 512 characters in a block). If *n* is followed by a **c**, the size is in characters instead of blocks.

`-type` `type-char`	True if the type of the current file is **`type-char`**, where **`type-char`** has the following values and associated meanings:

b	Block special files (that is, tape drives)
c	Character special files (that is, terminals)
d	Directories
f	Regular files
l	Symbolic links
s	Socket

`-user` `username`	True if the file belongs to **`username`**

Example

Entering

```
find . -print
```

displays the name of all files and all subdirectories under the current directory. Entering

```
find . -name test -print
```

displays the pathname of all files or subdirectories under the current directory whose name is **test**. Entering

```
find . -name \*.doc -print
```

displays all files or subdirectories under the current directory whose name has a **.doc** extension. Entering

```
find . -perm 700 -print
```

lists all the files in your home directory with their permission set to 700 (only the owner has read, write, and execute permissions). Entering

```
find /user/lbird -type f -exec grep -l sunspots {} \;
```

displays the name of all files under the directory **/user/lbird** (note the use of **f** to eliminate anything that is not a file) that contain the word **sunspots**. The **grep** command searches each file for **sunspots** and, since **-l** is specified, only prints the name of the file and not the line containing **sunspots**. Note the use of **{}** to mean the current file and the **\;**, which must follow any command to **-exec**. Entering

```
find . \( -user bsmith -o -user lbird \) -ok cp {} ~/temp \;
```

searches through the working directory and its subdirectories for files belonging to either **lbird** or **bsmith** and prompts for confirmation before copying them into the directory **~/temp**. Entering

```
find . -type d -print
```

lists all the subdirectories of the working directory. Entering

```
find . \! -name '.' -type d -print -prune
```

lists all the main subdirectories of the working directory, but does not list the sub-subdirectories as the previous example does. Entering

```
find . -type f -size +500c -atime +30 -ok rm {} \;
```

searches through your home directory for files larger than 500 characters that have not been accessed in the last 30 days, and asks whether you want to delete them.

See Also

chgrp, chmod, ln, ls, passwd

finger

Syntax

```
finger [options] [username]
```

Description

The **finger** command, with no user name specified, displays information about each user that is logged in. The information listed is as follows:

- Login name
- Full name
- Terminal name (preceded with an '*****' if write permission is denied)
- Idle time
- Login time
- Location (which is taken from the comment field from the file **/etc/ttytab**)

If a user name is specified, the information is displayed about that user only. User name can be specified as a first name, last name, or an account (login) name. When a user name is specified, the following information is also displayed:

- The user's home directory and login shell
- The time the user last logged in
- The terminal and terminal information from **/etc/ttytab**
- The last time the user received and read mail
- The contents of the file named **.plan** (if it exists) in their home directory
- The projects listed in the file named **.project** (if it exists) in their home directory

Options

    -m   Matches only user name (not first or last name)

    -l   Outputs long format

    -s   Outputs short format

Example

Entering

```
finger
```

displays information about all users currently logged in. Entering

```
finger lgoodman
```

displays information about user **lgoodman**. Entering

```
finger larry
```

displays information about any user who's first, last, or login name is **larry**.

See Also

who

fold

Syntax

```
fold  [-maxwidth] filename
```

Description

The **fold** command breaks lines at the maximum width as indicated by *maxwidth*. The default width is 80 characters. The *maxwidth* should be a multiple of eight if tabs are present; if it is not, you should use the **expand** command before using **fold**. (If you don't, when the tab character is printed it will move the print head over eight spaces, which will throw off the row widths.) The **fold** command is useful for displaying files on screens with widths less than 80 characters wide, or for setting the width of a file. (For instance, a file's width might be made narrower to set it off from a file it is merged with.)

Options

The **fold** command takes no options.

Example

Entering

```
fold -20 filename1 > filename2
```

copies **filename1** into **filename2**, but first adjusts the lines to a width of 20 characters.

grep

Syntax

```
grep [options] [-e expression] filename
```

Description

The **grep** command searches the file indicated by **filename** (or the standard input) for lines containing **expression**. If **grep** finds a line containing **expression**, it displays the line (if more than one file is specified by **filename**, the file name precedes the line).

The **grep** command can search a file for the string **word**, for instance. When searching for **word**, it also finds **word**y, **word**less, and **word**s. If you want to locate **word** by itself, specify **word** in single close quotes, ′ **word** ′ (note the beginning and ending spaces inside the quote). To specify the beginning of a line use the carat (**^**), and use the dollar-sign for the end of a line (**$**). To specify any of several characters, enclose the characters in square brackets. **[Bb]ill** matches **bill** or **Bill** and **[A-Z]ill** matches any uppercase letter followed by **ill**. **[A-za-z]ill** matches any letter (upper- or lowercase) followed by **ill**. A period (**.**) matches any single character (letters and special characters such as !, @, # . . .). Within a range delineated by square brackets, a caret (**^**) means any character except those in the brackets, so [^0-9] matches any non-digit. An asterisk (*****) matches zero or more preceding characters. The string **ab*c** matches **a** followed by zero or more **b**s followed by a **c**. For example, **abc**, **abbc**, and **ac** all match **ab*c** (note that the **ac** has zero occurrences of **b**). The string **ab.*c** matches **ab** followed by zero or more of any other character followed by **c**. For example, **abac**, **abdtzc**, and **abc** all match **ab.*c**.

To specify any special character ($, ^, [,], or \) precede it with a backslash (\). To use any of these special characters, you must enclose the string you are searching for in delimiters. A delimiter is a way to specify the beginning and ending of a string. The delimiter can be any character, such as **~**, **#**, or **/**, so long as the delimiter does not appear in the string.

Options

-c	Displays a count of matching lines rather than displaying the matching lines
-h	Inhibits the displaying of file names
-i	Ignores the case of letters (for example, treats **A** as **a**)
-l	Lists only the file name of files with matching lines
-n	Lists each matching line preceded by its line number from the beginning of the file
-v	Lists lines that do not match the search string

Example

Entering

```
grep SunOS *
```

lists any files in the current directory that contain the word **SunOS** (note the capitals). To search for the string **SunOS** regardless of the case of the letters, enter

```
grep -i sunos *
```

To search for files which contain numbers, enter

```
grep '[0-9]' *
```

Note the use of the single close quote to begin and end the search string; this enables the use of the square brackets ([]) to denote the range of zero to nine.

To search C program files for comments, enter

```
grep '/\*' *.c
```

The backslash is used to escape the wildcard usage of the asterisk. Also note the use of the single close quote (') as a delimiter since this command looks for a slash (/), and needs the backslash (\) to precede the asterisk (*). To search for users on your system who do not have passwords, enter

```
grep '^[^:]*::' /etc/passwd
```

This example searches the **/etc/passwd** file for any number of characters besides colons followed by a double colon at the beginning of lines.

head

Syntax

```
head [-count] [filename]
```

Description

If you are not sure what is in a file, using **head** shows you, or if you can not remember which file begins with some particular text, **head** can help you find out, without loading many different files into a word processor or editor. The **head** command sends the beginning of a file (or the standard input) to the display (or the standard output). How many lines get sent is determined by *count*. If *count* is not specified, **head** sends 10 lines. Whether standard input or a file is used depends on whether a file name is added. If a file name is not specified, the standard input is used. If more than one file is specified, **head** begins each file's display with **==>***filename***<==**.

Options

The **head** command takes no options.

Example

Entering

```
head -2 file1 file2 file3
```

prints out the first two lines of each file indicated, such as:

```
==> file1 <==
  I. Introduction
For the image coding application, strictly speaking, all
==> file2 <==
The output of a discrete information source is a message
that consists of a sequence of symbols.  The actual message
==> file3 <==
Boolean logic is the logic we are all familiar with, the
logic we all think of when we think of mathematical logic.
```

See Also

cat, **more**, **tail**

history

Syntax

```
history [options] [n]
```

Description

The **history** command displays a list of previously entered commands in the order of oldest to most recent. The shell stores a list of commands in the order you enter them. Erroneous commands, such as spelling errors, are stored in the **history** list as well as correct commands. You can repeat a command by entering **!***n*, where *n* is the number of the command in the **history** list that you wish to repeat. Entering **!!** reexecutes the last command. It is also possible to edit a command from the **history** list.

Options

    `-r`   Reverses the order of commands listed to most recent first

Example

Entering

```
history 5
```

prints out the five most recent commands you entered. Such a list may look like this:

```
3 cd ~/book/chap.14
4 ls -al
5 cAT log
6 cat log
7 rm log
```

id

Syntax

```
id
```

Description

The **id** command displays your user name and id, and your group name and id.

Options

The **id** command takes no options.

Example

Entering

```
id
```

might display

```
uid=1230(lgoodman)  gid=204(cntrcts)
```

See Also

`finger`, `who`, `whoami`

jobs

Syntax

```
jobs [-l]
```

Description

The **jobs** command reports the status of background and stopped jobs. A job consists of the commands specified on a single command line; this may involve several processes, each consisting of an executable program along with its data, files, and directory. Each process has a set of open files (the files in use), a working directory, and a unique process ID (PID) number.

The **jobs** command labels each job by a number in brackets. A plus sign (**+**) indicates the current background job, usually the first job placed in background. A minus sign (**-**) indicates the next job. All other jobs are unmarked. A job may be listed as **Running**, **Stopped**, **Terminated**, **Done**, or **Exit**.

Example

With several jobs running in background, entering

```
jobs
```

displays a list similar to the following one:

```
[1]   +     Running      find / -type f -print > ls.all
[2]   -     Running      grep -i 'keep busy' * > grep.out
[3]         Running      cat * > waste.space
```

See Also

`ps`

kill

Syntax

```
kill [-signal] process_ID_number
```

Description

A program is an executable file. When a program is loaded into memory and executed, it is called a process. If you and a coworker are both running a CAD package, there are two processes—one is yours, the other your coworker's.

A signal is a message sent to a process. For instance, if a program begins execution, and you want to stop it before it's done, you can send it a signal to stop. You may also want to stop a process for just a while, and later resume. Signals are also used when two or more processes are co-operating and need to send messages to each other.

Various system signals are defined within SunOS. Two defined signals are SIGKILL and SIGTERM. SIGKILL is the ninth defined signal (indicated by **-9**), which tells a program to abort itself. A process must shut itself down if it receives a SIGKILL message. SIGTERM is the fifteenth defined message (**-15**) and requests that a program shut itself down. A process may ignore a SIGTERM, but it can not ignore a SIGKILL.

The **kill** command terminates a process, as specified by its process ID number. Usually **kill** sends a signal **-15** to the process. Sometimes a process is harder to terminate, then a signal **-9** is needed. To determine the correct process, use the **ps** command.

Example

If you were running a process in the background, such as the following:

```
find / -name test -print &
```

entering

```
ps
```

would display a list similar to this one:

```
PID TT STAT  TIME COMMAND
15021 p0 S   0:00 -csh (csh)
15100 p0 R   0:02 find / -name test -print
15101 p0 R   0:00 ps
```

Notice the **find** command has a process ID number of 15100. To terminate this process, enter

```
kill 15100
```

The screen should display this line:

```
[1]     Terminated          find / -name test -print
```

If the **kill** command did not terminate this process, you would then enter

```
kill -9 15100
```

See Also

ps

leave

Syntax

```
leave [[+] time]
```

Description

The **leave** command reminds you of upcoming appointments by letting you set an alarm. Once you have set a time, **leave** reminds you of an appointment several times before the specified time, at the specified time, and every minute thereafter for up to ten minutes.

The time is specified as one of two formats: absolute or relative. An absolute time is in the form *hhmm*, with *hh* being hours and *mm* being minutes. All times are converted to a 12-hour clock and assumed to be in the next 12 hours. A relative format begins with **+** and sets the alarm for the indicated *time* from now. If no time is given, **leave** displays

```
When do you have to leave?
```

If you enter a Return without specifying a time, **leave** exits without setting an alarm.

Options

The **leave** command has no options.

Example

If it is Monday, October 5, 1992 at 3:20pm, then entering

```
leave +10
```

sets the alarm for 10 minutes from now. The system responds with

```
Alarm set for Mon Oct 5 15:30:00 1992
```

On the same day, entering

```
leave 1715
```

sets the alarm for 5:15 p.m. The system responds

```
Alarm set for Mon Oct 5 17:15:00 1992
```

See Also

```
cal calendar
```

ln

Syntax

```
ln [-fs] filename1 [filename2]
ln [-fs] filename(s) directory
ln [-fs] sourcefile1 newlink
```

Description

When you create a file on disk, SunOS places the file name in the appropriate directory and creates a link (or pointer) that points to the physical file. The **ln** command creates a link (or pointer) between the file named *filename1* and the name *filename2*. This makes it possible to refer to the same file by two different names. One person may prefer to name a file **phone.list**, while another prefers to call the file **numbers**. The **ln** command makes it possible for both names to point to the same file. The **ln** command can be used to point to the same file from different directories. If you are working on a project, and want to access a file from the **proj1** directory as if it were in your home directory, you could create a link from your home directory to the **project** directory.

There is an important difference between creating a link to a file and copying the file to another directory. With linked files, when one copy of the file is updated, all links to that file are simultaneously updated, whereas with a copy of the file, all copies must be updated individually. If you change the permissions of a file, any links to that file have their permissions changed also. Links are removed with the **rm** command. As long as a file has at least one link remaining, the file itself is not deleted.

The first form of the **ln** command creates a link called *filename2* to the existing file *filename1*. If *filename2* is not specified, the link is created in the current directory with the file name *filename1*. In the second form, **ln** creates a link in *directory* to *filename(s)*. In the last form, a symbolic link is made which may point to directories.

Options

-**f**   Forces a hard link to a directory. Only a superuser may use this option.

-**s**   Creates a symbolic link, which is useful for pointing to directories

Example

If you are working on a file and want to call it **sanitation**, while a coworker wants to call the same file **garbage**, create a link to garbage called **sanitation**:

```
ln garbage sanitation
```

In your home directory you can make a subdirectory, **project**, linked to the already existing **/proj1** directory by entering

```
ln /proj1/* project
```

See Also

rm, cp

login

Syntax

```
login [username]
```

Description

The **login** command signs the user identified by **username** onto the system. By requiring users to login, it is possible to protect the system from unauthorized use and to tailor the system to each user. This command may be used to change from one user to another in the middle of a session. If used without **username**, **login** will request a user name. In either case, login then prompts for a password.

Example

Enter

```
login lbird
```

to log in as **lbird**. The user indicated by **lbird** must be a valid user on the system in order to log in.

See Also

`logout,` `passwd`

logout

Syntax

`logout`

Description

The `logout` command terminates a SunOS session. By requiring users to log out, the system is protected against unauthorized use and is able to reallocate resources no longer in use (such as memory and CPU time).

See Also

`login`

lpq

Syntax

`lpq [-Pprintername] [-l] [+[n]] [job_number] [username]`

Description

The `lpq` command displays the contents of a printer queue. SunOS takes files to be printed and places them into a queue (a storage place in memory). This allows you to print out a file or several files while working on the same file.

The `lpq` command reports the user requesting the print job, the current position in the queue, the name of the file to be printed, the job number (needed to remove the job from the queue), and the size of the print job in bytes for each of the jobs in the queue. If the *job_number* is specified, `lpq` reports only on that print job. If *username* is specified, `lpq` reports on all print jobs requested by that user.

Options

-P*printername*	Used when more than one printer is connected to the system. When more than one printer is present, each printer uses a separate queue. If no printer is specified with the print request, the default is used.
-1	Requests print queue information in a long format. If multiple machines are sharing a printer, specifies from which machine the print request originated.
+*[n]*	Displays the status of the queue every *n* seconds until the queue is empty.

Example

To list jobs waiting in the print queue, enter

    lpq

which displays

```
Rank   Owner     Job   Files              Total Size
1st    dangell   56    ./friends/whales   34443 bytes
2nd    dangell   57    ./friends/dolphins 12452 bytes
```

where the files listed have previously been entered into the print queue.

See Also

    lpr, lprm, pr

lpr

Syntax

    lpr [options]

Description

The `lpr` command sends files to the print queue to be printed. This allows you to work on a file, print it out, and then while it is still printing out, continue to work on the file. The file prints in the same state as when you gave the **print** command. It also makes it possible to print out several files.

Options

`-Pprintername`	Used when more than one printer is connected to the system. Each printer uses a separate queue. If no printer is specified with **lpr**, the default printer is used.
`-#n`	Prints the number of copies specified by *n*
`-Jjobname`	Prints the string indicated by *jobname* as the name on the first page. Normally **lpr** prints the name of the file on the first page.
`-Ttitle`	Uses *title* instead of the file name for the page header indicated by **pr** (**pr** is a formatting utility)
`-in`	Indents the printed output the number of spaces indicated by *n* (the default is eight spaces)
`-wn`	Sets the page width used by **pr** to the number of columns indicated by *n*
`-r`	Removes the file from the directory after enqueuing it
`-m`	Sends mail to you to indicate that the file has been printed out

-s	Creates a link instead of copying the file to the queue. If the linked file is modified after the **lpr** command but before the file is actually finished printing, the changes show up in the printed output. Files larger than one megabyte are truncated unless this option is used. (Note: the **-s** option only works with named files; it will not work with output from a pipe.)
-p	Uses the **pr** command to format the file prior to printing
-l	Prints control characters instead of interpreting them. For example, a form-feed will show up as a **^L** instead of forcing a page break.
-v	Specifies that the file contains a raster image

Example

Entering

```
lpr text.file
```

prints out the file **text.file** to the default printer.

See Also

pr, **screendump**, **lpq**, **lprm**

lprm

Syntax

```
lprm [-Pprintername] [ - ] [job_number]
```

Description

The `lprm` command removes the print job indicated by *job_number* from the print queue.

Options

`-Pprintername`   Used when more than one printer is connected to the system. Each printer uses a separate queue. If no printer is specified with the `lprm` request, the default is used.

`-`   Removes all of your print jobs

See Also

`lpq`, `lpr`

ls

Syntax

```
ls [options] filename
```

Description

The `ls` command lists the files and subdirectories of a directory, as well as additional information about each file. The output is sorted alphabetically. When the *filename* argument is not added, the contents of the current directory are listed.

Options

`-a`   Lists all entries. Without this option entries beginning with a dot (.) are not listed.

`-A`   Same as -a, except that the entries for the current directory and the parent of the current directory are not listed.

`-c`   Lists files sorted by the time of creation

-d   If the `ls` argument **filename** is a directory, lists only its name.

-F   Marks directories with a trailing slash (**/**), executable files with a trailing asterisk (*****), and links with a trailing at sign (**@**)

-g   Shows the group ownership of the file (used with the **-l** option)

-l   Lists files in long format. This gives the permission modes, number of links to the file, owner of the file, and time of the file's creation or last modification.

-r   Reverses the order of the sort, listing files in reverse alphabetic order

-R   Recursively lists any subdirectories encountered

-t   Sorts by time of last modification instead alphabetically, listing oldest files and directories first

-u   Sorts by the time of the last access instead of the time of last modification when used with the **-t** option

Example

Entering

```
ls -altR
```

displays a long listing of all the files in the current directory and all subdirectories of the current directory, sorted by the time each was last modified.

man

Syntax

```
man commandname
```

Description

The **man** command displays information about commands from the online reference manuals usually located in the **/usr/share/man** directory. Not all systems have the manuals on line, but for those that do, this is a convenient command.

Example

Entering

```
man find
```

displays information on the **find** command.

mesg

Syntax

```
mesg [options]
```

Description

The **mesg** command reports on the status of message posting to your screen.

Options

    n   Disables posting of messages to your screen through the write command

    y   Enables posting of messages to your screen through the **write** command

Example

Entering

```
mesg
```

displays

```
is y
```

or

```
is n
```

Entering

```
mesg n
```

displays just the prompt and disables posting messages to the screen.

See Also

```
write, talk
```

mkdir

Syntax

```
mkdir directoryname
```

Description

The **mkdir** command makes directories.

Example

Entering

```
mkdir directory1
```

creates a directory named **directory1** in the current directory. If **mkdir** cannot make a requested directory, it displays an error message. For instance, the command

```
mkdir .
```

causes the screen to display the message

```
mkdir:.: File exists
```

The error is that **mkdir .** is telling the computer to make a directory with the name . (dot). Dot already refers to the directory in which you are currently working.

See Also

chmod, rm, rmdir

more

Syntax

    more [options]

Description

The **more** command displays files one screenful at a time. This is useful when trying to view large files, which **cat** displays too fast to read. Using **more**, the display pauses after each screenful, until you enter either a Return or another command that **more** can interpret.

Commands

The **more** command interprets various keystrokes as commands. The numerical argument by default is one, but you can repeat any command by preceding it with *n*, the number of times you want that command repeated. The following list explains keystroke commands that can be used with **more**.

h	Displays help for **more** and a description of the **more** commands
nb	Skips back *n* screenfuls, then displays a screenful
n/pattern	Searches for the nth occurrence of *pattern*
ns	Skips *n* lines, then displays a screenful
q or Q	Exits the **more** command
Return	Displays another line
Space	Displays the next screenful

z	Same as a space, except that if *n* precedes **z**, *n* sets the new default for the number of lines per screen.

Options

-c	Clears the screen before displaying the file
-d	Displays an error message rather than ringing the terminal bell if an unrecognized **more** command is used
-l	Treats form-feeds (Ctrl-l) as any other character, not as a page break. Without this, **more** treats form-feeds contained within the file as page breaks.
-*linecount*	Displays the number of lines indicated by **linecount** as a screenful instead of the default (typically 24 lines)
+*linenumber*	Starts display at the line indicated by **linenumber**, instead of the beginning of the file
+/*pattern*	Starts display at the two lines before the line containing **pattern**. Note that there is no trailing slash (**/**). (If one is included, it becomes part of the search pattern.)
-s	Squeezes the output, replacing multiple, consecutive blank lines in the file with a single blank line

Example

Entering

```
more .login
```

displays your `.login` file, pausing at the end of each screenful. A good use for **more** is to use it with a pipe at the end of a command line; that way you can slow down the output to allow time to read. For instance, entering

```
grep ' ' *.c | more
```

displays all lines in C source files in the current directory which contain a space. The **more** command allows you to read each screenful. If you enter the above command, type **q** to quit the **more** command.

See Also

`cat`

mv

Syntax

```
mv [options] filename1 filename2
```

or

```
mv [options] directoryname1 directoryname2
```

Description

The **mv** command moves or renames *filename1* to *filename2* (that is, it makes a copy, then deletes the original file). If you are moving or renaming directories, **mv** moves all of *directoryname1* to *directoryname2;* if *directoryname2* does not exist, **mv** creates it. The **mv** command can be used to rename a file. It is also possible to use **mv** to copy a file over another file, thus deleting the old file. If you copy a `.login` file from someone else's home directory into yours, their `.login` file will replace yours.

The **mv** command returns to the system prompt if successful. It is a good idea for new users to use **mv -i**, as **mv** by itself does not give feedback to the user, which can lead to unknowingly deleting files. If you always want to use the **-i** option with **mv**, enter **alias mv** `'mv -i'` into your `.cshrc` file. This will cause **mv -i** to be run whenever **mv** is entered.

Options

-**f**   Forces removal even if the file or directory permissions don't allow it

-**i**   Asks for confirmation before replacing an existing file or directory

Example

Entering

```
mv /socrates/questions /delphi/answers
```

removes the file named **questions** in the directory **socrates**, places it into the **delphi** directory, and renames the file **answers**.

See Also

rm, **cp**, **alias**

newgrp

Syntax

```
newgrp [group]
```

Description

The **newgrp** command changes a user's group identification. Only the group ID is changed; the user remains a member of all groups previously assigned. The user remains logged in and the current directory is unchanged, but the group ID of newly created files is set to the new effective group ID. With no **group** specified, **newgrp** changes the group identification back to the group specified in the user's password file entry.

Options

The **newgrp** command takes no options.

Example

Entering

```
newgrp wildbunch
```

changes your group to the **wildbunch** group, which must already be set up by a System Administrator.

See Also

chgrp

nice

Syntax

```
nice [-n] command(s)
```

Description

The **nice** command runs commands at low priority. Since SunOS is a multitasking system, it needs to know which jobs have priority. For instance, a user typing at the keyboard generally deserves priority over a file being printed to a printer. Various jobs are assigned various priorities. So if you decide to search the entire file system for a file you've misplaced, you can tell the operating system to give the command a low priority using the **nice** command.

The *-n* argument tells **nice** how nice to be. The larger the number used for *-n*, the lower the priority the command gets and the slower it runs. *-n* should be in the range of zero to twenty; if no *-n* is present, **nice** defaults to ten.

Options

The **nice** command takes no options.

Example

Entering

```
nice grep jabberwocky *
```

executes the **grep** command with a lower priority than usual, although you may not notice the difference. The **nice** command is especially useful when running jobs in the background.

nohup

Syntax

```
nohup command [arguments]
```

Description

The **nohup** command runs a command immune to **hangup** signals and quits. The action of logging out sends a **hangup** signal that terminates all your processes. To keep a job running after you log out, precede the command with **nohup**. To execute a pipeline or list of commands, the list or pipeline must be in a script file. **nohup** recognizes only one command per line. Entering **nohup** *command1; command2* applies **nohup** only to *command1*. Note that entering **nohup** (*command1; command2*) is syntactically incorrect.

Example

If you enter commands into a file named **script**, then entered this command

```
nohup sh script &
```

the commands are run in the background, and will continue to run even if you log out.

See Also

ps, **jobs**, **kill**

notify

Syntax

```
notify [%job_number]
```

Description

The `notify` command notifies you when the status of the current job or a specified job changes. SunOS usually informs you of a change of status, such as a background job finishing, before displaying a shell prompt. The delay in notification if you do not use `notify` may be considerable; for instance, if you are editing a file, it may be awhile before you return to the system prompt and are notified. By using `notify`, you will be informed of a change in status of a job even if you are in the middle of an editing program.

If you do not specify a job number, the current job (the first background job entered) is assumed.

Example

Entering

```
notify
```

turns on notification for the current job (the first background job entered). Entering

```
notify %3
```

turns on notification for the third background job you started. (Entering `jobs` displays a list of the background jobs and their numbers.)

See Also

`jobs`

passwd

Syntax

```
passwd
```

Description

The `passwd` command changes your login password. It prompts you for your old password, then for the new password, then for the new password again. Only a system administrator can change your password without knowing your current password.

When changing your password, you should change it to a word with at least six characters—five characters if you use both upper- and lowercase. Remember, case counts, as do spaces and other control characters. You should avoid using names, dates, social security numbers, and so on as passwords, since they are easy to guess. You should also avoid using words in the dictionary! One clever person decided to translate an entire dictionary using the same algorithm as the **passwd** command. This allowed him to look in the **/etc/passwd** file, find the encrypted passwords, look them up in his translated dictionary, and then log in under another user's name.

Example

The following illustrates a sample password-changing session. Enter

```
passwd
```

The system responds with

```
Changing password for lgoodman
Old password:
```

When you enter your old password, it is not displayed on the screen. The screen then displays

```
New password:
```

Enter the new password. Note that it is not displayed. Then you reenter your new password at this prompt

```
Retype new password:
```

and your old password is changed. If you enter a different password the second time, the system responds with this message

```
Mismatch - password unchanged
```

and your password remains unchanged. If you fail to enter enough characters for the new password, the system responds with the message

```
Please use a longer password.
```

If you reenter the same password each time this prompt is displayed (usually three times), your password is changed even if it is less than six characters.

paste

Syntax

```
paste [options] filename1 filename2
```

Description

The **paste** command merges corresponding lines of several files. Each file is treated as a column, or series of columns, and the columns are concatenated horizontally. Compare the action of **paste** (horizontal merging) with that of **cat** (vertical merging). The **paste** command replaces the newline character at the end of the first line in the first file with a tab (or another character with the **-d** option) and then appends the first line in the second file, and so on.

Options

-d*list*   Without this option, the newline characters at the end of each line (in each file) except the last one are replaced with a tab. This option allows the use of characters other than the tab character. The characters in *list* are substituted for the newlines. *list* is used circularly; when it is exhausted, it is restarted from the beginning. *list* may contain special escape sequences: **\n** (newline), **\t** (tab), **** (backslash), and **\0** (an empty string, not a null character).

Example

If a file called **men** contains the following list

```
Anthony
Othello
Romeo
Larry
```

and a file called **women** contains this list

```
Cleopatra
Ophelia
Juliet
Rhonda
```

then entering

```
paste -d' & ' men women
```

results in this display:

```
Anthony & Cleopatra
Othello & Ophelia
Romeo & Juliet
Larry & Rhonda
```

See Also

cat, **pr**

pr

Syntax

```
pr [options] [filename]
```

Description

The **pr** command prepares files for printing. The output is separated into pages. Each page has a header consisting of the date and time, the file name, and the page number.

Options

-h *string*	Uses *string* instead of the file name in the header
-l *n*	Sets the page length to *n* lines instead of the default page length of 66 lines

Example

Entering

```
pr textfile | lpr
```

paginates and prints the file **.cshrc**. Entering

```
pr -h 'My C Shell file' .cshrc
```

paginates and prints the file **.cshrc**, with **My C Shell file** as a header instead of the file name **.cshrc**.

ps

Syntax

```
ps [options]
```

Description

The **ps** command displays information about processes. Informally, processes can be thought of as jobs the system is running. The **ps** command usually only shows processes you are running.

If you enter

```
ps
```

a display resembling this one appears:

```
PID TT STAT  TIME COMMAND
9084 p2 S    0:00 -csh (csh)
9346 p2 R    0:00 ps
```

Your display may be different. The following list explains the information that appears in the example display:

PID	Process ID number
TT	Attached terminal (usually the one you logged in on)
STAT	State of the process
TIME	CPU time used by the process
COMMAND	Command associated with the process

Options

-a Displays information about all users' processes, not just yours

-u Displays the user name associated with the processes, as well as percent of CPU time used (**%CPU**), percent of available memory used (**%MEM**), information about various types of memory used (**SZ** and **RSS**), and time the process was created (**TIME**)

Example

Entering

```
ps
```

displays information about the processes you are currently running. Entering

```
ps -au
```

displays information about processes running by anyone on the system, as well as information about which user is running the process.

pwd

Syntax

```
pwd
```

Description

The **pwd** command displays the pathname of the current directory.

Options

The **pwd** command takes no options.

Example

Remembering that **cd** changes the current directory to the directory specified, entering

```
cd /usr/lgoodman/book
```

then entering

```
pwd
```

displays

```
/usr/lgoodman/book
```

See Also

```
cd
```

rasfilter8to1

Syntax

```
rasfilter8to1 [options] [infile [outfile]]
```

Description

The **rasfilter8to1** command reads the raster file *infile* (which is 8-bits deep) and converts it to *outfile* (which is 1-bit deep). An 8-bit file is either a color file or a black-and-white file with 256 levels of gray (from black to white). A 1-bit file is a black-and-white file with no grays, just straight black and straight white. The conversion can be either dithering or thresholding. *Dithering* means alternating black and white dots close together to simulate gray, and *thresholding* means taking all gray values above some threshold and converting them to white and converting all grays below that threshold to black. This command is useful for viewing 8-bit raster files on devices that can only display monochrome images (such as printers).

Options

-d	Uses dithering instead of thresholding
-rgba *threshold*	Sets the threshold for red, green, blue, and average pixel color values. The average defaults to 128, and the individual thresholds default to zero.

Example

The command

```
screendump | rasfilter8to1 | lpr
```

takes the image from the screen, converts it from an 8-bit deep image to a 1-bit deep image, and prints the results on the printer.

See Also

rastrepl, **screendump**, **screenload**

rastrepl

Syntax

```
rastrepl [infile [outfile]]
```

Description

The **rastrepl** command reads the raster file *infile* and converts it to the raster file *outfile*, which is twice as large in height and width. Pixel replication is used to magnify the image. The output file is the same type of file as the input file.

Options

The **rastrepl** command takes no options.

Example

The command

```
screendump | rastrepl | rasfilter8to1 | lpr
```

takes the screen image, doubles its size, converts it from 8-bits deep to 1-bit deep, and prints it out.

See Also

rasfilter8to1, **screendump**, **screenload**

rm

Syntax

```
rm [options] filename
```

Description

The **rm** command deletes one or more files. You must have write permission in the directory which contains the file or files, but you need not have write permission for the file. The **rm** command returns to the system prompt if successful unless the **-i** option is used. It is a good idea for new users to use this option, as **rm** runs without giving feedback to the user, which can lead to unknowingly deleting files. If you want to always use the **-i** option with the **rm** command, enter

```
alias rm 'rm -i'
```

into your **.cshrc** file. This will cause **rm -i** to be run when **rm** is typed in.

Options

-**f**   Forces removal even if the file or directory permissions don't allow it. A file can have write permission disabled to keep the file from being overwritten or erased. If you try **rm** on a file that has its protection set to disable writing, then **rm** will not delete the file. If the -**f** option is used, the delete will occur regardless of what permissions are set

-**i**   Asks whether to delete each file or to examine each directory if the -**r** option is used

-**r**   Recursively deletes the files and subdirectories associated with a directory, as well as the directory itself

Example

Entering

```
rm lgoodman/temp
```

removes the file **temp** from the directory **lgoodman**. Entering

```
rm -r lgoodman/book
```

removes all the files from all the subdirectories of **book**, as well as the subdirectory **book**.

See Also

mv, **cp**, **alias**

rmdir

Syntax

```
rmdir directoryname
```

Description

The **rmdir** command removes directories. The directory must be empty, meaning it cannot contain files or subdircctories.

Example

```
rmdir tmp
```

removes the directory **tmp** from the current working directory.

See Also

mkdir, **ls**, **rm**

screendump

Syntax

```
screendump [options] [-f frame_buffer] [-t type] [-xyXY n]
[filename]
```

Description

The **screendump** command reads the contents of a frame buffer and writes the display image to the file named **filename**.

Options

-c	Dumps the frame buffer contents without making a temporary copy in memory. The frame buffer must not be changed during the dump. (Normally a copy of the frame buffer is stored in memory to allow changes to the frame buffer after the dump command is issued but before it's complete.)
-e	Sets the output raster-file type to **2**, **RT_BYTE_ENCODED**. This usually saves a significant amount of space as compared with the standard output.

-o	Dumps the frame buffer overlay plane only
-8	Dumps the frame buffer color planes only
-f **frame_buffer**	Dumps the specified frame buffer device (the default is **/dev/fb.**)
-t **type**	Sets the output raster-file type (The default is **1, RT_STANDARD.**)
-x *n* or **-y** *n*	Sets the x or y coordinate of the upper-left corner of the area to be dumped
-X *n* or **-Y** *n*	Sets the width or height of the area to be dumped

Example

The command

```
screendump screen.image
```

writes the current console contents to the file named **screen.image**.

See Also

rastrepl, **rasfilter8to1**, **screenload**

screenload

Syntax

```
screenload [options] [-f frame_buffer] [-xyXY n]
[-h bit_pattern] [-i color] [filename]
```

Description

The **screenload** command reads a SunOs standard raster file and displays it in a frame buffer. The **screenload** command is able to display monochrome images on a color display but not color images on a monochrome display. If the input image is larger than the resolution of the display, **screenload** clips the bottom and right edges of the image.

Options

-d	Prints a warning if the display size does not match the raster-file image size
-o	Loads the image on the overlay plane of the display. (Ignored if the display does not have an overlay plane.)
-p	Pauses and waits for the user to press Return before exiting
-r	Reverses the foreground and background of the output image. This is useful when loading a screen-dump made from a reverse video screen.
-f *frame_buffer*	Displays the image on the specified frame buffer device
-x *n* or **-y** *n*	Sets the x or y coordinate of the upper-left corner of the image on the display to the given value
-X *n* or **-Y** *n*	Sets the maximum width or height of the displayed image
-b	Fills the border area with a default pattern of solid ones
-g	Fills the border area with a pattern of desktop gray
-n	Inhibits filling the border area
-w	Fills the border area with a pattern of solid zeroes

-h *bit_pattern*	Fills the border area with the bit pattern described by *bit_pattern*
-i color	Fills the border area with the given color (The default value is 255.)

Example

The command line

```
screenload screen.image
```

loads the raster image contained in **screen.image**.

See Also

rasfilter8to1, **rastrepl**, **screendump**

set

Syntax

```
set [variable [= value]]
```

Description

The **set** command, without *variable* or *value*, displays the values of all shell variables. Shell variables are used from within the shell, as opposed to environment variables which may be used within programs as well as the shell. Shell variables are used to save typing in long commands often. For instance, a path variable tells the operating system where to look for executable files or scripts so that you don't have to type a path with each name of a program or script.

The **set** command followed by *variable* assigns a null value as the current value of *variable*. The **set** command with *variable* followed by-*value* assigns the value indicated by *value* to the variable indicated by *variable*.

Options

The **set** command takes no options.

Example

Entering

```
set
```

displays the current value of any defined shell variables, with a display like the following:

```
argv ()
cwd  /usr/lgoodman/book
home /usr/lgoodman
path ( . /usr/ucb /bin /usr/local/bin /usr/lgoodman/bin)
printer   hp13
prompt    /usr/lgoodman/book >
shell     /bin/csh
term dec-vt100
user lgoodman
```

Entering

```
set prompt = 'What now?'
```

sets your prompt to **What now?**, which is displayed after every command or program is finished.

See Also

```
setenv
```

setenv

Syntax

```
setenv [variable [value]]
```

Description

The **setenv** command is used to assign a value to an environment variable. SunOS uses environment variables to keep track of information such as your home directory, the location of your mailbox, and the type of terminal you are using. Entering **setenv** without indicating a variable and a value displays all the defined environment variables with their values. Entering

setenv with a variable but no value sets the environment variable indicated by the variable to an empty or null value. Entering **setenv** with a variable and a value assigns the value specified to the environment variable specified.

Options

The **setenv** command takes no options.

Example

Entering

```
setenv
```

lists the values of the current environment variables. An example listing is

```
TERM=dec-vt100
HOME=/usr/lgoodman
SHELL=/bin/csh
USER=lgoodman
PATH=.:/usr/ucb /usr/bin:/usr/local/bin:/usr/lgoodman/bin
LOGNAME=lgoodman
PWD=/usr/lgoodman
PRINTER=hpl3
MAILER=Mail
EDITOR=/usr/local/bin/emacs
```

Entering

```
setenv TERM ansi
```

sets your terminal type to **ansi**. (ANSI is a set of standards, in this case a set of interfaces for providing terminal controls, such as the command to clear the screen or the command to set the cursor at a particular line and column position.) This is used by programs such as **vi** to control your terminal display.

See Also

```
set
```

sleep

Syntax

```
sleep time
```

Description

The **sleep** command suspends execution of a process for a specified number of seconds.

Options

The **sleep** command takes no options.

Example

Using **sleep** you can execute a command at some later time, such as the following:

```
(sleep 600; echo try that phone call again )&
```

which does nothing for 600 seconds (ten minutes), then displays

```
try that phone call again
```

See Also

at

sort

Syntax

```
sort [options] [-o outfile] filename
```

Description

The **sort** command sorts lines within the specified file and writes its output to either the screen or the file specified with the **-o outfile** option. Output lines are sorted character-by-character, left-to-right. If more than one file is specified as input, the files are sorted and collated.

Options

-b	Ignores leading blanks
-d	Sorts by ascending dictionary order (upper-case letters first, then lowercase). Only letters, digits, and blanks are significant in comparison. The default is to sort using ASCII order, where all ASCII characters are significant.
-f	Folds uppercase and lowercase letters, causing case to be ignored
-i	Ignores characters outside the ASCII range 040 to 0176 in nonnumeric comparisons
-n	Sorts by numeric order
-r	Reverses the collating sequence

Example

Entering

```
sort -o sorted namelist
```

sorts the file **namelist**, and writes the output to the sorted file **sorted**. Entering

```
sort dept[a-f] -o sorted.depts
```

sorts the six files, **depta** through **deptf**, and stores the output into the file **sorted.depts**.

See Also

tr, **uniq**

spell

Syntax

```
spell [options] filename
```

Description

The **spell** command checks a file for spelling errors. The output is an alphabetized list of all words that cannot be found in, or derived from, the system dictionary file.

Options

-b Accepts British spellings, such as "centre," "colour," and "travelled"

-v Prints all the words not literally in the system dictionary. Words that can be derived from the dictionary are displayed, showing the plausible derivation

-x Prints every possible stem for each word

Example

Entering

```
spell resume > corrections
```

reads in the file **resume**, checking for spelling errors, and writes any words not in the dictionary to the file **corrections**.

See Also

sort, **uniq**

su

Syntax

```
su username
```

Description

The **su** command temporarily switches your user ID to that of **username**. The **su** command prompts for a password, just as if you were logging in, and with a correct password changes your user ID and group ID to that of **username**. The **.login** file for *username* is not read, but the `.cshrc` file is. The current directory is not changed, but the HOME variable is changed.

Example

To change to user bjoy enter

```
su bjoy
```

and then enter the appropriate password for bjoy at the prompt

```
password:
```

See Also

`login`, `logout`

tail

Syntax

```
tail [options] [filename]
```

Description

The **tail** command sends the end of *filename* to the screen. The user can specify how many lines are sent. If the number of lines to be sent is not specified, **tail** sends ten lines. Whether standard input or a file is used depends upon whether or not the *filename* argument is used. If the *filename* argument is not specified, the keyboard (or standard input) is used.

If you have a file which stores transactions, using **tail** you can quickly review the most recent activity.

Options

+|-n   With no number specified, **tail** outputs the last ten lines of the input. If **+n** is present, **tail** outputs the number of lines, characters, or blocks from the beginning of the input; if **-n** is present, **tail** counts back from the end of the file.

1   Refers to lines when added after **+|-n**

b	Refers to blocks when added after **+** | **-***n*
c	Refers to characters when added after **+** | **-***n*
r	Outputs the lines in reverse order

Example

Using the file named **phonelist** and entering

```
tail -31 phonelist
```

displays

```
Thomas, Ginger (408) 555-2323
Williams, Greg  (408) 555-2916
Young, Charles (415) 555-2380
```

Entering

```
tail -23c phonelist
```

displays

```
Charles (415) 555-2380
```

Note that if options **l**, **b**, or **c** are used, they must immediately follow any **+** \| **-***n* with no intervening spaces.

See Also

cat, **more**, **head**

talk

Syntax

```
talk username [tty]
```

Description

The **talk** command establishes a two-way, terminal-to-terminal communication path. It allows users to send messages back and forth by typing them in.

Options

The **talk** command takes no options.

Example

Entering

```
talk lgoodman
```

displays the following on lgoodman's terminal:

```
Message from Talk_Daemon@system at time
talk:   connection requested by yourname@system.
talk:   respond with:  talk yourname@system
```

system is your computer's system name. **time** is the current time. **yourname** is your login name. The other user (in this case lgoodman) should then enter

```
talk yourname
```

This establishes the link between your terminals. To exit, just enter your system's interrupt character (on some systems press Control-O). Note that pressing Control-L redraws the screen while using the **talk** command.

See Also

mesg, **who**, **write**

tar

Syntax

```
tar [key] [options] [tar_filename] [blocksize]
[exclude_file] [-I include_file] [filename1] [filename2 ...]
[-C directory filename3] [filename4]
```

Description

The **tar** command archives and recovers files. It can create, add to, list, and retrieve files from an archive. The first option following **tar** is the key. The key specifies these actions: create (creates a new tarfile); write (writes the designated files to the end of the tarfile); table of contents (lists the table of contents of the tarfile); update (adds the named files to the tarfile if they are not already present or current); extract (extracts files from an archive file). One of these must be entered. After the key comes any modifiers. An archive file may reside on a system disk, floppy disk, tape unit, or anywhere else SunOS can write or read a file.

Common places to archive files are tape drives and floppy disks. One of the marvels of SunOS is that these devices can be written to or read from with no more effort than a file. The **/dev** directory has several "files" in it that are really devices such as a tape drive, terminal, system disk, or floppy disk drive. **/dev/rfd0a** is really a floppy drive, and **/dev/rst0** is really a tape drive.

The **tar** command knows about directory structures and can preserve absolute, relative, or no directory information. If the files specified to archive are given with a full path, that information is preserved, and when the file is recovered, it is placed back into the correct directory. If the files are specified with a relative path at the time of the archive, they are placed in the directory with the same relative path from the current working directory at the time of the recovery. If, at the time of the archive, the files are specified from the current directory with just a file name, they will be placed into whatever the current working directory is at the time of recovery.

The **tar** command keeps track of a great deal of information besides the file's contents. It keeps track of things like a *checksum*, which is a number used to help insure data integrity, the permissions associated with the files, their creation dates, and so on.

Examples of device names commonly found on Sun workstations include:

Device Name	*Device*
/dev/rst0 or **/dev/rst8**	¼" tape cartridge

Device Name	Device
/dev/rmt0 or	
/dev/rmt8	½" reel-to-reel tape
/dev/rfd0	3-½" diskette

After performing a backup or a retrieval on some devices, the system typically rewinds the tape and resets the file pointers for diskettes. To prevent rewinding, the device name should be preceded with an *n*, such as **/dev/nrst0**.

Keys

c   Creates a new archive file. This overwrites anything previously stored on the media (overwrites files on floppies, for instance).

r   Appends the named files to an existing archive file. Any existing files in the archive are not changed. This does not work with ¼" tape.

t   Prints the names of any specified files as they appear in the archive file. If no files are specified, this key displays a directory of all files contained in the archive file.

u   Performs an update, appending files to the archive only if they are not already present or if they have been modified since they were last written to the tape. This option runs slowly due to the checking it must perform. This does not work with ¼" tape.

x   Extracts files from an archive file. Given a file list, this option only extracts the files specified. With no file list, this option extracts all the files in an archive.

Options

e   Returns a positive exit status in the event of an unexpected error

f	Uses the next argument as the name of the file to read or write as the archive file (instead of the default of /dev/rmt8). If – is used, the standard input or standard output is used; thus **tar** can be used in a pipe.
F	Excludes all directories named **SCCS** from the archive
FF	Excludes all **SCCS** directories, all files with **.o** as their suffix, and all files named **errs**, **core**, and **a.out**
h	Follows symbolic links, which allows linked files to be treated as if they were normal files or directories. Without this option **tar** does not support symbolic links.
i	Ignores directory checksum errors
l	Displays error messages if links to archived files cannot be resolved. Without this option, error messages about unresolved links will not be displayed.
m	Does not extract modification times with files. Sets the modification time to the time of the extraction.
o	Suppresses information specifying owner and permission modes normally placed into the archive. Such information makes previous versions of **tar** generate error messages like **<filename>/: cannot create**.
p	Ignores the present **umask** and recovers files with their original permission modes. This is only used with the **x** key.
v	Displays the name of each file archived or extracted. When used with the **t** key, displays a listing similar to **ls -l**.

w	Waits for user confirmation before taking any action. Displays the action to be taken followed by the file name and waits for a **y** entered from the keyboard. Anything other than a **y** causes no action to be taken for the named file.
-I	Uses *include_filename*, the next file name, as a list of files, one per line, entered on the command line for the **tar** command. Excluded files take precedence over included files. See the **-x** option.
-X	Uses *exclude_filename*, the next file name, as a list of files, one per line, to be excluded from archive by the **tar** command. Multiple **-X** arguments may be used, with one *exclude_filename* per argument. Excluded files take precedence over included files.
014578	Selects an alternate drive on which the tape containing the archive is mounted. Note that 2, 3, 6, and 9 are not valid drives.

Example

To archive your home directory to the default tape drive (**dev/rmts**), and overwrite anything else on the tape, enter

```
tar cv ~
```

To extract the files from a floppy diskette into the current directory, enter

```
tar xvf /dev/rfd0a
```

To read the files on a ¼" cartridge tape drive, enter

```
tar tvf /dev/rst0
```

To update files on a floppy drive, enter

```
tar uvf /dev/rfd0a .
```

See Also

chdir, **ls**, **cpio**

tee

Syntax

```
tee [options] [filename]
```

Description

The **tee** command replicates the standard output. This command is usually used in a pipe. A pipe (|) is a way to connect the output of one command or program to the input of another command or program. The standard input is usually the keyboard, but by using pipes, you can get input from the output of a command or program instead. Sometimes when constructing long pipes, it is desirable to save intermediate results. If you form a **tee** in the pipe, you can siphon off some of the information and direct it to a file.

Options

-a   Appends the output to the specified file instead of overwriting the existing contents

-i   Ignores interrupts

Example

Entering

```
pr final.draft | tee report.printed | lpr
```

prepares the file **final.draft** for printing, saves a copy of the formatted file as **report.printed**, and sends a formatted copy to the printer.

See Also

`lpr`, `ls`, `pr`, `wc`

time

Syntax

```
time [command]
```

Description

The **time** command times how long a command takes to run, or with no command specified, tells how much time has been used for the current process.

Options

The **time** command takes no options.

Example

Entering

```
time
```

displays something like

```
8.1u 13.2s 3:30:42 0% 0+208k 108+44io 73pf+0w
```

Most of this is undecipherable except to system administrators, but some is useful for the average user. The **8.1u** added to the **13.2s** gives the total CPU time used by the current process (the times are in seconds). The **3:30:42** means that the process has been running for 3 hours, 30 minutes, and 42 seconds. To time a command, add the times indicated by **u** and **s**.

See Also

`date`

touch

Syntax

```
touch [options] filename
```

Description

The **touch** command sets the access and modification time of the file ***filename*** to the current time. ***filename*** is created if it does not exist. The **touch** command is often used with the special programming command **make** to force a complete rebuild of a program.

Options

-c   Does not create ***filename*** if it does not exist

Example

Enter

```
touch *.c
```

to change the access and modification of any files with the .c extension in the current directory.

tr

Syntax

```
tr [options] [string1 [string2]]
```

Description

The **tr** command copies the standard input to the standard output, translating occurrences from ***string1*** into corresponding characters in ***string2***. A common use of **tr** is to convert a file to all uppercase or lowercase.

Options

-c Complements the set of characters in *string1* with respect to the set of ASCII codes 1 - 255 (so that **tr -cd 0-9** means to delete everything that's not a number)

-d Deletes all characters in *string1*. For example, **tr -d '^A-^Z' < in.ctrl > out.txt** can be used to strip all control characters from a file (for printing a file, for instance)

-s Squeezes strings of repeated characters from *string2* to single characters

Example

Entering

```
tr A-Z a-z < mixed.case > lower.case
```

translates the file **mixed.case**, containing both upper- and lowercase, into the file **lower.case**, containing only lowercase letters. Entering

```
tr -sc A-Za-z '\012' < in.file > out.file
```

translates the file **in.file** into a file, **out.file**, with one word per line. Note that this example has no effect on the case of the characters contained in any of the files.

See Also

expand

tty

Syntax

```
tty
```

Description

The **tty** command prints the pathname of your terminal's device file.

Example

Entering

```
tty
```

displays something similar to

```
/dev/ttyp1
```

unalias

syntax

```
unalias pattern
```

Description

The **unalias** command discards aliases. Any aliases which match **pattern** are discarded, so **unalias *** discards all previous aliases.

Options

The **unalias** command takes no options.

Example

If you have previously aliased **ls** with

```
alias ls ls -l
```

which displays a long listing anytime **ls** is entered, you can undo the **alias** with

```
unalias ls
```

See Also

alias

uncompress

Syntax

```
uncompress [options] [filename]
```

Description

To recover a compressed file, use **uncompress**.

Options

-c   Writes to the screen (or standard output). Does not change any files. (The **zcat** command is equivalent to the **-c** option.)

-v   Displays the percentage of reduction

Example

Given a file, **report.text**, with a size of 4608 bytes, entering

```
compress report.text
```

results in a file, **report.text.Z**, with a size of 2696 bytes. To uncompress this file, enter

```
uncompress report.text
```

Note that with the **uncompress** command the **.Z** extension is optional.

See Also

compress

umask

Syntax

```
umask [mask]
```

Description

The **umask** command displays or sets the file creation mode **mask**. The numbers are like the numbers used for **chmod**, except that with **umask**, the numbers represent the permissions which are not granted, whereas with **chmod** the numbers represent the permissions which are granted. Because SunOS is a multiuser system, there are built-in safeguards to keep users from accidentally (or even deliberately) deleting another user's files. These safeguards protect against unauthorized reading, writing, copying, deleting, and executing of files.

The modes are given in either of two formats for this command. An absolute mode is an octal number formed by summing the following octal numbers representing the enabled permissions. There are three fields, one for the owner of the file, one for the group to which the file belongs, and one for everybody else.

0   Grants read and write permission for files, and read, write, and search permission for directories

1   Grants read and write permission for files and directories

2   Grants only read permission for files, and grants read and search permission for directories

3   Grants only read permission for files and directories

4   Grants only write permission for files and write and search permission for directories

5   Grants only write permission for files and directories

6   Grants no permissions for files, and grants only search permission for directories

7   Grants no permissions (denies all permissions) for files and directories

By default, files are given mode 666 (rw-rw-rw-), which gives everyone read and write access. Directories are given the mode

777 (rwxrwxrwx), which gives everyone read, write, and search permission.

Options

The **umask** command takes no options.

Example

```
umask
```

displays the current setting of the file creation **mask**. Entering

```
umask 002
```

sets the file creation **mask** so the owner and group have all privileges, while the rest of the world has only read permission.

See Also

chgrp, **chmod**, **chown**, **ls**

uniq

Syntax

```
uniq [options] [input_filename [output_filename]]
```

Description

The **uniq** command is used to remove or report on adjacent duplicate lines within a file. Normally **uniq** removes the second and succeeding repeated lines, passing everything else through to the output. To remove duplicate lines, they must be adjacent.

Options

-c   Precedes each line by a count of the number of times it occurred in the input

-d   Displays one occurrence of just the repeated lines from the input

-u   Displays just those lines which were not repeated in the input

      +*n*   Ignores the first *n* characters when comparing lines

      -*n*   Ignores the first *n* fields, together with any blanks before each field. A field is a string of characters separated by space or tab characters.

Examples

Entering

```
cat singers musicians | sort | uniq > people
```

combines the files **singers** and **musicians**, sorts the combined file, eliminates any duplicates, and stores the results in the file **people**. Entering

```
cat singers musicians | sort | uniq -d > diverse
```

combines the files, sorts them, and saves only duplicate lines, thus showing entries common to two or more files.

See Also

sort

units

Syntax

```
units
```

Description

The **units** command converts between units of measure. (Be aware that the money conversions are not current.) For a complete list of known units, look in the file **/usr/lib/units**. Note that the **units** command only does multiplicative scale changes; thus it can convert Kelvin to Rankine, but not Celsius to Fahrenheit. The **units** command operates interactively.

Options

The **units** command takes no options.

Example

Enter

```
units
```

and the **units** command displays

```
You have:
```

Enter

```
inch
```

and the **units** command displays

```
You want:
```

Enter

```
cm
```

and the **units** command displays

```
* 2.540000e+00
/ 3.937008e-01
```

To terminate the program, enter a Control-D.

vi

Description

vi is the visual text editor present on all SunOS systems. See Chapter 5 for a detailed discussion on vi and Chapter 6 for a discussion on the text formatting commands **nroff** and **troff**.

Types of Units

Character   Whatever is stored in a single byte, which is a unit of memory. The letter "a" is a character, a space is a character, and a tab is a character.

Word	A string of one or more characters separated on each side by a punctuation mark, space, tab, digit, or newline character (Return). A word can also be defined to include adjacent punctuation marks. These punctuated words are separated by the space, tab, or newline (Return) characters only.
Line	A string of characters separated by a newline character (Return). A line, as defined by vi, can be more than the width of a line of text displayed across your screen.
Sentence	A string of characters that ends at a period, exclamation point, or question mark, followed by two spaces or a newline (Return) character. If only one space follows the period, exclamation point, or question mark, **vi** doesn't recognize it as the end of a sentence.
Paragraph	A group of one or more lines of characters preceeded and followed by a blank line. Two newline (Return) characters in a row create a blank line in the text, which **vi** considers as the division between two paragraphs. A paragraph can be a single line or up to 45 lines.

Cursor Movement Commands

Command Key	Cursor Movement
Spacebar	Forward one character position
l	Right (forward) one character
h	Left (backward) one character
j	Down to same position in line below; moves left to last position

Command Key	Cursor Movement
k	Up to same position in line above; moves left to last position
w	Forward to first letter of next word
W	Forward to first letter of next word, including punctuation
b	Backward to first letter of previous word
B	Backward to first letter of previous word, including punctuation
Return	Forward to beginning of next line
$	End of current line
0	Beginning of current line
(	Back to beginning of current sentence
)	Ahead to beginning of next sentence
{	Back to beginning of current paragraph
}	Ahead to beginning of next paragraph
H	Home, or left end of top line on screen
M	Middle, or left end of middle line on screen
L	Lower, or left end of lowest line on screen
G	Last line in work buffer
*n*G	Move to line number *n*
Control-U	Up half screen
Control-D	Down half screen
Control-F	Forward (down) almost a full screen
Control-B	Backward (up) almost a full screen

Command Key	Cursor Movement
Control-Y	Scroll up one line at a time
Control-E	Scroll down one line at a time

Commands for Inserting Text

Key	Insert Location
i	Before cursor
I	Before first nonblank character on line
a	After cursor
A	At end of line
o	Open a line next line down
O	Open a line next line up

Delete Commands

Command Key	Deletion
x	Character at cursor
X	Character before cursor
dw	To end of word
dW	To end of word, including punctuation
db	To beginning of word
dB	To beginning of word, including punctuation
d Return	Two lines, current and following
dd	Current line
d0	From cursor to beginning of line
d$	From cursor to end of line
d)	To end of sentence

Command Key	Deletion
d (	To beginning of sentence
d}	To end of paragraph
d{	To beginning of paragraph
dL	To last line on screen
dH	To first line on screen
dG	To end of the file
d1G	To the beginning of the file

Change and Replacement Commands

Command	Change or Replacement
r	Replaces character at cursor
R	Replaces characters until Esc is pressed
cw	Adds change to end of word
cW	Adds change to end of word, including punctuation
cb	Adds change from beginning of word to cursor
cB	Adds change from beginning of word, including punctuation, to cursor
cc	Changes current line
c$	Adds change from the cursor to the end of the line
c0	Adds change from the cursor to the beginning of the line
c)	Adds change from the cursor to the end of the sentence

Command	Change or Replacement
c(	Adds change from the cursor to the beginning of the sentence
c}	Adds change from the cursor to the end of the paragraph
c{	Adds change from the cursor to the beginning of the paragraph

Yank Commands

Command	Text Yanked
yw	To end of word
yW	To end of word, including punctuation
yb	To beginning of word
yB	To beginning of word, including punctuation
y Return	Two lines—current and following
yy	Current line
y0	From the cursor to the beginning of a line
Y	From the cursor to the end of a line
y)	To end of sentence from cursor
y(	To beginning of sentence from cursor
y}	To end of paragraph from cursor
y{	To beginning of paragraph from cursor.

Search Commands

Command	Description
/**pattern** Return	Search forward for **pattern** in file
?**pattern** Return	Search backward for **pattern** in file

Command	Description
n	Find next pattern in same direction
N	Find next pattern in opposite direction

Useful Set Options

set all	Displays the complete list of options, including options you have set as well as vi's default settings
:set Wrapmargin=n	Specifies the size of the right margin used to wrap text as you type, and saves manually entering Return after each line. A typical value for n is 10 or 15.
:set nu	Displays line numbers of a file
:set ic	Specifies that pattern searches should ignore case
:set window=n	Sets the number of lines shown in the screen window where n is the number of lines
:set list	Displays invisible characters, with tabs displayed as **^I** and the end of each line (Returns) displayed as a **$**.

wall

Syntax

```
wall [options] [filename]
```

Description

The **wall** command writes to all logged-in users (as such it is usually used by the System Administrator for important messages). The standard input is read until a Control-D is entered. It is then sent to all logged-in users preceeded by the message

"Broadcast Message ...". If **filename** is specified, the input is taken from the indicated file instead of from the standard input.

Options

    -a   Writes to all terminals, even pseudo-terminals

See Also

  mesg, **write**

WC

Syntax

```
wc [options] [filename]
```

Description

    The **wc** command counts the lines, words, and characters in *filename*. If *filename* is not specified, **wc** counts the standard input. Words are separated by spaces, tabs, or newlines (carriage returns).

    The **wc** command is very useful in piping. You can use the **who** command, which lists the users currently logged in (giving one user per line) and pipe its output to **wc**, which then counts the number of lines by entering **who | wc -l**. This counts and displays the number of currently logged on users.

    Combining **ls**, a command to list the files in a directory, with **wc**, a command to count lines, as follows

```
ls | wc -l
```

counts the number of files in the current directory.

Options

    -l   Counts the lines in the specified file

    -w   Counts the words in the specified file

    -c   Counts characters in the specified file

Example

The command

```
wc file1
```

displays

```
227  876  6220 file1
```

which means there are 227 lines, 876 words, and 6220 characters in the file **file1**. Entering

```
wc -l file1
```

displays

```
227 file1
```

which means there are 227 lines in the file **file1**.

```
wc -c file1
```

displays

```
6220 file1
```

which means there are 6220 characters in the file **file1**.

which

Syntax

```
which command
```

Description

The **which** command locates a command and displays its pathname or alias. The **which** command cannot find built-in shell commands such as **history** and **set**.

Options

The **which** command takes no options.

Example

Entering

```
which vi
```

displays

```
/usr/ucb/vi
```

If you have aliased **ls** to **ls -aF !***, entering

```
which ls
```

displays

```
ls:        aliased to ls -aF !*
```

Entering

```
which set
```

displays a path similar to this:

```
no set in . /usr/ucb /bin /usr/bin /usr/local/bin
/usr/lgoodman/bin
```

where everything after the **no set in** is a possible path setting, and the **which** command could not find a command named **set** in the path.

who

Syntax

```
who
```

Description

The **who** command displays the login name, terminal name, and login time for each user currently logged in.

Options

The **who** command takes no options.

Example

Entering

```
who
```

displays something like

```
nbacon     tty6 Feb 29 09:18   (nbacon_tty)
rgoodman   tty3 Feb 29 13:12   (rgoodman_tty)
egoodman   tty9 Feb 29 08:10   (ecyr_tty)
```

See Also

```
whoami
```

whoami

Syntax

```
whoami
```

Description

The **whoami** command displays your login name.

Options

The **whoami** command takes no options.

Example

Entering

```
whoami
```

displays something like

```
lgoodman
```

See Also

```
who
```

write

Syntax

```
write username [tty]
```

Description

The **write** command allows you to send a message to another user's terminal (if they have allowed it through the use of the **mesg** command).

If the user is logged into more than one terminal, you must specify *tty*, which is a terminal number.

Type **write *username***. After entering a carriage return, enter your message, then finish by typing Control-D.

Options

The **write** command takes no options.

Example

Entering

```
write bheslop
lunch in 10 minutes?
^D
```

(where ^D means holding down the Control key and pressing the D key) displays on bheslop's terminal

```
Message from lgoodman on tty0 at 11:50 ...
lunch in 10 minutes?
```

See Also

mesg, **talk**, **ps**

APPENDIX A

Booting Up and Halting

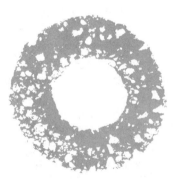

 THIS APPENDIX EXPLAINS HOW TO BOOT UP YOUR system (get it running), and how to halt your system (intentionally stopping the execution of system software) so that you can turn the power off safely. It assumes that you have already installed your system according to the installation manual pertaining to your machine.

Booting Your System

You normally don't have to boot your system because Sun workstations are designed to run continuously, preventing wear on system components. Each time you turn on the power, the machine reboots itself so that you can start using it again. In most cases, the system is set up to boot automatically from a local disk or over the network. However, when your machine is set up to boot from a tape or diskette, you need to insert the appropriate disk or tape for the boot procedure to work. In certain uncommon circumstances, a machine may become unresponsive; when you have no other alternative, you can reboot the machine to get it running again.

Emergency Rebooting Procedure

Always allow 60 seconds between turning off the power and turning it back on again. This pause prevents possible damage to power supply components in your machine.

When the machine doesn't respond to keystrokes, such as Control-C, then press Stop-A (The Stop key is the accelerator key located in the upper-left corner of the keyboard.) If you are using a keyboard other than a type 4 keyboard, press L1-A. If a special boot prompt (>) is not displayed, check the cables connecting the components of the system. If the system still doesn't respond, try turning off the power, waiting 60 seconds, and then turning the power back on. As a last resort, contact your system administrator or Sun Customer Service (1-800-USA-4SUN). Once the boot prompt is displayed, type **b** and press Return to reboot the machine. A system login screen or prompt indicates that the system has booted properly and is awaiting a user to log in.

Rebooting a Terminal

On a machine that has a terminal as a console rather than a Sun keyboard and bitmapped monitor, you need to press Break instead of Stop-A (L1-A) to obtain a boot prompt (>). Once you have a boot prompt, type **b** and press Return to reboot your system. The system should respond with a series of system messages. The final system message should be a system login prompt, which indicates that the system has booted properly and is awaiting a user to log in. When system messages indicate a problem, or when the system messages fail to appear, contact your system administrator, or as a last resort call Sun Customer Service.

Halting Your System

Halting a Sun workstation means intentionally stopping execution of the system software. You may want to halt a machine in certain circumstances, such as when you

- Install a new release of the operating system
- Install new hardware
- Move the system to another location
- Anticipate a power outage

You should always halt the machine before turning any of the power switches off. When you halt your machine properly, you protect the machine from damage and prevent the loss of your data. The following list explains the steps for halting a system:

1. Save any files you are presently editing with applications running on your machine and quit any applications that will lose information when the machine halts.

2. Become the superuser by entering **su** at the system prompt, and then entering the **hostid** or the password assigned to a superuser.

3. Enter the command **/etc/halt**. The **halt** command presents the system boot prompt (**>**) in case you decide to reboot, rather than turning off the power.

4. Turn off the power to all units in the following order: Monitor, external drive unit (if you have one), and system unit.

Emergency Halting Procedure

To halt a system that does not respond properly to the keyboard or to the mouse, follow these steps:

1. Press Stop-A. (If you are not using a type 4 keyboard, press L1-A.)

2. Press **N**, then press Return.

3. Enter the command **sync**, then press Return.

4. Turn off the power to all units in the following order: monitor, external drive unit (if you have one), and system unit.

APPENDIX B

Installing and Configuring the DeskSet

IN THIS APPENDIX YOU WILL FIND INSTRUCTIONS
for installing, configuring, and starting the SunView DeskSet or
OpenWindows environments.

DeskSet Hardware and Software Requirements

In order to install the SunView DeskSet, you must have the
following:

- A Sun workstation or server—for example, a Sun 3,
  Sun 3x (mc68020); Sun 4, Sun 4c (SPARC); or Sun
  386i (80386) computer

- A mounted hard-disk drive that contains over 1.5Mb of empty storage space for the DeskSet environment. This allows you to include binaries for all three Sun workstation architectures: mc68020, SPARC, and 386i.

- A tape or floppy-disk drive to read the DeskSet environment tape

- SunOS version 4.0 or later. If you have a Sun 386i workstation, you must be running SunOS version 4.0.1 or later.

The OpenWindows environment demands a minimum of 8.0Mb of main memory, and can be configured to take 13.2Mb of disk space in a minimal configuration and 36.5Mb of disk space if completely installed. Regardless of your configuration, in order to install and run OpenWindows, you must have at least 20.0Mb of swap space. Swap space is disk or memory space that allows a process to be swapped from disk to memory or from memory to disk.

Before Beginning the Installation Procedure

To correctly install the OpenWindows or the SunView DeskSet, you need to be familiar enough with SunOS to change directories and to use vi or another text editor to change a file's contents. During installation you must supply information to the installation script. Be ready to supply the following data. If you do not know any of the following information, ask your system administrator for help.

- Whether your media drive is local or remote and, if remote, on what machine the media drive is mounted

- The device name. The most common media drives and their device names are listed here:

  - An SCSI ¼" cartridge tape drive (usually named rst0 or rst8)

- A ½", nine-track, 1600 bpi tape drive (usually named rmt0)

- The type of workstation (or workstations) you will use to run the DeskSet: Sun 3 or 3x; Sun 4 or 4x; or Sun 386i

- The name of the directory that will contain the DeskSet environment, for example, **/home/sundesk** or **/usr/sundesk**

- Your root password, if you have one, so you can log in as a superuser to begin the script

You can create your own directory for the DeskSet if you want. If you do not create your own directory, one will be created for you as part of the installation process.

Installing the SunView DeskSet

If you are going to overwrite an old version of the DeskSet environment, do not run the installation script from the directory into which you are planning to load the DeskSet. If you are running an old version of the DeskSet environment, be sure to exit SunView before you begin the installation.

The following steps explain installing the SunView DeskSet and setting your environment variables using the C Shell. To begin the installation of the SunView DeskSet, follow these steps:

1. Become superuser on your workstation.

2. Enter

   ```
   extract_unbundled
   ```

   (This is a SunOS command that is normally found in the directory named **/usr/etc**.)

3. The script returns this prompt:

   ```
   Enter media drive location [local | remote]:
   ```

   Enter **l** if the media drive is local or **r** if it is remote.

4. When the following prompt appears

   ```
   Enter Device Name (et0, rmt0, rfd0c, rfd0g) : /dev/r.
   ```

   enter the remaining characters of your tape drive following the letter **r**.

5. A message is displayed telling you to mount the release media. Insert and lock the tape cartridge in the tape drive and press Return. The **Shell** window clears and the DeskSet copyright notice is displayed.

6. The script asks if you want to continue. Enter **y** for yes or **n** to stop installation.

7. A warning is displayed, instructing you not to run this script from the same directory into which you want to install the DeskSet. Another message is then displayed, instructing you to enter the full path for the destination directory and reminding you that you must have write permission for the directory. If you are running the script from a directory containing the old installation of the DeskSet you are going to overwrite, do the following: Exit the script by typing Control-C, exit SunView, then rerun the script **extract_unbundled** from some other directory. Do not run it from the directory that has the old installation of DeskSet environment. If you are not in the same directory, enter the full path of the destination directory.

8. A confirmation message is displayed, showing the choices you have made so far. Enter **y** to continue with installation or **n** to stop installation. The script now checks to be sure enough space is available on the media drive. If there is not enough space, the number of bytes available in the different partitions is displayed. You are then asked for a new destination. Installation then starts with the architecture-independent files.

9. Next you are asked to enter the architecture(s) you want. The installation program checks space availability and begins installation. For each architecture a set of subdirectories within the destination directory is created. The DeskSet and its files are extracted from the tape, listed as they are extracted, and copied to the subdirectories. The installation script then returns this prompt:

        Do you want to install any more architectures? [y,n]

The script continues asking you to specify an architecture until you enter **n**. After installing all the architectures you want, a check is made of the installation by verifying the existence of certain key files. If this verification fails, installation is aborted.

10. The following messages are now displayed:

```
Please remember to add /DeskSet_pathname/bin to your
path variable BEFORE /bin and /usr/bin to be able to
use the Deskset tools.

ALSO:

In order to use the Deskset, you will need to run in-
stall_deskset.

Would you like to run install_deskset [y|n]?
```

Another message is displayed telling you this installation script appends entries in a file named **/etc/magic** and creates a file called **etc/filetype**, where binder information is kept. If you do not answer **y** to continue the operation, the DeskSet will not work correctly. Type **y** to continue. If you do not run this installation script now, you can run it at a later time by changing to **$DESKSET/bin** and typing **install_deskset**.

The DeskSet is now installed.

OpenWindows Installation

The process of installing the OpenWindows environment is quite similar to installing the SunView DeskSet, except that variables are set automatically. The software media for installing OpenWindows differ in that they provide the program for one specific machine rather than all architectures. Before beginning to install OpenWindows you need to become a superuser and create a directory named **/home/openwin** (or, if you are using a Sun 386i computer, **files/local/386/openwin**). You can then begin installation by performing the **extract-_unbundled** command and then responding to the installation script's prompts.

To install the minimal OpenWindows configuration, you need to install the following components and subsets:

- The Base X/11/NeWS Component
- The X11/NeWS Users' Subset
- The XView Users' Subset

After installing OpenWindows, you also need to install the File Manager so it can work correctly in the OpenWindows environment. To install the File Manager, become superuser, change directories to **$OPENWINHOME/bin/xview**, and enter

```
install_filemgr
```

Setting SunView DeskSet Environment Variables

Once you've installed the DeskSet, you must set the appropriate environment variables, **DESKSET** and **PATH**, before you can run the DeskSet. If your **DESKSET** variable has already been set, but you have installed the DeskSet in a different directory, you will need to modify the variable.

If you are using a C shell, add the **DESKSET** environment variable to the file named **.login** in your home directory. You will most likely find the **PATH** variable in the **.login** or **.cshrc** file in your home directory.

Use vi or another text editor to add the **DESKSET** environment variable line to the contents of the **.login** file. Type **setenv DESKSET**, followed by a space and the pathname to the DeskSet environment's directory, which is the destination directory you used during installation. For example, if you used the destination directory **/files/sundesk** during installation, type

```
setenv DESKSET /files/sundesk
```

Now use your text editor to look through the contents of **.login** and **.cshrc** for a line that starts with **set path =** followed by a collection of pathnames, each separated by a space, and enclosed by parentheses. The following is a typical set path line:

```
set path = (. ~/bin /usr/ucb /bin /usr/bin \
/usr/local/bin)
```

Use your text editor to add **$DESKSET/bin** before **/usr/bin, /bin, and $SUNDESK/bin**, if it is present. Be sure to put a space before the pathname to separate it from the other pathnames. For example, if you added the DeskSet pathname to the sample set path line presented above, the line would now read:

```
set path = (. ~/bin /usr/ucb $DESKSET/bin /bin \
/usr/bin /usr/local/bin)
```

When you're finished editing and saving these files, put these environment variables into effect by exiting and logging in to run your **.cshrc** and **.login** files and restart SunView. To check your installation, start the two dimensional SunView version by entering

```
sunview
```

or the three-dimensional (3D) version by entering

```
sunview -3D
```

If the DeskSet environment does not run correctly, check to make sure that these conditions exist:

- A binary file exists in the **bin** subdirectory in the Desk-Set directory.
- The **PATH** and **DESKSET** variables are set to the directory where you installed the DeskSet.
- **$DESKSET/bin** is placed in the set path line before **/usr/bin, /bin,** and **$SUNDESK/bin**, if it is present.

Setting OpenWindows Environment Variables

If you installed OpenWindows in a directory other than the default directory **/home/openwin**, you need to set the **OPEN-WINHOME** environment variable to the directory you installed. For example, if you installed OpenWindows in **/files/owin**, you need to enter

```
setenv OPENWINHOME /files/owin
```

in your **.login** file. To start using OpenWindows, enter

```
openwin
```

Starting a Tool

To start any one of the DeskSet tools from a shell in the Sun-View or OpenWindows environments, open a **Command Tool** or **Shell Tool** window and enter the command assigned to the tool you want to start.

Tool	*Command*
Binder	**binder &**
Calculator	**calctool &**
Calendar Manager	**cm &**
Clock	**clock &**
Command Tool	**cmdtool &**
Console	**console &**
File Manager	**filemgr &**
Icon Editor	**iconedit &**
Mail Tool	**mailtool &**
Performance Meter	**perfmeter &**

Tool	*Command*
Print Tool	`printtool &`
Shell Tool	`shelltool &`
Snapshot	`snapshot &`
Text Editor	`textedit &`
Tape Tool	`tapetool &`

To start a 3D version, use the following syntax:

```
toolname -3D &
```

You can also start an application by choosing the application option in the **Programs** submenu from the **Workspace** menu, as explained in Chapter 8, "Getting Started with the DeskSet."

Customizing the DeskSet

Once you have started the DeskSet, you can customize many aspects of your Sunview or OpenWindows environment through the **Properties** option from the **Workspace** menu. This option works differently depending on whether you are using OpenWindows or the SunView DeskSet. Both methods are described below.

If you are using the SunView DeskSet, choosing the **Properties** option displays the **Defaults Editor** window. You can choose from several categories of menus in the SunView Defaults Editor by moving the pointer on the circular arrows in the upper-left corner (labeled **Category**) and clicking the left mouse button. Each time you click the left mouse button, a different list of options is displayed. If an option displays circular arrows, you can cycle through the available options the same way you cycled through categories; otherwise move the pointer to the option and click the left mouse button to set the input point and enter your new value. Be aware, however, that many of the options in the SunView Defaults Editor are not specific to the DeskSet because the Defaults Editor is a non-DeskSet application.

If you are using OpenWindows and you select the **Properties** option from the **Workspace** menu, a **Properties** pop-up window is displayed. In OpenWindows you can select from five menus to customize your working environment using the **Category** menu button. To display the **Category** menus, move the pointer to the **Category** menu button in the upper-left corner and press the right mouse button. You can then drag the pointer to the menu containing the options you want to change. The following sections give a brief description of each of these menus and their options. If a SunView Defaults Editor equivalent exists, it is also mentioned.

Remember, if you want to save any changes you have made, you need to move the pointer onto the **Save** button in the Sun-View Defaults Editor window header or the **Apply** button in the **OpenWindows Properties** pop-up window and click the left mouse button. The next time you start SunView or Open-Windows, your changes will take effect.

Color   Provides a palette of 72 colors to define the colors for the workspace and windows, and allows you to create your own customized colors using three slider boxes to determine hue, saturation, and brightness. The closest equivalent in the Sun-View Defaults Editor is the **Root_Pattern** option, which allows you to turn a background pattern on or off, or display a gray background. You can also create a pattern with the Icon Editor and enter the file name to create your own background pattern in SunView.

Icons   Sets the default location where icons are displayed on your screen. The settings include **Top**, **Bottom**, **Left**, and **Right**. The SunView Defaults Editor equivalent is the **Icon_gravity** option.

Menus   With the **Drag-Right distance (pixels)** option, determines how far you need to move the pointer before pop-up windows are displayed. The default is set to 5 pixels.

The **Select Mouse Press** option allows you to determine whether pressing the left mouse button on a menu button selects the default selection of a menu (**Selects Default**) or automatically displays the menu (**Displays menu**). The default selects the default menu option.

Miscellaneous   The **Beep** setting determines whether an alarm sounds when error messages or dialog boxes are displayed. The available options are **Always**, **Notices Only**, and **Never**. The default is **Always**. The SunView Defaults Editor equivalents are the **Ignore_Optional_Alerts** and **Audible_Bell** options.

Set Input Area allows you to determine if applications become active when you simply move the pointer inside the window borders **(Move pointer)** or whether you need to also click the left mouse button **(Click Select)**. The SunView Defaults Editor equivalent is the **Click_to_Type** option.

The **Scrollbar Placement** setting lets you determine whether the scrollbar is displayed on the left or right window border. The default is the right window border. The SunView Defaults Editor equivalent is the **Scrollbar/Vertical_bar-_placement** option.

Mouse Settings   The **Scrollbar Pointer Jumping** option allows you to disable the pointer from jumping to the new scrollbar position when performing scrollbar operations.

The **Pop-up Pointer Jumping** option determines whether the pointer automatically moves to the pop-up window or to notices (dialog boxes).

The **Multi-click Timeout (sec/10)** option presents a slider box to calibrate the sensitivity of the left mouse button to determine what constitutes multiple clicks.

APPENDIX C

Using Diskettes and Tapes

THIS APPENDIX EXPLAINS HOW TO USE AND WRITE protect the two most common types of media for Sun workstations: floppy diskettes and ¼" cartridge tapes. (For information on storing and retrieving data to a diskette or cartridge tape, see the **tar** command in Chapter 14, "SunOS Command Reference.")

Using Diskettes

To use a formatted diskette, first insert the diskette into the drive, label side up. Push firmly to lock the the diskette into place. To eject the diskette from the drive, type **eject** at the command prompt and press Return. If the diskette does not work correctly, it may need to be formatted.

Formatting a Diskette

Formatting erases whatever is on the diskette.

When you purchase new diskettes, you must format them before using them to save your files. To format a diskette you must first know whether you are using a high-density (1.44Mb) diskette or a double-density (720K) diskette. If you are using a high-density diskette, insert the diskette into the drive and at the command prompt enter

```
fdformat
```

If you are using a double-density diskette, insert the diskette into the drive and enter

```
fdformat -L
```

Remember, the format of your diskettes must match the type of diskette you are using. You cannot format a high-density diskette with a double-density format.

Do not mix MS-DOS and SunOS files on the same diskette.

If your system has DOS windows, you can format a high-density diskette with an MS-DOS (Microsoft Disk Operating System) format by inserting the diskette into the drive, label side up, and entering

```
FORMAT A:
```

To format a double-density diskette with an MS-DOS format, insert the diskette into the drive, label side up, and enter

```
FORMAT A: /n:9
```

Write-Protecting Diskettes

Write-protecting a diskette prevents its contents from being erased or overwritten. To write-protect a diskette, follow the steps below:

1. Turn the diskette upside down and find the write-protect tab. The diskette is upside down when the

metal circle at the center of the diskette is showing. If you hold the diskette at the label end, the write-protect notch is in the lower-right corner.

2. Using a ballpoint pen, pull the tab towards the edge until you can see through the notch.

Once you have write-protected a diskette, information cannot be saved on it. When you want to write information on the diskette, you can change it back to its write-enabled status by pushing the tab back so that the hole is completely covered.

Using Tapes

To insert a ¼" cartridge tape into an external tape drive unit, hold the cartridge with the label side up. The tape head faces the slide lock on the left side of the slot. Press the cartridge firmly into the slot and pull the slide lock to the right so that it holds the cartridge in place.

When a cartridge is first loaded, it is a good idea to perform what is called a tensioning pass. This ensures an even distribution of tension throughout the tape. To run a tensioning pass, insert the tape into the tape drive and enter the following:

```
mt -f /dev/rst8 retension
```

To release the cartridge, pull the slide lock to the left.

Write-Protecting Tapes

To protect a ¼" cartridge tape so that it cannot be erased or written to, you will need a screwdriver or a coin. On the top of the tape is the word "SAFE" with an arrow and a notch for rotating the arrow. To write-protect the tape, insert the head of the screwdriver or coin in the notch and rotate the arrow to point to the word "SAFE". To enable writing to the tape, move the arrow so that it is pointing away from the word "SAFE".

INDEX

TO JOIN THE SYBEX MAILING LIST OR ORDER BOOKS
PLEASE COMPLETE THIS FORM

NAME _____ COMPANY _____

STREET _____ CITY _____

STATE _____ ZIP _____

☐ PLEASE MAIL ME MORE INFORMATION ABOUT **SYBEX** TITLES

ORDER FORM (There is no obligation to order)

PLEASE SEND ME THE FOLLOWING:

TITLE	QTY	PRICE
_____	____	____
_____	____	____
_____	____	____
_____	____	____

TOTAL BOOK ORDER ____ $____

CUSTOMER SIGNATURE _____

SHIPPING AND HANDLING PLEASE ADD $2.00 PER BOOK VIA UPS _____

FOR OVERSEAS SURFACE ADD $5.25 PER BOOK PLUS $4.40 REGISTRATION FEE _____

FOR OVERSEAS AIRMAIL ADD $18.25 PER BOOK PLUS $4.40 REGISTRATION FEE _____

CALIFORNIA RESIDENTS PLEASE ADD APPLICABLE SALES TAX _____

TOTAL AMOUNT PAYABLE _____

☐ CHECK ENCLOSED   ☐ VISA
☐ MASTERCARD   ☐ AMERICAN EXPRESS

ACCOUNT NUMBER _____

EXPIR. DATE _____ DAYTIME PHONE _____

CHECK AREA OF COMPUTER INTEREST:

☐ BUSINESS SOFTWARE

☐ TECHNICAL PROGRAMMING

☐ OTHER: _____

THE FACTOR THAT WAS MOST IMPORTANT IN YOUR SELECTION:

☐ THE SYBEX NAME

☐ QUALITY

☐ PRICE

☐ EXTRA FEATURES

☐ COMPREHENSIVENESS

☐ CLEAR WRITING

☐ OTHER _____

OTHER COMPUTER TITLES YOU WOULD LIKE TO SEE IN PRINT:

_____

_____

OCCUPATION

☐ PROGRAMMER   ☐ TEACHER

☐ SENIOR EXECUTIVE   ☐ HOMEMAKER

☐ COMPUTER CONSULTANT   ☐ RETIRED

☐ SUPERVISOR   ☐ STUDENT

☐ MIDDLE MANAGEMENT   ☐ OTHER:

☐ ENGINEER/TECHNICAL   _____

☐ CLERICAL/SERVICE

☐ BUSINESS OWNER/SELF EMPLOYED

CHECK YOUR LEVEL OF COMPUTER USE

☐ NEW TO COMPUTERS

☐ INFREQUENT COMPUTER USER

☐ FREQUENT USER OF ONE SOFTWARE

   PACKAGE:

   NAME _____

☐ FREQUENT USER OF MANY SOFTWARE

   PACKAGES

☐ PROFESSIONAL PROGRAMMER

OTHER COMMENTS:

_____

_____

_____

_____

_____

_____

_____

PLEASE FOLD, SEAL, AND MAIL TO SYBEX

SYBEX, INC.
2021 CHALLENGER DR. #100
ALAMEDA, CALIFORNIA USA
94501

SEAL

SYBEX Computer Books
are different.

Here is why . . .

At SYBEX, each book is designed with you in mind. Every manuscript is carefully selected and supervised by our editors, who are themselves computer experts. We publish the best authors, whose technical expertise is matched by an ability to write clearly and to communicate effectively. Programs are thoroughly tested for accuracy by our technical staff. Our computerized production department goes to great lengths to make sure that each book is well-designed.

In the pursuit of timeliness, SYBEX has achieved many publishing firsts. SYBEX was among the first to integrate personal computers used by authors and staff into the publishing process. SYBEX was the first to publish books on the CP/M operating system, microprocessor interfacing techniques, word processing, and many more topics.

Expertise in computers and dedication to the highest quality product have made SYBEX a world leader in computer book publishing. Translated into fourteen languages, SYBEX books have helped millions of people around the world to get the most from their computers. We hope we have helped you, too.

For a complete catalog of our publications:

SYBEX, Inc. 2021 Challenger Drive, #100, Alameda, CA 94501
Tel: (415) 523-8233/(800) 227-2346   Telex: 336311

The Text Editor Menus

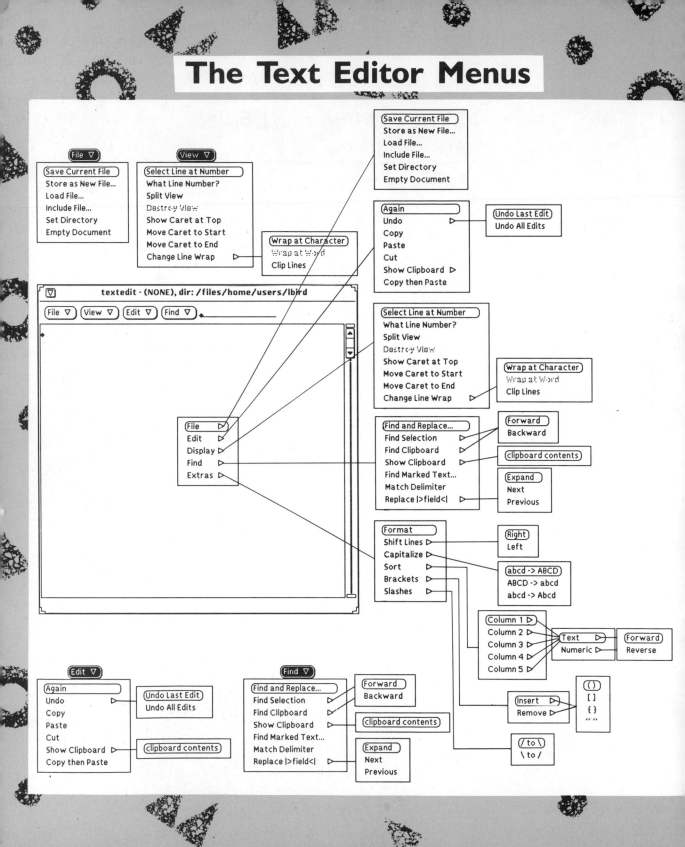

File ▽
- Save Current File
- Store as New File...
- Load File...
- Include File...
- Set Directory
- Empty Document

View ▽
- Select Line at Number
- What Line Number?
- Split View
- Destroy View
- Show Caret at Top
- Move Caret to Start
- Move Caret to End
- Change Line Wrap

- Save Current File
- Store as New File...
- Load File...
- Include File...
- Set Directory
- Empty Document

- Wrap at Character
- Wrap at Word
- Clip Lines

Again
- Undo
- Copy
- Paste
- Cut
- Show Clipboard
- Copy then Paste

- Undo Last Edit
- Undo All Edits

textedit - (NONE), dir: /files/home/users/lbird

File ▽   View ▽   Edit ▽   Find ▽

- File
- Edit
- Display
- Find
- Extras

- Select Line at Number
- What Line Number?
- Split View
- Destroy View
- Show Caret at Top
- Move Caret to Start
- Move Caret to End
- Change Line Wrap

- Wrap at Character
- Wrap at Word
- Clip Lines

Find and Replace...
- Find Selection
- Find Clipboard
- Show Clipboard
- Find Marked Text...
- Match Delimiter
- Replace |>field<|

- Forward
- Backward

- clipboard contents

- Expand
- Next
- Previous

Format
- Shift Lines
- Capitalize
- Sort
- Brackets
- Slashes

- Right
- Left

- abcd -> ABCD
- ABCD -> abcd
- abcd -> Abcd

- Column 1
- Column 2
- Column 3
- Column 4
- Column 5

- Text
- Numeric

- Forward
- Reverse

- Insert
- Remove

- ( )
- [ ]
- { }
- " "

- / to \
- \ to /

Edit ▽
- Again
- Undo
- Copy
- Paste
- Cut
- Show Clipboard
- Copy then Paste

- Undo Last Edit
- Undo All Edits

- clipboard contents

Find ▽
- Find and Replace...
- Find Selection
- Find Clipboard
- Show Clipboard
- Find Marked Text...
- Match Delimiter
- Replace |>field<|

- Forward
- Backward

- clipboard contents

- Expand
- Next
- Previous